BIDDING FOR THE 1968 OLYMPIC GAMES

A VOLUME IN THE SERIES

Culture and Politics in the Cold War and Beyond

EDITED BY

Edwin A. Martini and Scott Laderman

BIDDING FOR THE 1968 OLYMPIC GAMES

International Sport's Cold War Battle with NATO

HEATHER L. DICHTER

University of Massachusetts Press
Amherst and Boston

Printed in the United States of America

ISBN 978-1-62534-595-0 (paper); 594-3 (hardcover)

Designed by Sally Nichols
Set in Dante
Printed and bound by Books International, Inc.

Cover design by Rebecca Niemark, Twenty-six Letters
Cover art: Detail from East German team marching into the stadium at the 1968 Winter Olympics in Grenoble, France, behind the all-German Olympic flag and a sign simply reading "Germany" (Allemagne in French). © dpa—sports report. Courtesy of picture-alliance/ dpa | dpa.

Library of Congress Cataloging-in-Publication Data

Names: Dichter, Heather, author.
Title: Bidding for the 1968 Olympic Games : international sport's Cold War battle with NATO / Heather L. Dichter.
Other titles: 1968 Olympic Games
Description: Amherst ; Boston : University of Massachusetts Press, [2021] | Series: Culture and Politics in the Cold War and Beyond | Includes bibliographical references and index.
Identifiers: LCCN 2021017183 (print) | LCCN 2021017184 (ebook) | ISBN 9781625345943 (Hardcover) | ISBN 9781625345950 (Paperback) | ISBN 9781613768709 (eBook) | ISBN 9781613768716 (eBook)
Subjects: LCSH: Olympic host city selection—1968. | Olympics—Political aspects. | Olympics—Economic aspects. | International Olympic Committee. | North Atlantic Treaty Organization—Influence. | Sports and state—History—20th century. | Cold War—Influence. | World politics—1945–1989. | Olympic Games (19th : 1968 : Mexico City, Mexico)
Classification: LCC GV721.5 .D46 2021 (print) | LCC GV721.5 (ebook) | DDC 796.48—dc23
LC record available at https://lccn.loc.gov/2021017183
LC ebook record available at https://lccn.loc.gov/2021017184

British Library Cataloguing-in-Publication Data
A catalog record for this book is available from the British Library.

CONTENTS

ABBREVIATIONS

ATO Allied Travel Office

EEC European Economic Community

FIFA Fédération Internationale de Football Association

FILA Fédération Internationale de Lutte Amateur (wrestling)

FIS Fédération Internationale de Ski

FISA Fédération Internationale des Sociétés d'Aviron (rowing)

FITA Fédération Internationale de Tir l'Arc (archery)

FRG Federal Republic of Germany

GDR German Democratic Republic

IAAF International Amateur Athletic Federation (track and field)

IIHF International Ice Hockey Federation

IOC International Olympic Committee

ISU International Skating Union

IWF International Weightlifting Federation

MAE Ministère des Affaires Étrangères (France)

NATO North Atlantic Treaty Organization

TTD Temporary Travel Document

UCI Union Cycliste Internationale

UEFA Union of European Football Associations

UIPM Union Internationale de Pentathlon Moderne

PREFACE

The contest to host the 1968 Olympic Games revealed the power of sport to influence international diplomacy in the 1960s. Despite the International Olympic Committee's (IOC) claim that sport was apolitical, international sport challenged the North Atlantic Treaty Organization's (NATO) ability to promote a united front as Western nations disputed and negotiated Cold War policy in efforts to benefit from the soft power associated with hosting the Olympics and other major international sport events. Yet when Cold War politics left events in NATO states with a depleted field or forced international federations to relocate them to other countries or cancel them outright, their plans to gain soft power benefits from hosting these events in fact backfired. To prevent NATO member states from being excluded from organizing the Olympics and other world and European championships, international sport thus became the arena that allowed the West to accept East Germany by the 1968 Summer Olympics, paving the way for greater détente between the West and the German Democratic Republic (GDR, or East Germany). The erection of the Berlin Wall in August 1961 abruptly ended the German-German sporting relationship and brought international sport to a crisis point, with sport officials questioning the viability of NATO states as hosts for events. This book therefore considers these problems from two perspectives: how and why NATO and its member states confronted sport during the height of the Cold War and how international sport responded to this overt political interference. At the heart of the matter was the competition to host the 1968 Summer and Winter Olympic Games because six of the eleven cities bidding for the Summer and Winter Olympics were located in four NATO member states. The contest to select the Olympic hosts must then be considered within a larger context of other international sporting events in the years leading up to the IOC's vote—events marred by the German problem.

This project began during a 2010 visit to the National Archives in College Park, Maryland. In the State Department records I found documents that explicitly referenced NATO discussions regarding the problem of East German sport. Prior to my doctoral project on sport during the occupation of Germany, my master's thesis at the University of North Carolina–Chapel Hill had focused on the all-German Olympic team of the 1950s and 1960s. These State Department materials I found several years later confirmed the communist bloc's claims that NATO had brought politics into sport during this period and in fact that NATO and its member states were incredibly concerned about, and involved themselves in, international sport. I knew the moment I found these documents that I would return to some of those earlier ideas, but with a different focus. While the German question formed the central problem around which NATO discussions on sport focused, the contest for the 1968 Summer and Winter Olympic host cities became the larger and more complicated issue for the alliance as it impacted more states than a sporting event in a single country did.

One of the joys of this project is that it has taken me to archives in eight countries, although occasionally with the need to convince archivists that their diplomatic records did in fact contain discussions about the contest to host the 1968 Olympic Games. The foreign ministry files for seven countries were either at national archives or as separate archives at the ministries themselves. I am particularly indebted to the Utenriksdepartement staff in Oslo for declassifying their files for me before they were transferred to the Riksarkivet, as well as Karl Egil Hanevik for his help preparing for my Norwegian research trips. The staff at the Olympic Studies Centre in Lausanne was, as always, incredibly helpful on site and with additional email queries. Several international federations have kindly allowed me access to their files, which has allowed me to consider more than just the Olympic Games within this project. The staff at numerous other libraries provided support with other collections: the Bentley Historical Library at the University of Michigan, Detroit Public Library, Rauner Library at Dartmouth College, Lake Placid Olympic Museum, Oslo Skimuseet, les Archives de Grenoble, and Archives municipales de Lyon. All quotations originally written in English have kept their spellings, which may differ among American, Canadian, and British spellings. The translations in the book are mine, although sometimes the translations of news stories or documents by diplomats have been used.

Moving three times for different jobs—including across the Atlantic Ocean—slowed down my progress on this book, which could not have been completed without the financial support of the Society for Historians of American Foreign Relations (SHAFR), the Bentley Historical Library, Ithaca College, Western Michigan University, and De Montfort University. Funding from Ithaca College allowed me to hire Max Rottenecker, Kaitlyn Matrassi, and Jacob List as research assistants, who were invaluable in locating numerous French and German newspaper articles. Christopher Van Meter and Maria Paterno, student research assistants at Western Michigan University, helped with some of the German government documents. The Ithaca College library staff filled my numerous requests, including reel after reel of newspapers both common and obscure. De Montfort University's Institute for History covered the costs for the images included in the book. Samantha Finch and Brian Feltman helped to obtain some of the images during the pandemic, and Richard Steigmann-Gall kindly requested a book from his university library's storage during the pandemic to confirm some details as well.

Many people in Europe provided me with a place to stay and fun times after long days at the archives: Shelley Vaillancourt (who also allowed me to see other parts of NATO headquarters than the reading room), Steffi Seeh and Sandra Esser in Germany, Anna Groves-Kirkby and Fergus Cumming in England (before I moved there), and Solveig Straume in Norway. My De Montfort University colleagues Sophie Brockmann and Beatriz Pichel provided excellent advice and support in our writing group as we all worked toward completing our monographs. For someone who does not follow sports at all, Beatriz was an especially great friend, reading every chapter in the book, and some more than once. Additional thanks must be given to Kelly Shannon, Andrew Johnstone, Jason Parker, Molly Wood, Erik Huneke, and Sarah Teetzel for their feedback and advice as well. Working with Matt Becker and the entire University of Massachusetts Press staff has been a wonderful experience, and their support, along with the anonymous reviewers, has enabled this book to take its final shape.

BIDDING FOR THE 1968 OLYMPIC GAMES

INTRODUCTION

NATO AND SPORT?

In late February 1962 the city of Colorado Springs, Colorado, was in the final preparation stages for hosting the ice hockey world championships. In anticipation of this event, the State Department sent a memorandum to President John F. Kennedy's national security advisor about the public reaction to the recent exploitation of sport for political purposes. The State Department noted: "There has been some criticism to the effect that politics should not be injected into sports, with the implication being that it was the Western powers that introduced the political issue." However, the memorandum countered, "The fact is it is the Communist regimes rather than the Western governments which have sought to exploit sports for political purposes and brought this issue to a head. The [German Democratic Republic] has frankly attempted to utilize international athletic events to enhance its prestige and demonstrate the existence of two separate German states."[1] Two weeks later, on the same day the ice hockey world championships began, the Committee of Political Advisers at the North Atlantic Treaty Organization (NATO) addressed this same issue. During that discussion the Dutch representative commented: "Sports [have] political impact whether we like it or not."[2] Both of these views on sport and politics accurately summed up the situation in the early 1960s: that sport was something politicians and diplomats had to address and that it was a highly politicized weapon in the Cold War battle, especially because of its perceived impact on popular opinion.

This acknowledgment by foreign ministries of the place of sport within politics was in stark contrast to the publicly promoted view of the time about the separation of sport and politics. Yet international sport, and the organizations that governed the Olympic Games and individual sports, had a persistent and troublesome effect on relations with NATO. An intense conflict in international sport centered on the problem of divided Germany.

The efforts by the German Democratic Republic (GDR, or East Germany) to gain de facto recognition within the international system through sport came into conflict with the Atlantic alliance's policy of not recognizing the communist German state, which included restricting the travel of athletes representing East Germany. Almost every NATO member state hosted a major international sporting event during the 1950s and 1960s, giving them all a vested interest in the issue. As such, sport became an area where national self-interests prompted both large and small states within the alliance to try to change—or even go against—NATO policies.

The problem came to a head with the contest to host the 1968 Olympic Games. The four member states with candidate cities (the United States, France, Canada, and Norway) found it difficult to come to a consensus as they balanced NATO policies with national self-interest. This process revealed the increasing power of international sport organizations to influence diplomacy as these states were willing to bend their national policies and even break NATO agreements in order to host the Olympic Games. When Western diplomats attempted to influence international sport, sport leaders were appalled at this intrusion of politics. Sport's response to these efforts ushered in a détente between Western sport and East Germany, setting the stage for diplomats to accept détente more broadly by the end of the decade.

The excitement and the popularity of sport led foreign ministries to use sport as a form of soft power. Hosting international sporting events helped states with public image promotion and nation branding to project a specific image about their country to the world via global media coverage as well as directly to the spectators who came from abroad to attend the events.[3] The candidate cities for the 1968 Olympics—Detroit, Lyon, Buenos Aires, and Mexico City for the summer games and Lake Placid, Calgary, Grenoble, Oslo, Lahti, Sion, and Sapporo for the winter games—framed their bids accordingly as they tried to convince International Olympic Committee (IOC) members to vote for them. It was precisely these factors that led the foreign ministries and their representatives at NATO to become increasingly concerned with international sport and the role that it could play in foreign affairs during the Cold War. When GDR athletes did not receive the necessary travel documents to compete at international sporting events in NATO states, the other communist bloc states withdrew in solidarity or the international federations relocated those events to countries that did not impose travel restrictions on East German athletes. In these instances, NATO member states saw their soft power plans backfire. Instead of basking in the glory of organizing a successful international sporting event, depleted or relocated events led to little or no economic gains for local business and tourism alongside extensive criticism of the government and NATO in the domestic and international press.

Each time the GDR attempted to reinforce its legitimacy as a state, the implications for sport increased. The construction of the Berlin Wall in August 1961 caused an immediate crisis in sport as East Germany could not participate in two world championships in early 1962, including the ice hockey world championships in Colorado. However, it was 1963 when the problem converged from all directions: sporting events continued to be impacted by the inability of East German athletes to travel to events in NATO states; the IOC and international federations released a statement on sport and politics; and the IOC demanded a guarantee of free travel to the 1968 Olympics from all of the candidate cities. British IOC member Lord David Burghley, Marquess of Exeter, wrote to the Foreign Office at the start of 1963 to express his grave concerns on the matter:

> I feel that I should point out to you that the NATO policy on visas for East Germans is automatically ruling out all those countries from having either the Olympic Games or Area Championships. Where these, with their prestige, will go I leave to your imagination! I do hope that something may happen before October, when the International Olympic Committee will decide in Nairobi where the next Olympic Games are to be, for if the visa embargo remains, they cannot be in any NATO country, which will, apart from other obvious disadvantages, be highly unpopular with their very large sporting publics.[4]

Burghley rightly noticed how all of these factors—NATO policy, the Olympics selection, international sport more generally, and public opinion—came together over the German problem in ways that did not look favorably on the Western democracies.

THE COLD WAR, SPORT, AND SOFT POWER

Sport and politics impacting each other was not a new phenomenon by the 1960s, but the convergence of several factors from sport and international relations coalesced with the contest to host the 1968 Olympic Games, revealing the power of sport on diplomacy. International sport proliferated in the 1950s and 1960s spurred by cheaper air travel, the expansion of television, and decolonization. Newly independent states immediately sought to join the IOC, and international sport federations to solidify their status as members of the international system.[5] Technological advances with live broadcasts and then satellite transmissions, along with increasing ownership of television sets, also contributed to sport's growth in size, scope, and spectacle. The 1960 Rome Olympics, with live television coverage across Europe and nearly 1.5 million tickets sold, transformed "the Olympics into a truly global event."[6] Sport drew high ratings because it provided drama and unexpected outcomes.[7]

This expansion of sport and its global media coverage increased the desire of countries to host international sporting events. The Olympic Games and other major international sporting events allowed a city or country to gain valuable soft power benefits by projecting a specific image to the world.[8] Following the 1960 Rome Olympics, several cities declared their interest in hosting the 1968 games. This contest began in the early years of the decade, which coincided with a period of heightened Cold War tensions following the construction of the Berlin Wall and the Cuban Missile Crisis. The bidding process continued until the IOC selected the 1968 host cities in October 1963 and January 1964. When the 1968 Summer Olympics opened, they appeared via live satellite broadcast around the globe in color for the first time, bringing all of the drama vividly into the world's living rooms.

When East Germany could not participate in sporting events in the 1960s, the Soviet bloc accused NATO of interfering in sport. The democratic West, however, dismissed these claims as communist propaganda, deflecting the blame for political interference in sport back on them, as seen in the State Department's memorandum to President Kennedy. NATO and foreign ministry records, however, reveal the truth to those communist accusations. To understand this political involvement in sport, the issue must be considered as greater than a mere German-German problem, along with a recognition that NATO is more than a military organization. A multilateral approach to the alliance, the German question, and international sporting events therefore demonstrates the many ways sport and diplomacy impact one another and have affected the trajectory of both the Olympic movement and alliance politics.

International sport organizations also function as a type of NGO playing a diplomatic role.[9] The power of these sport NGOs, and especially the IOC, grew in the 1960s as their coffers increased from television and sponsorship contracts. By controlling a global commodity to which every country wanted access, the IOC and international federations participated in negotiations with diplomats who recognized the popularity of sport and its potential to shape public opinion. Indeed, the greater frequency of these discussions in the 1960s lent credence to sport leaders' inflated belief in their self-importance in the world. The prestige and public diplomacy of hosting the Olympic Games has led to a focus on why a bid was successful or failed, which at times has considered the diplomatic concerns or problems encountered during the bid and organizing phases.[10] A broader, multicity approach to Olympic bidding contests that incorporates the nonsport concerns that were discussed by the press at the time further reveals the complexities of the IOC's decisions in ways that a single-city approach cannot.

NATO's extensive concern with international sport reveals a broader expanse of what the alliance considered important to its work beyond the narrow confines of the military or security.[11] Diplomats monitored media coverage when states prevented East German athletes from competing at international sporting events and sought to counter negative publicity from damaged events and NATO's overt political interference in sport. The sporting events hosted in NATO states that are discussed in this book demonstrate the backfiring of soft power. Instead of reaping the benefits from hosting international sporting events, states viewed these politically marred events as damaging to themselves and the organization as a whole. NATO diplomats believed public opinion of the alliance mattered, and they used their fears about sport harming those public views to justify both changes to NATO policy and the desire to maintain travel restrictions on East German athletes. The media amplified the drama of Cold War sport and reported every instance when Cold War politics impacted sporting events or when the IOC and international federations took actions in response to politics.[12] The popularity of sport, governments believed, made it an area that could have a tremendous impact on public opinion in both directions.

Because of its membership in NATO, the Federal Republic of Germany could not act unilaterally regarding East Germany. The German question during the Cold War cannot simply be written from the East and West German perspectives or located solely along the Washington-Moscow axis; it must be considered within a broader international context. NATO's interest in international sport, along with its support of the Federal Republic, means that the East-West German sport relationship during the 1950s and 1960s must also take into account the actions of other states.[13] The Atlantic alliance necessitated that many states influenced the course of action, including multiple small states and the traditional larger powers.[14] The problem of East German participation in international sport demonstrates that Cold War divisions not only ran between East and West but within the Western alliance as well, requiring extensive negotiations year after year as NATO member states disputed the policy preventing East German athletes from traveling to international sport events. Each of the states contributed to the maintenance of or changes to alliance policies through NATO debates. The 1968 Olympic candidature process enabled two weaker states on each side of the Atlantic—Canada and Norway—to wield a greater influence than they typically held inside NATO or within the governance of international sport. After years of political wrangling, international sport ultimately provided the field in which the West accepted a separate East Germany by the end of 1968, paving the way for a broader détente between the two Cold War camps.

The East German decision to construct a wall in Berlin impacted German-German relations broadly during the Cold War; within sport, the wall effectively ended athletic cooperation between the two German states and, in particular, their ability to form a combined Olympic team, which the IOC had mandated since the 1950s.[15] The construction of the wall, which prevented East Germans fleeing with their feet, also had wider repercussions within the realms of diplomacy and sport, bringing these two groups of international actors together. At the heart of the issue was the freedom of travel. The GDR had severely restricted its citizens from traveling, primarily limiting their international travel to the communist bloc. Access between the Federal Republic and West Berlin had frequently caused heightened East-West tensions. The inability to travel to the West was one of the many reasons so many East Germans left the country, often via West Berlin.[16] The creation of the wall and NATO's subsequent travel restrictions thus prompted conflicting arguments over which Cold War side prevented the ability of East Germans to travel freely. The implications for sport as a result of the political actions taken in response to the Berlin Wall affected not only which athletes could participate in international sporting events but also where sporting events were held. Thus, selecting host cities for major events, in particular the 1968 Olympic Games, became a process no longer determined solely by the athletic world. Now international sport had to consider international politics in these decisions.

THE POLITICAL PLAYERS

Because of the competing interests promoted by multiple NATO members, this book combines an international history approach to diplomacy with a transnational approach to sport.[17] Using archival materials from NATO, several countries' foreign ministries, sport functionaries at the domestic and international levels, and newspapers, this project attempts to build a complete picture of NATO's involvement in sport during the early 1960s. Official NATO minutes largely denote the consensus achieved at a meeting or that discussion happened without a decision. The correspondence between the representatives who attended these meetings and their foreign ministries instead provides each member state's position and concerns, as well as insight into the discussions that happened outside of the formal North Atlantic Council or Committee of Political Advisers meetings. Complementing the official NATO files are the records from several foreign ministries: the State Department (U.S.), External Affairs (Canada), Foreign Office (UK), Ministère des Affaires Étrangères (France), Auswärtiges Amt (Germany), and Utenriksdepartement (Norway). The insight provided by the diplomatic representatives from the six major countries involved in the negotiations related to German sport and the 1968 Olympics, along with relevant sport organization materials, affords a sufficient basis for placing the other NATO countries within these events.[18]

This story follows several relationships emanating in multiple directions. At the center sits the NATO headquarters in Paris, with every delegation communicating with their foreign ministry—in particular, Washington, D.C., Ottawa, London, Oslo, Bonn, and Paris. Each foreign ministry also worked through bilateral relationships, with their embassies in the other NATO states meeting directly with other foreign ministries. At the same time, separate, smaller multistate consultations took place among the Americans, British, and French in Bonn, Berlin, and at NATO in Paris and with representatives from the Federal Republic as well. This web of diplomacy worked in all directions, revealing the complex nature of this truly international issue. Similar levels of consultations were occurring within sport organizations: among IOC members, between the IOC and the international federations, and between international federations and national governing bodies or individuals organizing their sporting events. These two networks overlapped when government members met or corresponded with sport leaders regarding the organization of international sport events and the problem of East German travel or the need to provide the necessary guarantees for Olympic bids.

With the IOC and international federations functioning as international NGOs, they also have affiliated bodies within each member country. The structure of international sport governance is largely replicated at the domestic level within each country, with national sport leaders representing the country at an international level. The IOC, headquartered in Lausanne, Switzerland, oversees the international sport movement primarily through the quadrennial Olympic Games. Working with the IOC are the international federations, which govern all of the aspects and events for a specific sport. International federations recognize the national governing body that oversees that sport within a country, and they also select the host cities for world championships and other international events. A country will have a national Olympic committee, which requests recognition from the IOC, and national governing bodies, which affiliate with the appropriate international federation. Many individuals have overlapping roles at the national and international levels, blurring the four levels of sport governance. As these sport leaders, who were almost always men in the 1960s, wore different hats as an IOC member and as an international federation president, such as Lord Burghley, for example, they had to balance concerns sometimes at odds with one another, as well as different directions taken within each organization.

Examining Cold War international sport issues within NATO complicates the traditional division of great powers from the weaker or small states.[19] By the 1950s, the United States was one of the two superpowers in the world, and also a dominant sporting power. The United States has hosted eight Olympic Games, more than any other country, and has won the most medals in history. As soon as Soviet athletes competed at the Olympics for the first time in 1952, the competition between the two global powers moved to the sporting arena. Soviet participation and American fears over communist influence in the Olympic movement in the 1950s prompted the U.S. government to brand international sport politically important.[20] From 1952 to 1972

Chicago businessman Avery Brundage served as IOC president and ensured his personal beliefs about the firm separation of sport and politics led the direction of the organization.[21]

France had been one of the traditional powers in global affairs and international sport, but World War II and decolonization transformed France into a middleweight power by the 1950s. Within NATO and Europe, France continued to assert its strength; similarly, its sport leaders remained in positions of power within international sport.[22] A Frenchman had founded the IOC in 1894, and French sport officials have served as presidents of more than a dozen international federations. However, France never exerted a comparable prowess on the actual playing fields. With the establishment of the Fifth Republic, President Charles de Gaulle "used sport to relaunch [France] as a rejuvenated nation," promoting greater mass participation as well as elite competition.[23]

Like France, Great Britain was one of the traditional great powers in the nineteenth century, and its global empire contributed to the development and spread of modern sport. Although the U.S.-Soviet rivalry diminished the country's importance during the Cold War, the country still played a role in postwar multistate governance structures. The country's ideas about amateurism and sportsmanship have served as underlying principles for international sport since its inception. Great Britain is one of the few countries to have sent athletes to every single Olympic Games, and London was the first city to host the Olympics three times. British sport leaders have held the presidency of more than ten international federations. Lord Burghley, a three-time Olympic competitor, played a particularly important role in sport as International Amateur Athletic Federation (IAAF) president from 1946 to 1976 and an IOC member from 1933 to 1982, serving on the executive board from 1951 to 1970 and as a vice president from 1954 to 1966. As a former member of parliament and the governor of Bermuda during the last two years of World War II, he maintained close connections with the British government, often speaking with Foreign Office staff about developments within international sport.[24]

In contrast to these three powers, Belgium and the Netherlands have assumed leadership positions within international sport at a far greater size than their political clout would suggest. Yet, as smaller states surrounded by traditional great powers, these states were essential to postwar European community building. The new supranational European organizations often selected Belgian or Dutch politicians as their leaders to prevent dominance by any single great power. Both countries were two of the three founding members of the first international sport federation, and Belgium is the only country to provide two IOC presidents. Since the nineteenth century men from both countries have also served as presidents or vice presidents of several international sport federations, influencing the nature and direction of sport at a global level. Both countries have a strong sporting tradition, each hosting the Olympic Games and numerous European and world championships. The Dutch and Belgian representatives to NATO were therefore frequent contributors to the NATO debates on the issue of travel by East German athletes.

Entering the diplomatic field later were both Canada and Norway. Canada did not establish a foreign ministry (the Department of External Affairs) until 1909, and Canada has promoted itself as a middle power on the global stages, both during and after World War II.[25] As the United States' northern neighbor, Canada was the only other NATO member from outside Europe. Under Prime Minister John Diefenbaker (1957–63), Canada sought to assert a place for the country on a global stage, under neither British nor American influence. This goal included bringing major international events to the country,[26] and the 1968 Winter Olympic bid from Calgary, Alberta, also fell within these efforts. Canada has had moderate success in several disciplines and has always been a dominant country in ice hockey. Other than for ice hockey and curling, Canadians have not held the presidency of an international federation, although many Canadians have served on the executive committees, thus reinforcing the country's position as a middle power.

Norway only gained its independence from Sweden in 1905 and was one of Europe's poorest countries until the discovery of oil in the 1960s, which enriched the country and enabled it to play a large role in international affairs, particularly through humanitarian aid. The German occupation during World War II left a strong anti-German sentiment inside Norway, which delayed the inclusion of German soldiers and officers in NATO's Northern Command, part of the alliance's military structure.[27] Within sport, Norway has consistently been a strong Winter Olympics participant, winning more Olympic medals in cross-country skiing, ski jumping, and Nordic combined than any other country. Norway has also played a leading role in the Fédération Internationale de Ski since its founding. This love of skiing even transcended politics. Even as Norwegians continued to be against the German military presence in their country as part of NATO's Northern Command, a public outcry occurred when East German athletes, including one of the best ski jumpers, were not allowed to compete in Norway.

With all of these differences in power among the countries, they were to some degree mitigated by the structure of NATO. Each country's permanent representative to NATO, the equivalent of an ambassador, represented the state at the North Atlantic Council, the highest level of the organization that approves final decisions or policies developed within the various committees. The Committee of Political Advisers, established in 1957 to encourage regular political consultation in nonmilitary areas to support unity among alliance members, was composed of each country's political adviser. NATO's assistant secretary general for political affairs led its meetings.[28]

The value placed on hosting sporting events by the rest of the alliance and the perceived damage to public perceptions of NATO demonstrate that the largest powers could not simply impose their will. For the 1968 Olympic bids in particular, Canada and Norway could, at times, have a greater influence than their size or population warranted. Both states wanted changes to the East German travel restrictions for athletes, but they did not work together to achieve this diplomatic goal. Their similar desires and interest in what actions the other was taking in the 1960s, however, foreshadowed later collaboration on international issues.[29] Of course, these four countries also had to contend with their NATO allies and the remainder of the world—and particularly the Soviet bloc—within international sport federations. In addition, as NATO states continued to deny entry to East German athletes, international sport federations increasingly relocated or awarded European or world championships to neutral or Soviet bloc states as Lord Burghley had predicted. The selection process for the 1968 Olympic Games became far more complicated for the potential host cities located in the four NATO member countries.

While the bidding for the 1968 Olympics, from NATO's perspective, only directly involved four countries, the larger issues that this working group addressed impacted all NATO members. Smaller states such as Norway, Denmark, and Belgium did not have the resources to host the Olympic Games, but they often sought to host European or world championships in individual sports. As a result, the problems related to the travel of East German athletes, representing a national team and seeking recognition of the GDR symbol, flag, and anthem, affected these states. Unlike the travel categories for academics, scientists, or politicians, the broad popularity of sport—particularly when East German athletes were medal contenders—

meant that travel restrictions against East German athletes received extensive media coverage. Thus, debates within NATO regarding sport entailed lengthy discussions with contributions from most, if not all, representatives. Even though the Americans, British, and French, via the Allied Travel Office (ATO) had since 1945 ostensibly controlled East German travel to the West, the Federal Republic of Germany had a strong influence on changes to ATO policies. Yet because NATO had agreed to support both the ATO and the Federal Republic's positions regarding East Germany, the rest of the NATO members wanted to ensure that their own interests, such as hosting successful international sporting events, were not compromised.

Against the complex diplomatic relationship among the four Western powers (United States, France, Great Britain, and the Federal Republic) in the early 1960s—the election of a young American president who wanted to chart a different path than his predecessor, Britain's failed application to the European Economic Community, and the Franco-German treaty—let alone broader European and North American relations, arose the problems of international sport and the bidding for the 1968 Olympic Games. The Olympic bid and the need for a united front among the candidate cities from NATO countries prompted different negotiating angles, yet they were never entirely divorced from these broader political concerns. For other NATO member states, hosting smaller sporting events allowed those countries to participate with a vested interest in discussions that typically had been reserved for the large quadripartite powers. The Cold War problems that beset international sport reinforced "the tight interconnection of local and global politics," one of the defining characteristics of the period.[30] The question of freedom of travel in Berlin ultimately impacted sporting events across two continents, as well as the bidding process for the 1968 Olympic Games—and the events themselves. What happened in a single city resulted in not only one of the Cold War's crisis points but moved well beyond a strictly political sphere to encompass the Western military alliance of NATO and the entirety of the international sport community. NATO diplomats and sport leaders in the 1960s both proclaimed their independence from one another, yet, as the German question and the bidding process for the 1968 Olympic Games demonstrate, these two groups worked closely together as their worlds became intertwined. Diplomats had to deal with sport matters, and international sport leaders had to contend with geopolitics, all as a global audience watched elite athletes compete for gold medals.

CHAPTER 1

TRAVEL RESTRICTIONS, STATE SYMBOLS, AND EAST GERMAN RECOGNITION IN SPORT

With the defeat of the Third Reich in 1945, the international community, including for sport, initially excluded occupied Germany, but with the creation of the Federal Republic of Germany in 1949, the country sought to return to international organizations. International sport federations and the IOC recognized the Federal Republic of Germany, largely as the resumption of a membership that had been terminated in 1945. This return of Germany to international sport largely took place from 1949 to 1952—albeit not at the same time or with the same level of smoothness across all of the international sport federations.[1] The German Democratic Republic, on the other hand, did not receive consistent treatment from these bodies and instead had to fight for recognition for several years. The Soviet Union, which had only recently joined the IOC and other international federations, and its communist bloc allies pushed for simultaneous recognition of the GDR alongside the Federal Republic.[2] Many international sport delegates from Western states pushed back at these efforts, attempting to support the stance taken by their West German colleagues who upheld the Hallstein Doctrine, their country's policy of not recognizing East Germany. Western sport delegates supported the line that the Federal Republic was the only legitimate and democratically elected German state, and therefore only one Germany should have membership within international sport organizations.

The IOC took this concept to the extreme, believing that all Germans should compete on one Olympic team.[3] Negotiations for an all-German Olympic team in 1952 broke down when the East German delegation, which had arrived in Copenhagen to negotiate with the West Germans and IOC representatives (IOC president J. Sigfrid Edström, vice president Avery Brundage, and chancellor Otto Mayer), failed to appear at the meeting. After waiting several hours, the IOC delegation, offended by the East German slight, consented to having only athletes from the Federal Republic participate as Germany in the 1952 Summer Olympics in Helsinki.[4] After replacing those sport leaders who had offended the IOC, East Germany received provisional recognition from the IOC and negotiated its participation on an all-German Olympic team for 1956 and subsequent games. This arrangement continued for the next decade but became increasingly more difficult as the Cold War intensified. The two states' sport leaders repeatedly debated how the all-German team would be represented and selected. Their agreement over the use of the black-red-gold tricolor for the flag and emblem came under question again with the introduction of the new East German flag with the communist symbol in the middle. Similarly, the East Germans advocated for playing the East or West German national anthem when an athlete won instead of Beethoven's Ninth Symphony. The two sides also argued where the selection events between East and West German athletes for every single sport would take place, with West Berlin a particularly thorny location. Finally, whichever German state provided the most athletes for the all-German team appointed the *chef de mission*, an important role at the games as the leader of the country's entire delegation.[5] Nonetheless, Edström's successor as IOC president, the American Avery Brundage, frequently promoted the fact that the IOC was able to overcome the problem of two German states, which politicians had been unable to solve.[6]

How each international federation treated East Germany became a contentious and frequent problem. Some international federations admitted East Germany early in the 1950s, although not always easily. Other federations, such as for rowing, only provisionally recognized East Germany, leaving them in a state of limbo for years. This issue was particularly acute when athletes representing an East German national team sought to compete in international events. The IOC's insistence on an all-German team for the Olympic Games meant that NATO states easily granted travel documents and entry into member states for all athletes on the combined German Olympic teams that competed in 1956 (Cortina d'Ampezzo, Italy) and 1960 (both Squaw Valley, United States, and Rome, Italy). European and world championships, however, received entries from individual athletes or teams officially representing the GDR—and thus had to confront its flag, symbol, and anthem. Because the GDR sought de facto recognition in any way it could, NATO member states regularly confronted this problem of East Germany and sport. Member states on both sides of the Atlantic had to invite all members of an international federation when hosting world championships, European championships (for all NATO members except the United States and Canada), or qualification rounds (such as for football's World Cup or Olympic tournaments).

The East German push for separate recognition within international sport brought the postwar German problem onto the world stage through two main areas: ability to travel and state symbols. International sport's acceptance of East Germany therefore came into direct conflict with NATO's explicit refusal to recognize the communist German regime. The introduction of a new East German national anthem and flag at the end of the 1950s increasingly drew NATO into the world of international sport as these state symbols are a highly visible element of sporting events. With NATO member states hosting numerous international sporting events, the alliance could not avoid confronting the potential recognition of these symbols of the East German state. The uneven treatment within international federations left the East Germans continually battling for recognition on several fronts while further decreasing support for the alliance among the general public unfamiliar with the intricacies of international sport. As the GDR sought to use sport to achieve its goal of international recognition, NATO countered these efforts by restricting the ability of East German athletes to travel to competitions. NATO's actions may have hindered East German efforts at the end of the 1950s and start of the next decade to use sport to achieve political aims, but they ushered in a new era where international sport forced diplomats to take frequent action.

TRAVEL RESTRICTIONS

Germany joined NATO in 1955 following the dissolution of the Allied High Commission, which had existed since 1949 when the three occupation zones combined. The Federal Republic gained full sovereignty over its affairs with the termination of the Allied High Commission and the establishment of formal ambassadorial relations with its former occupiers.[7] While NATO finalized the Federal Republic's accession, the alliance was already implementing the nonrecognition of East Germany in sport. The Italian delegation informed its NATO allies that Italy had refused to issue visas to an East German rugby team for an April 1955 tournament "on the grounds that Eastern Germany was not recognised as a sovereign state."[8] Just days before the 1957 wrestling world championships began, the Turkish foreign ministry also refused to issue visas to the East German athletes.[9] Although these were isolated incidents in the early years of NATO, by the end of the decade the issuing of visas and travel permits to East German athletes frequently arose as a discussion point within NATO meetings. The imposition of a travel ban for sport, imposed by the tripartite powers (the United States, Great Britain, and France) but upheld by all NATO member states, served as a form of retaliation for actions taken by East Germany more generally. Although multiple countries confronted the issue of East German travel in 1959, the international sporting events held in the United States garnered the most publicity. The broad appeal of sport—covered extensively in newspapers and attended by tens of thousands of spectators—forced NATO to confront the public perceptions of its travel restrictions on East Germany, which no longer remained a quiet policy impacting few people.

A year before the Federal Republic joined NATO, the alliance had already agreed to support the Federal Republic's nonrecognition of East Germany, commonly known as the Hallstein Doctrine.[10] Named for Walter Hallstein, a state secretary in the the Federal Republic's foreign ministery, this policy sought to prevent countries from establishing diplomatic relations with East Germany. The underlying belief within the government was that recognition of the GDR would signal the permanent status of a divided Germany.[11] Most states and international organizations did not recognize the GDR in the 1950s, whereas they did recognize the German state with its government in Bonn, actions that the Federal Republic claimed reinforced the lack of legitimacy of East Germany and its government. Without a formal peace treaty ending the World War II and finalizing postwar state boundaries, combined with the difficult position of supporting West Berlin deep inside East German territory, the Americans, British, and French retained reserve powers within the Federal Republic even after 1955.[12] West German sovereignty was not therefore wholly complete as the three former occupation powers continued to hold tripartite meetings in Bonn and also met with Auswärties Amt representatives in regular quadripartite meetings. The Americans, British, and French still controlled, via the Allied Travel Office (ATO), the decisions regarding East German citizens wanting to visit or transit through countries that fell outside of the Soviet bloc or were considered nonaligned.

During their regular quadripartite meetings in Bonn, matters regarding East Germany frequently arose, and the four countries then reported at

NATO meetings any relevant agreements made in Bonn. Acting this way contravened the very concept of NATO, where all member states made mutual decisions. When East German issues arose at NATO, the major powers' desires held sway, although they tried to couch their ideas in ways that would bring all NATO states on board and minimize debate. The smaller states at times voiced their concerns, which the quadripartite powers sometimes took into consideration as they revised or finalized policies back in Bonn. Travel by East German athletes to sporting events in NATO countries fell into this area as the tripartite powers set the travel restrictions imposed on East Germans. The rest of NATO, however, pushed back on these regulations when their national interests and domestic public opinion of the alliance came under attack.

Because the tripartite powers still controlled travel authorization, this practice became the method through which the West could damage internal support for the East German regime from its general population. The ATO, located in West Berlin, reviewed applications from East Germans for travel to or through NATO states and issued Temporary Travel Documents (TTDs) when they deemed the individuals and trips acceptable. Limiting travel or access to West Berlin had been a tactic employed by the Soviet Union during the occupation and again in the 1950s and 1960s. In response to the introduction in June 1948 of the Deutschmark as the new currency in the three western zones, the Soviets completely closed all land and sea routes into West Berlin. The Western Allies overcame this blockade by sending all supplies to West Berlin via an eleven-month airlift.[13] A decade later the Soviet leadership again threatened the idea of travel to and communication with West Berlin with Nikita Khrushchev's Berlin ultimatum of 1958. Wanting to separate West Berlin from the Federal Republic (and thus NATO's support), Khrushchev demanded the demilitarization of Berlin and its transformation to a "free city."[14] These threats ultimately came to naught, but the ability to travel freely became a central issue in how NATO dealt with the GDR.

Not only was the ability to travel subject to tripartite oversight, but the symbols with which a person traveled also became entangled with the issue of East German recognition. In 1958 the Federal Republic requested that its NATO allies issue visas (which were needed in conjunction with TTDs) on the travel document and not inside East German passports.[15] With the celebration the following year of the tenth anniversary of its founding, the GDR introduced new state symbols (addressed later in this chapter) and encouraged more of its citizens to go abroad (although not allowing for free travel). These two aspects were part of a concerted effort by the East German government to gain more recognition, or at least symbolic recognition, while it still lacked formal state recognition from most countries. A passport accepted by other states' officials to enter a country, the playing of a national anthem on foreign soil, and the flying of a country's flag abroad all implied de facto recognition. The GDR therefore publicized any example of this type of de facto or symbolic recognition as part of their efforts to gain de jure, or actual legal, recognition.

State symbols and travel restrictions further complicated the East German issue in sport because the country's status varied greatly across international federations (Table 1). The Fédération Internationale de Football Association (FIFA) granted separate recognition to East Germany in 1952, allowing both East and West German teams to qualify for and compete in FIFA-sanctioned tournaments.[16] The Fédération Internationale de Ski (FIS), in a close 18–17 vote with one abstention, accepted East Germany in 1951, which ultimately caused several problems in the 1960s because athletes from both German states excelled in the various skiing disciplines.[17] Other international federations, particularly when delegates from NATO states dominated the executive board, kept the East Germans at bay by either rejecting East German applications for membership or only granting provisional or temporary recognition (but not full membership) for much of the 1950s. The International Amateur Athletic Federation (IAAF), under the direction of Great Britain's IOC member Lord Burghley, maintained a similar position as the IOC. Relying on the IAAF rules, which "do not permit of the affiliation of more than one member from any country," the IAAF recognized only the track and field federation from the Federal Republic in August 1950, rejecting the East German application the following year on the basis of this rule.[18] By 1955 East German athletics officials finally agreed to a situation similar to the situation in Burghley's own country, where the four home nations controlled the sport within their borders, but they came together under the aegis of Great Britain in international organizations.[19] The international federation for rowing, Federation Internationale des Societes d'Aviron (FISA), for instance, granted the GDR temporary membership in 1955 but stipulated that only one German boat could compete in each category at European and Olympic regattas. East Germany only had this "temporary" situation resolved a decade later in 1965, when FISA finally voted to grant them full and separate recognition.[20]

TABLE 1. Year international federations on the Olympic program recognized the German Democratic Republic

FEDERATION	YEAR	STATUS
Fédération Internationale de Ski	1951	Full member
Fédération Internationale de Volleyball	1951	Full member
Association Internationale de Boxe Amateur	1952	Full member
Fédération Internationale Basketball Amateur	1952	Full member
Fédération Internationale de Canoé	1952	Full member
Fédération Internationale de Football Association	1952	Provisional membership in late 1951; full member 1952
Fédération Internationale de Lutte Amateur (wrestling)	1952	Full member
Fédération Internationale de Natation Amateur (swimming)	1952	Full member
International Yacht Racing Union	1952	Full member
International Skating Union	1953	Full member
Fédération Internationale de Judo	1954	Full member
Ligue Internationale de Hockey sur Glace/International Ice Hockey Federation	1954	Full member
Fédération Internationale des Socitétés d'Aviron (rowing)	1955	Temporary recognition in 1955; full member 1965
Union Cycliste Internationale	1955	Full member
Fédération Internationale d'Escrime (fencing)	1956	Full member (11 for, 10 against, 16 abstentions)
Fédération Internationale d'Handball	1956	Full member
Fédération Internationale de Hockey sur Gazon (field hockey)	1956	Provisional recognition in 1952; full member 1956
International Amateur Athletic Federation	1956	"Germany" the member country, with the delegates and votes split between the FRG and GDR federations
Fédération Internationale de Gymnastique	1957	Full member
Fédération International de Luge de Course	1957	Full member when international federation founded in 1957
Fédération Internationale de Bobsleigh et Tobogganing	1957/ 1972	Full membership in 1957; membership revoked in 1958; full membership granted again in 1972
Fédération Internationale Haltérophile et Culturiste/International Weightlifting Federation	1958	Full member
Union Internationale de Pentathlon Moderne	1958	Provisional recognition in 1958; full member 1961. GDR federation founded only two months before UIPM recognition
Union Internationale de Tir (shooting)	1959	Full member
Fédération Equestre Internationale (equestrian)	1960	Provisional membership 1955; full member 1960
Fédération Internationale de Tir l'Arc (archery)	1961	Full member. GDR federation only founded in 1960

Dates in the middle column are from the Bulletin of the National Olympic Committee of the German Democratic Republic IV/1965. Fédération Internationale de Bobsleigh et Tobogganing and Fédération Equestre Internationale are not included in the original document but were added for the comprehensive list of Olympic sports at the time. Additional status notes were added by the author.

—Source: Bulletin of the National Olympic Committee of the German Democratic Republic IV/1965, page 28, box 5, folder 19, JSM, RSCL.

The East German problem increasingly appeared at the sporting events themselves. A year before it held the 1960 Winter Olympics, Squaw Valley hosted test competitions in preparation for the games. While some athletes welcomed the opportunity to learn the terrain and become familiar with a venue before the Olympic Games, many skiers remained in Europe and competed in events there. For East German skiers, however, the event served a political and diplomatic function. The East German ski team attempted to compete at the North American Ski Championships in early 1959, but they had not replied to the organizers of the event until approximately one week before the championships began. Their response was "well past [the] thrice postponed entry deadline and too late for [the organizing committee] to accept their entries."[21] The organizers had mailed the initial invitations for the championships in October, and they had sent another letter to the East Germans on December 22, again with no response. When the East Germans finally responded in February to the invitation, nine days before the event was to begin and long after the deadline for receiving entries for the competition had passed, they did not contact the organizing committee but instead the National Ski Association of America, which was not in Squaw Valley.[22] Nonetheless, the president of the National Ski Association of America tried to facilitate visas for the East German skiers at the end of January, shortly before the event began.[23] The State Department directed its mission in Berlin, and thus its ATO representatives, to defer action on these visa applications unless they applied as part of an all-German team, in which case their applications could be expedited. The State Department also instructed its diplomats to sit on the visa applications instead of refusing them outright because it was "preferable from publicity point of view."[24] The U.S. mission in Berlin took this approach, even with daily enquiries from the East Germans about their visa status in the days leading up to the event.[25]

The East German press propagandized the incident, blaming the United States government for the inability of the East German skiers to compete in Squaw Valley. For over a week the East German state newspaper *Neues Deutschland* emphasized the refusal of visas for the GDR skiers, claiming, "The reasons—which no one made secret—are exclusively of a political nature: They want to prevent the appearance of a team from the GDR in the USA and also not deviate from the principle that members of a worker-party will not have approved a visa to the USA."[26] The East German ski federation also held a press conference in East Berlin on February 18 on the inability of its athletes to participate in the pre-Olympic event and another one the following week, three days after the championships began. American diplomats believed the second press conference was merely the East Germans "obviously trying keep issue alive for propaganda purposes."[27] Rather than publicize their own tardiness and misunderstanding to the press, the East Germans emphasized only the fact that the United States failed to issue visas for the East German skiers. The *New York Times*, on the other hand, never mentioned the lack of East German skiers, likely because most European skiers did not travel to the United States for the event. In contrast, the paper fully covered the process of the Soviet ski team obtaining visas in order to compete in the United States for the first time.[28] Until 1958 when the U.S. government removed the security requirement that all Soviet citizens entering the country be fingerprinted, the USSR had refused to compete in sporting events in the United States.[29] The Soviet Union supported the East Germans in their attempts to use the visa denial to foment Cold War divisions within sport. The Soviet representative to FIS even suggested that FIS boycott the 1960 Winter Olympics—a proposal no one took seriously because of the importance of the Olympic Games on the international sport calendar.[30]

Unlike the minor event in Squaw Valley, the problem of an East German team not being able to travel to the United States arose again later in 1959, this time for a world championship. At its 1958 congress the Union Internationale de Pentathlon Moderne (UIPM) selected Hershey, Pennsylvania (home of the world-famous chocolate company), to host its 1959 world championships. Modern pentathlon, an event created for the 1912 Stockholm Olympics, involves pistol shooting, fencing, swimming, equestrianism, and running—skills necessary for military officers of the time. As such, almost all of the competitors, as well as the organizers, during the sport's first several decades were military officers.[31] UIPM also agreed to provisionally recognize the recently formed East German federation despite concern from the United States and other countries. UIPM, however, stipulated that their recognition of East Germany was subject to IOC rules for the Olympic Games, which demanded an all-German team.[32] When the UIPM secretary visited the United States in March 1959, the world championship organizers, who were also U.S. Army officers and in contact with the State Department, unofficially informed the UIPM secretary that East Germany was not invited to the world championships in Hershey because the U.S. government did not recognize the GDR as a country.[33] The State Department, while emphasizing its positive support of the event and international sport in general, also shifted the blame for any political difficulties to the East Germans. They informed the local organizers that the State Department "places high value upon international sporting events as a means of creating wider understanding among peoples," including with the Soviet Union and Eastern European states. However, the East German regime would use the participation of a "national" team at a competition in the United States "for propaganda designed to create the impression that the so-called German Democratic Republic was winning a greater measure of acceptance abroad and designed to convince the East German population of the inevitability of Communist rule." The State Department also commented: "The position of the East German sportsman is a tragic one, for he finds that his interests and skills are exploited to accomplish the political purposes of the regime." Even though East Germany could not send its own team, the State Department said it "would be pleased to receive the visa applications" from any East Germans wanting to compete as individual members or part of an all-German team.[34] With most modern pentathlon athletes and officials active military members, this event had the potential to create a major problem if the United States permitted not only an East German team to compete but especially a team composed of members of the GDR's military.

The American modern pentathlon officials immediately informed the UIPM of the State Department's position, and the international federation in turn contacted the East German federation to try to find a solution to this problem.[35] The UIPM rightly assumed that the creation of an all-German team for the world championships would not interest the East Germans but nonetheless strongly encouraged them to nominate three athletes and submit their visa applications.[36] The East Germans followed this recommendation but failed to receive visas from the U.S. mission in Berlin in part because the individuals were members of the communist party but also because, by submitting their applications together, the mission considered they constituted a team rather than individual athletes.[37] The East Germans sent a letter of protest to UIPM, whose executive committee discussed whether to remove the world championships from Hershey a mere two weeks before the event began. The executive committee agreed to share the chain of events and East Germany's protest letter at the congress, which took place the day before the world championships opened. Following a long discussion the UIPM delegates confirmed that the 1959 world championships would continue (the UIPM and athletes were, of course, already in Hershey), that future hosts would need to guarantee participation to all UIPM members, and that a letter of regret would be sent to the East Germans.[38] Modern pentathlon has never been a sport that garners much attention, and as the world championships opened in Hershey, Americans' focus was on baseball's postseason and the college and professional football seasons, leaving minimal coverage on the sport pages in newspapers, even those local to the event. In addition, with UIPM's requirement for an all-German team, in contrast to the skiing events organized in Squaw Valley earlier in the year, the GDR was not able to rally much public opinion in support of their cause with this event.

These two instances of travel being refused particularly concerned the East Germans because the United States was preparing to host the 1960 Olympic Games. East German sport leaders now feared their athletes who made the Olympic team would not be permitted to travel to the United States, which would leave only athletes from the Federal Republic representing Germany at the games. As long as the athletes were part of an all-German team and not a separate East German team, the State Department affirmed it would approve travel documents. Nonetheless, both the State Department and the Italian foreign ministry believed that once in their countries for the 1960 Olympics, East German athletes and officials would take political action.[39] The official send-off for the East German contingent of the all-German Olympic team competing in Squaw Valley had included Minister for State Security Erich Mielke and two Politburo members (including future GDR leader Erich Hoenecker), justifying the American and Italian concerns. At this event, "Particular stress [was] placed upon contribution by GDR Olympic athletes to prestige of the GDR. Honecker pointed out 'GDR athletes competing for first time in USA. You are going to this country as envoys of peace and understanding, as representatives of the first workers and peasants state in history of Germany.'"[40] The East German government used the two cases of their athletes not receiving travel documents to participate in events in the United States in 1959 to highlight the country's unfair exclusion from the international system. However, these proclamations by East German leaders on the political value of its athletes competing on the all-German team in Squaw Valley justified the State Department's fears over East Germans propagandizing sport.

After a year of NATO and the ATO increasingly confronting the problem of East German travel, the Federal Republic raised the issue within NATO in March 1960. The German representative to the Committee of Political Advisers criticized the actions of the "Pankow régime" for concentrating "on fields which appear to be non-political, such as trade, cultural and scientific exchanges and sports . . . in order to create the impression that it has been accepted into the community of nations, thus paving the way for eventual formal recognition, which is the ultimate aim of these exchanges." He continued, "It is the generally accepted Communist doctrine that every sphere of social activity has a political content and that the merits of trade, arts, science and sport are to be judged by their political and propaganda value."[41] Indeed, the East German regime held a huge rally with five thousand people at the Dynamo Sport Hall in East Berlin after welcoming the returning Squaw Valley Olympians after the games. With this event the regime had tried "to exploit the athletic prowess and accomplishments of the Soviet Zone representatives on the All-German Olympic Team." Several speakers, mostly politicians and East German sport officials, attempted "to convince the audience that the performance by gold-medal winners Helmut Recknagel and Helga Haase resulted from the benevolence of the State and proved that the world has accepted the GDR." The American staff member from the Berlin mission who attended this event noted that while the crowd had a genuine enthusiasm for the athletes, the regime's attempts "to twist this enthusiasm to political benefit" failed, with one-third of the crowd departing during one forty-minute speech.[42] This "self-advertisement," as the British Committee of Political Advisers representative called the East German actions, was increasingly taking on "a political power" about which NATO states needed to be vigilant.[43] By placing East Germany's recent efforts to politicize sport in context with the regime's other actions, NATO member states in April 1960 reaffirmed their support for the limits placed on East German travel at the behest of the Federal Republic and tripartite powers.[44]

A few months later when East Germany encroached on the quadripartite status of Berlin in September 1960, the tripartite powers imposed greater restrictions on East German travel, and the Federal Republic also stopped issuing West German passports for residents of East Germany.[45] The East Germans announced that they would not recognize Federal Republic passports for travel through East German territory (typically between West Berlin and West Germany) and that these individuals would be required to hold an East Germany–issued transit permit.[46] The Americans, British, and French considered the imposition of countermeasures, proposed by the American embassy in Bonn in this context. The British embassy reported back to the Foreign Office: "There is clearly something to be said for the American Ambassador's argument that the right policy at this point is to hit back as hard as we can in order to leave no doubt about our resolution and our readiness to take counter-action, and to deter further restrictions by the implication that we are prepared to go even further in future." Yet, as the embassy noted, "the balance of advantage is in favour of the more prudent course of turning the screw gradually. There is no assurance that the East Germans would in fact be deterred by the relatively minor measures which we could mount against them. The more likely result would be to accelerate the spiralling process of restrictions against West Berlin and to leave us with no weapons to fight the next round."[47] A week of discussions among the tripartite powers (sometimes including the Germans) ensued with diplomats across the four capital cities. On September 23, 1960, sport became one of the nine categories of travel that they agreed to ban, along with trade, agriculture, medical and scientific, professional (professors, teachers, students, lawyers), political, cultural, press, and tourism. People applying to travel for health, emigration, compassionate grounds, contractual labor, and family visits would still receive TTDs.[48]

Individually, the nine categories of banned travel might not have amounted to a significant blow to East Germany, nor would each category on its own have much reach. Taken together, they affected a broad swath of the population and could hurt the GDR economically while also thwarting efforts to engage in soft power abroad. The East German government sought to champion its athletes' participation in the Squaw Valley Olympics as a victory for its recognition, but this example was only valuable to the regime because its athletes twice failed to compete in the United States the previous year. Sport was an essential component to these new travel regulations because of the recent addition of the GDR's state symbols. Even though scientists might have more and deeper person-to-person interactions while abroad than a team of elite athletes, sporting events received far more publicity than an academic conference. A team of football players wearing a national uniform emblazoned with the country's emblem and standing at attention in front of the new flag listening to the national anthem was a clear and powerful image, visible to tens of thousands of spectators in the stadium and reproduced in newspapers and on television. The state symbols on the athletes' uniforms promoted the GDR and made clear that its existence was greater than what the Federal Republic tried to claim. Sport by far produced the most frequent and passionate debate within NATO and in the press on both sides of the Iron Curtain because of its popularity and global visibility.

STATE SYMBOLS AT SPORTING EVENTS

During the GDR's tenth anniversary celebrations in October 1959, the East German state introduced a new flag with the emblem of the worker and peasant state in the middle of the black-red-gold German flag. The addition of the communist symbol differentiated the East German flag from the Federal Republic's plain black-red-gold flag, which was the same flag used during the Weimar Republic (1918–33). The Bonn government considered this new East German flag to be a symbol of the division of Germany, in contrast to the tricolor on its own, which, they believed, alluded to national unity in freedom.[49] The Federal Republic introduced a ban on flying the East German flag, including at sporting events.[50] The new East German flag quickly became a problem for any area that prominently used flags, both in NATO countries and neutral states.[51] The introduction of new state symbols therefore caused further challenges to East Germany's ability to participate in international sporting events, including events held outside of NATO countries. When NATO states could not restrict the entry of an East German team, the Federal Republic sought the support of its allies' diplomats to persuade their sport officials to take actions to prevent the East German flag from flying and anthem from playing.

National flags are a major part of the pageantry at international sporting events. Venues typically hang from the rafters or around the top of a stadium all of the flags from the countries competing at the event. During the victory ceremony the flags from the countries of the first, second, and third place athletes are raised while the national anthem of the winner plays. In addition to these visibly displayed symbols of the nation, all international federations had rules requiring world championship organizers to invite all recognized member national federations—which included East Germany for those federations that by the late 1950s had granted separate recognition to the GDR. This mandate to invite East Germany therefore brought with it the flag and anthem issue.

The basic black-red-gold flag had been used for the 1956 all-German Olympic team, but East Germany's adoption of a new flag complicated the negotiations for the next iteration of the combined team for the 1960 games. The East German Olympic Committee now claimed it "cannot be expected to march behind the flag of another state in view of the fact that they have their own flag." With the rest of the communist bloc supporting the East German demand for a neutral decision, the IOC sought a compromise: the black-red-gold with the five Olympic rings in the middle.[52] The Federal Republic government, however, did not approve of this idea, declaring "that it would be 'irreconcilable with national dignity' to go along with this compromise" because of the widespread political implications.[53] They also claimed that the use of a third, neutral German flag for the Olympics would acknowledge that two German states existed, which went against the Federal Republic's position that it was the only legitimate German state. Chancellor Konrad Adenauer, Foreign Minister Heinrich von Bretano, and Minister of the Interior Gerhard Schröder met with Karl Ritter von Halt, president of the National Olympic Committee and an IOC member, and Willi Daume, president of the German Sport Federation, for several hours in November 1959 to discuss the flag issue. Although von Halt and Daume argued that "sport must neither be subject to nor play an active part in Foreign Policy," as the Germans relayed to IOC president Avery Brundage, the fact that they were discussing this issue with the highest members of the government belied that idea.[54]

Adenauer preferred no German flag in any form fly around the stadium, appear in front of the all-German team as athletes marched into the stadium, or be raised when German athletes medaled over some form of a flag that contravened official government policy. He said the government could accept the Olympic flag on its own, which von Halt and Daume felt belonged to all nations and which the IOC would not accept. They did not believe the Olympic rings on the German flag would be dishonorable but instead "the flag would be decorated with the honorable emblem of the olympic idea to unify all nations."[55] If the Federal Republic rejected the flag solution proposed by Brundage and prevented a combined German team from competing in 1960, then only an East German team would compete at the games—and march behind its own communist state flag.[56] For these reasons von Halt and Daume implored Brundage to publicly announce that the IOC's decision would stand.[57] Because the Federal Republic's sport officials could not relinquish their right of recognition to the GDR and hand the East Germans

FIGURE 1. "The German Flag Controversy," *New York Times,* December 13, 1959, E2.

their international legitimacy, they "defied a 'recommendation' by the Bonn Government not to accept Mr. Brundage's proposed solution" to the flag dilemma.[58] Brundage commended the acceptance of the all-German Olympic flag, telling both German Olympic Committees that he considered this agreement "a victory for sport over politics."[59] In reporting the German flag controversy and the decision taken over Adenauer's objections, the *New York Times* published five cartoons (Figure 1), three of which showed the flag options. The other two were reproduced from West German papers: one showed Adenauer and a sport official physically fighting over the Olympic rings staying on the flag in one instance, while the other showed a pleased East German leader Walter Ulbricht and Khrushchev pointing to the GDR symbol in the middle Olympic ring.[60] Two weeks earlier *Neues Deutschland* had published a cartoon (Figure 2) with a displeased Adenauer shaking the flagpole flying the German flag with the Olympic rings, demonstrating the West German chancellor's stance on the flag.[61] The IOC had been able to impose its will because of the requirement for an all-German team, but the flag issue had once again forced the IOC to become involved in the German problem.

FIGURE 2. *Neues Deutschland*, November 25, 1959, 2.

The flag and anthem became particularly difficult to regulate when East German athletes not representing the national team competed in NATO states. An East German volleyball club was scheduled to play against a French club team on October 18, 1959, at the Coubertin Stadium in Paris. When the Paris Police Prefecture prevented the East German flag from being raised and anthem from playing, the East German club refused to play. The East German press decried this scandal, claiming it was the Federal Republic's ambassador in Paris who prevented the flag from flying, while the West German press lamented that the police were left with the task of dispersing a few thousand spectators who came to the venue but did not see any volleyball action.[62] The French Ambassador in Bonn felt the need to explain at the quadripartite meeting this "misunderstanding" so as "not to destroy the favorable impression which had been produced by the intervention of the French police."[63] Just weeks later a handball and volleyball team each received TTDs to play in events in France, but the ATO granted them "only on the condition that the new flag of the GDR does not appear during these games."[64] The handball team violated this agreement when it played in a venue that had hung the GDR flag, which the French government only realized after *Neues Deutschland* had reported it.[65] This blatant disregard for French authority prompted a desire by the French to take a harder line on issuing TTDs and visas to East German athletes, including rejecting any future applications from this club. The Ministère des Affaires Étrangères also had Maurice Herzog, the secretary of state for youth and sport, send a directive to all prefects and sport organizations in France banning the East German anthem and flag at sporting events.[66] Upon hearing of these incidents, the British embassy in Bonn commented that the "tough line" taken by the French would likely strengthen the Federal Republic's position regarding sporting events.[67] Indeed, the clarification on the ban on flying the East German flag in the Federal Republic, shared with NATO two months later in January 1960, included the requirement to intervene "whenever the flag is displayed in public; this includes sport events, exhibitions, and fairs."[68] The visits by East German teams to France in the autumn of 1959, with police intervention in one instance and the flying of the GDR flag in the other case, thus contributed to the great attention paid to this symbol of the communist German state.

By the end of 1959 *Neues Deutschland* printed a map of Europe with GDR flags planted in all of the locations where the East German flag had been flown at sporting events, attempting to show the growing de facto recognition for the country. Many of these places lay behind the Iron Curtain or in neutral countries, although quite a few were in NATO states: France, Great Britain, Norway, Belgium, Denmark, and the Federal Republic. Several of these events, however, were with clubs or individual athletes and not national teams. One event was for youth swimmers, and one "event" was merely a training week for ski jumpers. Three of the flags planted on the map were for events that had not yet taken place (the 1960 European speed skating championships in Davos, Switzerland; the 1960 Holmenkollen ski jumping event in Oslo; and a skiing event in Finland).[69] These examples of de facto recognition were, thus, relatively minor and, aside from the handball match in Paris, did not merit discussion within NATO.

To prevent these kinds of incidents from becoming public relations disasters, some sport organizers opted not to fly any flags at their events so that East Germans could not protest their unfair or unequal treatment. Instead of hanging the flags of every competing state, the European figure skating championships in February 1960, in the Bavarian town of Garmisch, opted to forego all flags in order to prevent recognizing the East German flag in the Federal Republic.[70] When the Italian city of Genoa hosted an international regatta in February 1960 to which both West and East German boats had been invited, the organizers consulted with the Italian Foreign Ministry regarding flags and suggested German boats use the flag of the all-German Olympic team. While the West German boats readily accepted this idea, the East Germans responded with a three-page polemic telegram insisting on flying the East German flag. The Italian Foreign Ministry informed the yacht club they "did not care how they solved the problem so long as no East German flag was flown in Italy. The yacht club accordingly telegraphed the East Germans that if they wanted to participate they could fly the German Olympic flag."[71] The new flag quickly became a symbol behind which the GDR could rally its population, especially when NATO states took action to prevent it from being flown. Nonetheless, by the spring of 1960 the German delegation at NATO assessed East Germany's recent efforts: "The Soviet Zone Régime has simultaneously been intensifying its efforts abroad to get closer to recognition direct or indirect. . . . Attempts to utilise sport in these endeavours, and to obtain agreement to the hoisting of the new Soviet Zone flag at sports events, have for the most part been unsuccessful."[72] The GDR's introduction of a new flag had led to some agitation and news stories, but NATO governments had supported the nonrecognition of the East German flag when they became aware of its possible appearance at events within their borders.

Sporting events held outside NATO member states were not immune to the problem of the two German states as the Federal Republic remained concerned with the public appearance of East German state symbols. Even before the GDR introduced a new flag, the national anthem became an issue at sporting events. Two weeks before the 1958 IAAF European Championships began in Sweden, the Auswärtiges Amt sought the help of its tripartite allies to ensure the "Becher Hymn" would not be played on the podium for any East German victories. Even though a combined German team was participating in this event in Sweden, a neutral state not aligned with either Cold War bloc, the two German athletics federations had not been able to agree in their meetings on which anthem would be played when their athletes won. The West Germans wanted the compromise of Beethoven's Ninth Symphony played, as was done for winners from the all-German team at the 1956 Olympics. The East Germans, on the other hand, sought to have their anthem played for GDR victories and the anthem of Federal Republic played when its athletes won. The Auswärtiges Amt therefore sought the assistance of its allies in Bonn. Should the East German anthem be played, the Foreign Ministry representative argued, it would be the first instance at a sporting event and "would constitute an unhappy precedent."[73] The Federal Republic especially sought British support since Lord Burghley was IAAF president and an IOC vice president.[74] The Auswärtiges Amt believed achieving this "compromise" of a neutral song played after any German victory in Stockholm would be a victory for the Federal Republic's politics.[75]

While in Copenhagen en route to Stockholm, Lord Burghley accepted a drinks invitation at the British embassy, where the ambassador requested Burghley's assistance in supporting the West German stance regarding the anthem. Lord Burghley agreed that this scenario was the best course of action, although he could not guarantee that the IAAF "would fall in line," but he would do his best to achieve this result.[76] The State Department as well reached out to its IAAF member Dan Ferris, who also sat on the federation's Executive Committee and was in Stockholm for the event. Ironically, the State Department—itself getting involved in international sport at the behest of one of its allies—instructed its embassy in Stockholm to tell Ferris that the "Soviet Zone regime [was] attempting [to] gain political advantage for self through effort [to] give itself separate identity in what should be exclusively sporting event."[77] Although unable to convince the East Germans to accept the "Ode to Joy" (Beethoven's Ninth Symphony) compromise, the IAAF ultimately decided to play anthems for all winners except for athletes from Germany. Any victorious East or West German would instead receive a trumpet fanfare while the previously agreed-upon German black-red-gold flag (without any emblems in the middle) flew. The East Germans reluctantly agreed to this decision, but, as the West German embassy reported back to Bonn, openly grumbled about this situation.[78]

East Germany continued to push for its new flag and anthem to be used at international sporting events, and they again became a major problem at two 1961 world championships in neutral countries: speed skating in Gothenburg, Sweden, and ice hockey in Geneva and Lausanne, Switzerland. In December 1960, two months before Sweden hosted another major sporting event, the West German consulate in Gothenburg reported that the program for the speed skating world championships listed the GDR by name in accordance with the International Skating Union's list of members. The Federal Republic requested the program be changed, which the organizers stated could not be done.[79] The Auswärtiges Amt diplomats, realizing that the East German flag and anthem were likely to appear at this event as well, repeatedly spoke with the organizers to prevent the East German flag from flying or anthem from being played.[80] The Federal Republic's consulate in Gothenburg also attempted to enlist the American consulate and Swedish Foreign Minister in these efforts, but to no avail.[81] The Federal Republic's consul general walked out of the banquet held in Gothenburg's city hall the night before the world championships began after seeing the GDR flag alongside all of the other competing countries' flags. The following day the West German team withdrew from the event minutes before the opening ceremony in protest of the East German flag flying around the stadium.[82] During the opening ceremony East German athletes marched into Ullevi Stadium with its communist emblem in full view—an image *Göteborgs-Tidningen* printed on its front page.[83] *Neues Deutschland* also carried the story on its front page: "Bonn flag bearer rebuffed; GDR flag in Gothenburg" but without a photograph.[84]

With East Germany gaining the upper hand in Gothenburg with the withdrawal of the West German skaters, the government of the Federal Republic and its sport leaders immediately turned their attention to the ice hockey world championships starting a few weeks later in Switzerland. The International Ice Hockey Federation (IIHF) had accepted East Germany in 1954 as a member, and both German teams qualified for the 1961 world championships. A week before the tournament began West German diplomats attempted to convince the tournament organizers to remove the East German flag from the venues or use the all-German Olympic flag, but their efforts failed.[85] On the opening day of the tournament the Auswärtiges Amt issued a press release stating they did not approve of the participation of a Federal Republic team if the GDR flag appeared at the rinks. The statement also reiterated that "sporting events should be kept out of the sphere of political controversy."[86] After several conversations and letters between Willi Daume and the Auswärtiges Amt, including foreign minister Heinrich von Bretano, the ice hockey team remained in the tournament since the two German teams were not in the same pool and thus not scheduled to play each other. If the teams met in the knockout stage, then the West German athletes would simply leave the ice instead of acknowledge the raising of the East German flag at the end of the match.[87] The negotiations between the government and sport leaders revealed the challenges of upholding the

Hallstein Doctrine in sport. The West German government could not force private entities in a different country to take down another country's flag. If the West German team withdrew from the tournament, that action would only embarrass the Federal Republic and not accomplish anything, as the East German flag would remain inside the venue.

The Federal Republic's least desired scenario became a reality as both teams' mediocre play resulted in a game between the two German teams on the tournament's last day to determine their final places. The IIHF reminded both German federations that they must respect the winning team's flag and anthem following the game's conclusion and threatened the Federal Republic with expulsion if it refused. The Federal Republic's ice hockey leaders suggested not holding a victory ceremony to avoid any incident, but the East German federation rebuffed this proposal, insisting it had the right to be recognized if victorious—and thus as a state.[88] Rather than risk losing and the possibility of having to recognize the GDR flag and anthem, the West German team forfeited the game. Inside the Federal Republic the press wrote that the country's sport leaders regretted that the IIHF and GDR had not accepted their "sporting and fair" proposals that would have provided an alternative to the flag and anthems of the traditional victory ceremony. By not playing the game, the Federal Republic prevented the de facto recognition of the GDR flag and anthem while simultaneously avoiding a violation of IIHF rules—and thus averted expulsion from the international federation. The IIHF gave East Germany a 5–0 "walkover" victory, resulting in a fifth-place finish for the GDR, and the West German hockey team fell to last place. The IIHF also made the West German hockey federation reimburse the rink for any costs incurred from the game's cancellation.[89]

With these actions the West German ice hockey federation brought the Hallstein Doctrine directly into international sport, a point which the global press highlighted. *Svenska dagbladet*, the major Swedish paper, reported this "flag war" on its front page.[90] The *Times* (London) reported that "some members of the west German team . . . were visibly upset when they heard of the decision to withdraw" and that loud boos from the crowd followed the announcement that the game would be cancelled.[91] The negative tone in the Swiss papers, the Federal Republic's embassy in Bern commented, should not be taken too seriously as the disapproval was largely from the disappointment of the cancellation of the game on short notice.[92] *New York Times* columnist Robert Daley, reporting from the tournament in Switzerland, focused on the emotional role of flags and anthems in fomenting nationalism at sporting events. The West German forfeiture prevented the "politically insupportable" action of potentially having the East German anthem "played to celebrate a West German defeat."[93] Daley used this incident to argue for abolishing the postgame victory ceremony using flags and anthems—an action that would have made it easier to uphold the Hallstein Doctrine in sport but not entirely. The West German team had played against its government's wishes on a rink that displayed the GDR flag, which they could ignore—until the two teams had to play each other. Only then did the West German sport officials act in accordance with their government's policies. The government's press release after the West German forfeiture took a different tone than the one from the start of the tournament. Now the government was "fully behind" the freely made decision of the German team's leaders, which was part of an effort to prevent the misuse of sporting events to force the division of Germany.[94] Even though the Federal Republic attempted to blame East Germany for bringing politics into sport with the 1961 ice hockey world championships, it was clearly their own policies that brought the Cold War German problem to the Swiss ice rink.

East Germany propagandized this incident, arguing that the Federal Republic was the state that introduced politics into sport. *Neues Deutschland* placed the ice hockey story on its front page, claiming that "the West German sports leadership has once again confirmed with its cancellation of the sports match on Sunday for all of the world that it is compliant to Bonn's politics of the Cold War." The paper claimed that instead of hurting the GDR, "millions of West German sportsmen will be more isolated with the application of the Hallstein doctrine in international sport."[95] By excoriating the Federal Republic (and drawing Adenauer into the affair) for mixing politics with sports, the East German regime hoped to improve its own international stature following the ice hockey championships. The official state newspaper did not mention any of East Germany's own efforts to introduce politics into sport, instead blaming the West German government entirely.[96] As the French mission in Berlin reported, many people in East Berlin strongly criticized what happened in Switzerland, calling it "an unprecedented scandal organized by Cold War enraged Bonn, who want at all costs to politicize sport."[97]

The introduction of a separate flag and national anthem enabled the GDR to use sport even more frequently in its quest for legitimacy within the international system. NATO member states now had to confront East German state symbols anywhere in the world instead of having to address this issue only when hosting a sporting event inside their borders and determining whether to permit East German athletes to enter the country. The ice hockey incident prompted further diplomatic discussion, including at NATO, regarding how to deal with East German sports teams. The German representative on the Committee of Political Advisers advocated strictly enforcing NATO's previously established guidelines, arguing that the "surest way of handling problem was to exclude GDR teams." If the other governments "did not find this possible then he suggested visas be issued only on condition anthem not be played, nor flag flown etc."[98] Travel and state symbols thus became entangled in the larger effort to prevent the recognition of East Germany, but the nature of elite sport and the national pride associated with victory at a global level were inherently intertwined with the very same situations that NATO sought to prevent.

CONCLUSION

While the 1961 IIHF world championships and the accompanying German drama were taking place, the tripartite powers agreed to relax the travel restrictions that they had imposed on East Germans six months earlier. With the support of the Federal Republic, the ATO still maintained strict control to avoid facilitating travel that would directly or indirectly help achieve East German goals.[99] Sport thus fell in this gray zone with the lifting of the September 1960 restrictions. The Portuguese were hoping to have an East German youth team participate in an upcoming Union of European Football Associations (UEFA) tournament that they were hosting.[100] In response to the announcement of the lifting of the travel restrictions and Portugal's desire to grant visas to the East German team, a larger discussion ensued at the NATO Committee of Political Advisers meeting regarding the travel of East German sports teams. The British, Dutch, Norwegian, and Danish representatives "were inclined to favor allowing team to come so long as it was carefully controlled and no national flags or anthems permitted."[101] The British argued that while they did not want East German athletes to exploit sport for political purposes, they felt refusing visas for sport teams "would have a disproportionately harmful effect on public opinion and, thus, would not be in the best interests of the Alliance."[102] Sport clearly drew the interest and input of all NATO member states.

While no major diplomatic incidents happened within sport during most of the 1950s, by 1961 NATO had increasingly been forced into taking action with respect to East German nonrecognition within international sport. As the Belgian representative stated in support of the continued ban on East German athletes, their participation "would almost inevitably lead to unpleasant incidents."[103] The Belgians were about to reject the visa application of an East German field hockey team, but they reiterated they would be in a difficult position if other NATO countries allowed visits by similar groups. The Belgian Foreign Ministry wanted an assurance that all NATO countries would deny visas to East German national sport teams. The Belgian delegation feared that after refusing visas to an East German team, if "at a later date, one of their NATO partners permitted the East German team to compete in their country, the Belgian Government would be placed in a very embarrassing position."[104] This kind of domestic backlash would harm the overall support for the alliance, which was already low.

Even with these highly propagandized incidents regarding East German sport, domestic sport organizations in NATO member states did not shy away from inviting East German athletes to events. As the IIHF world cham pionships were ending, the East German ice hockey federation approached the Norwegian federation, the group B (second tier) world championships, about scheduling two exhibition games in Norway the week after the tournament in Switzerland ended. Knowing there was not enough time for TTDs to be issued, the East German ice hockey federation asked the Norwegian mission in Berlin to issue visas in East German passports, which the Norwegians flat out rejected. The ATO, when asked by the East German ice hockey federation, also reiterated that it was doubtful TTDs could be issued in such a short amount of time. Two days later—and just one day before the first of the two scheduled exhibition matches—the Norwegian mission in Berlin received a call from the Norwegian Immigration Office, requesting that they approach the ATO. A member of the Norwegian mission staff then visited the ATO, asking them to issue TTDs and said that if not, the Norwegian Ministry of Justice had just agreed to admit the East German team without TTDs or visas. Because the travel ban had recently been rescinded, the ATO agreed to issue the TTDs, valid only for Norway.

While the ATO expedited the TTDs as a special favor to their Norwegian friends, the ATO was not pleased that the East Germans had succeeded in securing travel documents by directly contacting the Norwegians and bypassing the ATO processes in a carefully calculated tactic. After the ice hockey team arrived in Norway, the East German press reported that its anthem and flag appeared during its victory over the Norwegian team in the first match. This scenario was in direct opposition to the support Norway had made earlier that month at the Committee of Political Advisers meeting when NATO agreed to lift the travel ban but maintain support for some restrictions.[105]

NATO governments recognized that the groups organizing sporting events were private, which meant government officials struggled to demand the removal of East German flags or the prevention of its anthem from being played. Indeed, the Utenriksdepartement felt that "when it comes to avoiding sporting events where East Germans are participating not being exploited politically, there is not much one can do from the Norwegian side."[106] When sport leaders had a close relationship with their government—National Olympic Committee president Willi Daume in the Federal Republic, IOC vice president and IAAF president Lord Burghley in Great Britain, and FIS vice president John Stanley Mullin in the United States, for example—NATO had a greater chance of its position being upheld within the realm of sport. An internal Norwegian assessment of the ice hockey invitation and games revealed a breakdown in communication across the various ministries, but also an understanding at the time that if the East German team could not arrive in Norway and the games were cancelled, the government could expect a negative reaction from the public.[107]

By the late spring of 1961, the problem of East German sport had become a frequent topic within NATO and its members' diplomatic corps. Calling sport the "most troublesome category of past few weeks," the State Department noted, "There seems to be some recognition of this problem now among NATO members. In the absence of agreed, uniform practices many members will be reluctant to expose themselves to domestic criticism by taking stiff line."[108] When the Belgian Foreign Ministry denied visas to East German cyclists, they did so because "Belgium was not interested in aiding East German sportsmen." However, as the Belgian Foreign Ministry complained to the American Embassy in Brussels, they were "irked" when other countries failed to uphold the policy or claimed athletes required visas because it was in a country's "national interest." While willing to support a common line, the current NATO policy was not clear, the Belgian diplomat complained.[109] Indeed, the NATO policy only recommended, "If it seemed desirable visa offices could, when granting visas, warn visitors that they should, while in the receiving country, abstain from all political activity (e.g. showing of the East German flag, playing of the national anthem)."[110] Actions across the alliance were therefore uneven. The dramatic change in the political situation later that summer, with the hardened border around West Berlin and restrictions on the freedom of movement, ultimately provided clarity of NATO's position to East German sports teams. With that came even more publicity, which diplomats believed had the power to damage the alliance.

CHAPTER 2

THE BERLIN WALL AND THE ENDING OF FREE TRAVEL IN SPORT

The political victory gained by East Germany with the 1961 ice hockey championships did not last long. More than three million GDR residents had fled to the Federal Republic, primarily via West Berlin, prompting the East German regime on the night of August 12–13, 1961, to fortify the border between the two parts of the city with barbed wire in preparation for the construction of a concrete wall. The GDR leadership viewed the construction of the Berlin Wall as a way to secure its own borders and solidify the regime's legitimacy with its citizens.[1] The Federal Republic was outraged at the physical representation of the Iron Curtain and considered it yet another way the illegitimate regime restricted the rights and freedoms of Germans in Berlin. The Cold War had already penetrated international sport, but the appearance of the Berlin Wall shattered the illusion that sport and politics should remain separate—although international sport still attempted to function along these lines. The (West) German Olympic Committee met on August 16, just three days after the world awoke to the Berlin Wall. They claimed the East German action stopping freedom of movement violated international sport ideals, declaring the construction of the Berlin Wall "contrary to the fundamental principles of humanity and, in our field, means a violation of all the principles of the world of sport."[2] They immediately ended all sport interactions with East Germany. The GDR sport officials, however, blamed the break in German-German sport on their West German counterparts, arguing it was the sport leaders in the Federal Republic who had terminated sport relations with East German athletes. The East German statement, made on August 19, completely left out any reference to the East German actions in Berlin from the preceding days that might have prompted the Federal Republic's sport leaders to take such a position.[3]

In addition to closing the intra-German border and ending German-German sport contests, the Berlin Wall also solidified NATO support of the

Federal Republic and its policies. The American, British, and French representatives comprising the Allied Travel Office (ATO) reimposed the travel restrictions on East Germany that they had first implemented in September 1960 and lifted in March 1961. The ATO again banned the authorization of Temporary Travel Documents (TTDs) for East Germans whose applications fell under the categories of sport, trade, professional, political, cultural, press, and tourism.[4] NATO readily accepted these renewed restrictions in fields where East Germany could easily gain propaganda or financial benefit as retaliation for the GDR hindering freedom of movement with the Berlin Wall. This support of ATO policy meant East Germans from any banned category would receive neither a TTD from the ATO nor a visa from the country that they wanted to visit. The ATO only issued the TTD if a visa from the destination country was forthcoming, but NATO countries could withhold issuing a visa if a TTD would not be granted (Figure 3). Because East Germans needed both a TTD and visa to travel to NATO countries, this process created a circuitous problem for East Germans but a way for NATO member states to deflect blame when East Germans could not travel to events within their borders.

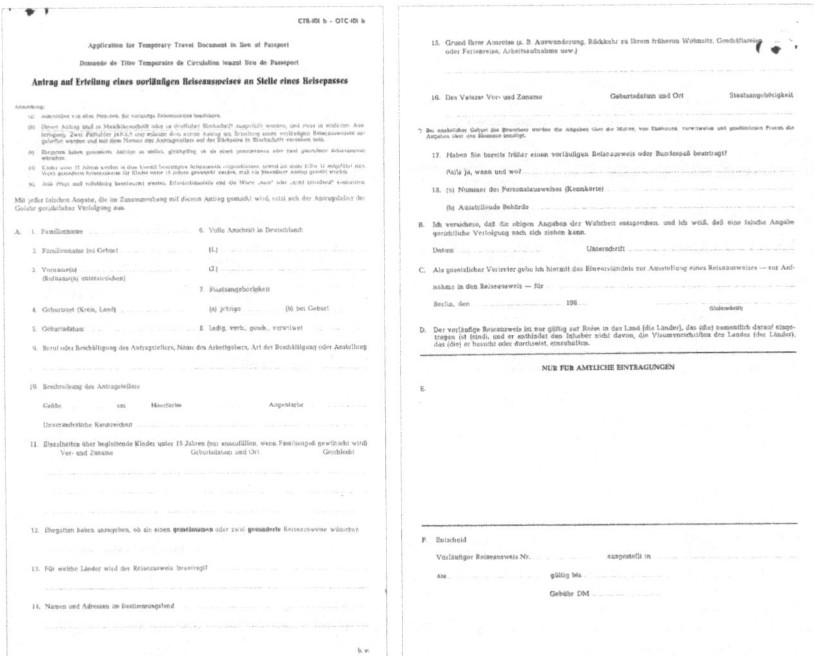

CTB-101 b - OTC-101 b

Application for Temporary Travel Document in lieu of Passport

Demande de Titre Temporaire de Circulation tenant lieu de Passeport

Antrag auf Erteilung eines vorläufigen Reiseausweises an Stelle eines Reisepasses

Anmerkung:

(a) [illegible]

(b) [illegible]

(c) [illegible]

(d) [illegible]

(e) [illegible]

Mit jeder falschen Angabe, die im Zusammenhang mit diesem Antrag gemacht wird, setzt sich der Antragsteller der Gefahr gerichtlicher Verfolgung aus.

A. 1. Familienname

2. Familienname bei Geburt

3. Vorname(n) (Rufname(n) unterstreichen)

4. Geburtsort (Kreis, Land)

5. Geburtsdatum

6. Volle Anschrift in Deutschland:

(1.)

(2.)

7. Staatsangehörigkeit

(a) jetzige (b) bei Geburt

8. Ledig, verh., gesch., verwitwet

9. Beruf oder Beschäftigung des Antragstellers, Name des Arbeitgebers, Art der Beschäftigung oder Anstellung

10. Beschreibung des Antragstellers

Größe cm Haarfarbe Augenfarbe

Unveränderliche Kennzeichen

11. Einzelheiten über begleitende Kinder unter 15 Jahren (nur auszufüllen, wenn Familienpaß gewünscht wird)

Vor- und Zuname Geburtsdatum und Ort Geschlecht

12. Ehegatten haben anzugeben, ob sie einen **gemeinsamen** oder zwei **gesonderte** Reiseausweise wünschen

13. Für welche Länder wird der Reiseausweis beantragt?

14. Namen und Adressen im Bestimmungsland

b. w.

15. Grund Ihrer Ausreise (z. B. Auswanderung, Rückkehr zu Ihrem früheren Wohnsitz, Geschäftsreise oder Ferienreise, Arbeitsaufnahme usw.)

16. Des Vaters* Vor- und Zuname Geburtsdatum und Ort Staatsangehörigkeit

*) [illegible]

17. Haben Sie bereits früher einen vorläufigen Reiseausweis oder Bundespaß beantragt?

Falls ja, wann und wo?

18. (a) Nummer des Personalausweises (Kennkarte)

(b) Ausstellende Behörde

B. Ich versichere, daß die obigen Angaben der Wahrheit entsprechen, und ich weiß, daß eine falsche Angabe gerichtliche Verfolgung nach sich ziehen kann.

Datum Unterschrift

C. Als gesetzlicher Vertreter gebe ich hiermit das Einverständnis zur Ausstellung eines Reiseausweises — zur Aufnahme in den Reiseausweis — für

Berlin, den 196

(Unterschrift)

D. Der vorläufige Reiseausweis ist nur gültig zur Reise in das Land (die Länder), das (die) namentlich darauf eingetragen ist (sind), und er entbindet den Inhaber nicht davon, die Visumvorschriften des Landes (der Länder), das (die) er besucht oder durchreist, einzuhalten.

NUR FÜR AMTLICHE EINTRAGUNGEN

E.

F. Entscheid

Vorläufiger Reiseausweis Nr. ausgestellt in

am gültig bis

Gebühr DM

FIGURE 3. Application for TTD. TTD application included as attachment to letter, W. B. J. Ledwidge to J. E. Killick, April 20, 1960, FO 371/154256, TNA.

These decisions taken in August and September 1961 changed the international sporting landscape, although the ramifications of the hardening of the Cold War did not become apparent until early 1962. The world championships for Alpine skiing and ice hockey, held in France and the United States, respectively, became mired in the controversies related to East German travel. Global media coverage of these events portrayed both countries and NATO negatively, further decreasing support for the alliance within NATO member states as people could not understand why NATO would block athletes from competing in a sporting event. The East Germans propagandized these incidents in their quest for recognition for as long as possible. The French and U.S. governments attempted to shift the blame for the East German athletes not being able to enter their countries onto other entities, and the ATO also released press statements placing the decision elsewhere. The back and forth among the ATO, foreign ministries, NATO, and event organizers left East German athletes—who may or may not have applied for the necessary travel documents in time—hanging in the lurch.

The travel restriction and continued refusal of NATO to recognize the symbols of the communist East German regime meant that other world and European championships slated to be held in several NATO member states felt the repercussions of the Berlin Crisis keenly. International federations, viewing what happened to the ice hockey and skiing championships, argued their sports were above politics and tried to keep the Cold War out of their activities. The Berlin Wall and NATO travel policies made that impossible if a federation had recognized East Germany and then allocated an event to a NATO member state. Sporting events either continued as planned, but with fewer competitors and diminished success as a major international sporting event, or the international federation relocated events to other countries where all athletes—but, in reality, just the East Germans—could be guaranteed the ability to travel there. That so many international sporting events in almost every NATO member state confronted this issue in 1962–63 demonstrates just how acute this problem was. The local regions hosting these international sporting events had hoped to gain positive public relations and benefits from expanded tourism in the short and long term. When the NATO travel restrictions damaged or relocated events, however, the local area did not receive the anticipated benefits associated with organizing international sporting events. The national government and NATO bore the brunt of the criticism in the press as these soft power efforts backfired publicly. In response, international federations increasingly favored selecting host cities in Eastern European or neutral states, a concern to international sport leaders and diplomats from NATO member states, who now saw their dominant position within international sport starting to wane. Suddenly sports and sporting events that rarely garnered publicity or the interest of governments now became major issues addressed at the highest echelons of the diplomatic corps.

THE FIRST CASUALTIES OF THE BERLIN CRISIS: SKIING AND ICE HOCKEY

The United States and France were each hosting a world championship in early 1962: ice hockey in Colorado Springs, Colorado, and Alpine skiing in Chamonix, France. The International Ice Hockey Federation (IIHF), as already seen in the previous chapter, and the Fédération Internationale de Ski (FIS) had both granted the GDR separate recognition in the early 1950s.[5] Three potential elements of hosting these events troubled both the French and American governments, if any of them actually happened, as potentially providing the GDR with de facto recognition: an official East German team using GDR passports to enter the country, the flags of all participating countries hanging around the venues, or, in the case of an East German victory, its anthem playing. While the hypothetical forms of de facto recognition all involved state symbols, travel became the way these concerns played out. Restricting East German travel would prevent any symbolic recognition at the events themselves. The American and French foreign ministries, along with the tripartite ATO, worked extensively to ensure that none of those scenarios happened and that East Germany could not participate in either of these world championships. Both events, as part of the reaction to the shock of the Berlin Wall, went ahead without East German athletes; one maintained its international federation support, whereas the other controversially lost its official designation. The ice hockey and ski federations each attempted to chart a path to keep the Cold War German problem at bay, yet neither organization was able to do so. Although diplomats acted in support of their country's policies, they recognized public perception of government involvement in sport was negative and, if known, could damage NATO's reputation. Diplomats and NATO therefore sought to deflect or even hide from the public their actions with respect to preventing East German participation in the 1962 ice hockey and Alpine skiing world championships. Instead of the local areas benefitting from hosting these world championships, the events received negative publicity and a diminished field of competition as a result of this political interference.

In 1959 FIS had awarded the 1962 Alpine skiing world championships to Chamonix, the French village in the Alps that had hosted the first Winter Olympic Games in 1924. John Stanley Mullin, a FIS vice president from the United States, believed the French venue had received votes from the communist bloc in exchange for supporting their other proposals raised at the 1959 Congress.[6] This event was one of the best opportunities for excellent results by French athletes in 1962, which prominent journalist Raymond Marcillac noted in his article, "Reasons to hope for French sport" at the beginning of January.[7] With the changed political situation by early 1962, the fate of the event became entangled with the realities of the Cold War. FIS required world championship hosts invite all FIS member countries, which included East Germany. The recently reimposed travel restrictions, however, meant that the East German team could not receive the necessary documents to enter France. French ski officials and the Ministère des Affaires Étrangères (MAE), however, feared FIS would cancel the world championships or relocate the event to another country if East German skiers could not compete.[8] The French high commissioner for youth and sport, Maurice Herzog, went on record questioning the idea of cancelling the event: "Who will be the victims? Athletes from all over the world whose training has been going on intensively for months, but also our country and especially Chamonix where nothing has been spared for this international competition is a great success."[9] Threats from communist bloc ski federations to boycott over the inability of East German skiers to participate prompted FIS to call an emergency meeting on February 4 in Bern, Switzerland. French diplomats requested support from their NATO allies and other states with FIS members at the meeting to ensure the world championships would continue as scheduled.[10]

The emergency FIS meeting focused entirely on the problem of East German skiers competing at the world championships in Chamonix. The French delegate stated that "everything possible was being done in the attempt to get the visas for the German crew, but that in this situation the decisions came from much higher places and could not be blamed on the French Ski Association."[11] In a seven to five vote divided along political lines, FIS agreed to give France forty-eight hours to accept an alternative document in lieu of East German passports so East German skiers could enter the country. If not, FIS would strip the Chamonix event of the "World Championships" designation. The federation also agreed that if Chamonix lost the world championship title, then that event would not be contested that year in any country. This decision ensured the world championships would not be moved, nor would another event on the calendar take that designation.[12] To help achieve the goal of having Chamonix continue as the world championship host with East German participation, FIS president Marc Hodler of Switzerland sent telegrams to the MAE, French president Charles de Gaulle, American president John F. Kennedy, and British prime minister Harold Macmillan requesting urgent authorization of French visas and tripartite ATO approval.[13] He also wrote, "We take liberty to remind efforts of international sports federations to promote friendly relations between people of all political systems STOP Are grateful for your assistance in our task helping us to respect our own laws and statutes."[14] By contacting world leaders, FIS hoped political intervention could solve these problems and the event could proceed as originally planned.

Newspapers covered this impasse extensively, often highlighting how the governments were ignoring these pleas. In Alberta, Canada, the *Lethbridge Herald's* headline screamed "World Ski Championships Appear to Be Doomed," with the article beginning, "Hopes that the world Alpine ski championships will surmount the political barriers threatening their existence have all but disappeared in the face of an inflexible travel ban by the NATO allies against East Germany."[15] Newspapers on both sides of the Iron Curtain and neutral states all reported the lack of response from the Western governments to the FIS telegrams.[16] Munich's *Süddeutsche Zeitung*, in an article titled "The Cold War in Sport," quoted the frustrated French ski federation member, who said, "It is unfair that we should suffer because of political developments. After all, France did not build the Berlin Wall, but rather the Soviet Zone has."[17] In contrast, the East German state-run press wrote that FIS hoped the three Western statesmen would do all they could "to keep sport free from this political tug-of-war," and that FIS recognized who had erected barriers on the eve of the world championships.[18]

Diplomats were, in fact, working on this issue but did not want to appear publicly to be influencing sport. The State Department instructed its Bern embassy to respond to Hodler to convey NATO's position regarding the travel of East German athletes.[19] France continued to maintain the NATO and ATO travel policies and refused to acquiesce to the ski federation's demands. FIS therefore announced the removal of the world championship designation from the Chamonix events. Skiers from four communist states (Czechoslovakia, the USSR, Poland, and Yugoslavia) immediately left France.[20] Over twenty countries still completed in Chamonix, including all of the top competitors, but the event lost its prestige. A lack of snow left the organizers scrambling to arrange for more than one hundred men to transport snow to the Chamonix slopes until two days before the event began when fresh powder coated the mountain. Heavy snow during the event called one day of races and disrupted the schedule, and an electrical failure "interrupted the television coverage of the event, the electric scoreboard and the public announcement system."[21] This outcome, the *Times* (London) reported, caused consternation to the hoteliers and shopkeepers in Chamonix, who had "regarded the award of the 1962 championships a rich prize for the resort."[22] Foreign correspondent Robert Daley wrote in the *New York Times*, "The spirit has gone out of the town and also out of many persons who had planned to come here. Some hotels are half empty and crowds at the events so far have been sparse. Taxi drivers are not getting fares. Everyone, except perhaps some of the racers, is deflated."[23] International politics were having a clear economic impact locally.

The media criticism of the French government regarding Chamonix frustrated the MAE. The denial of travel documents to the East German skiers was not a unilateral French decision; if this event had been held in any other NATO state the outcome should have been the same. The French ambassador in Bonn raised the French concerns with respect to the upheaval in sport and public opinion caused by this affair.[24] MAE officials also approached the American embassy in Paris about the "considerable domestic pressures over [the] threat to withdraw [the] world championship from Chamonix."[25] The French government did not want to bear the brunt of the blame for the lack of East German participation, diminished competitive field, and weak financial benefits for local business when other countries contributed to the common NATO policy. As the host of the first world championships impacted by the Berlin Crisis, however, they did.

The Western press criticized the FIS decision, which troubled ski officials.[26] U.S. Coach Bob Beattie told reporters that with the best skiers at Chamonix, "it will be the championship." With "the same races, the same courses, the same schedule," to them "just the label will be changed."[27]

Coaches advocated that their athletes, who had trained for two years to then not be able to compete for the world championship, would be the real losers. Inside FIS some representatives argued the removal of the "world championships" title would also have to be removed from the Nordic skiing world championships in Zakopane, Poland. This negative publicity prompted FIS to restore the world championship designation for Chamonix. Shortly before the Chamonix event ended, FIS released a press statement that they had "concluded that the present difficulties are caused by political acts and retaliations on which neither the affiliated national associations nor the F.I.S. have any influence whatsoever and which could not be foreseen" when FIS had awarded the event to Chamonix in 1959 or when they last met in late spring 1961.[28] While pleased with this outcome, the American FIS vice president Mullin lamented that "the first announcement of the cancellation of the World Ski Championships received world-wide attention, and the later reversal of this stand received comparatively little attention in the press."[29] Even though the Chamonix event retained the world championships designation, the image of both FIS and France remained tarnished. *Le Monde* even called FIS "fragile" after the problems from Chamonix and said that "it would take very little to shatter" the federation.[30]

While France dealt with the problems surrounding Chamonix, the United States was simultaneously confronting the same issue as Colorado Springs prepared to host the 1962 ice hockey world championships at the famous Broadmoor Resort. The event organizers, like the Swiss the year before, had to invite East Germany. One member of the organizing committee was U.S. Army Major General Marshall S. Carter, who later served as the director of the National Security Agency (1965–69). Carter's responsibilities included liaising with the State Department regarding East German participation. By late November 1961, more than two months before the events in Chamonix, State had informed Carter that, "barring some dramatic change for the better in the Berlin situation," the ATO would not issue TTDs for the East German ice hockey team to compete in Colorado Springs. Even if NATO relaxed the travel restrictions, the State Department told Carter it would still not sanction entry of a "national" team representing the GDR into the United States.[31] In December the IIHF released the group schedules for the world championships, which included both German teams.[32] The Soviet sports paper *Sovietskii sport* reported this positive development, and the major Soviet daily *Pravda* noted the East German invitation but without any editorializing comment.[33] The *Winnipeg Free Press* article reporting on the IIHF meeting and group schedules was headlined "Officials Hope to Bar Cold War from Rockies."[34] Publicly it appeared East Germany would compete in Colorado, but the organizing committee also prepared for the opposite situation. Carter informed the State Department that "the committee was in complete agreement with the Department's position." The organizing committee was "counting heavily" on the ATO rejection of TTDs for an East German team so the organizers could place blame for their inability to participate elsewhere—either with the East Germans themselves for not securing the appropriate travel documents or with the tripartite ATO (and thus preventing the United States from appearing solely responsible).[35]

Complicating these preparations was the 1959 IIHF policy that permitted the relocation of an international tournament if a "host country refuses visas for any participating teams."[36] The organizing committee in Colorado Springs had already invested heavily in preparing the world championships and did not want to be left empty-handed; preparing to blame the GDR and ATO helped avoid that scenario. The Federal Republic's National Olympic Committee feared the IIHF would relocate the world championships or the United States would cave under pressure and change its policy to permit East German participation. They therefore requested Chancellor Konrad Adenauer raise this issue during his November 1961 visit with President Kennedy, where the Berlin Crisis was the main topic of discussion. With more pressing issues to address, Kennedy and Adenauer did not find time to discuss ice hockey. The German embassy therefore approached the State Department the following month, and the Americans reassured their German allies they had no need to be concerned that the United States would weaken its position.[37]

The ATO quickly became the central focus in the preparations for the 1962 ice hockey world championships. In December the East Germans picked up several TTD forms from the ATO in Berlin for the world championships in Colorado, and the East German sports pages frequently discussed the strength of the ice hockey team and its determination for the upcoming world championships. The encouraging remarks made by the American vice president of the IIHF in response to the announcement of the tournament groups, combined with the lack of completed TTD applications returned to the ATO nearly a month later, aroused suspicions among the staff at the U.S. mission in Berlin. This inaction indicated to the mission that East Germany knew its participation in Colorado Springs was "politically impossible" and was therefore delaying its TTD applications until the last possible minute "to be able to launch a heavy propaganda barrage on U.S. and West Germany 'political intrusions into world of sport' when the visas and TTD's are denied."[38] To ensure that the blame for the lack of GDR participation fell on the ATO and not solely on the United States, the American ATO representative requested the support of his French and British counterparts. Doing so, the American claimed, "would allow the U.S.A. to take refuge with respect to the IIHF, behind a tripartite decision taken by the Allied Travel Office in Berlin."[39] The United States representative to the quadripartite meetings in Bonn reiterated the firm American position, which also helped the French maintain their stance regarding the simultaneous drama regarding Chamonix.[40]

While the American ATO delegate pushed forward with the hard line on travel by East German sportsmen, the U.S. mission in Berlin also sent the State Department a lengthy warning in early January 1962 about the possible problems if they maintained this position. The mission cautioned against publicly emphasizing the ATO's role in refusing TTDs as the reason why East Germany would not be competing in Colorado Springs. Promoting that line, the mission argued, would undercut the effort to force NATO allies to actually uphold the nonrecognition and travel policy and refuse issuing visas themselves. Furthermore, East Germany and its communist bloc allies would see through this "subterfuge" and place the blame in this instance entirely on the United States. Attempting to make the ATO responsible for East German nonparticipation in order to maintain the financial success of the tournament was "wishful thinking" if the organizing committee believed "it can hold world championships in Colorado Springs without East Germans but with Soviet, Czechoslovak and other East bloc teams in attendance."[41] As long as the East Germans could not prove American subterfuge, the State Department replied, then the organizing committee hoped to forestall the transfer of the event to another country, such as neutral Sweden.[42] Indeed, the Canadian ambassador in Stockholm learned from the Swedish IIHF representative that if East Germany could not participate in the world championships, neither would the Soviet or Czechoslovakian teams. If that scenario happened and the event was no longer very "international," then the Swedish team might also consider not attending.[43]

In late January the IIHF called a meeting in Geneva and invited the East Germans to discuss their travel problem and whether Colorado Springs should remain as host. The East German ice hockey federation originally hoped the 1959 resolution guaranteeing entry to all member states would bolster its case. The British IIHF vice president J. F. "Bunny" Ahearne, however, said that resolution was only valid for the United States, and when the IIHF selected Colorado Springs to host, its backup was Canada and, as a last resort, the Federal Republic. Thus, if the IIHF stripped the event from the United States, East Germany would still face the same travel problems as the two backup locations were also NATO members. The IIHF ultimately offered the East Germans the possibility of quietly accepting not participating in the 1962 world championships in exchange for $20,000 (U.S.), a guaranteed fifth seed for the 1963 world championships in Sweden, and no invitation for the Federal Republic to the 1963 world championships. The GDR refused all of these offers, believing the "capitalist majority in the IIHF" was more concerned with the expected revenues to be gained from holding the world championships in the United States. Two long days of meetings, lasting until 2:30 a.m. the first day, did not produce any resolutions.[44]

Like the FIS meetings, these IIHF meetings received extensive press coverage, particularly in the regions where ice hockey was popular. The *Lowell (MA) Sun* referred to American and Soviet bloc officials as "playing a game of political ice hockey over whether an East German team can enter this country to compete in the world hockey championships."[45] The meetings yielded no official decision whether the world championships would remain in the United States or move to another country. Ahearne nonetheless informed the press at the conclusion of the Geneva meetings, "You can take it from me that the championships will take place in Colorado Springs."[46] Some North American papers reported on the possibility of the world championships moving to Canada after local hockey officials in Calgary and Edmonton offered to arrange the tournament on short notice, although the Toronto-based president of the Canadian Amateur Hockey Association responded that Canada's membership in NATO made that doubtful.[47] These actions prompted Canada's External Affairs to request its embassy in Washington approach the State Department about how it planned to respond to public questions so the Canadian response remained on point.[48]

The widespread coverage across the globe prompted the State Department to issue a press release to counter these claims. The statement read,

> It should be noted that there are two sets of procedures involved in the travel of East Germans to Western countries. Under long-established Allied regulations a resident of East Germany desiring to travel to the West must receive a temporary travel document (in lieu of a passport), issued by the tripartite Allied Travel Office in West Berlin, and a visa issued by the country to which he desires to travel. These two procedures are interrelated in the sense that if the individual applicant is not eligible for a visa, the ATO will not issue a temporary travel document. On the other hand, if the travel of certain categories of East Germans is, as a matter of ATO policy, restricted or prohibited, the question of a visa issuance does not really arise.
>
> Under existing policy established as a result of the erection of the Communist wall in Berlin and subsequent Communist restrictions on free circulation in Berlin, it is highly questionable that temporary travel documents could be issued to an East German ice hockey team. For this reason the issue of American visas is not a controlling factor.[49]

The American representative to the Committee of Political Advisers reassured his colleagues that the State Department only mentioned NATO as a background point during the question period of the press conference, but a *New York Times* journalist had included those details in his article.[50] If other NATO member states received questions regarding this policy, State recommended "indicating a relationship of cooperation between govt concerned and the Allied Travel Office but without making it too clear whether the TTD or the visa was governing factor."[51] The American comments did not mollify the concerns from their NATO colleagues, who increasingly faced pressure from their domestic sport leaders because these actions elsewhere could impact their own ability to host sporting events.[52]

This discussion at NATO regarding how to respond to press enquiries also included some off-the-record guidance as a result of the East German "Wall of Shame," which placed the responsibility and propagandizing squarely on the East Germans and Soviet Union.[53] The line maintained by both the Colorado Springs organizing committee and the State Department was that neither were responsible for the inability of the East German team to participate in the ice hockey world championships. Another body, the ATO, had made that decision—even though that body included American diplomatic representation. The IIHF president, the Canadian Robert LeBel, informed East Germany's ice hockey federation that the North American Executive Committee for ice hockey, composed entirely of Canadians and Americans, "unanimously upholds the right of America to carry on the championships."[54] With this telegram the international federation publicly accepted the explanation from the American organizers that the ATO and not the United States had refused to grant the necessary travel documents to the East German team. The United States had therefore not violated the 1959 IIHF resolution, and the tournament could proceed in Colorado instead of being transferred to another country.[55]

As it became clear in early February, a month before the tournament began, that the East Germans would not receive travel documents, protests appeared in newspapers across hockey-loving Canada. The *Toronto Globe & Mail* published James G. Reidford's political cartoon entitled "The Anti-Red Line" (Figure 4), depicting the construction of the Berlin Wall by the American-, British-, and French-controlled Allied Travel Board (the ATO), which granted—or refused—travel documents to East Germans. With the East German ice hockey team left stranded on the ice behind the wall, Reidford's cartoon blamed the Western Allies for the problems surrounding the 1962 IIHF World Championships.[56] As a Canadian and the IIHF president, LeBel still attempted to secure a reversal of the ATO's decision regarding East German TTDs, particularly as the Soviet and East German ice hockey federations increased their pressure on the international body. Relying on the IIHF's policy on neutrality in its constitution, which stated "the IIHF observes strict neutrality in political and religious matters," LeBel requested the ATO "consider our request and treat it on a base of sportsmanship and favor us with a decision that will please all hockey fans across the world."[57] LeBel and other Canadian hockey officials also wrote similar letters to President Kennedy and Canadian prime minister John Diefenbaker—all of which, of course, were to no avail (although Diefenbaker sent a polite reply).[58]

In late January rumors began to circulate that the Soviet and Czechoslovakian teams would withdraw from the event. At the weekly lunch meeting in West Berlin of foreign diplomats and journalists, the press attaché of the Soviet Embassy in East Berlin suggested that the USSR and Czechoslovakia would refuse to participate in the world championships in solidarity if East Germany could not participate.[59] Papers across the world speculated about the withdrawal of the communist teams.[60] The Eastern European press followed up these claims with questions regarding the event's finances,

FIGURE 4. "The Anti-Red Line," *Toronto Globe & Mail*, February 2, 1962, 6.

claiming the television broadcast contracts that the organizers had negotiated were dependent on Soviet and Czechoslovakian participation.[61] American diplomats, however, believed the Soviets had to balance the "political desirability of demonstrating solidarity with [their] East German brethren" with Soviet prestige, since predictions had the Soviet team performing well at the championships.[62] By early February the Soviet Union had already decided to withdraw from the Colorado Springs world championships but would not announce this decision until shortly before the tournament began to cause more problems for the American organizers and government.[63] Just over two weeks before the world championships opened on March 8, the ice hockey federations in the Soviet Union, Czechoslovakia, Romania, and Yugoslavia announced that they were withdrawing their teams in solidarity with East Germany.[64] East Germany's *Neues Deutschland* criticized the United States and its NATO allies, saying they had "discriminated against" the GDR.[65] The 1962 world championships continued without the five teams from the communist bloc, but the tournament only had two pools (Championship and Pool B) instead of three pools, as was the case in 1961 and 1963. Sweden became the world champion, defeating Canada in the final, and the United States placed third; the Federal Republic finished in sixth place.[66]

The 1962 world championships in Alpine skiing and ice hockey became the first major sport casualties of the Berlin Wall. With the tripartite powers reinstating travel restrictions on East German athletes, these two events forced the international sport community to confront the harsh reality of NATO policy. The Federal Republic followed these events closely, speaking with National Olympic Committee president Willi Daume several times and sharing the updates received at quadripartite and NATO meetings, but the German government allowed the Americans and French to shoulder the work publicly.[67] Both the French and American foreign ministries upheld the ATO and NATO policies regarding travel for East German sportsmen, even as the IIHF, FIS, and global media tried to pressure them to change their positions. As the host countries for world championships and also members of the tripartite ATO, the event organizers and diplomats all knew they had to speak carefully to prevent international federations from cancelling or removing the world championships over the inability of East German athletes to participate. The communist bloc used these events to further their own political aims, demonstrating their continued support of East Germany and their supposed moral superiority over the West with upholding the values of sport. International sport leaders had hoped that sport could rise above the politics of the Cold War. Instead, Cold War divisions hurt these two world championships through diminished competitive fields and significantly less revenue for the region and event. France and the United States also faced criticism in the press and from international federations for their actions. These two world championships thus made international federations take geopolitics seriously into consideration when selecting the host country for their major events.

THE AFTERMATH OF CHAMONIX AND COLORADO SPRINGS

The international sport community quickly responded to the Chamonix and Colorado Springs events but in different ways. For the few international federations which by the 1960s had not yet granted East Germany separate recognition, the problems that befell ice hockey and skiing were not as great of a threat. For most international federations, however, the inability of East German athletes and sport officials to travel to NATO countries increasingly brought the Cold War into their ability to carry out one of their most important functions: overseeing international competitions. Particularly in sports where communist bloc countries were dominant competitors—and the fear of a decimated competitive field was a real concern—international federations had to confront the reality of Cold War geopolitics. Wanting to prevent the financial losses of weakened competitions and extensive negative publicity, international federations increasingly considered relocating their events from NATO countries when East Germany could not participate. In several cases, they followed through with these plans. The change of the host country for many events and meetings began to erode the dominance that Western Europe and the United States held within international sport. Rather than confront the same challenges as the ice hockey and ski federations, several other international federations took steps to minimize the growing tensions among host countries, the ATO, and themselves.

The ice hockey world championships prompted other international federations to reconsider the allocation of their events scheduled to take place in the United States. Just two weeks after the ice hockey tournament concluded in Colorado Springs, seventeen East Germans submitted TTDs to compete at the 1962 wrestling world championships in Toledo, Ohio, in June. The Berlin mission reported to the State Department at the end of March: "Judging from the appearance of the TTD applications, a number of which were carelessly completed, lacking in photographs, etc., the East Germans do not believe that they have any chance of obtaining the TTD's and merely are submitting the applications so that they later can claim that the ATO has refused to issue the documents."[68] Indeed, the lack of any East German follow-up on the TTD applications by the wrestlers until two days before the competition began in June confirmed the Americans' "earlier impression that East Germans realized from outset that they had no chance of obtaining TTDs and were merely interested in establishing formal basis for possible subsequent propaganda attack against ATO."[69] Unlike for ice hockey or skiing, the Soviet team did not boycott the event or even threaten to do so. In this instance they only protested East Germany's exclusion at the international federation's meeting. Soviet wrestlers had dominated the 1961 world championships and again came away with more medals than any other country in Toledo. The French president of the international federation, Roger Coulon, commented, "I am pleased that in spite of the political complications, all of the Iron Curtain countries have come here in proof of their interest in sport."[70] In contrast to the extensive publicity given to Chamonix and Colorado Springs, East German media buried the story about their athletes' inability to participate in Toledo, not mentioning it until halfway through the single two-paragraph story after the wrestling championships ended. The article, "Wrestling against Discrimination," focused on the federation's decision to award future world championships to countries that could guarantee entry for all member federations.[71]

As the complete inability of East Germans to compete in world championships in the United States became clearer to the international federations that had recognized the German Democratic Republic, they began to relocate events from American cities to other countries to which East Germans would be able to travel. In September 1961, just one month after the Berlin Wall appeared, the International Weightlifting Federation (IWF) had selected Hershey, Pennsylvania, to host its 1962 world championships.[72] Five months later, the IWF realized the problems that this decision would likely bring to their sport. The two politically marred world championships prompted the British secretary general of the IWF, Oscar State, to contact the American embassy in London while the ice hockey world championships were underway in Colorado. Oscar State requested "assurances that competitors from East Germany will without discrimination receive visas to attend World Championships to be held in Hershey, Pennsylvania, later this year." The embassy responded with the guidance that the State Department had provided in late January with respect to the ice hockey championships, namely that applicants "are considered of individual merits in accordance with prevailing law," which in the case of East Germany also included a TTD provided by the ATO in Berlin.[73] Upon receiving this reply Oscar State then asked the ATO, "Our federation is considering holding our annual World Championships in Hershey, Pennsylvania, U.S.A. Before final approval can be given I must know whether competitors from the Soviet

Zone of Germany would be allowed to enter the U.S.A. Can you please give me a definite assurance that travel permits will be granted to them for this purpose?"[74] The ATO planned to respond to Oscar State with the same letter sent to the IIHF regarding their policies, stating that TTDs for sport teams have been restricted in response to the East German actions taken on August 13 (the construction of the Berlin Wall).[75]

Because the organizers in Hershey could not provide a guarantee that all athletes and officials would be permitted to enter the country, the IWF immediately asked them to relinquish the event. Budapest, already scheduled to host the European championships, agreed to organize the world championships as well.[76] This doubling up of events was normal for the IWF; only when the world championships took place on another continent were separate European championships held. Oscar State shared these developments with the IOC president and chancellor in early April 1962, explaining the event had been relocated to Hungary, which could "offer free access to all teams." State concluded his letter by commenting that "we have ensured that our World Championships will not be spoiled by the same unfortunate incidents as occurred at Chamonix, Colorado Springs, and one or two other cities."[77] IOC chancellor Otto Mayer supported this outcome, responding, "Your decision is a very good one and we hope it will be followed by other International Federations too."[78] Hershey, already the site of a world championships without East Germany (for modern pentathlon in 1959), lost its chance to hold another world championships in the aftermath of the Berlin Crisis.

Whereas the political problems surrounding the ice hockey and Alpine skiing events made headlines on both sides of the Iron Curtain, the transfer of the weightlifting championships from Hershey to Budapest received almost no media coverage. A very short article announcing the change of location to Budapest appeared in *Neues Deutschland* and in a wire story locally around Hershey—yet these articles appeared before Oscar State had conducted his correspondence with the London embassy and ATO.[79] With the changed venue of the world championships in Budapest, the IWF did not have to worry about Soviet bloc countries withdrawing. Even though no East German athletes medaled, fourteen athletes from the Soviet Union, Hungary, and Poland did.[80] The IWF understood the importance of the Eastern European participants in the sport, demonstrated by their success at the world championships, and why they had to move the event. Coverage of the world championships did not even mention that Budapest had not been the original host of the event.[81] Even though this event garnered minimal publicity, its forced relocation over the travel issue provided East Germany and the communist bloc a victory over the United States and NATO, setting a precedent for other international federations.

Similarly, the Fédération Internationale de Tir l'Arc (FITA) moved its 1963 world championships from a NATO member state to a country that did not impose travel restrictions. In the summer of 1962 the Grand National Archery Society, the governing body for the sport in Great Britain, received confirmation from the government that East German athletes at present could not obtain visas to enter the country for competitions. The archery governing body then contacted all FITA member countries asking about their likelihood of participating in the 1963 world championships in England. After receiving several negative responses as a result of the Cold War political climate, the Grand National Archery Society's Council met in September 1962. They agreed that if England hosted the world championships, "a number of important countries would be absent and that the meeting could not be regarded as being in the best interests or traditions of the sport. This regrettable conclusion has been reached purely as a result of the political situation." They therefore withdrew their offer to organize the 1963 world championships.[82] The FITA president, Inger K. Frith of Great Britain (the first female president of any international federation), immediately contacted all FITA member states regarding England's withdrawal in the hopes of securing a new host for the 1963 world championships. However, she ended her letter less than optimistically: "It should be pointed out the present difficulties over visas apply to all N.A.T.O. countries—half our Members."[83] Ultimately Helsinki, Finland, agreed to host the 1963 archery world championships, and East Germany competed in the event for the first time, albeit without much success.[84] The Nordic states had strong archery programs, and Finland won two bronze medals at the 1961 world championships. Helsinki had also previously hosted the world championships in 1955. FITA, like the weightlifting federation, prevented its world championship from turning into a disaster in the wake of the Berlin Crisis by moving the event to another non-NATO, and in this case nonaligned, country. Media coverage of the archery world championships, similar to weightlifting, did not mention the event's relocation.[85] These two federations, seeing firsthand the challenges arising from the ATO and originally selected host countries, took action to minimize the potential damage Cold War tensions would have on their world championships. Of course, moving the events to different countries was a clear acknowledgment of the impact of international politics on sport.

Other events, however, proceeded as planned in the NATO member states, including the smaller states that had no influence on the tripartite decisions regarding East German travel. The Union Cycliste Internationale's (UCI) secretary general, the Frenchman René Chesal, lamented that because UCI had recognized the two German states separately, its annual congresses and world championships often lacked East German participation.[86] The world championships for three of cycling's four disciplines in 1962 took place in NATO member states: track cycling (Milan) and road cycling (Salò) in Italy and cyclo-cross in Esch-sur-Alzette, Luxembourg. In all three cases East Germans could not obtain travel documents from the ATO; Luxembourg also denied the East German visa applications.[87] The East German cycling federation publicly called for the cyclo-cross event to be moved to another state, but like the other two world championships in February 1962, this event went ahead in the original host country.[88] UCI faced the same problem the following year as well, with the cyclo-cross world championships and its annual congress scheduled in France and the track and road cycling championships in Belgium, leaving the East Germans out of all but one of UCI's major events.[89] The travel ban even impacted junior teams, with the East German under-eighteen soccer team unable to participate in a 1964 continental junior tournament in the Netherlands.[90]

In contrast to the international federations that had recognized East Germany separately in the 1950s, the rowing federation followed the IOC's approach of requiring an all-German team. The Fédération Internationale des Sociétés d'Aviron (FISA) had approved the Federal Republic's membership in 1951 and, with strong guidance from its Swiss president Gaston Mullegg, agreed to base its future recognition of East Germany on the IOC's actions. The GDR continually sought recognition in FISA but received annual disappointment as the vote went against them until 1965.[91] The 1961 FISA Congress took place a mere ten days after the erection of the Berlin Wall, and the vote to recognize East Germany resulted in thirty-two against and twenty for, with seven abstentions—an unsurprising result in light of recent political events.[92] Rowing, one of the oldest international federations, did not have a world championship before the 1960s. FISA had held European championships since 1893 but only introduced a world championship event in 1962—which forced FISA to develop policies addressing the problems of the Cold War from the outset of this event.

As FISA prepared for its first world championships, the federation decided not to include flags, national anthems, or even medal ceremonies. FISA took this decision in order to promote athletic achievement instead. As Munich's *Süddeutsche Zeitung* commented, Eastern European countries had emphasized the anthem and flag problem too much in recent years. In order to preserve peace in sport, FISA's policy interested other international federations because of the frequent cancellation of international sporting events resulting from the anthem and flag problems.[93] This idea was not new. When West Germany forfeited its 1961 ice hockey world championship game against East Germany, Robert Daley had called in his *New York Times* column for abolishing the postgame victory ceremony of flags and anthems because it was both political untenable and not very sportsmanlike.[94] FISA president Thomas Keller, from Switzerland, even extolled the success of the lack of a medal ceremony at the rowing world championships at a meeting of the IOC Executive Board with international federation presidents in February 1963, noting FISA "simply called out the name of the winner. It seemed to work most satisfactorily and this innovation met with success."[95] Rowing's solution, however, remained an anomaly within sport, although one that FISA has continued to proudly promote for decades.[96]

NATO's hard line on travel by East German representatives within sport not only impacted the sporting events but also the international federations' meetings. The International Amateur Athletic Federation's (IAAF) November 1963 Calendar Congress moved from Lisbon to Sofia because the East Germans could not receive visas for Portugal.[97] That same month the East German delegates could not attend the Fédération Internationale d'Escrime (fencing) Congress in Paris.[98] During the June 1962 FIS council meeting in Copenhagen, the Calendar Committee met across the sound in Malmö, Sweden, because the East German member could not receive travel documents for Denmark but could travel to neutral Sweden. The close proximity of these two cities created an easy solution for this one meeting. The council discussed the East German visa question in Copenhagen, and American delegate John Stanley Mullin raised the likelihood of a similar problem occurring for the FIS Congress later that year in Athens.[99] When the East German delegates could not obtain TTDs for the meeting in Greece, the FIS council proposed a workaround in which the delegates from both German states would "undertake the journey to Athens as *one* delegation. After arrival in Athens, each separate association could then exercise all its rights as an ordinary FIS-member during the Congress."[100] East Germans traveling to other (nonsport) conferences in Athens had previously followed this model. The West German ski federation accepted this proposal, and the ATO approved TTDs for the four East German delegates because they would travel as part of an all-German delegation.[101]

The East Germans, however, did not agree to this solution, objecting to the "renewed political interferring [*sic*] of some N.A.T.O. countries to the importance of International Sport Federations."[102] The East German FIS delegates never picked up their TTDs and did not attend the Athens meeting.[103] Mullin commented that "it is apparent that the representatives of the east German Association deemed it more important to stand on the issue of recognition of the 'German Democratic Republic' than to attend the Congress, inasmuch as they have already agreed to participate in the 1964 Olympics as a joint team with west Germany."[104] Because their skiers had already competed twice as part of an all-German Olympic team, the East German delegates were hypocritical in their actions now. After the East Germans failed to pick up their TTDs, the British diplomats in Berlin expressed a similar sentiment as Mullin, noting that for the East Germans "the formation of all-German delegations is basically undesirable in that it tends to contradict their thesis of two German states."[105] Communist bloc members within FIS attempted to make an issue over the lack of East German delegates in Athens, but the rest of the FIS executive lacked any sympathy because the East Germans had disregarded the solution that was devised, which would have enabled their participation at the meeting.

As a result of all these travel problems, some international federations began to implement policies that required all event host cities be located in countries that would guarantee travel and participation by all international federation member states. The IWF implemented this policy at its meeting in Toledo, Ohio, after the East Germans could not participate in the 1962 world championships. They also selected Sofia, Bulgaria (freestyle), and Helsingborg, Sweden (Greco-Roman), for the following year's world championships, both of which—as a communist bloc and neutral country, respectively—would not have the same problems as the 1962 event.[106] In federations that did not create a specific policy, members remembered those instances when they voted to select host cities after the Berlin Crisis.

The IWF's response to the problems encountered with Toledo in 1962 revealed the biggest concern arising from the exclusion of East German athletes: that only neutral or communist states would host international sporting events because these countries could guarantee free entry for all athletes and officials. International federations increasingly realized sporting events and meetings needed to be organized in Eastern Europe or the neutral states of Finland, Sweden, Switzerland, and Austria which, as the secretary-treasurer of the IAAF noted, was "a most inconvenient way of running European sport."[107] Events could take place on other continents, but with the majority of sport leaders primarily residing in Europe, most European and international sport business was conducted in Europe. In the aftermath of the Chamonix debacle, FIS considered a proposal, submitted by four communist bloc federations, which demanded all future world championship hosts guarantee entry into their country. Recognizing that national federations cannot make guarantees on behalf of their governments, the delegates ultimately withdrew these proposals and FIS tabled the discussion, hoping no further difficulties would arise.[108] This scenario, as the American FIS vice president John Stanley Mullin remarked, would allow the communist bloc to "achieve the propaganda that only in Communist countries is sport free of the 'insidious influence of the NATO politics.'"[109] Sport leaders from NATO states realized this sentiment was increasing across all international federations, which had the potential to limit their traditional influence within sport.

International federations could not avoid the impact of the Berlin Wall and NATO's tighter travel restrictions. The Cold War and German problem forced international sport federations to deal with the ATO to (unsuccessfully) negotiate for East Germans to receive TTDs, plead with the governments in host countries, move their events to other countries, and pass new policies for future hosts to provide travel guarantees. *New York Times* correspondent Robert Daley questioned who would rush to organize an international sporting event having seen all of the losses in Chamonix.[110] International federations worried about this problem because it meant the potential loss of many traditional host venues. NATO diplomats saw the international federations move events out of their countries and worried about their potential inability to be selected to host future sporting events[111]—including the crown jewel of international sport, the Olympic Games.

CONCLUSION

International sport did not have a uniform response to the problem of East German travel after the appearance of the Berlin Wall. Yet, all of the international federations, depending on East Germany's status within them and where their event were scheduled, had to confront the reality of the Berlin Wall and divided Germany. The federations that had recognized East Germany outright faced the issue most acutely, as did federations for team sports or that Eastern European countries dominated. If an East German ban brought with it a boycott by the rest of the communist bloc, team sports had the greatest vulnerability, with disrupted group schedules when teams withdrew. Organizers were then left with an uneven number of teams and imbalanced groups, along with presold tickets for matches no longer happening. Individual sports such as cycling or archery could more easily cope with the loss of a few athletes (although the women's archery field for the 1963 world championships would have lost 25 percent of the participants from a Soviet bloc boycott had it not moved to Finland). When a significant number of the best athletes in a sport resided behind the Iron Curtain, such as in weightlifting, moving the event was essential for its viability. What transpired in 1962–63 within international sport demonstrated that the Berlin Crisis was not limited to a single city, the two German states, or even the two superpowers. East German participation and where sporting events could be held had become widespread problems affecting all NATO states and most international federations.

In order to prepare for future problems within international sport, diplomats from the quadripartite states began circulating a list of upcoming international sporting events to which the East Germans would likely be invited.[112] Similarly, the IOC was so concerned with the frequency with which the travel restrictions had affected international sport by December 1963 that it requested each international federation provide details about any events that "have been troubled by the refusal of Visas, the approximative [*sic*] dates, the places where your championships or other events took place and the athletes (resp. the country) (ies) who have been the victims of that discrimination."[113] The ensuing dossier compiled in Lausanne counted ten world championships, three European championships, six congresses, and eleven other cases affected by the refusal of visas to East German representatives between 1959 and 1963.[114]

Even before the IOC's creation of this exhaustive list, sport had already felt the impact of the travel restrictions on East Germans acutely. Member states' efforts to remind the public they had only implemented these policies in response to the GDR's physical division of Berlin with the erection of the wall were drowned out by the outcry of sporting events repeatedly being disrupted. At the February 6 NATO Committee of Political Advisers meeting—days before the world championships in Chamonix even began—the chairman said with respect to ice hockey and skiing, "This was the first time in which the Berlin situation had been brought home to the wider public because of their interest in sports." He thought NATO "should take advantage of this occasion to get across our case rather than be on the defensive."[115] By that time, however, NATO was already facing an uphill battle. Howard Iverson, a sportswriter for the *Lowell (MA) Sun*, wrote in his regular column on the same day the NATO Political Advisers met that "politics has reared its ugly head" in sport. Noting the problems affecting skiing, ice hockey, and likely wrestling, he lamented, "WHILE NOT WISHING to debate foreign policy with the state department, we can't help but feel that the travel ban on East German athletic teams wishing to compete in amateur world championships is somewhat ridiculous and detrimental to the good will that the free world usually seems anxious to promote."[116] This negative opinion regarding NATO's actions was not limited to Iverson or even the United States; the German representative to the quadripartite meeting the following week commented that "public opinion should be educated" to combat the fact that "press and public opinion was not wholly on the side of NATO Governments in this matter."[117] Diplomats at NATO and in the foreign ministries increasingly considered these problems arising within sport as damaging public opinion against the alliance. Instead of being lauded for hosting an exciting and successfully organized world championships, NATO states faced extensive press criticism for actions that impacted the quality of competition or the event's relocation to another country.

Trying to change negative public opinion when it came to political interference in sport was a challenge, even though international sport had long been promoted by both sport officials and governments as an arena where political differences could be overcome. The Americans, British, and French had used that approach during the German occupation, and the State

Department had frequently used athletes within goodwill tours across the globe in the previous decade.[118] Indeed, Iverson's column referenced these tours as a rebuttal to the concept of denying travel permits for athletes.[119] These examples, however, involved a government sending its own athletes abroad for friendly competitions or exhibitions. In contrast, direct political intervention in the running of an officially sanctioned international event did just the opposite of using sport as a form of public diplomacy and instead soured populations against a country's government. This increasingly negative coverage of NATO actions in the press prompted more member states to speak up within the multilateral organization with respect to the travel ban. Not wanting to lose the limited opportunities available to them to shine on the global stage by hosting an international sporting event, several of the smaller NATO members began to push back against the dominance of the quadripartite powers of the United States, Great Britain, France, and Germany. Sport thus provided the smaller states with the ability to be on a more even footing within the alliance.

CHAPTER 3

NATO'S SMALL STATES ASSERTING THEIR POWER

The fallout from Chamonix and Colorado Springs went beyond the international federations. The media across NATO member states reported at length the extent to which politics were impacting sport, often criticizing the military organization in the process. A wire story published across Canada and the United States about the impending doom in the days leading up to Chamonix began by placing the blame squarely on NATO: "Hopes that the world Alpine ski championships will surmount the political barriers threatening their existence have all but disappeared in the face of an inflexible travel ban by the NATO allies against East Germany."[1] *New York Times* sports columnist Robert Daley lamented in October 1962 that "this past year had been a bad one. East Germany has been refused visas for events in NATO nations, beginning with the world ski championships at Chamonix, France, in February. East German athletes are barred from NATO nations (as are all East Germans) as a reprisal for the Berlin Wall."[2] As negative press coverage proliferated on both sides of the Iron Curtain, NATO member states realized they urgently needed to confront the problem of travel for East German athletes to prevent further escalation.

The smaller states in NATO, Christian Neunlist has argued, wanted the Western Four (the United States, Great Britain, France, and the Federal Republic of Germany) to consult with them on matters within the organization, rather than merely report their quadripartitely made decisions to the Atlantic group.[3] The frustrations felt by other NATO member states with the Western Four became particularly acute when these actions affected their own sporting events. With virtually every NATO member state hosting international sporting events, East German travel restrictions became an issue in which all countries had a vested interest. This topic thus became a frequent and lengthy point of discussion at several levels of NATO in 1962, from informal bilateral discussions to the Committee of Political Advisers, and at the highest level, the North Atlantic Council. Norway and Canada took the lead in these meetings to push for change in NATO's travel policy toward East German athletes. The Committee of Political Advisers consisted of each country's political specialist posted to NATO headquarters in Paris, not experts on sport. These individuals, however, became quite knowledgeable about how international sport worked (whether they wanted to or not) as a result of the amount of time they spent on the issue.

During these NATO debates some states kept raising the concept of "national interest" when advocating for exceptions to the travel restrictions. For a smaller state like Norway, winter sport, and especially skiing, was one of those national interests. Norway considers itself the birthplace of skiing, and ski competitions are immensely popular.[4] Norwegian sport officials thus knew inviting the best skiers in the world to events in Norway would draw large crowds, including for the Holmenkollen ski festival in Oslo, one of the important annual ski jumping events on the international calendar. The smaller the country, the more important hosting a single international sporting event is. Winter sport federations are smaller in size and typically have fewer member states than the governing bodies that control the sports contested at the Summer Olympics. With climate and terrain well suited for winter sports, the problems of East German travel often arose in winter sports. Countries like Norway in skiing and Canada in ice hockey played dominant roles in the international federations for these sports. These two states thus raised these sports within broader NATO discussions on East German travel.

Damning coverage in the domestic press of these events when East Germans could not participate, combined with negative global coverage on both sides of the Iron Curtain, left NATO in a vulnerable position. With the idea of a multicountry military alliance costing precious dollars from each country's national budget, NATO already faced public opinion challenges on the home front.[5] The representatives at NATO believed the organization could not afford to have its reputation damaged further by sporting events and that relocating or diminishing one of the most exciting and prestigious international events a country hosted would weaken domestic views of NATO even more. This view of the issue prompted some states to fight vigorously for a change in the East German travel restriction policy on sport. With its strong position in winter sport competitions, Norway took a leading role in trying to change NATO travel policies, particularly once the ability of one of the world's best ski jumpers to participate in the Holmenkollen came under threat. Canada, not wanting to jeopardize its government-supported Olympic bid, supported Norway's efforts. These two states led a coalition of the self-styled "cold countries" within NATO that sought to change the alliance's policy in early 1962. These NATO debates, discussions between representatives in the private offices of NATO's headquarters in Paris, and the communications between foreign ministries and their NATO delegations reveal the challenges of finding consensus with so many competing national interests. In his history of NATO, Timothy Sayle has noted that when "leaders had to choose between preserving the Pax Atlantica or pursuing other national interests, they chose NATO."[6] Norway's repeated calls for skiing to receive an exception to the NATO travel policy on East German athletes demonstrates those tensions between national interests and the alliance and that, at least for sporting matters, smaller states did not always choose NATO. However, rather than repudiate the alliance on these issues, the smaller states fought to promote their views and change NATO policies against the position of the dominant Western Four, who held a broader consideration of Cold War actions and how they appeared to the public on both sides of the Iron Curtain.

SPORT MORE IMPORTANT THAN BERLIN?

As newspapers started to write about the travel ban for the East German ski and ice hockey teams in late January 1962, the American and French delegates to NATO's Committee of Political Advisers provided information about Colorado Springs and Chamonix so that member states could reinforce the official position and demonstrate to their publics a united front within the alliance. Reaffirming NATO's position, Political Affairs Committee chairman R. W. J. Hooper (United Kingdom) stated that "there was no question at this stage of relaxing the ban on the issue of TTDs to East German sportsmen."[7] Yet, less than a week later—just days before the Chamonix world championships began—the Norwegian delegation renewed the debate to relax the travel ban for East German athletes.[8] Norway led the charge to remove sport from the travel restrictions, or at least to grant exceptions to the ban when falling under the guise of national interest.

As the Chamonix and Colorado Springs dramas were unfolding, Norway prepared to host two international sporting events in early 1962: the European speed skating championships (February) and the Holmenkollen ski festival (March). With a strong Soviet team and the subsequent speed skating world championships in locations where East German athletes would not have problems traveling (Kuovola, Finland, for the women's world championship and Moscow for the men's world championship), the East Germans did not use this event for propaganda purposes. The East German skaters had only been provisionally entered for the Oslo event, but when they had received neither TTDs nor visas for Norway, they withdrew their four athletes, stating they were staying home to focus on the world championships.[9] Like the wrestling world championships later that year in Toledo, Ohio, the Soviet dominance in this sport trumped East Germany's needs for recognition, and the Soviets could not risk jeopardizing their own event in Moscow by withdrawing from the European championships, which also provided an important test before the world championships.[10] As Evelyn Mertin has noted, "The unity shown in sport was intended to demonstrate the general superiority of communism to a worldwide audience," but the Soviet-East German relationship was not always smooth, particularly if it placed Soviet sport superiority at risk.[11] The Utenriksdepartement prepared a "statement in case there is a question raised as to why East German athletes do not have access to travel to Norway" a week before the speed skating championships.[12] The Norwegian government would not issue a visa without a TTD, and Norway, through its military mission in Berlin, supported the policy that East German athletes would not receive TTDs from the Allied Travel Office (ATO).[13]

Even though the European speed skating championships did not face the problems that befell the world championships in Alpine skiing or ice hockey, Norway nonetheless raised within NATO the recent publicity surrounding the East German athlete travel ban. The Norwegian delegate to the Committee of Political Advisers stated he recognized the need to keep quiet the specific categories of banned travel and the desire not to place all responsibility on the ATO in order to prevent further backlash to NATO. However, he "could not understand why the UK and USA reps seemed unwilling to have it admitted in public that there was a NATO decision involved when they would admit that the restrictions were part of quote Allied policy unquote."[14] The American representative reiterated that the acknowledgment of a NATO policy would give East Germany an advantage in its pleas to international federations, which would likely result in all of the major competitions being held outside NATO member states. The German, French, and Italian representatives also supported the American position, with the Italian arguing that stating the exact rules would make a change or relaxation in policy more difficult.[15] These arguments failed to convince the Norwegian representative, who noted the press in many countries had already attributed these policies to NATO decisions. He thought NATO had now reached the stage where the alliance either had to accept responsibility for its decision or try to deny it.[16] These discussions continued at the next Committee of Political Advisers meeting four days later. All members agreed on the general position to take when questioned about this issue and that they would include "the key phrase 'the three Western Powers supported by their North Atlantic allies.'"[17] A unanimous lack of support nixed the American suggestion of a formal NATO statement on the matter. Instead, the Dutch representative noted, "more stress should be laid on the origins of the travel ban and less on the question of TTDs and which agency is responsible on the Allied side."[18] By focusing on the origins of the ban, NATO could deflect the focus on its actions and instead shift the narrative—and, NATO representatives hoped, public opinion—to focus on the East Germans and the construction of the Berlin Wall.

Smaller NATO states, seeing how the press covered the travel ban, did not fully agree with the strict requirements limiting East German travel. While this discussion focused narrowly on how to respond to press questions, the Norwegians pushed for a broader debate on the issue of East German travel for athletes, questioning whether the original NATO decision on this matter was wise. The Canadian representative reported back to Ottawa on the comments from the Norwegian representative at length:

> He thought the decision had been justified in response to the East German actions last summer and autumn but it appeared to him that the rigid application of this decision had led to an unfavourable reaction by the press and public opinion. In the field of sports he thought we might arrive at quote more intelligent unquote rules to apply the decision. In this field he emphasised that we were at a disadvantage in dealing with the communists.[19]

The Belgian representative spoke against flexibility because it would result in too many exceptions, and he advocated maintaining the strict regulation or removing the sport category entirely. The German representative continued to support the travel restriction for athletes because "the disadvantages did not out-weigh the advantages. Sporting events attracted the public notice and there was some advantage in bringing home to public opinion the facts about the nature of the DDR [GDR] regime and the reasons for not letting the regime make capital out of sporting events."[20] The French were fully aware of the disadvantages from the recent events surrounding Chamonix, as their representative commented, but it would be difficult for NATO to change its policy so "soon after so much publicity had been given to the world ski championships."[21] The chair ended the debate when he said that the "effects of Berlin situation have been brought home to public and thought this presented opportunity for Govts to explain publicly why restrictions imposed on GDR travel."[22] NATO should, Hooper noted, "take advantage of this occasion to get across our case rather than be on the defensive," and the Committee of Political Advisers would have a full discussion on these broader points at their meeting the next week.[23]

Each NATO delegation sought instructions from their foreign ministries to prepare for the discussions at the Committee of Political Advisers meetings on February 13 and 20. The UK Foreign Office suggested proposing that the travel restrictions on the sport category be lifted as soon as possible but realized that it was likely "too early for general agreement on any relaxation yet, when nothing has happened to alleviate the effects of the Wall or the threat against Berlin."[24] The American representative felt that in reality the British doubted East Germany would respond to this type of statement, but that the Western position would be more appealing from a propaganda perspective "by saying that if GDR would relax certain travel restrictions within Berlin, e.g. that prevent Berlin families from reuniting, then West would relax certain of its restrictions. Aim would be to put blame more clearly on GDR."[25] This British proposal, along with the Norwegian comments from the previous meeting, shaped the discussions at the February 20 meeting, when the Committee of Political Advisers finally had its "first thorough discussion of the Norwegian proposal."[26] NATO states largely aligned into two sides: a group of smaller states arguing for a change in NATO's position and the Americans, French, and Germans supporting the status quo.

The first group largely consisting of the "cold countries" in NATO of Canada, Denmark, Iceland, and Norway, along with Portugal (simultaneously dealing with a proposed visit from an East German football team) advocated for a relaxation of the travel ban. Drawing on the instructions articulated by External Affairs in Ottawa, the Canadian delegate emphasized four main points. First, the current NATO policy disadvantaged the West when hosting international sport, and the subsequent organizing of sporting events in neutral or Soviet bloc countries provided further propaganda disadvantages for NATO. Second, the extensive publicity surrounding international sport often led to "misunderstandings in public opinion in NATO countries. To less sophisticated minds it is difficult to understand the exclusion of sportsmen from a puppet régime like East Germany when those from the Soviet Union and other satellites are received."[27] With these reasons Canada proposed excluding from the travel ban not only East German athletes who formed part of an all-German team (who already received exemptions) but also East German athletes in sports where the international federation had fully recognized the GDR. The Danish delegate supported this position, noting that the great public interest in sport, combined with the exclusion of GDR athletes, left "a danger that the public at large might take a negative attitude to other countermeasures which NATO might wish to impose at a later stage."[28] Neither Canada nor Denmark had hosted any sporting events that had been impacted by the travel ban, but they recognized that maintaining this policy would soon affect them. Copenhagen was the site of the 1963 European rowing championships, and Calgary was bidding for the 1968 Winter Olympic Games.

The Western Four, with support from the Belgian, Greek, Italian, Luxembourger, Dutch, and Turkish delegates, argued against a change in policy at the present time. The German representative opposed the idea of NATO states permitting East German athletes to compete in events governed by the international federations that had recognized the GDR against the wishes of the Federal Republic's delegates. He reminded his colleagues that the imposition of the travel restrictions on East German athletes (and other groups of people) had been in response to the GDR restricting freedom of movement. Many delegates, including the American, admitted they would be willing to consider greater flexibility if they gained some concession with respect to travel from the Communist bloc, but "there was nothing in the present situation that would justify the West taking any initiative in relaxing the TTD ban."[29] What became clear from the comments was the great interest the public in any country had when international athletes came to compete.

While this debate centered on NATO policy itself, much of the discussion focused on publicity and the general inability of NATO to exert control over international sport. The American disagreed with the Canadian point that the international federation representatives from communist states would determine where sporting events would be held. Furthermore, the American noted, the participation of East German athletes in competitions behind the Iron Curtain provided far fewer political advantages than in events held elsewhere.[30] The Norwegian delegate responded that it was "wishfull [*sic*] thinking" by NATO to suppose that it "could impose our wishes on sports federations who tended in any case to be more sympathetic to Soviet than to NATO line."[31] NATO risked "becoming scapegoats as a result of [its] own policy" if it did not prepare for the sport world taking action.[32] The government representatives at NATO realized they could not dictate to sport organizations, which were private bodies and, at the international level, nongovernmental organizations. Yet they knew they had to take some action to try to prevent further damage to the alliance's reputation. The chair ended the discussion by noting "a distinction should be made between the merits of the problem and the question of tactics and timing."[33] With the majority of NATO member states believing the time was not appropriate to change policy, Hooper tabled discussion for another two weeks. The delay also allowed NATO to see how the ice hockey world championships in Colorado Springs developed and whether East Germans could participate in the Holmenkollen ski festival in Norway.

This fixation on timing became the biggest obstacle to Canada's and Norway's ability to convince NATO to change its policy regarding the travel restrictions on East German athletes. It had only been six months since the erection of the Berlin Wall. The Western Four viewed changing current policy as making a concession to the Soviet bloc and "showing weakness" when there is "no sign of reciprocal concession" rather than taking action to alleviate damage to NATO. The Canadians nonetheless saw a sliver of possibility with a comment from the French representative, who said he did "not think that positions on travel control were very far apart except in relation to timing." The Canadian delegation at NATO developed two new tactics and requested advice from Ottawa before the next Committee of Political Advisers meeting discussion. If NATO found "some concessions were forthcoming from the other side, we should find ourselves pushing on an open door" with respect to their earlier arguments regarding the flexibility in the travel policy. To make gains with the other political advisers at the present time, Canada suggested getting the committee "to agree now that at the first possible opportunity it would be suitable to make an exception along the lines of the draft amendment we have suggested."[34] This idea was that NATO would be able to take immediate action rather than always being on the defensive. The Canadian delegation's second proposal was the removal of the "national interest" exception, which countries had previously used to circumvent the travel ban. East German athletes had occasionally received national interest exceptions. For any action, however, the Canadian delegation believed that their "ability to influence the other members of the [committee] will be very much diminished if we are unable to address ourselves to the question of timing since this has become, in the eyes of a majority of the [committee], the crux of the problem."[35] Ottawa rejected the suggestion to remove the national interest exception "because it makes it more difficult to resist domestic pressures on the basis of agreed policy." External Affairs was more supportive regarding flexibility and timing but nonetheless feared the German delegation to NATO would strictly interpret action to mean the rescinding all East German restrictions from August 1961 instead of changing policy following "any positive sign of relaxation by the East Germans."[36]

Canada's hopes for the next Committee of Political Advisers meeting to address the timing of a policy change failed to materialize as the discussion opened with a majority of NATO delegations maintaining the belief that the timing was not right. The chair of the Committee of Political Advisers emphasized that "since no valid reason for relaxation had appeared, [the] question was largely academic."[37] The Norwegian representative vehemently disagreed and led the ensuing debate, arguing that "the psychological effect on public opinion of maintaining the present regulations, particularly in the category of sport, for too long" would damage the prestige of the West. The Canadian delegate fully supported the Norwegian position, noting the difficulty was in changing public opinion that "was not sympathetic to certain aspects of NATO policy." The German representative countered that a change in NATO policy at the present time would negatively impact public opinion within the Federal Republic, which "would assume that their NATO allies thought that football was more important than the fate of Berlin." The Belgian representative, knowing that his country did not host as many major international sporting events, did not want the larger or more powerful sporting states to benefit at the expense of less prominent sporting countries. He again argued that "it would be difficult to explain to Belgian public opinion, in the event of any relaxation for international championships, why TTDs were granted for international players but not to East Germans who wished to take part in, for example, a local tournament in Belgium." The chair summarized the debate at the end of the meeting by reiterating that the timing was not appropriate for a policy change because it would be interpreted as yielding to pressure. However, if "the Communists stopped behaving so badly, then there might be a case for some relaxation on the part of the West." The other possible justification for modifying the travel ban would be if NATO "could not maintain the present restrictions in the face of Western public opinion," but that at present this concern was not such a difficult problem.[38]

The issue of travel for East German athletes clearly challenged the ability of NATO members to come to a consensus about how they might change this policy; the only part where the representatives demonstrated any unity was that the present was not the right time to change their current position. The debate appeared to conclude on March 6 within the Committee of Political Advisers, which would now look to improve information to better convey NATO's position to the general public.[39] Since virtually all member states had repeatedly agreed the timing was not right to change the travel restrictions, in the face of continued criticism of this policy the various governments could in the meantime counter these accusations with the standard lines to which the delegates had consented. The Committee of Political Advisers cited public opinion as one of the main arguments for changing NATO policy and one that factored into both sides of the debate. They therefore believed each country could alter the public's views of the alliance by taking a more proactive approach to promote the idea that the NATO position was merely a response to East German actions, thus placing the blame for the entry of politics into international sport on the communist bloc.

HELMUT RECKNAGEL AND THE 1962 HOLMENKOLLEN SKI FESTIVAL

The annual Holmenkollen ski festival takes place every March in Oslo and is one of the major events on the ski jump circuit. East Germany had produced successful ski jumpers, including Helmut Recknagel, the 1960 Olympic champion on the individual large hill as a member of the all-German Olympic team (Figure 5). In 1957 he became the first non-Scandinavian to win the Holmenkollen, and he had won the event again in 1960 after his Olympic victory. At the 1962 Nordic skiing world championships he was the only German to win any medals, placing first in the individual large hill and third in the individual normal hill. The Holmenkollen organizers requested government help to ensure Recknagel could enter the country and compete again in 1962.[40] Concerns regarding Recknagel's ability to travel for ski jump competitions were not new by 1962; even before the Berlin Wall and renewed travel restrictions, he had been prevented from participating in the pre-Olympic test event in Squaw Valley in 1959 and the 1961 Holmenkollen ski festival.[41] As the Chamonix and Colorado Springs dramas unfolded, Norwegians realized the strong East German ski jumpers, including Recknagel, were in jeopardy of again not being able to compete in the Holmenkollen. Norway had previously used the national interest request when hosting the 1961 women's speed skating championships to ensure athletes from both German states could compete and returned to this idea again in 1962. Norwegian ski leaders tried to enlist the Utenriksdepartement and their NATO permanent representative to secure an exception to the East German travel ban for the ski jumper. They argued Recknagel's inability to compete at the Holmenkollen would damage Norwegian public opinion of NATO.[42] Norway's NATO delegation wanted to prevent another event from turning into a public relations problem for the alliance, but these efforts for Recknagel specifically, and to change NATO policy as a whole, brought national self-interest in direct conflict with the need for consensus building within NATO.

FIGURE 5. Ski jumper Helmut Recknagel at the 1960 Winter Olympics at Squaw Valley (USA). The all-German Olympic team emblem appears on the sleeve of his jacket. © dpa—Report. Courtesy of picture-alliance/ dpa | dpa.

In late January, seventeen East Germans submitted applications for travel documents so that they could participate in the Holmenkollen ski festival in March. The ATO, in passing along this list of names to the Norwegian military mission in Berlin, informed the Norwegians they would refuse these applications under current guidelines, although the East Germans would not receive the formal rejection for approximately another three weeks, closer to the event itself.[43] Having observed what was happening with Chamonix and Colorado Springs, the Norwegians were not surprised at receiving this information from Berlin. As the Holmenkollen ski festival neared, the East Germans realized they would likely not be able to participate. A *Neues Deutschland* article suggested that the TTDs would be rejected as a result of Bonn's efforts and would prevent Recknagel from competing.[44] The East Germans sought to stir Norwegian popular sentiment by reaching out to leading Norwegian ski officials. In late February the East German Ski Federation sent a telegram to Einar Bergsland, a Fédération Internationale de Ski council member from Norway, requesting his support for their visa applications. Bergsland immediately called the Norwegian foreign ministry seeking advice on how to respond. He replied to the East Germans that he would do "everything possible with the authorities to achieve the entry permit." Following the Utenriksdepartement's advice, however, Bergsland tempered the East Germans' expectations by also writing that it would be "difficult to assess the prospects for the result of our efforts."[45]

Although the Norwegian ski leader appeared to accept the government's position with this reply to the East Germans, he nonetheless continued to try to help Recknagel and the East German ski jumpers obtain visas. A few days after speaking with the Utenriksdepartement, Bergsland directly contacted Norway's permanent representative to NATO, Jens Boyesen. He told Boyesen the Polish and Soviet athletes scheduled to compete might withdraw if the East Germans could not participate.[46] Knowing Recknagel's presence would interest most Norwegians, Boyesen reached out to his West German counterpart at NATO, Gebhardt von Walther, to see if the Federal Republic would grant Recknagel an exception to the travel ban for the Holmenkollen. The foreign minister had previously instructed Boyesen not to make any official interventions, but following Bergsland's call, Boyesen reached out to von Walther on a private basis. The Norwegian foreign minister did not want Boyesen to take formal action because "the matter would not be profitable and . . . Recknagel's entry into Norway would not be useful from the point of view of NATO, although undoubtedly Recknagel's non-entry in Norway itself would cause great annoyance." In asking for an exception for Recknagel, Boyesen told von Walther "the non-issuance of the TTD would likely provoke a movement critical of NATO among the hundreds of thousands of skiers in Norway."[47] After consulting with Bonn, von Walther replied to Boyesen that the Auswärtiges Amt's "thoughtful consideration" resulted in the conclusion that "the exceptional issue of a TTD to Recknagel, which would have to be done in disregard of existing NATO-wide travel restrictions, would have most undesirable consequences."[48] Providing Recknagel with an exception would have gone against the agreed NATO policy and also fomented negative publicity inside the Federal Republic and other NATO member states whose sporting events had not received a travel exception for East German athletes. In addition, von Walther noted the French, who had felt the public backlash following the refusal of travel documents for East German skiers to compete in Chamonix, "would most certainly refuse [to issue] a TTD to Recknagel, even if the Federal Government would agree."[49] Following this response, the Norwegian diplomats, both at NATO in Paris and Oslo, acknowledged that at this point nothing else could be done to secure Recknagel's participation in the Holmenkollen.[50]

While von Walther emphasized public opinion inside the Federal Republic in his reply, Norwegian public opinion factored in Bergsland's, Boyesen's, and the Utenriksdepartement's actions as well. Yet, the day after von Walther had spoken with Boyesen, the Norwegian nonetheless raised the problem of Recknagel and the Holmenkollen at the North Atlantic Council meeting. Boyesen even called Recknagel "the most popular German who had ever stayed in Norway." A lengthy discussion followed, but without any change in NATO's position. The Canadian delegate noted it was "not Norwegian officials who were being troublesome but Norwegian public opinion which was becoming quote embittered unquote against NATO." NATO secretary general Dirk Stikker, however, summed up the discussion by noting that one must remember several sets of public opinion were involved—not just the Norwegian, but also the West German and East German at a minimum.[51] The Utenriksdepartement knew Recknagel's ability to participate would garner public attention and frequently spoke with Bergsland. The day after the Norwegian ski leader had informed the government that he had been working to minimize the negative coverage of the East German travel ban in the press, a sports column in the country's largest newspaper, *Aftenposten*, attempted to support the NATO position with respect to Recknagel's likely absence from the Holmenkollen. Although the paper noted, "It is common to say that the visas are a NATO issue," it was actually the East German "Wall of Shame" which precipitated these new travel restrictions.[52] By playing both angles at the same time, the Norwegian government hoped to minimize domestic criticism but also use that same public opinion to work for a travel ban exception.

As with the world championships for ice hockey and skiing, the sport leaders' efforts to have government officials obtain exceptions for East German athletes came to naught. Unlike the Fédération Internationale de Ski telegrams to prime ministers and presidents regarding the Chamonix world championships, Norwegian ski leaders convinced their country's diplomats to seek an exception to the travel ban. Norway's NATO delegation was unsuccessful in its efforts, leaving Recknagel and his East German teammates unable to compete in the 1962 Holmenkollen. Norwegian ski jumper Toralf Engen, the recently crowned world champion on the individual hill, secured victory at the Holmenkollen event as well. Some communists attempted to politicize Recknagel's absence by distributing placards with a photo of Recknagel on one side and details about his visa refusal on the other side, but the Oslo police shut down their efforts.[53] The American embassy reported back to Washington that Recknagel's exclusion "evoked no noticeable public demonstration."[54]

Concerns about a potential public backlash against NATO had prompted the efforts by Bergsland and Boyesen to seek an exemption for Recknagel's participation, but in the end neither the Utenriksdepartement nor NATO came under attack. Instead, the Norwegian press published articles that placed the blame for his absence from the competition on East Germany's original actions curtailing the freedom of its own citizens. The left-leaning *Arbeiderbladet*, which was close to the government, published an article supporting the rationale for the ban, questioning how Norwegians could accept an exception for a single athlete when common men and women were unable to visit their own relatives in West Berlin.[55] The country's largest paper, the more conservative *Aftenposten*, published an article titled "The Use of Recknagel," criticizing the small "east-oriented" minority who had been using Recknagel's case as propaganda against all Western cooperation. This article also followed NATO's recommendations and emphasized the East German restrictions, reminding readers that "the East German regime holds the entire population captive behind a continuous border barrier from the west by wall and barbed wire and a death zone, where everyone who shows up is shot on the spot."[56] The West German embassy in Oslo reported positively to Bonn about the Norwegian press coverage supporting the NATO line and that the West German ski jumpers performed admirably in front of King Olav V and more than eighty thousand spectators, even if none of them earned a podium place.[57] The Holmenkollen did not face the problem that befell the Chamonix and Colorado Springs events, and the domestic press primarily published articles in support of the government's position. Nevertheless, the difficulty of securing an exception for a single athlete or event reinforced to the Utenriksdepartement the need for a complete change in NATO policy.

THE CANADIAN PROPOSAL

While publicly the Norwegian government maintained the official line, within NATO the Norwegians were disappointed with their inability to secure Recknagel's participation in the Holmenkollen ski festival. The Norwegian delegation felt the secretary general had given no support to their position when Boyesen had raised the issue in the North Atlantic Council.[58] Even so, the council requested the Committee of Political Advisers return to this issue at its next meeting on March 13, just days before the Holmenkollen ski jump competition, which the committee had already planned to do. The Canadians used this opportunity to push for a relaxation on the East German travel ban on the idea of flexibility and timing. Canada and Norway thus challenged NATO unity over this issue of travel for East German athletes, with each state advocating for change from different angles.

The political advisers prepared for this meeting by seeking guidance from their respective foreign ministries. Canada's secretary of state for external affairs, Howard Charles Green, sent instructions (albeit reluctantly) to the Canadian delegation at NATO on how to approach this next stage of the discussion. Looking to gain support for their own stance and the government's desire for Canada to host the Olympic Games, Green wrote,

> While the Norwegians, at the moment, have a specific case which is creating difficulties for them and it is therefore difficult to distinguish the extent to which expediency colours their views, most of

> the arguments they have submitted are ones with which we can sympathize. I think, however, we should avoid discussion of particular cases such as the one raised by the Norwegians. The summation of the problem by the secretary general, that the question involved is one of principle rather than of expediency, cannot be ignored. If the principle involved, however, in its operation is in the long run more damaging to ourselves than to the East Germans or the Soviet bloc, it is essential to consider making alterations and it is precisely in this context that the timing of any charge is of paramount importance.[59]

Green therefore advised the Canadian delegation to again propose that greater flexibility for East German travel arrangements "should be kept under review and the question of when it is the right time to make specific changes should be given careful examination from time to time" within NATO. Ideally this timing should coincide "with any positive sign of relaxation by the East Germans of their restrictions and when there is a significant reduction of East German or Soviet Bloc pressure on the west."[60] Canada hoped to push the alliance away from the current consensus against taking any action at the moment toward their minority position, which was clearly influenced by their national interest. In contrast, the British wanted to see this issue brought to a close. The Foreign Office admitted that it could understand the particular circumstances related to Norway's concern with Recknagel and the Holmenkollen ski festival, but it did "not think that these outweigh the harmful effects which an exception may have on N.A.T.O. solidarity on this question."[61] Broader Cold War issues and alliance unity underlined this position.

To the relief of the British, the March 13 meeting saw the conclusion of this debate, with the discussion first focusing on the Norwegian concerns before moving to the Canadian proposal. The chair of the Committee of Political Advisers asked each delegation to go around the table and express their views regarding the Norwegian situation. Armed with a list of ten points from Washington to counter the Norwegian and Canadian claims, the American delegate emphasized that continuing the ban hurt East Germany because the "Regime lionizes its international champions and has even made Recknagel [a] member of [the] Volkskammer (Parliament)."[62] Excluding Recknagel and other athletes would damage the prestige that the East Germans hoped to gain from their participation.[63] After hearing the same arguments repeated by several delegates, with a majority against permitting an exception for Recknagel, the Norwegian delegate concluded by stating he had not asked for an exception for the East German ski jumper. Instead, he claimed, Boyesen had merely "brought up the ski championship rather as an illustration of the harm done by the current restrictions."[64] Norway's continued efforts to bring the world's best ski jumper to the Holmenkollen ski festival thus ended with the Norwegians' backtracking, stating that all of their arguments for more than a month were merely about policy rather than a specific request for an exemption for Recknagel. With the ski festival already under way, and Recknagel's event only five days away, the Norwegian delegation also realized it was out of opportunities to push for an exception.

The second part of the discussion centered on the Canadian proposal introducing flexibility into the travel restrictions for East German athletes. This proposal recommended two amendments to the sport category within the travel ban: (1) East German athletes competing as part of an all-German team and (2) East German athletes and teams attending international sporting events "organized by any federation which has a fully participating East German organization accredited to it."[65] The first part, which already happened in practice for the Olympic Games and a few international federations, was largely acceptable to NATO member states. The German representative naturally spoke in favor of the all-German teams: "If the East Germans were to accept the idea of all German teams this would indicate that they had relaxed some of their pretentions to be a separate state," but of course for that same reason very few cases of this exception would likely happen. The second exception, however, faced strong opposition. The Dutch representative began the debate, noting it was in NATO's "interest to try to force the East Germans to accept a single team from both parts of Germany for major sports competitions."[66] The Dutch representative feared adopting this proposal would actually "have the opposite effect and would put a premium on East German efforts to become independent in the field of sport and hence increase the pressure for recognition of the DDR regime." The Danish delegate similarly argued that creating this exception would be "self-defeating" by "fostering the very thing it wished to avoid" as East Germany would be encouraged to push harder for separate recognition within all sport organizations.[67] This action would "have the effect of introducing politics into sports federations in which East Germany was not" already represented, and NATO should therefore remove the entire sport category as a banned category for East German travel.[68] The nature and actions of international sport therefore became a central consideration in how NATO might change its policy.

In addition, the publicity angle remained a central aspect of the discussion. The British representative reiterated his previous arguments that a relaxation in the sport category was acceptable in principle but that it required a justification for the timing. He again emphasized the importance of promoting NATO's position, particularly "that the present restrictions were not directed against international sporting contacts as such, but were simply one of the unfortunate consequences of Communist policy in Germany."[69] The American delegate, relying on the instructions from Washington, argued firmly against the Danish suggestion of removing the sport category and the second Canadian exception. A retreat from the current NATO position, he said, particularly in the face of intensified pressures from the communist bloc, would be interpreted by the Soviets and East Germans "as weakness and evidence of Allied disunity."[70] NATO had tightened restrictions on East German travel in response to the erection of the Berlin Wall and East Germany's curtailing of freedom of movement. The alliance had previously agreed not to rescind the travel ban until East Germany took the first steps to roll back its own restrictions to prevent the appearance that NATO was cowering to the Soviet bloc. The American delegate also argued public opinion, in the long run, would ultimately shift to supporting NATO's views as long as member states maintained a firm position. The Norwegian representative "did not, however, share the optimism of [his] NATO allies on the prospects of channeling public opinion in the right direction."[71] Recognizing the lack of support for their initial proposal, the Canadian delegate stated that while he believed the entire sport category should be removed but that the timing was not right, it was nonetheless these propaganda concerns that had prompted Canada to create this proposal in a sense of compromise. Most importantly, however, the Canadian government did not want to see the travel ban remain indefinitely until East Germany ended its August 1961 restrictions (the removal of the Berlin Wall) in order for NATO to adjust its policy.[72] With stakes so high with the perception of NATO and its actions on the line, the timing of the alliance's actions was thus crucial.

Hooper finally concluded the debate, and this weeks-long discussion, by noting the Canadian proposal had been helpful in focusing attention on the problem. NATO was unlikely to find a "halfway house" with respect to relaxing the travel restrictions. Although a general consensus existed for all-German teams, Hooper believed future all-German Olympic teams were unlikely to happen again, particularly because "the whole of the East German effort in sport was to establish the identity and respectability of the DDR as an international entity, and it was unlikely that the regime would go into reverse on this point."[73] (Hooper was wrong on the future of the all-German team, although its formation for the 1964 Olympics was quite acrimonious, as will be seen in chap. 7.) Thus, when the timing was right for NATO to change the travel restrictions, it appeared the sport category would have to be an all or nothing change. Finally, in what was a bright spot at the end of a long debate against their proposal, the Canadians felt Hooper said "his most useful remark of the day": that based on the discussion's tone it was not realistic to expect to wait until all of the East German actions from August 1961 were undone before NATO relaxed its regulations. When Hooper then asked if anyone disagreed with this summing up, nobody did, giving hope to the Canadian delegation for their ideas in the long run.[74]

After six Committee of Political Advisers meetings and a North Atlantic Council meeting in which the Canadians and Norwegians had pushed for a change to NATO policy that would help their short-term goals for hosting international sporting events, the travel ban on East German athletes remained in place. Yet the weeks of debate revealed a general consensus: when the political timing was right, the Committee of Political Advisers would be amenable to returning to this issue. NATO's belief was that negative public opinion of its policy around what most people viewed as an apolitical area—sport—challenged the ability for the alliance to maintain a unified position when that same policy damaged countries' efforts to promote their own domestic agendas via the soft power of hosting international sporting events.

CONCLUSION

The Norwegian attempt to use the threat of negative public opinion over no East German skiers participating in the world championships and Holmenkollen as a way to change NATO policy—or at least receive a special exemption from the travel ban for Recknagel in 1962—was unsuccessful, as was Canada's effort to change NATO policy. These decisions did not, however, quell the debate inside NATO. Neither Norway nor Canada viewed these March 1962 decisions as the final outcome on the issue as they both continued to advocate for their views on East German travel because it served their national interests more than the alliance's position. The travel restrictions on East German athletes caused more problems and prompted more discussions within NATO than any of the other banned categories for travel because of the greater public interest in sport compared to other fields. In the summer of 1962 no media, either in East Germany or the West, published stories when the ATO denied TTDs to East German professors wanting to travel to an international meteorological meeting in Canada, an international physics conference in England, or an international poultry conference in Australia.[75] When scientists could attend conferences as part of an all-German delegation, such as to the International Union of Geophysics and Geodesy conference in Berkeley, California, in August 1963, *Neues Deutschland* publicized that its scientists attended. The East German state paper, however, omitted that its scientists attended as part of an all-German delegation because unlike sport, no television or magazine coverage of this event would illustrate this all-German element to the East German public.[76] Like these scientific meetings, sport was not a life-or-death issue within NATO, as evidenced by their treatment within the Committee of Political Advisers and not in the Military Committee. Political matters were nonetheless important when considering action taken by the multilateral organization. It was for this reason—that decisions related to sport would not make or break the organization—that these debates regarding the sport category for the East German travel ban are so revealing. All member states could voice their views, particularly with the hope that they could achieve a change in NATO policy.

Following the Chamonix and Colorado Springs debacles, the NATO states arguing for the removal of sport entirely from the travel restrictions, or at least for greater exceptions, expressed a concern that the continued ban would prompt international sport federations to hold their events only in communist bloc or neutral states. This scenario thus benefitted East Germany and the Soviet bloc and weakened NATO. Removing the travel restrictions would ease Cold War tensions, which aligned with Canada's efforts to pursue détente with the Soviet Union.[77] Indeed, as a Canadian External Affairs telegram to its NATO delegation noted, acknowledging "there was a NATO policy on this matter would give the East Germans an unnecessary advantage for any argument they might advance to hold international competitions outside NATO countries." Importantly for their position, the Canadian government intended to support Calgary's application to host the 1968 Winter Olympics and did "not wish any statement on policy issued which would prejudice our position in this regard. Our hope is therefore that any public statement made on this matter is phrased in vague terms indicating no clear relationship between the issuance of TTDs and visas."[78] Not antagonizing the communist bloc over sport could help with détente and hopefully win the Olympic Games for Calgary.

The inability of East Germany to make gains in other areas left sport the most prominent and, because of its widespread popularity and global media coverage, most visible field, particularly when East German athletes could not participate in international competitions. NATO governments and foreign ministries therefore closely monitored popular media coverage of this issue, which also factored into the NATO debates. Although Canada and Norway failed to achieve a relaxation of the East German travel ban for athletes in early 1962, this lengthy debate paved the way for future discussions, both within NATO and, importantly, among the Western Four during their quadripartite meetings in Bonn. As the travel ban on East German athletes continued to cause problems for NATO states throughout 1962 and 1963, the four member states with cities bidding to host the 1968 Olympic Games increasingly recognized that this NATO policy hurt their cities' chances of winning the biggest international sport event in the world.

CHAPTER 4

THE 1968 CANDIDATE CITIES CONFRONT OLYMPIC DEMANDS FOR FREE TRAVEL

The IOC opened the bidding process for the 1968 Olympics amidst all of the sporting events being impacted by the Cold War problem of NATO's non-recognition of East Germany. In the middle of the twentieth century, the IOC typically selected host cities five years before the games. A city declared its intention to bid for the Olympic Games by sending a letter to the IOC, often one to two years before the IOC's scheduled vote. Even as international politics marred world or European championships, several cities sought to bring the five rings of the Olympics to their town. Eleven cities entered the contest to organize the 1968 Olympics, with six of them from NATO members states (Figure 6). For the winter games, Lake Placid, New York; Calgary, Canada; Grenoble, France; Oslo, Norway; Lahti, Finland; Sion, Switzerland; and Sapporo, Japan, all wanted to bring the Olympics to their mountains. The metropolises of Detroit, Michigan; Lyon, France; Mexico City; and Buenos Aires, Argentina, vied for the Summer Olympics. With both Olympic Games still held in the same year, the contests to organize games ran concurrently.

In the midst of the candidature process for the 1968 Olympic Games, the IOC held an extraordinary meeting of its Executive Board and representatives from all of the international federations in February 1963 with a single agenda item: sport and politics. International federations had experienced political interference directly in their events and had requested the IOC organize a meeting to address this issue.[1] The IOC Executive Board regularly met with the international federations, but the growing problem of politics intruding on sport prompted this extraordinary gathering on only this topic. The inability of East German athletes to participate in sporting events held in NATO countries was just one of the many recent examples they discussed. Other instances included the refusal to invite Israel, Albania, and Libya to the Mediterranean Games, the Philippines' refusal to grant a

FIGURE 6. Cities bidding for the 1968 Summer and Winter Olympic Games.

visa to the Yugoslavian basketball team for the 1962 world championships, and the "deplorable incidents" from the Asian Games in Jakarta, Indonesia, where neither Israel nor Taiwan were able to participate.[2]

The meeting produced a statement for public release and included a declaration of seven points opposing political interference in sport to hinder the travel of athletes and officials. The declaration reiterated the IOC's commitment to opposing political interference in sport, including, if necessary, changing the location of the Olympic Games or canceling them outright.

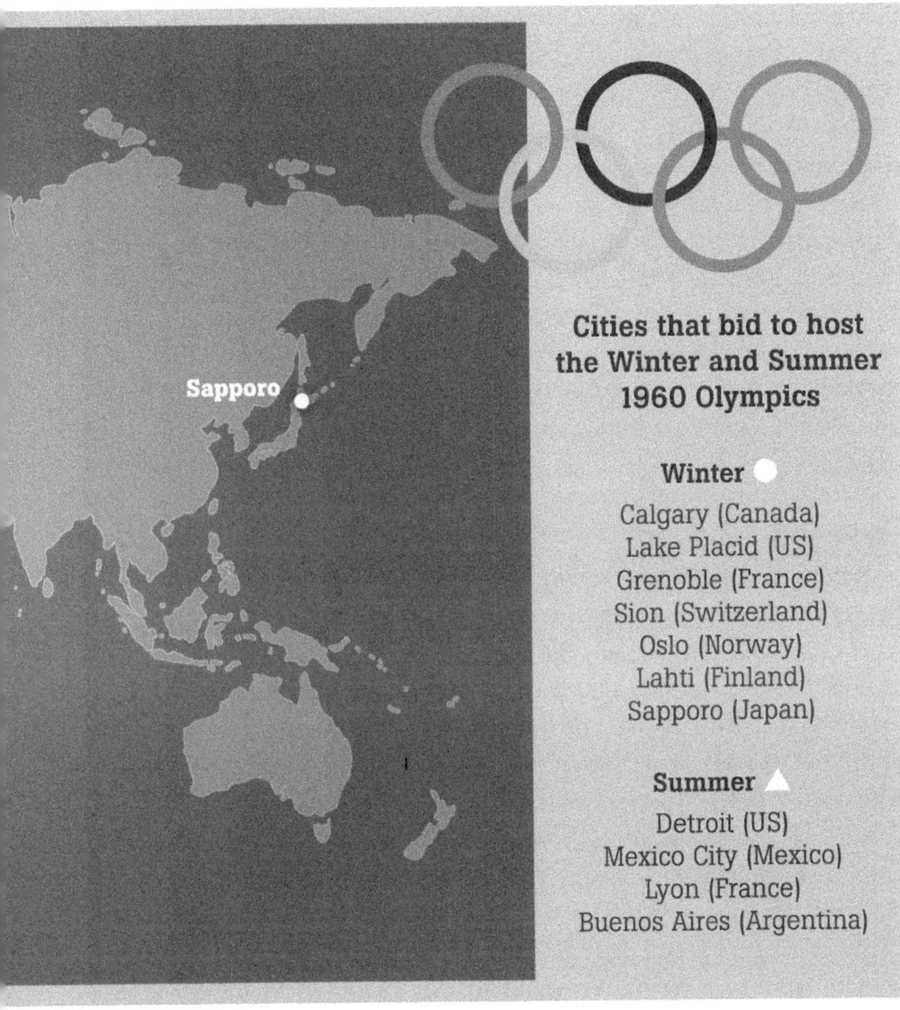

MAP BY CPORTER DESIGNS

Many of the international federations also included a similar rule, and the declaration urged the international federations that did not yet have such a regulation to add one. The statement also boldly declared: "The I.O.C. will not award the Olympic Games to any City nor grant its patronage to any regional Games unless free access is guaranteed."[3] The public statement satisfied international sport leaders, but the Western press did not report favorably on it. *New York Times* columnist Robert Daley felt this ultimatum did not solve the problem, writing, "It is unrealistic of the International

Olympic Committee and the sports federations to believe they can force governments to promise no further interference with what is by now of recognized political value."[4] Karlheinz Vogel, writing in the *Frankfurter Allgemeine Zeitung*, described the meeting as a big show and criticized the way the IOC addressed its problems.[5]

Having observed the frequency at which NATO's policy of not recognizing Germany was impacting sporting events, the IOC grasped the extent of the travel problems and became increasingly concerned about how these Cold War politics might affect the Olympic Games. The IOC therefore requested each city provide a governmental guarantee that all participants would be permitted to enter the country if selected as host. Over half of the candidate cities bidding for the 1968 Olympic Games were located in NATO member states, but none of these states wanted their cities' responses to unnecessarily exclude them from being selected as the host of the 1968 summer or winter games. The four NATO member states with candidate cities realized that they needed to work with each other, and with their other NATO allies, to ensure each of their responses satisfied the IOC and at the same time did not violate any NATO agreements. The alliance had framed its policy as retaliation against the East German regime because the communist state had taken away the freedom of travel from its own citizens, but now the IOC was primarily ascribing the limitations on free travel—at least with respect to East Germany—to NATO member states.

Both of these statements from the IOC—one broadly addressing the problem of sport and politics and the other specifically for the 1968 Olympic candidate cities—were a clear response to all of the sporting events impacted by geopolitics. Because so many of the affected sporting events resulted from NATO policies regarding East German travel and national symbols, the IOC's actions prompted a flurry of activity within NATO. The quadripartite group in Bonn had been developing a temporary relaxation of some of the travel ban categories, including for sport. The Western Four had hoped to inform NATO of this temporary change to the travel policy and have their allies accept it, but this IOC request prompted renewed debate in NATO to try to negotiate additional changes to the travel policy. At first NATO had not initially considered the joint IOC-international federation statement, but once the IOC's request for a travel guarantee from the bid cities came to their attention, this political statement also factored into their discussions. The Canadians and Norwegians again took the lead in the effort to change the NATO policy, with both countries keeping in view their 1968 Olympic bids. Canada, the only NATO member state with a city in the running for the 1968 Olympics that had never before hosted the games, immediately set to work to ensure this requirement for a travel guarantee, and the conflicting NATO policy, did not prematurely end Calgary's bid. The Norwegians pushed for more immediate action because the country was hosting other international sporting events that continued to be affected by the travel ban. These two IOC documents, coinciding with quadripartite negotiations to temporarily relax the travel ban on East German athletes and scientists, brought together the various strands of NATO's concern with sport all at once. Discussions in official NATO meetings, among the quadripartite powers in Bonn, and informally between diplomats at NATO's headquarters and in their capitals could not separate the three issues of changing the travel policy for East Germans, providing the travel guarantee to the IOC, and supporting the continued formation of an all-German Olympic team from each other. The response to both of these documents demonstrates the power of international sport organizations, and especially the IOC, to force foreign ministries and their diplomats not only to consider sport but also to take action on these matters, including modifying their policies. National self-interest in wanting to win the contest to host the 1968 summer and winter Olympic Games directly challenged NATO unity as the alliance again confronted the issue of free travel and debated the restrictions on East German athletes as Cold War policy.

THE OLYMPIC BIDS

Geography, topography, and venues play a major part in the Olympic host city selection process, but several other factors contribute to how IOC members vote. For the 1968 contest, candidate cities emphasized their facilities in their bid materials and hoped to boost tourism from both domestic and foreign visitors. A city's previous experience organizing sporting events also helped to demonstrate a level of expertise necessary for ensuring a smooth-running and successful Olympic Games. Each city emphasized its strengths, particularly if those features hinted at competitors' weaknesses. Only two of these cities would emerge victorious and organize the world's most prestigious sporting event, but complicating the process was the fact that half of the cities bidding for the 1968 Olympics were in NATO member states. Bid committees and their countries' foreign ministries increasingly worried about the implications of the Cold War as they watched other sporting events—often in their own countries—impacted by NATO's policies. In the meantime, however, these cities had to demonstrate to the IOC and international federations why they were superior to their competitors and should become the host of the 1968 Olympic Games.

Although the Winter Olympics happen first in the calendar year, the summer games were the IOC's original product. As the larger and more important event, the IOC prioritized the summer host city selection. For 1968, four cities vied for the Summer Olympics, with three of these cities in the western hemisphere and just one city in Europe.[6] The 1968 summer games competition was a contest between somewhat unequal candidates. Detroit drew on its industrial prominence as home of the American auto industry, whereas Lyon emphasized its sportiness. Both Mexico City and Buenos Aires pushed to be the first Latin American host of the Olympic Games, although each faced additional challenges: the altitude of the Mexican capital and the political instability of Argentina. The four summer Olympic Games candidate cities thus offered a different experience for the IOC members to consider.

Detroit's civic leaders aspired to host the Olympics and had bid for every summer games since 1940. Fred Matthaei, president of an automotive parts supplier and part owner of the National Football League's Detroit Lions, founded the Detroit Olympic Committee in 1936 and served as its chairman for nearly thirty years.[7] Joining Matthaei were representatives from the Big Three automotive companies (Ford, General Motors, and Chrysler), the energy company (Detroit Edison), a major pharmaceutical company (Parke Davis), and the city's largest bank (Detroit Bank & Trust, known today as Comerica). Detroit's many professional teams and nearby universities provided numerous venues for the Olympic events. The city proposed a compact games, with all venues within a fifteen-mile radius from the city center and proposed Olympic Village.[8] Although the city had not hosted any major international sporting events, it had extensive experience with national sporting events and several Detroit Olympic Committee members had attended the Olympic Games since the 1930s. Detroit's bid also had the support of local businessman (and Matthaei's successor as the president of his company) Douglas F. Roby, a prominent American sports leader who had also served as the Pan American Games president in the 1950s and an IOC member since 1952.[9]

France's candidate for the 1968 games was Lyon, the country's second largest city. In its official materials Lyon emphasized the city's commitment to sport, particularly through the extensive facilities for a variety of sports throughout the city.[10] At the October 1962 opening of the Palais des Sports de Lyon, a new indoor stadium with two arenas inside, Mayor Louis Pradel discussed the city's Olympic candidature.[11] IOC chancellor Otto Mayer attended this event, commenting, "This Palace honors the city of Lyon to which it adds a flagship for the candidacy of your city for the organization of the Games of the XIX Olympiad in 1968."[12] The city hosted a number of major sporting events, including the Sugar Ray Robinson–Georges Estatoff fight a month after the Palais opened, and had numerous events scheduled for 1963: international matches for the French national teams in basketball, handball, judo, and indoor athletics; the European Maccabi Games; and an international table tennis event. Local organizers had also been involved in other major international sporting events, including the 1959 Mediterranean Games in Beirut, the 1961 Friendship Games in Abidjan, Côte d'Ivoire, and the 1962 Alpine skiing world championships in Chamonix.[13] The city also hosted a pre-Olympic field hockey tournament in autumn 1963, inviting fifteen IOC members to the event so they could envision the games in Lyon.[14] In addition, one of Lyon's most famous residents was Maurice Herzog, who had written a best-selling book about his experience as part of the first expedition to summit Annapurna in the Himalayas. From 1958 to 1964 Herzog served in Charles de Gaulle's cabinet as the high commissioner for youth and sports, a role in which he ensured that the French government would financially support the Olympics if Lyon won.[15]

Buenos Aires wanted to bring the games to South America for the first time, emphasizing the benefits of the Olympics taking place in a new part of the world within their bid. The city had narrowly lost the election (twenty-one to twenty) for the 1956 Olympics to Melbourne, but it had hosted the first Pan American Games in 1951 and the first basketball world championships, as well as seven South American Football Championships (today's Copa América), including two postwar editions of the tournament.[16] However, political instability hindered Buenos Aires's candidacy. One German paper commented on Buenos Aires's chances that "sudden coups and Olympic Games get along poorly."[17] *New York Times* columnist Robert Daley discounted Buenos Aires because IOC members did not take the city's candidacy seriously "for financial reasons. They are too poor to stage so expensive a spectacle."[18]

The fourth candidate for the 1968 summer games was Mexico City, whose greatest challenge was its high altitude and concerns for how that would affect the athletes' performances.[19] The impetus for Mexico City's Olympic dreams largely came from the country's Olympic Committee president and IOC member, General José de Jesús Clark Flores, and other sport leaders who wanted "to increase Mexico's profile in the world of international sports."[20] Mexico City had previously bid for the 1956 and 1960 Olympic Games but received few votes in either contest. Mexico City planned a one hundred thousand–seat stadium, Estadiu Azteca (Aztec Stadium), which opened in 1966 and was a major part of Mexico's (successful) 1970 FIFA World Cup bid.[21] The city had experience organizing multisport events, including the 1954 Central American and Caribbean Games, the 1955 Pan American Games, and the 1962 modern pentathlon world championships.[22] To convince IOC members of Mexico City's ability to host the Olympics, General Clark had invited all of his Olympic colleagues to attend the 1962 modern pentathlon world championships. Almost half of the IOC members accepted, receiving free travel, accommodation, and meals for their personal visits, which enabled them to envision an Olympics in Mexico City.[23] Mexico City also framed its bid as a contrast to stereotypes of its northern neighbor. It was both a "modern and exotic" location, and by promoting Mexico as a "nation of the people" with "harmony between human beings," the bid sought to gain votes from IOC members from communist and newly independent former colonial states.[24] Although geographically located on the North American continent, Mexico was not a member of NATO and therefore positioned itself as a counter to the United States and a choice that could remain outside of Cold War issues.

The competition for the 1968 Winter Olympics was greater, with cities from four NATO member states bidding to host the games, along with Sion, Switzerland; Lahti, Finland; and Sapporo, Japan. The competition spanned three continents, with two North American cities and four European candidates, along with the lone Asian city attempting to bring the winter games to the Far East for the first time. Two of the candidate cities (Lake Placid and Oslo) had previously hosted the winter games. Four of the other countries had Olympic hosting experience in other cities; only Canada had never organized the games (either summer or winter). The cities all had the geography and topography necessary to organize the Olympics, and no clear favorite appeared within the crowded field, with each city promoting its winter sport credentials far and wide.

Lake Placid, the small village in the Adirondack Mountains in upstate New York, had hosted the 1932 winter games after Los Angeles won the bid for the summer games. The town now hoped to bring the winter games back to the eastern United States just eight years after Squaw Valley had organized them on the West Coast. Lake Placid highlighted not only its Olympic heritage but the town's thirty years of experience continuing to host major events annually for each of the sports on the Olympic program. With so many winter sport facilities already existing, Lake Placid's bid emphasized compactness. The town also highlighted its closeness to the Canadian border, noting the two nearest major international airports were in New York City and Montreal in an effort to break the traditional view of the United States as a vast country where only Americans would be the spectators.[25]

Grenoble, the largest city anywhere in the Alps, began preparing for its 1968 bid far in advance, with the mayor announcing Grenoble's intentions on December 30, 1960.[26] In its bid materials, Grenoble drew on its two thousand–year history as a city of crossroads to highlight its welcoming nature, as well as the city's importance in the development of winter sport in France.[27] The events themselves would be spread across three areas in the region, with the city of Grenoble as the Olympic hub with the large Winter Sports Salon, outdoor stadium, and main press area. The Olympic Village would be less than a mile from the stadium and other venues in the city. The sliding track was forty miles from Grenoble in L'Alpe d'Huez, and the skiing venues were elsewhere in the mountains.[28] The region had experience with organizing international sporting events, including the 1951 bobsled world championships and the upcoming 1964 European figure skating championships.[29] Like Lyon's bid, Grenoble also had the support from Herzog and the Ministry of Youth and Sport.[30]

Oslo, like Lake Placid, hoped to become just the second city to host the Winter Olympics for a second time, after having previously organized the 1952 winter games. The Norwegian Olympic Committee, with the support of the country's IOC member, Olav Ditlev-Simonsen, initiated the bid in the spring of 1961.[31] The bid materials emphasized the city's strong winter sport tradition, experience organizing events, and existing venues. In addition to the 1952 Olympics and the annual Holmenkollen ski jump event, Oslo had also hosted eight world championships (six for winter sports) and five European championships (all but one for winter sports) in the first fifteen years after the war. Only downhill and giant slalom skiing would take place outside of Oslo, seventy-five miles away in Norefjell. Oslo was keen to highlight that Norefjell's popularity had grown in the past decade since it had hosted those disciplines at the 1952 Olympics, and that the accommodations and amenities in that area had greatly expanded since then (attempting to fend off any criticism about earlier subpar offerings).[32]

Shortly after losing the selection for the 1964 Winter Olympics to Innsbruck in what many people considered a "token bid," businessmen and sports leaders in Calgary embarked on their effort to bring the 1968 games to the area.[33] The city's sport experience largely consisted of national sporting events and the occasional North American championships. To compensate for its lack of experience organizing international sporting events, Calgary highlighted its two million annual tourists, including half a million people who attended the Calgary Stampede in 1962, demonstrating the city's ability to handle large events. Although the Calgary Olympic Development Association officially led the bid, the Olympics would largely take place seventy-five miles west of Calgary in Banff, Canada's first national park. The Rocky Mountain terrain allowed Canada to compete with the candidate cities from the Alps. Some of the ski runs had already been cut, which Calgary emphasized had been done under the auspices of the Fédération Internationale de Ski (FIS). Calgary highlighted that its two existing facilities met international federation standards and name-dropped the influential individuals who had provided technical direction; the rest of the venues, however, were all proposed and did not yet exist.[34]

Three cities outside of NATO member states also wanted to host the 1968 winter games. Finland's fourth-largest city, Lahti, drew on its strength as a Nordic skiing site for its Olympic bid. Knowing the lack of mountains would hinder its ability to host the winter games, Lahti partnered with the Swedish city of Åre, which sits near the Norwegian border, for the Alpine skiing events. The inability of Finland to stage all of the events within the country, however, became a major criticism of Lahti's bid.[35] Lahti's bid drew on the city's experience organizing winter sports, including the 1958 Nordic skiing world championships, which was the third time the city had organized this event. The city had also hosted some of the 1952 Summer Olympics soccer matches.[36] Sion sought to return the Winter Olympics to Switzerland for the third time, following the 1928 and 1948 games. With the Matterhorn, one of the tallest mountains in the Alps, located nearby, the canton hoped holding the Olympics in Sion would bring significant publicity to the region.[37] Sion could not boast of any European or world championships having been held in the area, but it had organized several national and international sporting events.[38] However, rumors of the local population not supporting Sion's candidacy started to surface in the summer of 1963.[39] In December the mayor, after receiving letters threatening that he would lose the next election should he continue with Sion's bid, called the first referendum on whether a city should bid for the Olympic Games. The question of Sion's bid narrowly lost the referendum by 287 votes (out of nearly 26,000 votes cast), ending the city's bid barely a month before the IOC voted.[40] The Japanese Olympic Committee approved Sapporo's candidature for the 1968 winter games, which would coincide with the city's centennial celebrations in 1968.[41] Sapporo, with a strong winter sport tradition, should have organized the 1940 Winter Olympics, which were cancelled because of World War II.[42] The city had some venues but planned several new ones, and it had experience hosting the 1954 world speed skating championships.[43]

Sion's late departure left six cities in the final vote for the 1968 Winter Olympics. The candidate cities spanned three continents and varied greatly in size, from the small village of Lake Placid to the major metropolis of Sapporo with more than half a million residents. The American and European candidates viewed their continental competitors as their biggest competition, but they did not forget the strong candidate cities across the Atlantic. However, once the IOC selected the 1968 summer games host, the winter candidate cities then had to consider the geographical ramifications of that decision. Even with four candidate cities for the summer games, many newspapers—even outside the United States and France—believed this contest as really just being between two cities: Lyon and Detroit. Papers frequently dismissed Mexico City as a legitimate candidate because of its high altitude.[44] These stories ignored the fact that the city had hosted regional games as well as the modern pentathlon world championships, which required both men and horses to compete and which had taken place the previous year. Political support at several levels ensured Olympic bids would receive the necessary funding for the games to run smoothly and that any difficulties that might arise could be mitigated as soon as possible. With all of the political problems surrounding international sporting events in the early 1960s, especially with East Germany after the Berlin Wall appeared, political support for an Olympic bid took on even greater importance for the two 1968 contests.

CALLING ON GOVERNMENTS

Olympic bid committees routinely include government letters of support for their candidature to the IOC. With many international sport leaders blaming Western governments for refusing to allow East German athletes to travel to NATO states, the IOC began to question what those letters of support actually provided in this new period of increased political interference within international sport. The demand for guaranteed free entry into the host country for all athletes and officials sought to prevent the further encroaching of politics on sport. The bid committees did not want politics to jeopardize their years of effort to bring the games to their city, and they immediately began working on their responses to the IOC. The bid committees and their respective national sport leaders pursued multiple courses of action to ensure their governments would provide the letter and that it would state what the IOC wanted to hear.

The IOC's demand appeared to result from the joint IOC–international federation statement, but in fact this insistence on free access first arose a year earlier at the March 1962 IOC Executive Board meeting. IOC president Avery Brundage had invited FIS president Marc Hodler to inform the committee about what had happened with the Chamonix world championships. After hearing about the problems the skiing and ice hockey federations had faced, Brundage declared that he believed "the only possible solution would be for the IOC and the international federations to grant the Olympic Games and the world championships only to countries which make no restrictions on the granting of visas to all those who wish to participate." The Federal Republic's Karl Ritter von Halt, a member of the Executive Board, reminded his colleagues that the construction of the Berlin Wall had caused these problems and that the two German states would again form an all-German team for the Tokyo Olympics. Nonetheless, the Executive Board members present—four from NATO states (the United States, France, Federal Republic of Germany, and Great Britain) and one from neutral Sweden—agreed to write to all international federations "to urge them to grant their world championships only to countries granting visas to all nationals affiliated to the I. F. [international federation] and wishing to participate in these championships." In addition, the IOC followed this same principle when awarding the Olympic Games.[45] At the full IOC session held in Moscow that summer, the IOC members debated the topic of political interference in sport at length, ultimately agreeing that "the I.O.C. will only grant the organisation of the Olympics to a city which gives visas to all athletes and officials belonging to Olympic Committees recognised by the I.O.C. who send them with a view to participating in the Games." The IOC clearly aimed this statement to NATO and the problems East German athletes had faced. The following statement in the IOC's minutes noted that they had written to the Allied Travel Office (ATO), which had assured them "visas would be granted to East German athletes belonging to a unified German team."[46] Brundage's achievement of the creation of the all-German Olympic team could continue with the ATO's assurance, and he was once again able to impose his firm belief in the separation of sport and politics on the situation. Brundage feared international sport would otherwise "degenerate into a tool or a weapon in the cold war."[47] To prevent the Olympics from becoming a victim of Cold War politics, the IOC thus demanded every candidate city bidding for the 1968 Olympics guarantee free access to the games.

With a year of events impacted by the travel ban and the subsequent IOC–international federation statement, the IOC sent its request on March 14, 1963, to all of the candidate cities for both the 1968 summer and winter games. The brief letter read,

> We wish to inform you hereby that all Cities which propose to submit invitations to stage the Olympic Games (Summer or Winter 1968) must let us have, *before October 1st, 1963*, a certificate from their Government assuring the International Olympic Committee that all athletes, teams, officials, Jurys [*sic*], etc. from National Olympic Committees and International Federations recognized by the I.O.C. will be granted free entry without any restriction.
>
> Failing to such a formal declaration the candidature of a City will not be taken into consideration.[48]

The IOC's deadline to receive the travel guarantee was just before the vote on the summer games, scheduled for October 1963. Newspapers immediately published wire stories about this demand. The Canadian Press called External Affairs for clarification and issued a second story noting that Ottawa had not yet received the letter from Calgary but that the Canadian government would need to issue such a guarantee.[49] Robert Daley noted the increased frequency with which travel for sporting events has been impeded, but he also commented on the lack of teeth to the threat, writing, "But the I.O.C. does not state who is to sign such a certificate nor what sanctions it can apply if a certificate signed by some government executive today is repudiated by a different government official five years from now, on the eve of the games."[50] As one of the most active columnists covering international sport who had reported on the Chamonix saga, Daley astutely pointed out the challenges of the IOC's request.

After learning of this request, the president of the United States Olympic Committee expressed his concern regarding Detroit's bid to Michigan governor George Romney in early April. He emphasized the State Department's past actions refusing East German athletes could impact the city's chances for the 1968 Olympics. He noted that Detroit's opponents "would state unequivocally that they could issue visas to all the Olympic athletes of the various countries and we must be in the same position."[51] As parties to the official bid committee, Romney's office and the mayor of Detroit's office worked together to try to secure a letter from the State Department in response to the IOC. Romney wrote a letter directly to Secretary of State Dean Rusk to speed up the process of receiving the travel guarantee.[52]

When Calgary received the IOC's letter, the bid committee's public relations committee chairman sent a letter to External Affairs asking for more information "to understand thoroughly the present arrangements and regulations."[53] This report prompted the Interdepartmental Committee on the 1968 Olympic Winter Games to investigate how to provide this guarantee while still upholding External Affairs' policies. External Affairs deferred responding to Calgary's letter and instead requested Joseph Willard, the chairman of the Interdepartmental Committee, to inform the bid committee about the specific policies currently in place for citizens from East Germany, the communist bloc, and other states with which Canada did not have formal relations.[54] By passing this action on to Willard, External Affairs wanted to enforce the new policy that all correspondence relating to the 1968 bid should go to the Interdepartmental Committee and not individual government departments. In addition, having Willard, from the Department of National Health and Welfare, respond about Canada's travel regulations also diminished the chance of public comments on this policy sounding like they were a direct statement from the foreign ministry. External Affairs knew from recent NATO experiences that such a statement from one of its staff would bring unwanted negative publicity and hurt Calgary's bid.

At the next Interdepartmental Committee meeting the External Affairs representative noted his department "had no alternative but to enforce rigidly the rules governing entry from communist countries."[55] Because their goal was to facilitate a successful bid for Calgary, the Interdepartmental Committee, upon hearing this information from the External Affairs representative, "took the view that a 'tough' application of visa regulations could easily ruin Calgary's chances."[56]

Calgary's bid leaders met directly with External Affairs and the Interdepartmental Committee about the IOC's demand for a travel guarantee. They told External Affairs they had heard "Norway was going to raise the matter of lifting the ban on East German sports personnel at the forthcoming Ottawa NATO Council meeting and they would very much like us (Canada) to raise it first because whoever raised it would gain Kudos with the Eastern Europeans and more importantly possible votes for their site."[57] External Affairs had tried to present the current situation realistically to both the Interdepartmental Committee and Calgary's bid leaders. Upon hearing this information, however, the rest of the meeting attendees attempted to provide new suggestions for how External Affairs could take action within NATO to help Calgary. The External Affairs representative from the Interdepartmental Committee admitted to the undersecretary of state for External Affairs that "it certainly would be more dignified as well as sensible if any modification of restrictions on East German Olympic sports delegations was worked out on a planned basis rather than in competition."[58] Negotiating a solution with their NATO colleagues, or at least with the Norwegians, might be more beneficial than trying to fight against each other over travel policy in what was already an intense battle to become the Olympic host.

Following this meeting, the Calgary organizers submitted a formal request to the Interdepartmental Committee "for consideration and action" on the IOC's demand for a letter guaranteeing free travel.[59] Referencing the problems with the ice hockey and skiing world championships in Colorado Springs and Chamonix, the Calgary organizers noted they "can only assume that the bottleneck lies in the NATO policy concerning East Germany."[60] In their original candidature brochure prior to the March request for a travel guarantee, Calgary had responded to the IOC's standard question about whether any laws "would limit, restrict or interfere with the Games in any way" with the following statement:

> In Canada there are no laws, customs or regulations which would tend to interfere in any way with the Games or participation in them. All national teams, including the news representatives, which are recognized by the International Olympic Committee, are assured free entry by the Canadian government. It is proposed to give all delegations the option of utilizing regular visas or special I.O.C. Identification Cards. These will be issued in lieu of visas by the Organizing Committee with the approval of the International Olympic Committee. There will be no charge for the issue of these cards or visas.[61]

Noting that the United States, France, and Norway all faced a similar problem, Calgary then commented that "Finland, Japan and Switzerland would then be the only other interested sites that could get the Games," referencing just the winter games candidates.[62] Since the Canadians had not previously organized the Olympic Games or hosted any recent world championship, this information was helpful guidance for the Interdepartmental Committee.

External Affairs began requesting information from its embassies regarding the experiences of other recent Olympic hosts in an effort to understand how best to respond to the IOC's request. Ottawa sent letters to its embassies in Bonn, Vienna, and Washington and to its NATO delegation in Paris. Letting the embassies know the Canadian government heavily supported the Calgary bid, whose organizers were "anxious to have this problem settled as soon as possible since they are concerned that restriction in this area will result in losing the bid for the Games," Ottawa requested discreet inquiries to help in this matter.[63] External Affairs wanted to learn from Bonn the West German government's attitude regarding the formation of the all-German team, whether it would be continuing for the upcoming Winter Olympics in Innsbruck (the Canadians again apparently only cared about the winter games and not the Summer Olympics in Tokyo), and what kind of documents East German athletes used to enter West Germany to train for the all-German Olympic teams.[64] From its Washington embassy, External Affairs wanted to know how the East German athletes, spectators, and journalists were able to attend the 1960 Squaw Valley Olympics and whether they traveled with Temporary Travel Documents (TTDs) or some other documentation. They also wanted to know whether there were any instances of visa refusals for security reasons.[65] Recognizing the upcoming Winter Olympics were taking place in neutral Austria, the telegram to Vienna listed several questions: "Will the Austrian govt recognize the East German passport or require a docu[ment] similar to a temporary travel docu issued by the ATO in Berlin. Would the Austrians recognize an East German team participating separately or an all German team only? Will East German journalists and spectators be permitted to attend?"[66] External Affairs informed its NATO delegation it had heard indirectly that Norway was "interested in raising the question of relaxing the existing NATO rules on the ban of East German athletes, journalists and tourists in order to favour their bid to win the site of the 1968 Olympic Winter Games." They therefore requested the delegation find out whether this issue would be raised soon within NATO.[67]

From these efforts External Affairs gained additional insight into how the Canadians needed to proceed in order to help Calgary's bid. Although the NATO delegation did not directly speak with their Norwegian counterparts regarding this rumor, they learned about the impending relaxation to the travel restrictions on East German sportsmen. The American delegation at NATO also told the Canadians it anticipated no problem with the issuance of TTDs for an all-German Olympic team.[68] The embassy in Washington provided the details related to German travel in 1960, noting the special Olympic documents pertained to athletes, coaches, and officials at Squaw Valley, whereas journalists and spectators applied for visas through the regular process.[69] The Austrians, a neutral state after 1945 that maintained decent relations with states on both sides of the Iron Curtain, would be issuing "ordinary visas in East German passports accepted as identity cards without any implication of recognition of state in doing so" for both athletes and spectators.[70] The replies to Ottawa helped External Affairs determine the best course of action.

An Auswärtiges Amt representative had a lengthy discussion with the Canadians in Bonn, confirming the all-German team participated in the 1960 Olympics and would again be formed for the upcoming Innsbruck games. The German representative was, the Canadians perceived, intentionally vague with respect to past details, but he explained for future events East Germans would receive TTDs and could enter the Federal Republic on them. The representative was hopeful with regards to the upcoming changes to the travel policy, confirming the rumors that the Canadians had heard. He also stated the East Germans had recently shown a more cooperative attitude on travel matters. The Canadians reported back to Ottawa that, on the whole, the Federal Republic officials felt "the prospects were very good that a pattern of all-German participation in international sports events and scientific gatherings would be established and if so no [REPEAT] no problem would be likely to arise in connection with the 1968 Winter Games." The report from Bonn, however, concluded that "on the other hand 1968 was a long way away and it would be difficult for anyone to provide a guarantee that the DDR [GDR] would continue throughout this period to behave cooperatively."[71] The embassies' knowledge about past experiences was valuable for External Affairs to understand how other Olympic hosts had dealt with this problem, but the warning from Bonn highlighted the greatest unknown.

While External Affairs gathered this information from its foreign posts, the Interdepartmental Committee established an ad hoc subcommittee "to assess the implication of Canadian rules and regulations governing entry into Canada of person from foreign countries to determine the changes necessary for Canada to guarantee unconditional entry of participants to the Games."[72] Representatives from National Health and Welfare, External Affairs, the Royal Canadian Mounted Police, and Citizenship and Immigration comprised its membership. These individuals carefully crafted a lengthy memorandum for the cabinet on the IOC's request for a certificate guaranteeing free entry for Olympic teams and officials. The memorandum began by emphasizing the support promised to Calgary should the city win the right to organize the 1968 winter games, with an earlier draft of the memorandum noting the nearly 9 million Canadian dollar contribution from the federal government. The document then outlined the problem confronting Calgary's candidature: current federal regulations restricting entry to Canada for individuals from communist states and states that Canada did not recognize (North Vietnam, North Korea, Outer Mongolia, Mainland China) and the additional NATO restrictions on East Germans. Attempts to compromise with the IOC regarding the letter guaranteeing free travel, the ad hoc subcommittee had concluded, "are not likely to yield positive results but may be harmful to the Calgary bid."[73] Further underpinning the importance of Calgary's bid, the memorandum informed the cabinet that "the prestige which Canada will gain by having the Olympics and the encouragement thereby given to amateur sport, will compensate for any internal security risks posed by liberalizing entry procedures and any embarrassment which may result by the use in Canada of symbols (flags, national anthems) of countries which we do not recognize."[74] The representatives from four government agencies understood the significant soft power benefits that hosting the Olympic Games in Calgary would bring to Canada. With other NATO member states also having cities bidding for the 1968 Olympics, "the time is ripe for giving encouragement, within the forum of NATO, to an easing of restrictions against East Germans for the purpose of participating in the Olympics." The memorandum therefore recommended Canada take the lead within NATO to press for changes to address the travel problem raised by the IOC. The subcommittee also recommended a new immigration procedure be used just for the 1968 Olympic Games in Calgary based on Olympic precedent, which used the creation of Olympic identity cards instead of traditional government-issued passports and visas.[75]

Along with the procedural aspects of addressing entry into Canada for the Olympics, the Interdepartmental Committee also recognized the possibility that an inability to provide this guarantee could damage the country's (and NATO's) reputation abroad. In advocating for Canada's NATO delegation raising the need for a common agreement regarding East German travel, the memorandum to the cabinet noted that "failure to do so is likely to bring discredit on NATO without any evident benefits."[76] The External Affairs representative recommended a circular be sent to all of Canada's foreign posts outlining the efforts being taken in Canada to provide the IOC with the travel guarantee. When questioned on this issue, they could note the challenges with the current regulations but that the "Government's staff show an optimistic face and indicate that they anticipate no problems."[77] Providing this guidance would allow Canadian diplomats to not only help Calgary's bid but also contribute to public diplomacy efforts to depict Canada more positively abroad, as well as combat any negative views of NATO that had resulted from sporting events impacted by Cold War politics and the East German travel ban.

The IOC's demand for a travel guarantee, although sent to bid committees, forced them to work more closely with their governments. IOC president Avery Brundage was adamant that the Cold War problems that had impacted the international federations would not befall the Olympic Games, and requiring candidate cities to provide a guarantee of free access to all Olympic athletes and officials would, he believed, force countries to uphold that promise. If a country could not provide the guarantee, then the city would no longer be in the running to organize the 1968 Olympics. Detroit saw an urgency with responding to the IOC and sought help from the governor to coordinate with the State Department. Calgary, in contrast, already had a member of External Affairs on the Intergovernmental Committee supporting the city's bid. With the federal government directly involved in bringing the Olympics to Canada for the first time, External Affairs embarked on a global fact-finding mission to ascertain how it could best focus its efforts to support Calgary's bid and not have NATO's restrictive policies thwart the city's chances. These two candidate cities' initial reactions shaped the different approaches taken within NATO. Canada's determination to raise its global profile, to which Calgary's Olympic aspirations aligned, led to the country focusing on its national self-interests—and thus challenging NATO unity and the alliance's policy toward East Germany.

RELAXING THE BAN, TAKE II (1963 EDITION)

While the bid committees (and the Canadian Intergovernmental Committee) fretted over how to respond to the IOC's travel guarantee, the quadripartite powers were discussing a temporary relaxation of the travel ban for some categories of East Germans. Whereas the Calgary bid committee had heard rumors that the Norwegians would raise this idea within NATO, it was in fact an agreement made in Bonn by the four powers, who then presented the idea to their NATO colleagues for approval. The quadripartite group had intended for the temporary travel ban relaxation to be limited in scope—just the categories of sport and science/medicine—and duration, until September 1963. Knowing a few events within these two categories were scheduled in the coming months, ending this relaxation in September would allow the four powers to assess this "experimental relaxation" in six months' time.[78] Initially affecting just four events, with the European rowing championships in Copenhagen being the only sporting event, the temporary relaxation of the East German travel ban quickly became subsumed by broader concerns raised with the IOC's public statement and letter to the 1968 bid committees. These two documents changed the nature and focus of these policy debates. None of the four NATO states with candidate cities wanted them excluded from the IOC's consideration, but they each brought different views to the debate over NATO's travel policies for East German athletes. What should have been a simple test case to relax the East German travel ban instead turned into a complex set of parallel negotiations in Paris and Bonn, along with additional bilateral discussions across NATO capitals, with each state pushing its own agenda. This effort to temporarily relax NATO's travel ban on East German athletes once again pitted Canada and Norway against the Western Four as the desire for the prestige associated with hosting the Olympic Games came into conflict with NATO policy.

In late April 1963 when the four powers were almost finished with the changes to the travel policy, the Americans proposed including the 1968 Olympic Games within the relaxation policy, which would be in effect through September 1963. Although the IOC had given an October 1 deadline, both the Detroit bid committee and the State Department wanted to submit Detroit's letter before the IOC Executive Board's June meeting. The American representative wanted to ensure the candidate cities from NATO states could all provide letters that would not hurt their chances, and including the Olympic Games in this trial relaxation policy would bolster the effectiveness of their letters to the IOC. Even though they also had both a Summer and Winter Olympics candidate city, the French representatives in Bonn disagreed. The French thought that it could be embarrassing to mix the Olympic case with the events that would fall within the time frame of the temporary relaxation. That the 1968 Games were actually years away would actually prevent it from being included in this travel ban relaxation, which was limited to the summer of 1963.[79] The U.S. delegation in Bonn realized from these discussions that including the 1968 Olympics in this travel ban relaxation would tie the games to the conditional relaxation, which was not what they had intended. They therefore excluded the Olympic Games from the travel relaxation.[80]

With the four powers thus in agreement on the scope of the temporary relaxation, they shared this new policy with NATO. In preparation for the Committee of Political Advisers meeting on May 2 when the travel relaxation policy would likely be discussed, Ottawa instructed its delegation to act in such a way that would help Calgary's bid. The Canadian government had wanted the travel policy changed so Calgary could provide a complete guarantee to the IOC, and they were particularly concerned for East Germans who may or may not be part of an all-German team by 1968. Knowing the selection of the winter games would not take place until January 1964, Ottawa stated a temporary relaxation only until September 1963 with strict limitations as presented was both "irrelevant and unsatisfactory" even though it allowed for the submission of the guarantee. The Canadians should support any proposal including a provision for the 1968 Olympics, and if no other delegation raised that topic, the Canadians should do so. The "subject must be raised at least in initial discussion, in view of political importance attached to candidacy for 1968 Olympics in [Canada] and, we presume, in other NATO countries who are also candidates." External Affairs believed that the letter to the IOC "requires sweeping statement covering all possibilities, i.e. separate East German team as well as all-German team." Thus, if the Committee of Political Advisers should actually reach a favorable decision where a sweeping guarantee is approved, the Canadian delegation should support such a measure. If, however, the discussion concluded that a trial relaxation or the guarantee should reach negative conclusion, the Canadian delegation should reserve its position.[81] External Affairs was doing all that it could to help bring the Olympics to Canada, pushing its NATO delegation to advocate for the position that benefitted Calgary's bid.

The Americans also prepared to address the issue of the 1968 Olympics at the meeting, with Washington instructing its NATO delegation to comment at the meeting that no agreement for an all-German team existed yet for 1968. The delegation should therefore note the "specific requirement for participation on that basis in order qualify for TTDs might be viewed by International Olympic Committee as imposing unacceptable limitation on free travel to 1968 games." The Americans could acknowledge the ability of East Germans to travel to potential candidate cities may influence the selection of the site, but 1968 was still quite some time in the future. Finally, the American representative should state "that in light of past experience sufficient flexibility exists in making arrangements for Olympic Games to anticipate that adequate provision will be made for participation by East Germans."[82]

The French presented to the Committee of Political Advisers the carefully crafted text granting a trial relaxation through September 1963 of the travel ban in the categories of science and sport if an event met certain criteria. East Germans would be granted TTDs from the ATO and visas by the host country to four events—three scientific conferences and the European rowing championships—as long as they applied as part of all-German delegations and no flags, emblems, or anthems from East Germany would appear at the events.[83] (Presumably the latter provision only referenced the rowing event and did not apply to electrotechnicians, geophysicists, or crystallographers.) The European rowing championships, scheduled for August in Copenhagen, was the one sporting event included because the international federation had taken a cautious approach to the GDR, granting it provisional recognition in 1955 but requiring all-German teams along Olympic lines. The East Germans continued to push for their own recognition, but the international federation had twice voted down that proposal, in 1958 and again in 1961.[84] The French delegate emphasized that the advantages of this new proposed flexibility included making it easier to hold international meetings in NATO countries, removing an aspect of the TTD restrictions "which was particularly misjudged by public opinion," and contributing "to keeping international scientific and sporting meetings free from political overtones."[85] The blame for no East German participation would, in these instances, now fall on East German shoulders and not on NATO because it would be the East Germans' decision not to participate within a previously agreed-upon all-German delegation.[86] With this new position, NATO hoped to receive less criticism in the press and not have its events damaged by negative publicity when East German athletes could not participate.

The rest of the NATO delegations accepted this trial relaxation, with many of them emphasizing their approval of the text that specified "in other cases where the same conditions exist, the granting of TTDs could be envisaged."[87] The Norwegians stated they were pleased to see the travel ban relaxation but wished it went further, noting that several international federations would, during the period of the temporary relaxation over the summer of 1963, decide the location of many of the sporting events for 1964. It was important, they emphasized, "that the organisers of such meetings should not be discouraged from holding their events in NATO countries because of pressure of the T.T.D. ban."[88] The Norwegians were selfishly thinking of two European championships already scheduled to take place in Norway and two future events for which Oslo was bidding.[89] The quadripartite powers responded to the enthusiasm for a broader relaxation that "there would be no automatic extension of the current provisions, but a new examination which would take into account each of the cases considered."[90] NATO thus appeared to come to a consensus over the temporary travel ban relaxation.

The discussion quickly followed from the trial relaxation to the 1968 Olympics and the need to provide the IOC with a travel guarantee, with the Americans making their statements following Washington's instructions and the Canadians and Norwegians in particular asking questions.[91] The

Canadian delegation made all of the points that Ottawa wanted raised, followed by a "lively" discussion about the travel problem as it related to the 1968 Olympics.[92] The committee tasked the Canadians with circulating the IOC's letter in full to all of the delegations so the topic could be addressed at another Committee of Political Advisers meeting. In total, the Committee of Political Advisers spent nearly ninety minutes discussing the temporary travel relaxation and the concerns related to the 1968 Olympic Games.[93] As with the previous instances when NATO addressed East German sport and travel, the political advisers did not come to any conclusions in their first discussion on the issue, and the debate was far from over.

The next week's Committee of Political Advisers meeting on May 7 saw a return to the temporary travel relaxation, with cracks now appearing in the consensus that they had reached in their previous meeting. The Belgian representative, supported by his Dutch, Norwegian, and Italian colleagues, confirmed his government's support for the travel relaxation but reiterated the change to NATO policy should be by an entire category, not by individual exceptions. These delegations thus desired a blanket exception for the categories of science and sport, rather than this short list of four events.[94] The Norwegians, following instructions from Oslo, had sent a letter to the French representative raising the question of including the upcoming events scheduled in Norway in the travel relaxation. The Norwegians argued the European shooting championships, scheduled for August 1963, both fell within the period of temporary relaxation and had an all-German team the previous year in Belgrade, Yugoslavia, and should therefore also be included in the travel relaxation. The tripartite powers again reiterated their willingness to review all applications that fell within the noted parameters and would consider this event.[95] However, one of the future events to which the Norwegians alluded was the bid for the 1968 Olympics, which again entangled this question—and how to respond to the IOC's letter requesting the travel guarantee—with the more general travel policy and the temporary relaxation. The chairman cut short the inconclusive discussion by requesting the committee return to the issue the following week to address the questions posed by the Norwegians.[96]

To prepare for the next Committee of Political Advisers discussion on May 14 the various foreign ministries and embassies conducted separate meetings and corresponded at length to establish their own positions and ascertain how other countries would respond. The Committee of Political

Advisers chairman, R. W. J. Hooper, called an informal meeting with the quadripartite powers, which would enable him to anticipate the nature of the discussion and prevent it from being derailed by other representatives. The German delegation agreed to investigate the circumstances related to the European shooting championships, and if it met the same criteria as the other four events, the ATO would issue the necessary TTDs. All four representatives agreed the 1968 Olympic Games was the "most complicated question" because of the "vigorous competition among cities wishing to host both summer and winter games and in view [of the] terms [of the] IOC letter requesting governmental certificate regarding free entry 'without any restriction' by athletes, officials, etc. of all national Olympic committees and federations recognized by the IOC." They generally agreed the text of the letters should be "as near identical as possible" but recognized how challenging that could be considering the guarantee that the IOC requested covered more than just East Germany, alluding to the growing problems in international sport regarding divided Korea as well as China and Taiwan.[97] The French expressed their desire for the response to reiterate the terms of the letter that the ATO had sent to the IOC in May 1962. That letter had stated, "If conditions remain as at present, the three Western Powers would have no objections whatsoever to the issuance of the necessary documents on behalf of athletes from East Germany who wish to participate in the 1968 Olympic Games as members of a single, all-German team, as was the case in 1960."[98] The other representatives at the meeting felt the 1962 letter was too limited and placed restrictions on what circumstances would lead to the issuing of the TTD, whereas the current request from the IOC called for an unconditional certificate. This informal meeting of the Americans, British, French, and Germans at NATO concluded that the best result from the upcoming Committee of Political Advisers meeting was a general agreement for the responses to the IOC to be coordinated along with the creation of an informal working group composed of the four countries bidding for the 1968 Olympics.[99]

On May 13, the day before the Committee of Political Advisers next met in Paris, the quadripartite powers also coordinated their positions in Bonn. The Auswärtiges Amt had investigated the European shooting championships in order to respond to the urgent Norwegian request.[100] An all-German team had not actually competed in 1962 in Belgrade, so unless an all-German team would be formed for the 1963 European shooting championships, East German athletes would not receive TTDs for that event.[101] With respect to the other events Norway had raised, the British lamented, "There remains the problem of international events taking place after the trial period, but for which guarantees of free entry are required to be given within the period."[102] Whereas only the French advocated using the earlier 1962 ATO letter to the IOC just a few days earlier at the informal quadripartite meeting at NATO without agreement from the others, at this meeting in Bonn the Americans proposed using that same framework. The Americans suggested, "If conditions remain as they are, the three Western Powers would not raise any objection when the time came to providing the necessary documentation for athletes from East Germany taking part in the 1968 Olympic Games within the framework of an all-German team, as was the case in 1960." By adding the phrase at the beginning about conditions remaining as they are, the tripartite powers had the ability to return to the previous restrictions if they were not satisfied with the temporary relaxation. All four powers were in agreement with this position, which they would put forward at NATO the following day.[103]

Meanwhile the Canadians continued to gather intelligence from their foreign posts to provide their NATO delegation with as much information as possible. The Canadian embassy in Washington sent a representative to speak with the State Department on the same day as Hooper's informal meeting with the quadripartite powers in Paris. The State Department representative commented it might be necessary for NATO or the countries "most directly concerned" to reach an agreement on the details to be included in any response to the IOC.[104] The Canadians left the meeting with the sense that the Americans would make every effort to ensure Detroit and Lake Placid were "not prevented from being host candidates for 1968 Games because of requirements laid down by IOC." At one point the State Department representative had said to the Canadian that "even if East Germans insisted on separate representation at these games, some way would be found to allow them to participate."[105] The latter comment, which concluded the Washington embassy's telegram back to External Affairs in Ottawa, hinted that the Americans would not be too obstructionist when it came to the reply to the IOC—an important aspect since the Canadians were desperate to reply positively and bring the Olympics to Canada for the first time. External Affairs consented to the informal coordination with the US, France, and Norway about how to respond to the IOC. However,

Ottawa cautioned, "The difficulty we foresee in a formula of this kind is that while it will place the four NATO countries on an equal footing, unless it is ingeniously clever it will not give the NATO countries the same rating as non-NATO countries who are prepared to give an unrestricted certificate."[106] Similarly, the Canadian embassy in Oslo approached the Utenriksdepartement, returning with a sense of the greater Norwegian concern for the upcoming sporting events in Norway, and particularly the impending decision for the site of the 1966 Nordic skiing world championships, which Oslo was hoping to host. The Norwegian foreign ministry also stated it did not have a formal position regarding the response to the IOC's letter, which it had only received from its NATO colleagues and not from the Oslo bid committee.[107] Whereas the Canadians focused solely on the 1968 Olympic bid, the Norwegian concern was broader, including Oslo's Olympic bid as well as its other potential sporting events, especially a bid for its national sport of skiing.

The Norwegians had in fact raced into action after the May 7 Committee of Political Advisers meeting, not wanting to have their views suppressed by the strength of the quadripartite powers. With the selection of the location for 1966 Nordic skiing world championships at the FIS Congress in Athens later that month—the same congress that would also be addressing (for the last time) the problems from Chamonix—the Norwegians wanted to press for a resolution within NATO with a sense of urgency.[108] The Norwegian representative on the Committee of Political Advisers had a lengthy conversation with his French counterpart, coming away from the meeting with an even stronger impression of how slow and difficult it was for the quadripartite powers in Bonn to achieve any decisions. Furthermore, the Norwegian cautioned his ministry back in Oslo, the efforts (by the Belgians, Norwegians, or other NATO delegates) to push too hard for changes to the TTD regulations were counterproductive, only solidifying the entrenched position of the tri- and quadripartite powers.[109] This concern about pressure within the Committee of Political Advisers likely contributed to the cautious Norwegian response to the Canadian approach in Oslo.

Following this week of informal diplomatic discussions, the Committee of Political Advisers returned to the issue of travel by East German athletes for the third consecutive week in May 1963. The committee fairly easily agreed with the quadripartite powers' responses to the two non-Olympic events that Norway had raised (the 1963 European shooting championships and Oslo's candidacy for the 1966 Nordic skiing world championships). The Committee of Political Advisers accepted the response drafted by the Bonn group for future non-Olympic events that fell outside of the temporary relaxation, as long as conditions remained as they currently were. The Norwegians agreed to inform their FIS representatives that the international federation could contact the ATO directly for a response that, while not a complete guarantee, at least provided an assurance that East German athletes could participate in the 1966 Nordic world championships should Oslo be awarded the event.[110] The Norwegians pressed for this type of response to FIS as the federation was "particularly sensitive" following the exclusion of the East German team from Chamonix. The Canadians noted the representatives from the ATO powers "were obviously somewhat uncomfortable in front of this clear demand." The French representative eventually assented that FIS could expect the ATO's response as long as the conditions remained unchanged for this international sporting event.[111] Norway thus achieved a partial victory in its efforts to host the 1966 Nordic skiing world championships with this concession from its NATO colleagues.

The discussion then turned to the bids for the 1968 Olympic Games, with the chairman opening the conversation by saying that while he had thought that the previous year's ATO letter to the IOC had settled this issue, having seen the recent IOC's letter demanding the guarantee had perhaps changed that view. The Americans, as one of the most recent Olympic hosts, expressed their concern about the East German "hangers-on" who were not explicitly members of the 1960 all-German Olympic team. The East Germans, the Americans noted, had tried to include political activists and intelligence personnel on the list of officials for Squaw Valley. Because of these broader problems to which an unqualified guarantee might lead, the Americans wanted this issue to be studied further and doubted the IOC statement could be accepted as it stood. The Norwegian representative also commented that "his authorities were opposed in principle to the issuance of the assurances in the broad terms demanded by the IOC," while the French representative noted a "blank cheque in the terms demanded by the IOC was not in accordance with international usage."[112] After hearing these three views from states with cities that had received the IOC's letter, the chairman recommended the (quadripartitely previously agreed to) creation of a working group composed of the four states with candidate cities. The entire Committee of Political Advisers agreed to the formation of this new subcommittee, which would draft a response to the IOC, which the committee as a whole would ultimately review.[113]

Hooper was optimistic the creation of the working group would remove interminable discussions over the trivialities of wording a letter to a sport organization from Committee of Political Advisers meetings. The working group would hopefully craft the response to the IOC in a more timely manner with only four countries involved instead of all fifteen NATO representatives. Whereas the Americans and French had been formally discussing this topic with the Germans and British in Bonn and Paris, the Canadians and Norwegians were now involved in a formal capacity in Paris with the establishment of this working group. No longer just two states fighting against the Western Four within the entire NATO structure, Canada and Norway would now push their position as half the members of this smaller working group. Within three months of the IOC releasing its statement on politics and sport and sending its letter to the candidate cities requiring a travel guarantee, both the quadripartite powers and NATO had taken them into consideration in their negotiations over the temporary travel relaxation. Furthermore, the creation of this NATO working group to coordinate responses to the IOC was an even greater demonstration of the increasing power of the IOC to influence diplomacy.

CONCLUSION

In late May 1963, after the formation of the working group, Hooper commented that the Committee of Political Advisers "seemed likely to have a good deal more trouble in store on the subject of all German representation"[114]—and how right he was. Not only were the 1964 Olympic Games barely a year away, but all of the candidate cities for the 1968 Summer and Winter Olympics were in the final stages of their bids, trying to win IOC members' votes. Any formal NATO response to either of the IOC's documents (the travel guarantee demand or the statement on politics and sport) was ultimately intertwined and dependent on the decisions taken and common language to which the four members of the working group agreed. The Americans and French expected, as parties to both the quadripartite Bonn group and the new NATO working group on the 1968 Olympic Games, to have the greatest influence in shaping the position taken by NATO on the issue of international sport. Their opinions, however, were not accepted unchallenged, as the other two powers in each of those groups (the British and Germans in Bonn and the Canadians and Norwegians in Paris) still contributed to shaping the agreements. The short deadline to accomplish any of these tasks before the IOC Executive Board's June meeting left the State Department as the main protagonist pushing for a finalized response to the IOC. In particular the experience of the ice hockey world championships in Colorado Springs, along with frequent correspondence with John Stanley Mullin regarding the situation in FIS, left the State Department with the recognition that its own policies alongside the NATO and ATO travel restrictions on East German athletes presented a significant hurdle for its candidate cities to overcome in their efforts to host the 1968 Olympic Games.

The Canadians and Norwegians, on the other hand, used the IOC's request for a travel guarantee as another opportunity to push for change in NATO travel policy. Both countries wanted a greater relaxation of the travel ban, which aligned with each of their national self-interests. Although Oslo and Calgary were both candidates for the 1968 winter games, their desire to change NATO's policy went beyond that single event. Canada had never hosted the Olympics, and bringing the games to Canada was part of a broader effort by Prime Minister John Diefenbaker's government to enhance the country's position globally. Norway, while supporting Oslo's bid, also had more urgent concerns with the upcoming European and world championships slated to be held in the country. Having already experienced the difficulties when East German athletes could not participate in the events previously held in Norway, and seeing international federations move events to other countries, the Norwegian government had a clear understanding of the impact of these policies—and how a relaxation of the travel ban could remove those problems. For Norway, being selected as the host of the 1966 Nordic skiing world championships was in some ways more important than the Olympic bid because of the country's love of skiing. The stiffer competition for the winter games also made Oslo a longshot in that contest, whereas Oslo had a much stronger bid to win the skiing event. Norway's support for a greater travel relaxation policy therefore factored into its desire to prevent international federations from excluding NATO countries as hosts of events, as well as to ensure that the 1966 Nordic skiing world championships could be held in Oslo.

Frustrations with growing political interference in sport had prompted the IOC to act in early 1963, releasing a public statement with the international federations on sport and politics and requesting all candidate cities bidding for the 1968 Olympic Games provide a guarantee of free travel. The IOC did not address either of these documents specifically to NATO, but the messages contained in them achieved their intended effect. These two documents reached the governments of NATO's member states, and they responded accordingly. The State Department knew it needed the support of its international sport federation representatives to overcome this challenge to hosting another Olympic Games in the United States and cultivated these relationships to this end. The Canadians, lacking the prior experience of hosting the Olympic Games that over half of their NATO allies had, nonetheless recognized from their country's well-placed international sport officials that their own immigration laws as well as the NATO restrictions on East Germans significantly hurt Calgary's chances to host the winter games. The race against the clock, combined with the typically slow pace of multistate diplomacy and decision-making, tested the resolve of many NATO member states during the summer of 1963 as the contest to host the 1968 Olympic Games entered its final stages.

CHAPTER 5

THE NATO WORKING GROUP ON THE 1968 OLYMPICS

Three days after the Committee of Political Advisers agreed the four countries with Olympic bids should form a working group, those representatives met informally to begin drafting a coordinated response to the IOC that each candidate city could use. The members of the temporary NATO working group on the 1968 Olympics spent the next few months in extensive consultation with each other and their respective bid committees and sport leaders. Although seemingly a simple enough task to draft a letter that all six candidate cities could use, the national pride and soft power benefits that accompany organizing the Olympic Games further complicated the efforts of the working group. Canada, the one working group member that had not yet hosted the Olympics, was desperate to organize the games and was willing to upset its allies to do so. Whereas all four members of the working group had a city bidding for the winter games, only the United States and France were in the running for the summer games. These two states thus had more direct competition with each other while simultaneously needing to work together if they wanted to ensure their responses did not benefit the non-NATO cities also pitted against them.

By the time the working group convened in mid-1963, NATO's travel restrictions on East German athletes had disrupted several international sporting events. The working group members feared these experiences would prejudice IOC members to vote for the bid cities outside NATO (Mexico City or Buenos Aires for the summer games or Lahti, Sion, or Sapporo for the winter games). These concerns lent even more importance to the wording of the responses to the IOC, which needed to provide a travel guarantee for athletes and officials at the 1968 Olympic Games. American diplomats expressed a sense of urgency for the group to begin working right away because the upcoming June IOC Executive Board meeting could respond to a coordinated letter. If the IOC found any parts unacceptable, NATO cities would still have time to send a revised letter by the October 1 deadline.[1]

The lack of a coordinated effort from the other NATO candidate cities and desire by each country to be victorious in this Olympic contest, which required appeasing the IOC, hindered the working group's progress. The underlying implications of flag raising and anthem playing that the German Democratic Republic would claim as de facto recognition made sport the most complicated field among all of the categories included in NATO's travel ban. Although the East and West German Olympic Committees had, in 1963, resumed contact and agreed to form an all-German team again for the 1964 Olympic Games, it was clear to both diplomats and sport leaders that each iteration of the all-German Olympic team was fraught with more difficulties and problems. Nearly fifteen years of two separate German states, whether the Federal Republic and IOC recognized the GDR or not, made NATO diplomats question how much longer the combined German team would last. Providing a travel guarantee based on a concept (the all-German Olympic team) that itself might not exist in five years further complicated the issue. The high stakes of hosting the Olympic Games—two weeks of the world's media broadcasting from the host city, an influx of international visitors, carefully crafted images encouraging future tourism, and the domestic pride fostered by organizing a mega-event—made coming to a consensus even more challenging for the working group.

As the cities lobbied IOC members in the final few months to secure their votes, the governments did not want to take any action that would counter those efforts. The other NATO candidate cities anxiously awaited the IOC's response to Detroit's early letter to ascertain whether its wording had hurt Detroit's candidacy and thus how their own reply should be crafted. With the IOC Congress voting for the 1968 summer games in October, the working group spent five months meeting and having informal conversations with each other, sending frequent telegrams back and forth with their foreign ministries and seeking insight from their country's sport leaders and bid committees. All four states desired the national pride and soft power benefits generated by winning the right to host the Olympic Games. The United States attempted to lead the working group with a common approach, but the self-interest of each country to host the Olympic Games ultimately led to a shift in positionality of states with respect to the travel restrictions in general. That NATO created a working group about the 1968 Olympic candidate cities and the delegations' constant worry about how the IOC would respond to their letters demonstrated the increasing strength of nongovernmental organizations, and especially international sport organizations within diplomatic negotiations. As governments elevated the importance of sport within their overall political aims, the foreign ministers and heads of government became involved in these negotiations. The working group's struggles to come to a consensus, however, revealed the challenges of maintaining unity and upholding the alliance's policies. The four governments waited for the IOC's decisions before finalizing their letters, allowing international sport to dictate the course of intra-alliance diplomacy.

THE WORKING GROUP GETS TO WORK

In the halls of NATO in Paris, the diplomats from the four countries, along with the occasional input from their German and British colleagues, began working on their response to the IOC. Although the IOC had requested a reply by October 1963 when the it would select the site for the 1968 summer games, the Detroit bid committee wanted to submit its letter before the June IOC Executive Board meeting. Detroit wanted an earlier submission in case the IOC had a problem with Detroit's response. If that happened, the city could then submit a revised letter without hurting its chances. This early deadline left the newly formed working group less than a month for four countries to come to a consensus. To support this end, the State Department became the driving force within the NATO working group for Detroit's self-imposed June deadline to be met by all of the candidate cities. Canada's intense desire to host the Olympics, combined with broader French efforts to undermine NATO unity, however, derailed Detroit and the State Department's efforts.

One of the biggest difficulties confronting the working group with how to respond to the IOC was whether governments would be willing to make a commitment for an event five years in the future.[2] The Allied Travel Office (ATO) had imposed travel restrictions on East Germans in 1960, removed them five months later, and then reinstated them after the Berlin Wall went up in August 1961. NATO member states were therefore reluctant to provide a guarantee when they could not predict what actions the Soviet bloc states would take in the ensuing years. Both the Committee of Political Advisers and the working group agreed the IOC's request "for unqualified governmental certificate of entry" for all athletes and officials participating in the 1968 Olympic games was "inconceivable."[3] External Affairs in Ottawa, satisfied with the establishment of the working group, was also pleased that other delegations finally "recognize[d] that there is a serious problem posed for NATO countries in replying to IOC demand." Yet, however unreasonable Ottawa or other states might have felt the IOC demand was, the Canadian government believed any "attempt by NATO members to give equivocal reply to it will likely lead to 1968 Olympics being held in non-NATO country." The IOC's demand created a dilemma for the four countries. Refusing to provide a clear guarantee, the Canadians believed, would lead to the IOC excluding the candidate cities from NATO countries, whereas "the refusal to honour a commitment made is only likely to bring discredit on the country concerned and on NATO."[4]

At its first meeting the working group agreed to the basis of their position but little else. The national governments and not city governments needed to send these letters, as an assurance from cities could be neither unconditional nor broad in scope as required by the IOC.[5] They generally agreed that the letter should start with a statement to the effect that a "broad unequivocal certificate requested by IOC was inconsistent with responsibilities of governments and that normal controls over entry of individuals would have to be applied to Olympic games but that these normal controls would be applied on non-discriminatory basis." Beyond those points, however, the working group did not find much consensus. What should follow next in the letter—namely how to state any of these limitations—was a major point of contention. The French again presented the stance they had posed in earlier meetings, wanting to refer to the position taken by the ATO in its 1962 response to the IOC. The Canadians and Norwegians were "unwilling to be that specific, pointing out in particular that ATO requirement for all-German team was inconsistent with IOC position and might disqualify their cities."[6] With a starting point at least established, each of the four countries sought guidance prior to their next meeting in two weeks.

The State Department wanted to ensure the text of the letter was strong enough to prevent the IOC ending any city's candidacy because the government did not provide a travel guarantee.[7] The proposed American text read,

> We have received your let[ter] regarding the forthcoming decision concerning the site of the 1968 summer and winter Olympic Games,

> which points out that the ability of participants to travel to such games would be decisive in the selection of the site. As a result of consultation with the govt of (blank) I (mayor) am authorized to state that while the 1968 Olympic Games are now several years in the future, the (blank) govt anticipates in the light of past experience in developing satisfactory arrangements, that adequate provision will also be made for travel to the 1968 Olympic Games by participating athletes, teams, officials, juries, etc, from the National Olympic [Committee] and international federations recognized by the IOC.[8]

Upon receiving this revised letter, the Canadians shared with the Americans their dissatisfaction with the letter, particularly that "evasive replies would be unlikely to have any influence" on the IOC and its president. A shorter, earlier version proposed by the American delegation at NATO, which had also not satisfied the State Department, had greatly troubled the Canadians.[9] Although they noted the improvements in this revised draft, the Canadians still felt it lacked the straight-forward reply demanded by the IOC.[10]

The Canadian embassy in Washington approached the State Department directly regarding the draft, particularly since the Americans in Paris had informed their Canadian colleagues that the text had originated in Washington. Again Canadian diplomats informed the Americans this draft letter did not provide the straightforward guarantee requested by the IOC. The State Department representative tried to assuage the Canadians' concerns by noting that both countries' positions were not really that far apart, as both states did not want admission of East Germans to prevent American and Canadian cities from being Olympic candidate cities. He also stated that the Canadian view was what the State Department considered a "fallback" position they should attempt only after all other efforts come to naught. They discussed several details about the letter and related issues: the likelihood of future all-German teams, the prospects of the non-NATO candidates for the 1968 games, the desire to have the reply submitted earlier in case changes needed to be made, and the problems of the other divided countries. The Canadians reported to Ottawa their doubts the Americans were "prepared to go as far" in meeting the IOC's request for a guarantee. They noted all hope was not lost as the Americans believed there was "a halfway mark between outright capitulation to IOC demands and a statement sufficiently restrictive to prevent western cities from being candidates for the 1968 Olympics"—mainly that East Germans participate as members of an all-German team.[11] The Canadians wanted a letter that would help, not hurt, their chances to host the Olympic Games as the government had put its full support behind Calgary's bid. They hoped these additional direct conversations with the State Department would relax the firm American position on wording that did not provide the guarantee the IOC requested.

At the working group's second meeting on May 28, they considered the positions of the IOC and international federations in the suggestions for next revisions. The Norwegians shared the details of the recently concluded Fédération Internationale de Ski (FIS) meeting in Athens, when FIS finally laid to rest the problems of Chamonix and also approved a new policy regarding politics and organizing skiing events. Based on FIS's actions and his government's discussions with its sport leaders, the Norwegian representative believed the proposed American text "might meet the requirements of the IOC for the 1968 Olympic Games."[12] The Canadians reiterated the same points they had shared with the Americans privately at NATO and in Washington: a straightforward response to the IOC was essential. They argued that all NATO states sending the same letter "would probably lead to the 1968 Olympics being held in a non-NATO country."[13] The Canadians would only be persuaded to use the language of the draft letter if the Americans could provide concrete evidence, such as an assurance from Brundage that the IOC would accept this letter. Otherwise, the Canadian representative stated, it would "not be acceptable to place CDN govt in a position where it could be accused of having lost the 1968 Olympics for Calgary by failure to give the sort of assurance which was required."[14] By specifically emphasizing Calgary's bid within their comments, the Canadian delegation made clear to its working group colleagues that it prioritized self-interest and national pride in these negotiations.

The Canadian position, however, did not go over well with the working group. The Americans were prepared for Canada's statement, but as the Canadian representative quickly realized, his position "was particularly unwelcome" to his French and Norwegian colleagues. The French responded by describing "the commonly agreed position on TTDs [temporary travel documents] as being fundamental to the western position on Berlin" and questioned whether the IOC had considered the possibility that the presence of an East German team might lead French, West German, and other Western European teams to not participate. While the

Canadian representative doubted this scenario would actually happen, he did suggest External Affairs consider this possibility and mention it to the Calgary bid committee.[15] The French also asked whether Canada was prepared to "renounce common NATO line on TTDs."[16] The working group thus realized Canada's desperation to host the Olympic Games and assert itself more prominently on the international stage, both athletically and politically. The Canadian delegate admitted to his colleagues in the working group that Prime Minister John Diefenbaker had promised Calgary the government "would do 'everything necessary' to advance Calgary candidacy."[17] This support for Calgary's Olympic aspirations aligned with Diefenbaker's broader aims of Canada taking a greater role in international affairs.[18] However, Diefenbaker had just lost the April 1963 election and Lester Pearson succeeded him as prime minister. As this transition happened in the midst of the candidate cities developing their replies to the IOC, the Canadian representative said his delegation was in a "difficult domestic position" because Diefenbaker's guarantee had been made to Calgary unbeknownst to the rest of the government. Pearson had campaigned on restoring "the diplomatic credibility that Diefenbaker had squandered" and improving relations with Canada's NATO allies.[19] Canada's position on the wording of the travel guarantee letter illustrated this diminished standing in the eyes of its allies. Yet, even as Pearson's cabinet was still settling in to their roles, they were "not prepared [to] be less forthcoming" in terms of their support for Calgary's bid.[20]

With the representatives now understanding Canada's position better, the working group then turned its attention to the actual letter. The Norwegians stated that with the recent NATO decision to continue supporting the creation of all-German teams, a "general letter along lines US draft was right approach since our all German team policy was known and well received and governments could not give unequivocal assurance regarding future entry of kind demanded by IOC." The proposed American text served as the basis for the discussion, although the French and Norwegians objected to the inclusion of "National Olympic Committees" and the "completely open-ended commitment regarding entries of non-athletes." They felt "explicitly accepting attendance [of] officials [from] National Olympic Committees will undermine all German team formula and will give more endorsement to separate East German participation than vague language."[21] The negotiations for each all-German Olympic team had included the athletes as well as the number of individuals from the East and West German Olympic Committees who accompanied the team at the games. A blanket acceptance here could result in the East Germans attempting to bring more people who would otherwise not receive travel authorizations because of their political roles. Instead, they recommended a more general final phrase: "that adequate provision will also be made for travel by participants to the 1968 Olympic Games."[22] The representatives generally agreed their governments could support the draft, albeit with a greater hesitation from the Canadians. All four delegates reported the proposed changes to their foreign ministries for further guidance or acceptance.

The State Department was quick to respond the next day (May 29), particularly with the urgency being pressed by the Detroit bid committee to have a letter to present to the IOC just one week later. Detroit hoped that having the entire Executive Board receive the letter would exert a moderating influence on IOC president Avery Brundage and chancellor Otto Mayer. Detroit believed Brundage had a penchant for "impulsiveness" and that Mayer was "prejudiced" against the city. Detroit officials also sought State's assistance in pushing the other NATO candidate cities—or at least one of the other cities—to send its letter by the June Executive Board meeting. Multiple letters, they believed, would "make it clear to IOC that all NATO cities will give same assurance" and not hurt Detroit or any other NATO candidate city's chances. The State Department supported Detroit's rationale for the earlier June deadline and instructed its diplomats to "urge strongly" within NATO that all candidate cities also submit their letters by June "to protect Detroit's position."[23] The United States was trying to lead a common policy in the working group, and having more than one NATO city submitting an early letter would demonstrate that united front. The other cities could send an early letter to reinforce the NATO position, or they could let Detroit be the only candidate to do so, gaging the IOC's response to the wording before finalizing their own letters. The conflict between maintaining NATO unity and self-interest in winning the 1968 Olympic Games was great, and the bid cities and governments only had one week to act to meet the early June deadline.

The Americans had emphasized the need for NATO unity the previous month in meetings with its quadripartite colleagues in Bonn and Paris, just as the State Department had noted this concern in the meeting with the Canadian embassy officials. The Canadian officials in Washington had left that meeting with the belief that it was "hardly likely US Govt would sacrifice US chances to host 1968 games over issue of travel of East German athletes"—a point that the Canadians had heard loud and clear in that meeting.[24] The Canadians thought the plan to present Detroit's letter at the June meeting was risky and, unless they were "reasonably sure that [the IOC's] Lausanne meeting would behave as State hoped it would do," the plan could backfire. The Canadian embassy felt this plan posed too great a risk to Calgary's bid and the government in Ottawa would not be willing to similarly submit a letter. External Affairs also noted that apart from the risk, the government could not meet the June 5 deadline from an administrative standpoint because the cabinet had instructed External Affairs not to respond to Calgary regarding the letter's text without receiving full ministerial approval. However, Ottawa informed its representatives to the working group that they would "be delighted" if Detroit sent its letter to the June meeting as a test case or if other American representatives on the IOC could have a moderating influence on the IOC's demand.[25]

On the morning of May 30, just two days after the previous working group meeting, the Americans immediately called another working group meeting for that same day after receiving the instructions about the urgency of the letter's timing.[26] At this meeting called on short notice, the Americans pressed for an acceptance of the text discussed two days prior so the IOC would have more than one letter at its meeting. The debate continued much as the previous one. The French and Norwegians again expressed concern over explicitly providing detailed assurances, although they acknowledged the phrasing protected the NATO position regarding all-German teams. However, they felt using the IOC's exact language in their own reply would lead the IOC to believe the NATO states were completely acquiescing to their demands, including separate participation by the East Germans. NATO "would then face possibility of charges of bad faith when we later make explicit our support of all-German-team concept."[27] The Americans argued the language still sufficiently maintained support for an all-German team, and the French and Norwegians both stated they believed their governments would be able to accept this text as the response. The Canadian delegate to the working group, who personally did not have problems with the U.S. draft response, said he could not predict whether his government would concur. The other members realized the Canadian government again did not want to take any action that might damage Calgary's chances of securing the 1968 Winter Olympics. All members of the working group agreed to obtain a response from their governments within 24 hours regarding the text and whether they would agree to have multiple letters sent to the IOC before its meeting in six days' time. The Americans left this meeting believing that the "Canadian attitude is key to this problem" and requested the U.S. embassy in Ottawa speak with External Affairs to gain support for the American position.[28]

Instead of handling this issue in Ottawa, the State Department called in Canadian embassy officials and placed pressure on their northern neighbor in an attempt to maintain alliance (or at least working group) unity. Again the Canadians expressed concern with the riskiness of the June submission of the letter, along with the inability to obtain the complete government approval of such a letter in time.[29] Three State Department representatives tried to persuade the Canadians that submitting the letters in the next few days was in fact the best tactic and less risky, particularly as other European IOC members could provide a moderating influence on Brundage. The American officials also stated their concern Brundage might simply sit on independently submitted letters until October, at which point there would be no opportunity to revise them.[30] While the State Department officials acknowledged the Canadian concern that the IOC's rejection of letters in June might "result in irreparable damage to Calgary's candidacy," they considered that result highly unlikely, particularly since the cities would still have time to submit a second letter.[31] Finally, the State Department requested that if the administrative difficulties prevented Calgary from submitting a letter within the next few days, perhaps Ottawa could at least authorize an expression of support for the proposed letter.[32]

Without another working group meeting, each delegation at NATO informed the others of the official response of their government. The Norwegians accepted the draft letter in principle but still needed to speak with their country's sport leaders.[33] In Oslo the Utenriksdepartement told the Canadian embassy about their surprise at the reversal of the American position, believing the Americans were now willing to go much further than Norwegian authorities had expected. The Norwegians now expressed concern that the West Germans might react adversely to the U.S. position. Of course, with any new decision with respect to the Olympics, the Norwegians would then press for it to be applied to the other events Norway would be organizing in the coming years.[34] For a country whose identity was based on winter sport and that hosted several international sporting events annually, the Norwegian concern was broader than the contest for the 1968 Olympics.

Although the Canadians did not budge before the IOC Executive Board meeting in June, they informed the American delegation at NATO they did not object to Detroit sending its letter. However, they emphasized this acquiescence did not constitute Canadian approval of the text. The Canadians also used the excuse that they could not provide their approval because Pearson's cabinet had not provided the necessary approval. Norway similarly noted that it could in principle accept this letter, but since the text still had to be cleared by Norwegian authorities, Oslo would not be able to submit a letter before the IOC meeting. The French agreed to submit their letter on behalf of Lyon in time for the meeting, as long as Detroit confirmed it was going ahead with its letter.[35] The Ministère des Affaires Étrangères was dismayed at the Canadian position and instructed its NATO delegation to press upon the Canadians the problems of their position, particularly that it would undermine NATO.[36] Complications within the French bureaucracy unrelated to the IOC letter, however, prevented the letters supporting Lyon's and Grenoble's bids from being sent.[37] France's delay appeared to the others to reinforce Charles de Gaulle's general attitude toward NATO and efforts to establish coordinated policies during a period of repeated political crises—mainly that de Gaulle's actions were trying to break the NATO alliance.[38]

Ultimately Detroit was the only NATO candidate city to submit a letter to the IOC in June. American pressure on its colleagues at the last minute to send their letters came to naught. The Americans had hoped the working group would facilitate a coordinated response to the IOC in a short time frame, but national self-interest, which had also motivated the American push for an early letter submission, prevented the working group from achieving consensus in its first few weeks. Any hope that the working group or the candidate cities had for a positive response from the IOC Executive Board regarding Detroit's letter quickly faded as other business dominated the meeting. Detroit could only hand over its response, but the Executive Board did not address the letter or the issue of the travel guarantees at its meeting at all.[39] In less than a month the four NATO states bidding for the 1968 Olympic Games had come together to develop a response in line with their alliance commitments. Their extensive discussions with one another and their foreign ministries brought them closer to a common position, but not in full. The United States attempted to direct a common approach (which they hoped would bolster Detroit's bid), but the other states were not as willing to follow the Americans wholesale. France ran into bureaucratic delays, and Canada's adamant support of Calgary's bid at any cost contributed to the country's refusal to support the wording pushed by the Americans. The United States remained the only country to act with the urgency of time and concern that the exact wording might not be sufficient.

FINAL LETTERS

The lack of action at the IOC Executive Board meeting in early June left Detroit and the other NATO candidate cities in limbo with how to move forward. Instead of a quick and decisive response to spur the other NATO candidate cities to send comparable letters, the Executive Board's inaction prolonged NATO discussions as Detroit and the State Department anxiously awaited a reply. Lyon and the winter games candidate cities still had four months to submit their letters. These delays, along with the continued Canadian desire to bring the Olympic Games to Calgary at all costs, further challenged the ability of the alliance to remain united, leading to the breakdown of the working group's efforts to develop common language for all of the travel guarantee letters. The IOC's (in)actions and decisions directly influenced how the four governments ultimately responded by modifying their policies to better position their cities to win the Olympic contest.

News stories covering the IOC Executive Board meeting reported the IOC's concerns about NATO travel restrictions on East German athletes. A *New York Times* article prompted the Canadians at NATO to ask their American colleagues if "this article should be taken to imply that the [letters] from the mayors of Detroit and Lyon had been found unacceptable."[40] Canadian diplomats in Washington learned from the State Department that the American representative who attended the IOC meeting had characterized it as being in "shambles," dominated by arguments over the possible candidacies of Berlin and Vienna for the 1968 summer games. With this atmosphere not "propitious to submit" the letter, the American representative had not presented Detroit's letter to the IOC chancellor until the very end of the day when everyone was leaving. The State Department official admitted to the Canadians that "one of main advantages of their manoeuvre had been lost for IOC would now be able to examine [the letter] and criticize it at their leisure."[41] All of the working group countries shared this sentiment as they waited to hear how the IOC responded to Detroit to determine how they should each proceed.

To help regain some of the benefits of an early letter submission, the Americans encouraged the other three countries to send their responses to the IOC as soon as possible. The State Department believed doing so "would [make it] clear to IOC that NATO is presenting solid front on this issue," and then "the IOC will be compelled to react more quickly and perhaps less negatively."[42] The State Department also wanted Detroit's follow-up to the IOC to take place after other NATO bid cities, and especially Lyon, had sent their letters in the hopes of gaining a more favorable reply.[43] External Affairs was "not substantially in favour of this USA idea" and instructed its NATO delegation to ascertain the possibility of pushing the IOC for an assurance that an all-German team would continue. If the IOC granted the guaranteed the existence of the combined German team for the 1968 Olympics, External Affairs believed, it should then not be difficult for the working group states to acquiesce to the IOC's demand. Ottawa also stressed the importance of reaching "a satisfactory arrangement concerning the certificate required by the IOC" in NATO "without further delay." This Canadian push for a resolution, and not merely sending the same letter as Detroit had, was a result of the new Pearson cabinet wanting "to ensure that Calgarys chance of obtaining the Games are equal to those of other applicants within or without NATO."[44] Although the Canadians had spoken directly with the Americans about alternative options for their letter, they now bypassed the working group and went straight to the full Committee of Political Advisers to bring more states around to its view.[45]

The Canadian delegation sent a letter to all of its NATO colleagues about their concerns with the American stance and Detroit's letter. They also stated that Calgary, if required to take rapid action, would respond in accordance with the IOC request.[46] This Canadian statement and continued efforts to submit a more liberal response to the IOC frustrated several foreign ministries. The State Department directed its NATO delegation to urge their Canadian counterparts to refrain from sending their letter acquiescing to the IOC demands until Detroit received a response from the IOC, and at the same time continue to press the French and Norwegians to submit similar letters as Detroit to show the united NATO front. Still hoping the IOC would consider Detroit's letter acceptable, the State Department feared that the Canadian alternatives would "undercut entire concept of TTDs and might cause IOC to abandon its commitment to all-German team for Olympics." NATO diplomats did not know how committed the IOC really was to the concept of the all-German Olympic team, and the State Department did "not wish to disturb this policy by having ATO make statement IOC prima donnas might resent."[47] The Foreign Office felt the ATO did not need to send another letter to the IOC on this topic, nor did they believe this matter warranted an urgent discussion in the Committee of Political Advisers as the Canadians had proposed. As such, they instructed their delegation to avoid playing a leading role at the NATO meeting because "it is of more concern to NATO members bidding for 1968 Olympic Games than it is to us."[48] The Utenriksdepartement advised its delegation to adopt a cautious attitude, especially pending a reaction from the American and German delegations. The Norwegians felt "it would be unfortunate if the Canadian authorities were to go outside the TTD system," but they still favored a broader change to remove the entire banned TTD category of sport.[49] With the many sporting events Norway regularly hosted, the country's interests went beyond the narrow confines of the 1968 Olympic bid. The awarding of the 1966 Nordic skiing world championships to Oslo diminished the city's chances of organizing the 1968 Winter Olympics, leaving its diplomats more interested in a broader change to the travel regulations than the Canadian goal, which was specifically for the Olympic Games.

Armed with instructions from their foreign ministries, the political advisers debated the Canadian letter in their June 17 meeting. The Canadian opened the discussion by emphasizing the IOC was unlikely to provide an early response to Detroit's letter and "half measures or temporizing replies were very difficult to justify in light of public opinion on subject of restrictions of travel for sports purposes." In order for NATO states "to stand a chance" of winning the contests to host the 1968 Olympic Games, it would be better if their replies corresponded "as closely as possible with the requirements of the IOC." The French rebutted the Canadian proposals, arguing they "would jeopardize the entire system of travel control" and "did not take sufficient account of the principles which led to the adoption of NATO system of restrictions on the travel of East Germans." The Americans supported the French and noted "it was important to avoid letting the IOC think that it could play one NATO country off against another." Although the Americans reminded NATO not to cede its power to an external organization, the IOC had clearly forced NATO to take action. The fact that NATO was again debating these points, and that Canada was contemplating a drastically different response to the IOC in an effort to support Calgary's bid, demonstrated the increasing power of international sport to influence diplomacy. In contrast to the Canadian line, the American representative said he could "not agree that the matter was so urgent as to prevent waiting for a reaction to Detroit [letter] and [repeated] that the chances of acceptance of Detroit formula would be better if all candidate cities used it."[50] The British and Norwegian delegates contributed as instructed, and the Danish representative commented that his government, understanding the Canadian position, believed they all needed "to avoid any action that would force Olympic Games to be held outside NATO area."[51] The committee chair, R. W. J. Hooper, summed up the meeting by agreeing that "it would be deplorable if the TTD system kept NATO countries from being hosts to Olympic Games." He acknowledged broader changes to the travel system might be desired by some members, but even they were against any action taken outside the TTD system. The chairman also admonished Canada from taking unilateral action in his closing remarks. Undeterred, the Canadian delegate requested the subject return on the following week's agenda.[52]

This Committee of Political Advisers debate forced Canada to reconsider its stance. Recognizing "the almost completely negative response to our suggestions," the Canadian delegation relayed to Ottawa additional insight gained on the possible courses of action.[53] Canada had not hosted many international sporting events in recent years, and none that the East German travel ban had impacted. While the country's delegates had contributed to NATO discussions on the travel policy and often supported relaxation, the issue had not, until this need to respond to the IOC, really mattered in any serious way to the Canadian government. The repercussions for circumventing the TTD system, however, could be immense. Within NATO, Canada would "assume responsibility for terminating a form of pressure on East Germany which other members of the alliance consider to have been reasonably successful and wish to consider." This action would then have further ramifications, such as "starting a process which will call into question present system of oral agreements within NATO and result in pressure to develop a system of written agreements." Reprisals could follow as well, especially within international sport. The U.S. and European representatives on the IOC Executive Board could be pressured by their own governments "to exercise what would amount to a veto over Calgarys candidature if we breach the TTD system." Indeed, the Norwegian representative's remark that Canada should "not underestimate the strength of European feeling in the matter of opposing East German pretensions and manoeuvres" was particularly striking to the Canadian representative because it "came from the rep who has been the most vocal hitherto in attempting to terminate the travel control system." The Canadian delegation argued to Ottawa that the risks for going outside the TTD system were "sufficiently great" and Canada should try to avoid that route. Instead, Canada should urge the State Department to obtain a reaction from the IOC to Detroit's letter.[54]

The desire to support Calgary forced an impatient External Affairs to develop multiple options for how to respond to the IOC's letter, with varying degrees of maintaining NATO unity or pursuing its self-interested goal of bringing the Olympics to Canada, whatever the cost. In a memorandum prepared for the cabinet, External Affairs detailed the situation regarding NATO discussions and the text and status of Detroit's letter. The memorandum proposed three courses of action for Calgary: (1) submit the text of Detroit letter, (2) state the guarantee of free entry without restrictions, but that it "is issued on the understanding that the present IOC recognition of all-German teams," or (3) provide an unconditional guarantee. External Affairs sent this proposed memorandum, along with comments on each course of action, to its NATO delegation for its input before submitting to the cabinet. External Affairs recommended the second option, noting that preserving the concept of the all-German team "should decrease our unpopularity with some of our NATO allies since it would be more in line with NATO principles than the certificate demanded by the IOC."[55] The NATO delegation, however, countered this claim. While this option would be less objectionable than the third, they advocated the memorandum contain the "implication of lingering displeasure" with the second course, and that "It would certainly not [REPEAT] not make [Canada] popular."[56] The memorandum also argued the unconditional guarantee of option three "in no [REPEAT] no way can jeopardize Calgary's chances for the Olympics." External Affairs' rationale behind this route was that the other NATO states bidding for the 1968 games "can afford to be less forthcoming than Canada because they have all at one time or another been host to the Olympic Games or to world champion sport meets. . . . A loss of the

Games by Calgary because of NATO rules may create considerable difficulties."[57] The NATO delegation expressed concern with this assessment of the situation as well, wanting External Affairs to make clearer to the cabinet "that there be no [REPEAT] no illusion as to difficulty in NATO of going it alone in respect of travel control." They also countered the suggestion Calgary's chances would not be jeopardized by option three was "misleading." Instead, the delegation reiterated again "if we anger NATO partners by a unilateral action we cannot [REPEAT] not expect sympathy of their nationals in IOC," particularly because "all NATO countries concerned have serious domestic problems in respect of travel control on sportsmen, scientists and other categories now hindered by the rules."[58] External Affairs incorporated some of the NATO delegation's concerns into the final version of the memorandum submitted to Pearson's cabinet but still advocated Calgary send a letter following the second course.[59] Although they did not select the third option with its brazen disregard for NATO unity, External Affairs still prioritized national self-interest with its recommendation.

Back in Paris NATO discussions continued at the next two Committee of Political Advisers meetings, with representatives reiterating previously presented positions and nothing new of substance.[60] The biggest question was the IOC's response to Detroit's letter. Even though the State Department felt Detroit had become a "stalking horse for other NATO candidate cities," the Americans reassured their colleagues Detroit would follow up on the matter if it did not hear from the IOC by the end of June.[61] Detroit used local businessman and IOC member Douglas F. Roby to ascertain Avery Brundage's sentiments regarding the city's letter. When Roby and the IOC president spoke a month after Detroit had submitted its letter, Roby learned the IOC chancellor had kept Detroit's letter to himself and had not shared it with the IOC president or the Executive Board. Roby immediately sent a copy of Detroit's letter directly to Brundage and also wrote to the IOC chancellor to confirm the text was satisfactory.[62] The U.S. delegation then shared these details with its NATO colleagues and reiterated its plea for patience to await the IOC's response before taking any other action. The Americans clearly directed that comment at the Canadians, who recommended to Ottawa to delay any cabinet action on the matter.[63] Canadian diplomats pestered their American counterparts at NATO and in Washington for updates throughout June and July, hoping to forestall any concrete action in Ottawa that might cause greater problems within the alliance.[64]

By late July the State Department became "increasingly concerned" Detroit remained—two months later—the only NATO host city to have submitted a travel guarantee letter to the IOC. The State Department, which in late June had leaned on the French embassy in Washington, was particularly concerned with the lack of a French response not only because the French had also agreed to submit a letter before the June Executive Board meeting to reinforce the NATO position but more importantly because Lyon was Detroit's competitor for the summer games.[65] In late July the Americans again pressured the French delegation at NATO, emphasizing Lyon's "delay in submission is (1) unfair to Detroit, (2) creating bad impression on American side, and (3) likely have unfortunate results when combined with increasing Canadian impatience and IOC delay in answer Detroit letter."[66] The American efforts to maintain a unified front among the four states were unraveling.

In the meantime, State learned from Roby the reactions to Detroit's letter. Brundage felt the letter was sufficient, but he believed the entire Executive Board needed to consider the matter.[67] The IOC chancellor wanted the word "travel" to be changed to "visas." The State Department, on the other hand, believed the word "visas" was "too restrictive as not assuring actual entry into U.S."[68] Both Roby and the mayor of Detroit explained in separate letters to the IOC chancellor this difference between "entry" and "visas" with respect to U.S. immigration statutes and asked whether the revised sentence with "entry" would be satisfactory.[69] The American delegation informed its NATO colleagues on July 30 of Brundage's views. Without a firm response accepting the Detroit letter, however, the Americans doubted whether the Canadians could restrain the impatience in Ottawa to provide as much assistance to Calgary's bid as possible by taking independent action.[70] The French also warned the Canadians against taking any action counter to other NATO members, urging them to wait until after Lyon sent its hopefully forthcoming letter to the IOC.[71]

With no firm response by the IOC to Detroit's updated letter, combined with the lack of a Committee of Political Advisers meeting at NATO until late August because of summer holidays, diplomatic action regarding the 1968 Olympic selection also largely took a vacation until a month before the IOC deadline. Ottawa, however, continued to work feverishly on the matter. External Affairs accepted the recommendation from its NATO delegation to delay submitting the memorandum to the cabinet, which advocated a letter differing significantly from Detroit's—but it did not want to wait much longer. At most External Affairs was willing to delay presenting the memorandum to the cabinet until mid-August. Unless the State Department provided "substantial confirmation in writing from the IOC that the Detroit formula is acceptable," then Canada would forge ahead with its own version.[72] The Canadian embassy in Washington informed the State Department of this impending deadline, in essence giving State an ultimatum regarding Detroit's letter or else Canada would forge its own path.[73]

Without a concrete assurance from the IOC regarding the acceptability of Detroit's updated letter, Paul Martin, secretary of state for External Affairs, presented to the cabinet on August 16 a revised memorandum regarding the approach Calgary should take in its letter.[74] Because Canadian policy placed additional restrictions on individuals from communist states applying to visit the country, External Affairs had to revise its immigration policies more broadly for Calgary's Olympic bid than merely taking into account East German athletes.[75] Ottawa set a final deadline of August 31 for an update on Detroit's letter, and any new information would be taken into consideration during the discussion Calgary officials and a government representative planned to have with Brundage during his September visit to Canada. At this time Calgary would ascertain directly from Brundage which draft letter would be acceptable. If Detroit's revised letter was sufficient, then Calgary would follow suit with a similar letter. If not, then Calgary would use Detroit's text but with an additional statement that the Canadian government would be amenable to providing more precise guarantees should the IOC require it. If Brundage did not support that text either, then Calgary would use the version that specifically mentioned the requirement of the all-German Olympic team. Finally, should Brundage not find any of those three options viable, then Calgary would submit an unconditional guarantee, and External Affairs would inform its NATO allies of this decision in advance.[76] Canada was willing to cede to the IOC the decision-making process on how it would act, allowing an international sport organization to dictate the terms of the travel guarantee the Canadian government would provide—which would be in direct violation of the NATO policy which Canada had previously agreed to uphold.

With Pearson and his cabinet approving this course of action on August 21, the relevant government officials convened a meeting in Ottawa the following week with Calgary representatives and Sidney Dawes, Canada's

IOC member. The chairman of the Interdepartmental Committee, Joseph Willard, and M. H. Wershof, the assistant undersecretary of state for External Affairs, provided the Canadian Olympic officials with the updated details regarding the cabinet's decision. The Calgary officials decided on the version of Detroit's letter that included an additional sentence acknowledging Canada's willingness to provide more precise guarantees should they be required. Dawes, however, noted that Brundage's schedule had changed and the IOC president was no longer visiting Canada. This news prompted Wershof and Dawes to immediately call Brundage to discuss the acceptability of Calgary's proposed letter. Brundage stated on the phone that both Detroit and Calgary's letters were acceptable to him, although he could not state equivocally whether the IOC would share his views. Nonetheless, he could guarantee that, should the IOC not accept Calgary's letter, it would not invalidate Calgary's candidature since winter games cities would still have another three months to submit a revised letter before the January vote. Upon hearing Brundage's remarks, the attendees at this special meeting agreed to issue Calgary's letter immediately.[77]

With Brundage's opinion determining the final version of the Canadian letter, Ottawa informed its representatives in both Washington and Paris of the letter that Calgary would soon be sending to the IOC.[78] Calgary's letter used the same text as Detroit's, but then included the following sentence: "The Canadian Government is most anxious to welcome athletes from all over the world for the 1968 Winter Olympics, and if the International Olympic Committee requires further expression of the Government's willingness to accommodate and facilitate the entry of athletes, we would be glad to give such a request very sympathetic consideration when the precise nature of these assurances are (sic) indicated to us."[79] Recognizing this development might not receive a favorable response from their NATO colleagues, Ottawa also instructed both representatives to not only share that Brundage supported this letter but also that the Canadians believed the other NATO cities—particularly Lake Placid, Grenoble, and Oslo as winter games candidates—would be issuing letters similar to Detroit's because they supported the U.S. stance, even though none of those other cities had yet submitted their own letters. If any of them now decided to submit different letters, Ottawa requested they receive adequate warning.[80] This last instruction indicated the recognition by the Canadian government that its decision to place its national self-interests above NATO unity might upset its alliance partners.

Canada's actions, not surprisingly, did not go over well at the State Department, which expressed displeasure directly to the Canadian embassy and at NATO.[81] Additionally, the IOC chancellor finally sent the Detroit mayor a reply on August 24 about the text of the revised letter. While accepting the word "travel" for "entry," Mayer still wanted "without any restrictions" added to the text. Alluding to the problems from Colorado Springs' ice hockey world championships, Mayer did not want the United States to use that "past experience" as its point of reference for how to act. Lastly, Mayer stated the guarantee must come from the federal government and not the city of Detroit.[82] State informed the Canadian embassy of these details and that the letter would be signed either by the secretary of state or attorney general.[83] Mayer's response, however, did not reach NATO prior to the September 3 Committee of Political Advisers meeting, when the Americans simply stated their displeasure with the text of Calgary's letter and that they had no further updates from the IOC. They finally shared Mayer's reply with the rest of their NATO colleagues at the Committee of Political Advisers meeting two weeks later.[84]

Canada's departure from maintaining a unified NATO front left the other three states to send final letters to the IOC, which also provided opportunities for the countries to circumvent NATO policy. State prepared a memorandum for the Department of Justice, along with a letter to be signed by Attorney General Robert F. Kennedy that alleviated the IOC's concerns with Detroit's original June letter. The letter, which Kennedy signed, explained that while certain individuals might be ineligible to enter the United States, the government had a provision that would permit a waiver of this restriction for "any *bona fide* participant in the Olympic Games." These individuals might have a restriction on their movement once inside the United States, but, as Kennedy unqualifiedly assured the IOC, these restrictions would not impair participation in the Olympics.[85] When the United States shared this letter with their NATO colleagues on September 17, the Canadians commented on the tone at the end of the letter, which they felt "would lead to very encouraging interpretation of US text."[86] The delegation did not criticize the new American letter because, as it reported back to Ottawa, "the farther it goes the more room we will have comfortably to protect interests of Calgary."[87] Indeed, this more lenient stance taken by the Americans gave Calgary more latitude should it be necessary before the winter games vote. The State Department had instructed its delegation to inform its NATO colleagues without asking for approval and to ensure the delegation did not imply that the letter would be changed.[88] The French requested Kennedy's letter not be sent for a few days to allow the delegates to consult with their authorities and report any concerns directly to the Americans.[89]

The French confronted the American delegation at NATO the next day, stating they felt the letter was "so general in terms that [the] specific point of all-German team is lost and letter appears to give assurances for which IOC had asked." In addition, the French were concerned Kennedy's letter "would give impression of liberal assurances and would have unfortunate consequences in giving Canadians feeling that they were now free to act as they wished in spite of agreed policy re East German travel, and that existing policy itself might now become difficult to administer and would be to some degree eroded."[90] The State Department considered these French objections but refused to budge and requested the Geneva consulate send an advance copy of Kennedy's unchanged letter to the IOC.[91] The German and British representatives expressed concerns and suggested some minor changes, which the U.S. delegation believed would not alter the message. However, the telegram regarding the German and British reservations arrived after the letter had been pouched to Switzerland.[92] The desire to host the Olympic Games was so great that the Americans even refused to make the minor changes suggested by the other quadripartite powers.

With this seemingly altered American perspective, the French also admitted to the Americans that Lyon was now considering a more liberal letter so as not to be disadvantaged by Detroit's new position. The French government ministers concerned with various Olympic bid preparations had already agreed on September 11 to submit a letter to the IOC that stated France would grant entry to athletes from East Germany as long as they competed as part of an all-German team.[93] The French had consulted with the German embassy in Paris about including this idea, which the Auswärtiges Amt supported for both Lyon's and Grenoble's letters.[94] The Ministère des Affaires Étrangères recommended the paragraph about the all-German team be removed "to avoid the French answers being more restrictive than those of Detroit and Calgary."[95] France's letter, on behalf of both Lyon and Grenoble, ultimately included one paragraph using Detroit's previously agreed-upon text but then included a second paragraph. This additional text stated that "the French Government is prepared to grant entry visas to French territory to athletes who will be admitted to the Olympic Games by the International Olympic Committee, under the conditions provided for by the regulations currently in force."[96] In explaining its letter to the Americans, the French representative at NATO noted the phrasing regarding the IOC's existing regulations referred to the present requirement for the all-German team. Furthermore, the French considered the U.S., Canadian, and French letters as all maintaining the "same position, in spite of different wording."[97]

After learning about Kennedy's letter at the September 17 meeting, the Norwegians "expressed regret at [the] turn of events and concessions made."[98] They now believed the four states were "relatively free in how they will handle the matter."[99] Just a few days earlier the Norwegian foreign ministry was considering how to explain to the city of Oslo why it could not provide a complete guarantee, but the new American letter prompted the Utenriksdepartement to change course and draft a letter that would meet the IOC's request.[100] After confirmation Kennedy's letter had been sent, the Norwegian Ministry of Justice submitted a letter to the IOC that drew on text from both Detroit's and Calgary's letters. The letter stated, "While the 1968 Olympic Games are now several years in the future, the Norwegian Government anticipates that adequate provision will be made for entry into Norway," but then concluded, "The Norwegian Government is most anxious to welcome athletes from all over the world for the Xth Olympic Wintern [*sic*] Games and would hereby express its willingness to facilitate the entry of all bona fide participants in these Games."[101] By having a comparable letter to Detroit and Calgary, the Norwegians felt "all three would stand or fall together in such a way as to leave matter open for further negotiations if necessary," as the Canadian embassy in Oslo reported back to Ottawa.[102] Of course, by stating their "anxious" desire and "willingness to facilitate the entry of all" athletes so boldly, the Norwegians as well placed their self-interest in seeing Oslo host the Olympics again above alliance policy.

Although each country submitted their own letter, the four states broadly conveyed the same sentiment, particularly as they used the same text as the basis for each of their letters. How the IOC would interpret these subtle differences, however, remained to be seen. In reflecting on the final letter submitted on behalf of Detroit and Lake Placid, State reminded its NATO delegation that "other NATO countries had not provided united front that we had been urging for months. We continue to believe that letter with more restrictive text could have been used if all NATO candidate cities had submitted identical letters."[103] A completely united front by the NATO candidate cities, which the working group was intended to preserve, was ultimately thwarted as the four states prioritized their self-interests of hosting the Olympic Games. The Canadians in particular were the most outspoken against conforming to the NATO line. They also delayed informing their NATO colleagues (aside from the United States) about Brundage's remark that if the IOC deemed Calgary's letter unacceptable, they would have time to submit a revised letter before the January 1964 selection of the winter games.[104] Whereas the United States, France, and Norway had already hosted several international sporting events and had previously confronted the East German travel issue directly, the Canadian government was revising its entire travel and immigration policy in support of Calgary's Olympic bid. With the other three NATO countries all having winter candidate cities, the Canadians were definitely not team players in this case.

CONCLUSION

In the final weeks leading up to the deadline for the IOC to receive letters providing government guarantees, IOC president Brundage informed Detroit that Mexico City and Buenos Aires, the city's non-NATO competitors, had submitted guarantees, and winter games candidate Sapporo had also submitted a letter with an unconditional guarantee.[105] In fact, while the four NATO states coordinated their efforts to respond to the IOC, they also wanted to take into consideration how the other candidate cities were responding to this request. Canada took the lead in reaching out to its embassies in the non-NATO countries with bid cities, seeking to ascertain when the other candidate cities would send their letters and whether they would provide an unconditional guarantee.[106] By mid-July Ottawa had learned four of the five non-NATO governments had either submitted their letters to the IOC or would be able to provide a guarantee because national policies did not prohibit entry from any specific countries.[107] Although External Affairs never explicitly stated so, knowing other cities—and especially Sapporo, Lahti, and Sion for the winter games—could provide the unrestricted guarantee surely factored into the Canadian willingness to go against its NATO colleagues to boost Calgary's chances.

Although the American diplomats had urged their NATO colleagues to submit letters as early as possible to maintain a united front to the IOC, the other three countries did not take any serious action until the final weeks before the deadline. While they negotiated in May and early June regarding the text of the letter, only Detroit (and not even Lake Placid) made an attempt to ascertain whether the agreed-upon wording would meet the IOC's demand. Canada, France, and Norway were willing to allow Detroit to serve as the test case before they placed their own cities' candidatures in jeopardy, as evidenced by the slow course of action internally for each of them. Canadian impatience with a lack of certainty regarding Detroit's letter further fueled the desire to bring the Olympics to Canada at all costs, contributing to Canada's willingness to provide an unrestricted guarantee and thus flout NATO regulations should it be necessary. U.S.-Canadian relations, which had been strained during the Diefenbaker years, had started to improve during the summer of 1963 after Lester Pearson's victory in the April election.[108] Even so, Ottawa still maintained some points of contention with its southern neighbor, including this differing view on how to respond to the IOC. The French and Norwegians, on the other hand, monitored the American and Canadian actions and comments, only seriously working on their letters in those last few weeks. France, which had felt the impact of the travel ban acutely with the skiing world championships in Chamonix and had ardently advocated maintaining the strict position on East German athletes, now softened its position in its letter to the IOC so Lyon or Grenoble could host the Olympic Games. Norway as well had shifted its positionality in its view with the tone taken in its letter.

The intense spotlight of global and domestic media on the Olympics brought the actions of the foreign ministries under scrutiny, and the diplomats knew these government guarantees had to be worded carefully and precisely. The East German state paper recognized the IOC's demand for a travel guarantee from the candidate cities was aimed at NATO and commended the IOC for its serious upholding of the Olympic spirit.[109] The Canadian government was particularly concerned with the optics surrounding the vote for the 1968 winter games, and especially how the letter would impact Calgary's chances. One August 1963 memorandum to the secretary of state for External Affairs noted "the International Olympic Committee is known to be crotchety and independent, and if Calgary should lose its bid because the Government has not been forthcoming enough in its guarantee of free entry, every precaution should be taken that the Federal Government is not made a scapegoat. Criticism in the sports pages of the nation would be unfortunate and particularly damaging in Western Canada, where hopes undoubtedly run high."[110] This fear of domestic criticism frequently appeared in the Canadian telegrams, memorandums, and discussions pushing External Affairs to take a more lenient stance in its letter and be willing to completely disregard alliance policy.

The debate surrounding how NATO countries should deal with the IOC's request for a guarantee revealed the importance of sport and the strength of nongovernmental organizations within international relations. National self-interest in supporting domestic Olympic bids—which in mid-1963 meant complying with the IOC demand for a travel guarantee for all athletes and officials—prevented the four working group member states from maintaining a united front. At one Committee of Political Advisers meeting when they discussed the Canadian proposal of circumventing the TTD system, the chairman commented that if Canada "took action interpreted by other Alliance members as breach of Alliance agreement" then it "could lead to other breaches and eventual collapse of system."[111] If one state completely disregarded NATO policy for an international sporting event as Canada clearly wanted to do in order to host the Olympic Games, Hooper anticipated several other states would do so as well because of the frequency with which members had requested an exemption for sporting events they were hosting. This scenario—a single state's rogue action—had the potential to destroy completely an agreed-upon alliance policy, in this case the consensus on restricting East German travel. This issue had become increasingly contentious at NATO as more states wanted top East German athletes at their events or, particularly in the case of the four working group members, to be able to host the pinnacle of international sporting events: the Olympic Games. Once the governments sent their letters, however, the diplomats could only wait for the IOC to consider these travel guarantees as it voted for the host cities for the 1968 games.

CHAPTER 6

THE 1968 OLYMPIC HOST CITY ELECTIONS

By the time the IOC gathered in October 1963 in the Federal Republic spa town of Baden-Baden for its congress, all of the candidate cities had submitted letters providing a government guarantee for all athletes and officials to travel to the candidate city should the IOC select it as the host, albeit with different wordings from the cities in NATO countries. As seen in chapter 2, several international sporting events had taken place in NATO member states without East German athletes—sometimes without any teams from the Soviet bloc. In other instances, the events had been transferred to other countries. Although not deterred from applying for European or world championships in individual sports, cities and sport leaders (domestically and within the international federations) nonetheless paid close attention to what the IOC did. As the organization that oversaw the world's biggest sporting event, the IOC made decisions that influenced how the international federations acted, including how to deal with East Germany and countries that prevented athletes from participating by not authorizing appropriate travel documents.

All of the candidate cities bidding for the 1968 Olympic Games planned on making their formal presentations at the IOC session in Nairobi, Kenya, in the summer of 1963. Kenya, however, threatened to refuse entry to IOC members from apartheid African states.[1] While the IOC anticipated making quorum for the meeting, IOC chancellor Otto Mayer noted that such a low number was "not enough to take such important decisions as the choice of a City for the 1968 Games."[2] The IOC therefore moved the session to Baden-Baden, where in October they would select one of the four candidate cities to host the summer games. That the Federal Republic had been the source of so many issues related to politics and international sport apparently was not a problem when selecting a new venue for the IOC session. A few individuals balked at the change of location because they had already purchased flights to Nairobi. With the new site in Germany, however, a larger number of IOC members would more easily be able to attend as the majority of members were European. The candidates for the winter games, as had been announced in February 1963, made their presentations at the IOC meeting right before the opening of the 1964 Winter Olympics in Innsbruck.

IOC members enjoyed visiting the historic German spa town for five days (and a full week for members of the Executive Board) as well as spending two weeks in Innsbruck, Austria, for their next meeting and the 1964 Olympic Winter Games. In addition to members taking these all-expense-paid trips for the IOC sessions, candidate cities mailed bid books and other materials to them, sent representatives across the globe to visit IOC members for in-person lobbying, and occasionally invited IOC members to visit their city on a free trip under the guise of attending an international sporting event.[3] The campaigning continued until the vote took place, with each candidate city having a dedicated space to showcase itself at the IOC session. Diplomats stationed in both Germany and Austria provided support as needed for the candidate cities in their efforts to win and, in case of securing the games, preparing the obligatory victory party.

Whereas in Baden-Baden the focus was on the IOC and its business, in Innsbruck the organization met in the days immediately preceding the Olympic Games, where the excitement and anticipation of the sporting event itself contributed to the atmosphere. The IOC nonetheless conducted its business, including selecting the host for the next winter games just as Innsbruck's Olympics began. As they weighed their options in both of these votes, the IOC considered the actions of these politicians and diplomats. Governments at local, regional, and national levels routinely provided support (financial and otherwise) for Olympic bids. With the 1968 Olympic selections, however, the problem of East German travel required explicit government guarantees regarding entry policies with respect to athletes and officials participating in the Olympic Games. The IOC liked to believe that sport and politics could remain separate and publicly espoused that claim. As the outcomes of these votes clearly demonstrate, geopolitics and the actions of diplomats factored significantly in Olympic host selection. IOC members remembered the East German travel problem and NATO's actions with respect to numerous world and European championships when they cast their ballots. While venues, experience, and funding still mattered in the selection process, both votes for the 1968 Olympic host cities were, in reality, political decisions.

THE SUMMER SELECTION IN BADEN-BADEN

Global politics provided the background in Baden-Baden as the IOC met. That the Congress met in Germany was a direct result of the growing anti-apartheid movement and Kenya's refusal to issue visas for white sport leaders from African apartheid states.[4] While all IOC members and international federation representatives from African states could travel to the Federal Republic, the German problem remained in members' minds as the cities wanting to organize the 1968 Olympic Games competed for their attention. Although four cities were on the ballot, no one considered Buenos Aires a serious candidate because of political instability and a lack of reliable funding. Everyone wondered whether the IOC would select the country of the modern Olympic movement's founder (France), the country of the current IOC president (United States), or a brand-new host country (Mexico). As the IOC and the world's press descended on the German spa town, the bid committees, often with the help of politicians yet trying to eschew global politics, made their final pitches to bring the Olympic Games to their cities.

The bid committees arrived in Baden-Baden for the final presentation to the IOC and also built exhibits to convince IOC members of the merits of their city. Detroit sent a sixty-person delegation and created an exhibit that included "a 12-foot-long model of a redesigned Michigan State Fairgrounds, with a $25-million, 110,000-seat stadium," alongside "dramatic photos of Detroit and Michigan athletes in action."[5] The Detroit exhibit displayed a panorama of the United States and the city that "slid across two TV-like screens." The *Detroit News* noted four men had left Michigan a month earlier and "babied" the display across the Atlantic Ocean and Germany. In Baden-Baden "auto and advertising company heads, a real estate tycoon, utility, public relations and film company executives" assembled the exhibit in what the paper called "the highest paid construction crew in building trades history." (This characterization surely amused readers in the heavily unionized city.) In contrast, the Mexico City committee "flew in a crew of Mexican workmen and hired extra German carpenters," and Lyon used twenty French paratroopers to construct its exhibit. For its exhibit, Mexico City built "an elaborate Aztec room with carpeted floor, massive chairs and table, plus dozens of paintings, color photos and murals depicting Mexican history from the days of Cortez."[6] These enormous and intricate exhibits were an attempt by the candidate cities to demonstrate their ability to organize all of the aspects necessary to host the Olympics. Buenos Aires's lack of seriousness as a candidate was apparent as their exhibit, which consisted of a "four-projector slide presentation with taped English commentary," received no coverage in the press.[7]

In addition, the cities all hosted receptions for IOC members, some more lavish than others. One Canadian sport leader in Baden-Baden remarked, "There was nothing unusual about the Buenos Aires reception, nor about the Detroit reception," and the *New York Times* reported Detroit was "the only candidate not staging lavish receptions."[8] At the Lyon reception the French paratroopers wore "Louis XIV costumes with white stockings and wigs. They served as footmen guarding the grand staircase that led to the mezzanine of the Kurhaus and the French reception for delegates to the meeting of the International Olympic Committee (IOC)."[9] In addition, Lyon emphasized its gastronomy, bringing renowned chef Johannes Nandron and two of the country's award-winning sommeliers, along with the best vintages of Beaujolais wine. At this reception the Lyon committee's technical director emphasized that all of Lyon's sport facilities already existed and were ready for anyone to inspect them.[10] Guests and journalists clearly understood this comment as a knock against Detroit, whose bid centered around a large stadium not yet constructed. Working against Mexico City's favor was the appearance, two days before the IOC voted, of an anonymous pamphlet on the disadvantages of Mexico City's altitude and the problems it would cause athletes.[11] Many IOC members had long since made up their minds, but the candidate cities hoped these exhibits and their final presentations would persuade any undecided members or secure votes on the subsequent ballots if their preferred city was no longer in the running.

German president Heinrich Lübke opened the Baden-Baden Congress on October 16 and welcomed the IOC to the town.[12] Two days later, on October 18, each city made a forty-five-minute presentation to the IOC members and representatives from the international federations with sports on the Summer Olympic program, followed by a question-and-answer period.[13] The cities presented in alphabetical order: Buenos Aires, Detroit, Lyon, and Mexico City.[14] The Buenos Aires presentation, with the smallest delegation in Baden-Baden, was fairly unimpressive, noting they would be an Olympics "of simplicity, Spartan style but with the best and full stadiums."[15] Four Argentine sport leaders spoke alternately in French and English and ran too long, in part because the simultaneous translation system was not working, which prompted the delegation to cut their slideshow. (Avery Brundage permitted them to show their 13-minute slideshow after the lunch break before Lyon's presentation.[16]) IOC members said privately to journalists that "the Argentine representatives might have talked too much and showed too little."[17] Detroit's presentation had 31 minutes of movie footage, including a filmed speech by President John F. Kennedy. In the remaining 14 minutes, Mayor Jerome P. Cavanaugh and Michigan governor George Romney "set out just what Detroit can put on to deserve the greatest athletic show on earth."[18] Detroit's color movie, one unnamed IOC member said to a journalist, left the other three cities' presentations appearing "dull."[19] Lyon's presentation began with a nearly 30-minute color movie focused on the city's long cultural heritage, followed by speeches from the mayor of Lyon and the Préfet du Rhône.[20] Using no slides or video, Mexico City relied on speeches from five delegates who emphasized the medical evidence demonstrating the altitude of the city would not affect athlete performances (a counter to criticism and the anonymous pamphlet). They also highlighted the low daily cost of $2.80 per person for national Olympic committees if Mexico City hosted the Olympics.[21] IOC members felt the Mexican presenters were "sincere and sympathetic" and "impressed us all."[22]

In the evening after all of the presentations finished, the IOC members met again to select the host city. Olympic voting procedure requires a simple majority of the IOC members present to win; if no winner emerges on the first ballot, the city receiving the fewest votes does not move to the next round. The IOC continues to vote this way until a city receives enough votes to secure a simple majority. On the day of the vote the French paper *Le Monde* listed the betting for Mexico and Lyon "at roughly the same odds, at 2 to 1, whereas Detroit (at the moment) is at 12 to 1, and Buenos-Aires is at 15 to 1."[23] Mexico City won in the only round of voting with 30 of the 58 votes cast; Detroit received 14, Lyon 12, and Buenos Aires only 2. One IOC member commented to the press that "Detroit didn't have a chance despite that slick presentation piece which was the best we have ever seen."[24] The *Frankfurter Allgemeine Zeitung* ultimately concluded "Detroit had been accused of wanting to buy the 1968 Games with dollars; in Baden-Baden, the Americans could only conclude that Mexico had already made this purchase."[25] This comment alluded to the all-expense-paid invitation to attend the 1962 modern pentathlon world championships in Mexico City, which half of the

IOC members had accepted. The Mexico City delegation, upon hearing the announcement of their victory, shouted, applauded, and "danced a conga line around the room."[26] The Olympic Games would, for the very first time, be held in Latin America.

One month after Mexico City's shocking one-round victory in Baden-Baden, the French consul general in Chicago had a lengthy conversation with Brundage. Jean Beliard had held this diplomatic post in the IOC president's home city since 1957, and he had developed a relationship with Brundage over that time.[27] The IOC president was quite open and frank with the diplomat about why Mexico City had won and why the Detroit and Lyon bids had failed. Helping Mexico City was a feeling of sympathy among a large number of IOC members because the games had not been held in Latin America or in a Spanish-speaking country, along with the great enthusiasm among Mexicans and their youth for sport. In addition, Mexico City had several and high-quality hotels—in direct contrast to Lyon, one of the main factors that had hurt the French city's candidacy. Wider discussions happening in France surrounding amateurism, one of Brundage's biggest personal concerns within the Olympic movement, had also hurt Lyon's bid even though the city had no control over such debates. Detroit's loss was inevitable, Brundage stated, because "the whole world is hostile to the United States, and because of the flashy, ostentatious, far too 'American' presentation to which the Olympic Committee was subjected." Brundage, whom Beliard noted despised the current administration, criticized President Kennedy's comments in the candidature film as "pompous and misplaced."[28] Based on these comments, Brundage not surprisingly cast his vote for Mexico City, according to a list obtained by the French government of how each IOC member voted in Baden-Baden.[29] The fourth factor that favored Mexico City was its neutrality. Brundage noted that the country had "undertaken to honor all visa applications submitted to it, in particular by the delegation of the German Democratic Republic." Even though Detroit and Lyon had provided letters with guarantees from their governments, it became clear to Beliard that the phrasing of each city's letter, as well as the countries' previous actions, had influenced the IOC. Beliard criticized the hypocrisy of this explanation, with the IOC president assuring the French diplomat that the political reason alone did not decide the vote. Brundage nonetheless continued discussing the travel difficulties that East German athletes had faced.[30]

NATO policies may have been one of a few factors that influenced a majority of IOC members to vote for Mexico City over Lyon and Detroit, both located in the western alliance. Although Brundage provided the French consul general in Chicago with this rare, on-the-record insight into Olympic host city voting, how heavily the NATO travel policy weighed in each member's decision varied greatly. All eight members from communist states (from six European states and Cuba) voted for Mexico City, as did Brundage, another U.S. member, two Italians, and the two members from the Federal Republic (one of whom was Willi Daume, the president of the National Olympic Committee). Eight of Detroit's fourteen votes came from members from NATO countries, including hometown resident Douglas F. Roby, Canada's Sidney Dawes, and Britain's Lord Burghley. France's three members and Luxembourg contributed to Lyon's twelve total votes.[31] Mexico City's victory on the first ballot meant the IOC did not have to worry about any travel problems for its main event. Regardless of which city received their vote, IOC members breathed a sigh of relief as they left Baden-Baden, hoping the German problem could recede to the background as preparations for the all-German Olympic team for the 1964 Olympics continued in the lead-up to the Innsbruck games.

WINTER IN INNSBRUCK

With the selection of Mexico City for the 1968 Summer Olympics, the focus over the next three and a half months turned to the candidates for the winter games. The choice for the summer games of a city in the Americas—albeit not the U.S. candidate—had direct implications on the winter games field. Many people and the media speculated Mexico City's victory hurt Lake Placid and Calgary's chances and increased the likelihood that a European candidate—Grenoble, Oslo, Lahti, or Sion (which had not yet withdrawn)—would win the vote in Innsbruck. With four of the seven total candidate cities from NATO states, Mexico City's victory made those cities question the text of their letters guaranteeing travel. All of the cities had submitted their letters by the IOC's October deadline prior to the Baden-Baden meeting, but they now considered whether they should revise their letters to improve their chances. In addition to these political concerns, the bid committees also had to contend with new restrictions limiting their efforts to convince IOC members of the merits of their candidacies. The 1968 Winter Olympic selection in Innsbruck was thus a less ostentatious affair. IOC members had even more aspects to consider for the winter games host and needed several rounds of voting before they could declare a victor. The selection of the summer games host, and the extent to which the IOC factored in the travel ban and government guarantees, shaped the additional steps that the candidates for the winter games and their governments took to prepare for the Innsbruck vote.

The winter games bid cities, in Baden-Baden to promote their own candidacies as well, quickly reassessed their positions in the wake of Mexico City's victory. As soon as Detroit lost, the mayor of Lake Placid said from Baden-Baden, "We'll buy the Detroiters a beer when they come to Lake Placid. Their loss is our gain. We're in with a real chance now."[32] Both Lake Placid and Grenoble knew if their country's candidate for the summer games had won, their own bids would have in essence ended, as the IOC no longer wanted to attend Olympics in two different cities in the same country as they had in 1932 and 1936. European candidate cities felt the selection of Mexico helped their chances, as their representatives—still dominating the IOC and international federations—would be unlikely to select a second non-European city for the other Olympics in a single year. The editor of the French sport newspaper *L'Equipe* informed the French government after returning from Baden-Baden that the Fédération Internationale de Ski selection of the 1966 Alpine skiing world championships in Portillo, Chile, would also work against the non-European cities for the 1968 Winter Olympics.[33] With the most powerful winter sport federation having also selected Oslo to host the 1966 Nordic skiing world championships, this decision furthered Grenoble's chances. The German press reported Sapporo's bid committee felt its own chances significantly decreased with Mexico's selection and predicted a European city would end up hosting the games.[34] In contrast to the Lake Placid mayor, Calgary's mayor expressed concern that Mexico's selection "inevitably weakened our position a little" even though the city's "natural advantages are substantial."[35] The recent Olympics supported these sentiments. Since their postwar resumption, the Olympics had taken place in Europe if not once (1956 winter, 1960 summer, and 1964 winter) then for both editions (1948 and 1952).

The French gained insight into the Baden-Baden vote from Beliard, their consul general in Chicago, as part of their efforts to support Grenoble's candidacy for the winter games. At their meeting a month after Baden-Baden,

Beliard and Brundage engaged over the exact meaning of the letter that provided the travel guarantee for Lyon. At Baden-Baden the IOC declared Lyon's letter, which Maurice Herzog, the high commissioner for youth and sport, had signed not sufficient. Following several frantic phone calls and telegrams between Baden-Baden and Paris, French prime minister Georges Pompidou provided a new letter just two days before the IOC voted for the summer games host.[36] In contrast to the English letters from the other NATO candidate cities, Pompidou had submitted his letter in French, the IOC's other official language. Pompidou's letter stated, "The French Government is prepared to grant entry visas to French territory to athletes who will be admitted to the Olympic Games by the International Olympic Committee, under the conditions provided for by the regulations currently in force." Beliard reiterated to Brundage this letter provided "all the necessary assurances." Brundage countered it did not, with his concerns over the word "currently," which left "the door open for change" and demonstrated an arbitrariness on the part of the French Government with respect to the concept of "regulations which are currently in force." This debate over semantics continued for ten minutes before Beliard eventually convinced the American of his misunderstanding of the French text. When their conversation then turned to the assessment of the winter candidate cities, Brundage felt Grenoble had the strongest bid and dismissed for various reasons all cities except Grenoble and Oslo. However, Brundage noted, these two cities faced one obstacle: they were in NATO states and were unable to freely issue visas, as the U.S. State Department and Canadian Department of External Affairs had confirmed with their own letters supporting Lake Placid and Calgary. Beliard again assured Brundage that Pompidou's letter was an unequivocal guarantee. Brundage responded if that were the case, then "the chances of Grenoble would be great."[37] As a result of this conversation Beliard recommended to the Ministère des Affaires Étrangères strategies for how Grenoble should position its candidacy in order to secure the 1968 winter games.

The French were not the only country concerned with how much the East German travel issue factored into the IOC's decision. With a city from a non-NATO country selected to host the summer games, all four cities from NATO countries wondered whether their original letters regarding the travel guarantee were sufficient or, since they had another three months until the IOC voted on the winter games host, whether they should submit revised letters. Just days after the Baden-Baden meeting ended, the Calgary committee sought to ascertain from Avery Brundage and Canada's IOC members whether their letter was acceptable or, since the French letter (likely referring to Pompidou's last-minute guarantee) had been "an improvement over the Detroit letter as well as ours," whether their own "letter could be improved."[38] Upon learning their original letter satisfied the IOC's request, the Canadian government and Calgary organizers felt reassured.[39] Lake Placid did not send a new travel guarantee but obtained a letter from Lyndon Johnson a month into his presidency reaffirming the recently assassinated president's earlier support for the New York village.[40] Following Beliard's conversation with Brundage, Pompidou again provided what sounded much like a blanket guarantee for Grenoble. In this new letter a slight difference in wording from the last-minute letter for Lyon went significantly further than the original letter. Pompidou's updated letter read, "I have the honor to confirm that the French government is willing to grant entry visas to the French territory to the athletes admitted to the Games under the conditions existing in the regulations of the International Olympic Committee."[41] Unlike his previous letter, which had not satisfied Brundage, this new letter for Grenoble stated the French government would allow entry under the IOC's regulations—rather than using the phrase "currently in force," which Brundage had felt provided too much ambiguity.[42] The Norwegian delegation at NATO reported the text of Pompidou's new letter back to the Utenriksdepartement less than a week before the IOC voted in Innsbruck, commenting that the Norwegian side might issue a declaration with comparable wording if now deemed necessary.[43] The Norwegian government did not appear to take any action as Oslo's delegation decamped to Austria, but the French letter had raised their concern.

The lavish efforts of the four summer candidate cities in Baden-Baden prompted the IOC to impose restrictions on the winter candidate cities in an effort to limit such extravagance and possible bribery in the Olympic bid process. This new policy sought to prevent lobbying efforts by candidate cities in the remaining time before the January vote.[44] At the IOC meeting in Innsbruck, the final six winter candidate cities built far less elaborate exhibits than their summer counterparts had in Baden-Baden. Norway's main paper, *Aftenposten*, criticized Oslo's unimaginative display, staffed by just one person and displaying photographs and a pair of two hundred-year-old skis from the city's Ski Museum.[45] In contrast to the 3.5 tons of material Detroit shipped across the Atlantic, Lake Placid only sent a single ton of booth materials, which included an interactive four-by-six foot lighted map of the Lake Placid region illustrating the short distances between venues.[46] Calgary hoped its earlier efforts, prior to the restrictions, would help to persuade IOC members to support the Canadian city. The previous winter the Calgary bid committee had sponsored a flight for members of the European Journalists Association to see their excellent facilities firsthand and write stories to support tourism to the area and promote Calgary's bid.[47] Calgary also prepared for a possible victory party with help from Ambassador Margaret Meagher, the country's first female ambassador, to ensure they would have enough Canadian whisky to serve a party of three hundred people.[48] Sapporo had twenty people staffing its exhibit. *Aftenposten* commented on the exhibits by noting Grenoble had clearly advanced its candidacy if the IOC is impressed by greatness (although the paper never stated what the city had done that was so grandiose).[49] The Calgary bid committee's assessment after Innsbruck, however, noted how few IOC members actually visited the exhibits.[50] They were not as exciting and extensive as in Baden-Baden, likely prompting many IOC members to not bother seeing them.

On January 28 the six candidates made their thirty-minute presentations to the IOC, again in alphabetical order: Calgary, Grenoble, Lahti, Lake Placid, Oslo, and Sapporo.[51] Calgary's mayor went off script and made the city's presentation run longer than the time allotted. The rest of the delegation included members of the city's bid committee and the Canadian Olympic Association president, James Worrall.[52] Keeping in mind the financial support that contributed to Mexico City's victory, Calgary announced in its presentation a $150 travel subsidy per team and a $3 a day cost per person for athletes in the Olympic Village, a decrease from the $5 a day it was costing national Olympic committees in Innsbruck.[53] Grenoble's presentation also included the city's mayor, who spoke for exactly nine minutes, followed by a film from local cinematographer Jacques Lesage, who had also created the official film for the 1962 Alpine skiing world championships in Chamonix.[54] Lahti tried to emphasize that its need to hold Alpine skiing events in Sweden in fact fit within the IOC's principles of fair play and sportsmanship. The mayor ended his speech by proclaiming, "We trust that your solution will be such that we will be able to say to all the winter sportsmen of the world, to whom we guarantee free entry to our land: Welcome to the Winter Olympics of 1968 and the sunny snows of Finland's spring-winter!"[55] Unlike the high-profile speakers that Detroit included, local officials including the mayor made up Lake Placid's seven-man delegation. They emphasized the excellent facilities and strong athletes produced from the area, including two of the delegation's speakers who were well known to the IOC: Art Devlin, a World War II fighter pilot who earned three Purple Hearts before becoming an Olympic ski jumper in the 1950s and who was now part of the television broadcast team in Innsbruck, and Stanley Benham, coach of the U.S. bobsled team and a vice president of the Fédération Internationale de Bobsleigh et Tobogganing.[56] Oslo's mayor highlighted the new and low-cost accommodations for athletes as well as the travel guarantee for everyone, and the accompanying film to the city's bid showed the extensive winter sports in Oslo in "their natural setting or background."[57] Sapporo's delegation also included the mayor of the city as well as royal support from Japanese IOC member Prince Tsuneyoshi Takeda. The lack of familiarity with Asia within the IOC was obvious as one French member asked how far Sapporo was from Tokyo (one hour by jet plane).[58]

The vote in Innsbruck was also not without controversy, as an anonymous letter again circulated among IOC members, this time condemning Calgary's candidacy. The offending material claimed Banff "was nothing more than two hotels on some hills in Western Canada, about 65 miles from Calgary, which is no metropolis." The *New York Times* reported this claim was "not strictly accurate, but it was enough to kill any groundswell that might have developed" for the Canadian candidate.[59] Right before the vote, IOC president Brundage also received a "mysterious telegram" from "Anderson, Banff citizens committee" stating the city did not want the Olympics, which was the desire of only a few Calgary businessmen.[60] With six cities on the ballot it took three rounds of voting until a victor emerged. The first ballot saw Grenoble receive 15 votes, Calgary 13, Lahti 11, Sapporo 6, Oslo 4, and Lake Placid 2. The Japanese, Norwegian, and American cities all left the competition after the first round. On the second ballot Calgary took the lead with 19 votes, with Grenoble receiving 18, and Lahti 14. The final ballot, between the Canadian and French cities, resulted with Grenoble defeating Calgary 27 votes to 24.[61]

Grenoble's victory was in many ways not much of a surprise, confirming many of the sentiments previously expressed by sport leaders and in the press. Europe's dominance led to the selection of a city on that continent, particularly following the earlier decision for the 1968 summer games to go

GRENOBLE VILLE OLYMPIQUE

LE DAUPHINÉ libéré

Mercredi 29 Janvier 1964

En janvier préparez votre PUBLICITÉ DE TOUTE L'ANNÉE

0.30

Le Grand Quotidien d'Information des Alpes et de la Vallée du Rhône

Grenoble

Mise au point de Pékin : L'IDEE DE "DEUX CHINE" EST INACCEPTABLE

Paris maintient que son accord a été donné "sans condition préalable"

Le navigateur d'un « Vautour » quitte son appareil avec son siège éjectable

C'est probablement du 2 au 12 février 1968 que la capitale des Alpes françaises verra s'affronter l'élite des champions de sports d'hiver

ENCORE DES ENNUIS POUR NAESSENS

Bernard Ferran, le jeune miraculé de Prunete (Corse) à nouveau malade

(LIRE L'ARTICLE EN DEUXIÈME PAGE)

SUITE EN 5me PAGE

Suite en Dernière Page

MAGNÉSIE BISMURÉE DIGESTION ASSURÉE Poudre - Pastilles

AUX ASSISES DU RHONE

FIGURE 7. *Le Dauphiné Libéré*, January 29, 1964, 1. Courtesy of Hautes-Alpes Archives Departementales.

to Mexico City, and sympathy for Lyon's loss led to Grenoble's victory. French papers celebrated Grenoble's selection. The front page of *Le Dauphiné Libéré*, the regional paper published in the French Alps, wrote "Grenoble Olympic City" above the paper's masthead and then wrote Grenoble to mirror the five Olympic rings, large and in color on the front page (Figure 7). The sports section continued with a two-page spread with several articles and "Bravo Grenoble" across the top.[62] Paris's *Le Monde* emphasized the enthusiasm from Grenoble's residents and that the city, with "its location and hosting possibilities, deserved to be selected."[63] Others were not as excited. *New York Times* columnist Robert Daley noted the challenge of hosting the Winter Olympics: "The Winter Olympics these days appeal only to major cities such as Innsbruck and Grenoble, which can bid on behalf of several outlying communities. Or to places such as Squaw Valley and Banff, which scarcely exist as stations and where a fortune in real estate can be made by staging the games, or to peripheral distant places such as Sapporo or Lahti." He lamented on the choices with which the IOC had been left and their actual decision: "Is there really snow in Japan? Are there streets in Lahti? The voter sees no way out. And so Innsbruck now. So Grenoble four winters from now. Let us weep for the snows of yesteryear, for there is none on these downtown streets."[64] Daley's column highlighted the differences and challenges of hosting the Winter Olympics. Regardless of what sportswriters or fans might have felt, French sport leaders were pleased with the IOC's decision to award one of the 1968 games to their country, even after its involvement in preventing East Germany from participating in other events.

CONCLUSION

The selection of Mexico City and Grenoble as the hosts of the 1968 Olympic Games both provided the IOC with the familiar and something new. The Olympics had never been to Latin America or even a Spanish-speaking city (Barcelona had lost the race for the 1936 Olympics to Berlin). France had hosted the Olympic Games twice previously, in 1900 and 1924, but both times it was in the summer games in Paris. The first Winter Olympics had taken place in the French Alps in Chamonix, but originally it was simply an International Sports Week organized by the people running the 1924 summer games and only retroactively did it become known as the first Winter Olympics.[65] Yet many international sport leaders had attended a variety of events in both cities, and therefore neither city selected to host the 1968 games was truly unknown to the IOC. The candidate cities did everything they could in their efforts to host the Olympic Games, with Mexico City and Grenoble emerging as winners and leaving a slew of cities as losers. Some of the winter candidates continued harboring aspirations and eventually hosted the games (Sapporo 1972, Lake Placid 1980, and Calgary 1988), but in 1963 and 1964 the individuals behind all of the losing bids only felt disappointment. Successful bidders Grenoble and Mexico City had a few years of intense planning ahead of them—including having to confront global politics.

The NATO travel restrictions influenced the IOC as it selected the host cities for the 1968 Olympics. While several aspects contributed to Mexico City's victory, the country was nonetheless able to provide an unconditional travel guarantee, which its two serious competitors, who were both NATO members, could not. The lengthy conversations between the French consul general in Chicago and IOC president Avery Brundage allowed Grenoble to capitalize on Lyon's loss and ensured that Brundage and the IOC did not misinterpret the French wording of Pompidou's letter for Grenoble. The trading of votes between winter games candidate cities, shifting each round between two NATO candidate cities and a city in a neutral state, leaves the voting rationale less clear than the single round that resulted in Mexico City's victory. Grenoble was not only located in a NATO member state, but that state was also one of the tripartite powers that controlled the Allied Travel Office, which played a central role in the ability (or inability) of East German sportsmen and women to travel for competitions. France's position thus had the potential to cause problems for Grenoble during the four years the city prepared for the 1968 Olympics.

The all-German Olympic team was competing in Innsbruck (in neutral Austria) and later that summer in Japan. However, East Germany and its communist allies again requested the IOC fully recognize the GDR with a separate team, hoping the topic could be added to the agenda for the IOC's Tokyo meeting. With the 1968 winter games scheduled in a NATO member state and organized before the summer games in Mexico City, the IOC could not ignore the German problem. A decision to recognize East Germany before the 1968 games, while not a problem for Mexico, would put the Grenoble organizers in a difficult situation. NATO as well knew the IOC had selected a city in one of its member states for 1968, requiring the multilateral organization to continue focusing on international sport and the Olympic Games.

CHAPTER 7

DECISIONS REVISITED

The selection of Grenoble as the Winter Olympic host city forced the IOC to address the East German travel situation directly. Although two NATO member states (the United States and Italy) had hosted both of the 1960 Olympics, those games happened before the construction of the Berlin Wall and the subsequent increased travel restrictions imposed by NATO on East German athletes. The IOC was able to avoid the travel issue with the 1964 Olympics since they took place in a neutral European state (Austria) and an Asian country (Japan). Nonetheless, the formation of the all-German Olympic teams had become increasingly problematic with each iteration. In Innsbruck the East German athletes, closely supervised by their GDR superiors, "refused to mix socially with their fellow team members from the Federal Republic, refused to appear before West German television cameras or grant interviews to West German correspondents, and refused to wear their all-German insignia at victory celebrations," the American mission in Berlin reported.[1] Although the East and West Germans had held joint Olympic trials and selected the athletes to compete in the 1964 Summer Olympics in Japan, the difficulties of trying to work together became public when the team landed in Tokyo. The East and West Germans had failed to reach an agreement regarding which athlete should carry the German Olympic flag when the team marched onto Tokyo Plaza for the flag-raising ceremony a few days prior to the opening ceremony of the games. The *New York Times* reported the leaders of the combined team, Manfred Ewald of East Germany and Gerhard Stoeck from West Germany, "refused to shake hands when approached by photographers," with the paper also printing a photograph of a disheartened combined German team marching behind a sign bearing its name but no flag.[2] The IOC could anticipate similar challenges—if not more—in another four years with a continuation of the all-German Olympic team. Additionally, the IOC had voted for the Winter Olympics to take place in a NATO member state. Although the French government had provided a travel guarantee to allow athletes and officials to enter the country, much could—and did—happen during the four years before Grenoble in both politics and sport, forcing NATO to reconsider its approach and policies toward the GDR.

While NATO provided one form of security for member states, some of the European countries had also been developing other agreements to further the states' efforts to work more closely together. France and Germany, along with Italy and the Benelux states—all NATO members—had established the European Economic Community (EEC, the forerunner of the European Union) in 1958. Charles de Gaulle vetoed the British entry to the EEC in 1961, but by the end of 1963 additional efforts to create other forms of Western European alliances to provide strength and security without having to rely on the United States had failed. As Jeffrey Glen Giauque has noted, the quadripartite powers swung "between cooperation and competition" in the late 1950s and early 1960s, with a "constant shift in alignments between them."[3] These competing interests of stronger alliances, national interests, American pressure, and British wavering between the continent and its Commonwealth all factored into how the quadripartite powers approached the renewed discussions over East German travel, which began again in late 1963 and continued for another three years.

When the IOC met in 1965 in Madrid, the German problem again concerned the IOC, but this time in the context of its Olympic formulation instead of the travel problem. Knowing the IOC would consider East German recognition at that meeting, the Federal Republic mobilized its diplomats across the globe to prevent that outcome. In the meantime, NATO member states continued to host and bid for international sporting events. As a result, NATO, the quadripartite powers, and the Allied Travel Office (ATO) returned time and again to the issue of East German travel in order to revise the policy in ways that allowed their cities to organize sport competitions with East German athletes participating, while also still trying to maintain the nonrecognition of East Germany as a state. Diplomats sought to directly influence how the IOC acted, particularly with respect to preventing separate East German recognition and maintaining the all-German Olympic team. When these efforts failed, NATO had to react to the decisions taken within international sport and renegotiate their own policies. If NATO member states wanted to be able to host international sporting events following the IOC's decision in Madrid to recognize East Germany,

NATO had to relax its travel ban on athletes representing the GDR. Once again, the Norwegians not only supported this process but requested its earlier application so that sporting events scheduled to take place in Norway could benefit from these changes. The French, in the meantime, had to figure out how to square their own regulations with the IOC's decision to recognize East Germany in order to still be able to organize the 1968 Winter Olympics in Grenoble. International sport thus forced NATO to reconsider its policies in the face of a changing international reality, becoming by the end of 1968 the earliest field where NATO member states accepted détente with East Germany.

REVISITING THE EAST GERMAN TRAVEL BAN

The North Atlantic Council returned to the topic of East German travel just weeks after the IOC selected Mexico City as host of the 1968 Summer Olympics. The Norwegian representative noted, "The idea of all-German teams had now been overtaken by events, and its very principle was contradicted by the terms of the letters sent respectively by Mr. Herzog and Mr. Kennedy to the cities of Lyon and Detroit concerning the admission of foreign sports teams to the Olympic Games. By continuing to apply the travel restrictions as at present to athletes, artists and scientists, NATO countries were creating many unnecessary difficulties for themselves."[4] Indeed, other NATO states increasingly shared Norway's sentiment and pushed back against the quadripartite powers to an even greater extent. They believed each refusal of East German travel documents for sporting events in NATO countries damaged the alliance's reputation among their domestic populations. A different political and sporting landscape confronted NATO by the end of 1963, and the Berlin Wall was clearly not going away. Although the Federal Republic insisted on maintaining the nonrecognition of East Germany including in sport, the IOC's decisions forced the quadripartite powers and NATO to revise the travel policy for East German athletes. These new negotiations ultimately led to an acceptance of the reality of both the political and sporting landscape and a relaxed NATO travel policy for East German athletes.

While the bid committees and IOC members traveled to Baden-Baden, the quadripartite powers prepared for the scheduled reexamination of the trial relaxation of the Temporary Travel Document (TTD) ban on East

German athletes and scientists that they had approved in May 1963. The diplomats anticipated that their raising of this issue for these two narrow categories within NATO would almost certainly invite a broader discussion from other member states. Simultaneously, the Danish prime minister, in response to East Germany's Bertolt Brecht Theater group not being able to travel to Denmark, made several comments to Danish newspapers and in parliament that the country's NATO representatives would raise the issue of these travel restrictions and push for allowances to be made for artists and scientists.[5] (The State Department, however, told the British embassy in Washington that the Danish prime minister's "outburst" in parliament was merely "for the record only, and that the Danes would be quite happy if the present situation continued."[6]) Even before this Danish action, the quadripartite powers knew the refusal of travel documents for athletes, as with actors, resulted in criticism against NATO in the press, and most member countries stated they faced mounting pressure to further relax the travel ban each time an incident arose.[7]

The Auswärtiges Amt therefore requested its quadripartite colleagues coordinate their views to "effectively influence talks" at NATO once the alliance returned to the issue. Even in late September 1963—shortly before the extensive IOC discussions in Baden-Baden and months before the public disagreements over the all-German team at the 1964 Summer Olympics—the Federal Republic's representative at the quadripartite meeting stated the "all-German experiment had been only partially successful," but he personally "would not favor abandoning" the concept of the all-German team.[8] Three weeks of preparing a new policy statement resulted in the Auswärtiges Amt providing to the tripartite powers in Bonn a single sentence stating a travel relaxation for East Germans in several categories (scientists, artists, and athletes) would be implemented "on condition that a relaxation of the Soviet zone's ban on the corresponding groups or person from Berlin (West) is established, and that these are given the possibility of visiting East Berlin and the (Soviet) zone." Knowing their countrymen would need to present these ideas and state their position within NATO shortly, the British, Americans, and French were disappointed with the paltry sentence the Federal Republic had produced. Although the Auswärtiges Amt representative "knew that some members of NATO would not be satisfied with this step," he felt it would nonetheless "improve our public position," whereas going further on relaxing the travel ban would instead represent "a big victory for the other side."[9] The single sentence, however, provided the tripartite powers very little with which to work after having waited so long, the British embassy in Bonn informed the Foreign Office. Nonetheless, they all promised to seek comments from their governments urgently.[10]

The British, who desired a greater relaxation of the travel ban, hoped to convince the Americans via their embassy in Washington to push the West Germans to go further with their position. Fearing the French would "take a back seat," the British felt the responsibility to push the Federal Republic fell to themselves, although they hoped the Americans would join their efforts.[11] The British assessment of the French was fairly accurate, with the French merely reporting on the text and not providing commentary or requesting action to take.[12] The Americans also lived up to their expected action and, to the frustration of the British, sided more with the Federal Republic in this matter, largely wanting to maintain the travel restrictions unless the East Germans provided a comparable lifting of restrictions as quid pro quo.[13] One of the reasons behind the Americans' position was the belief that if they relaxed the travel restrictions on athletes, the East Germans might be encouraged to withdraw from their recent agreement to form an all-German team for the 1964 Olympics—and the winter games in Innsbruck were just three months away. Although Detroit had, just weeks earlier, lost out on organizing the 1968 summer games, Lake Placid's candidacy surely factored into the American concerns over the creation of the all-German Olympic team. If that agreement fell apart, it would nullify the guarantee that the Justice Department had provided in support of Lake Placid. Realizing they were unlikely to gain concessions from their quadripartite colleagues, the British embassy in Washington floated to the State Department the idea of accepting the Federal Republic's present proposal but with the condition of reviewing it again in six months.[14]

In their arguments to maintain the travel ban, the diplomats frequently cited the need to influence public opinion and counter the negative publicity leveled against their governments and NATO as a whole. *Neues Deutschland* had reported the Danish calls for a relaxation of the NATO travel ban in a front-page editorial. The U.S. Embassy in Bonn used this article to bolster support for maintaining the travel ban. The East German belief that internal NATO pressure alone would end the travel ban, the Americans argued, made the GDR "little disposed [to] make concessions" regarding the Berlin Wall. Instead, U.S. Ambassador George McGhee advocated "publicity explaining and supporting present ATO policy would serve notice that GDR should expect no relaxation of ban unless it makes comparable concessions."[15] The countries involved in the travel restrictions—and not East Germany—needed to direct the narrative to help persuade the public to support their policy, McGhee argued. The Americans hoped the Federal Republic "would take the lead in a 'public relations campaign'" to use arguments the Auswärtiges Amt had developed to support maintaining the current policy and to counter the false propaganda emanating from East Germany.[16] NATO foreign ministries believed they needed to combat the negative sentiments that appeared each time prominent East Germans could not travel by promoting NATO policy in a way that painted the alliance in a more positive light. The French foreign ministry, in conversation with a representative from the British embassy in Paris, agreed the Western powers needed to "make a much greater effort to explain their policy to public opinion." Rather than focus on the travel restrictions imposed by NATO, they should instead "say that the East Germans had adopted a totally unacceptable policy towards their own nationals."[17] East Germany only permitted individuals—be they from artistic, cultural, or sport groups—to travel abroad "to make propaganda for the regime." As such, he continued, "There was no reason whatever for the Western governments to encourage this by granting travel documents."[18] The French believed these arguments could easily persuade Western public opinion, and these actions would then bolster support for NATO and its actions.

While the quadripartite powers worked on a possible revision to their position regarding East German travel, the Danish permanent representative to NATO made an impassioned plea at the October 23 North Atlantic Council meeting for the East German travel policy to be relaxed. It had been two years since NATO had implemented the travel policy in response to the Berlin Wall, yet "the general public does not appreciate the necessity of these restrictions in the case of sporting events, such as [for instance] if the ban is applied to an East German football team entered in an international competition."[19] By placing the sport category front and center in the first paragraph of his comments and accompanying aide-mémoire, the Danish permanent representative emphasized the outsized role this topic had with respect to the Danes' understanding of public opinion of NATO. While the restrictions were "a natural and reasonable reaction in the unhappy circumstances" created in August 1961, these restrictions were "no longer quite accepted by public opinion as adequate in prevailing circumstances [and] could have effects contrary to those desired."[20] The Danish comments received support from several other delegations, notably the Norwegian, Belgian, Italian, and Canadian, and the North Atlantic Council agreed they and the Committee of Political Advisers should open a larger discussion on the travel restrictions.[21] Sport had been the most frequent point of discussion with respect to East German travel within the alliance, but NATO had also addressed the travel of artistic groups for performances and scientists wanting to attend academic conferences. The State Department had greatly mischaracterized the Danish prime minister's public criticism when it had reported it as merely political grandstanding. This statement in the North Atlantic Council forced the quadripartite powers to respond and bring the rest of the alliance members into the policy planning process.

The sport category within the travel restrictions was the most contentious, often providing the other representatives with the greatest amount of counterpoints to quadripartite arguments. Several other NATO member states felt the tripartite powers controlling the ATO granted travels requests to their three countries more frequently and leniently than East German requests to travel to events held in the rest of the alliance. The letters provided by the French and American governments in support of Lyon and Detroit in particular had factored into these accusations, leveled one month after Baden-Baden and two months before the Innsbruck vote.[22] American diplomats, however, believed arguing for the continuation of all-German delegations carried the most weight in the sport category. They again emphasized a change in the travel policy "would have serious implications for Olympic Games" because of the IOC's agreement to continue the all-German team for 1964.[23] Deviations by NATO in this area might prompt the IOC to revise its own stance to the detriment of the Federal Republic and the West in general.[24] The French supported the continuance of the current travel regulations, including the exception for the creation of all-German teams because it formed the understanding behind the French letters supporting Lyon's and Grenoble's Olympic bids.[25]

The extent to which the other NATO delegations pushed back in meetings against the quadripartite argument for maintaining the travel restrictions forced the Auswärtiges Amt to realize that some change in the policy might have to happen. Otherwise, NATO allies might "break ranks and make their own unilateral relaxations."[26] This British comment about unilateral relaxations, made in November 1963, while not directly about the ongoing Canadian efforts to provide an unconditional guarantee at that same time, provided an astute understanding of the present situation. Nonetheless, the Germans still insisted any relaxation on East German travel had to be balanced by a comparable lifting of restrictions on travel by residents of the Federal Republic or West Berlin into the GDR or East Berlin.[27] More than a month of tense discussions at NATO on the East German travel policy, which the Auswärtiges Amt representative to the quadripartite meeting admitted had been "creating harmful friction within NATO," pushed the Federal Republic to slightly shift its position.[28] Any change in policy, it felt, needed to be accomplished in such a way as to avoid the impression that the Soviets and East Germans had forced the alliance to back down by manipulating public opinion in the West.[29]

By late November 1963 the discussion within the Committee of Political Advisers turned to the idea of reverting to the pre–Berlin Wall regulations, when NATO member states imposed conditions on East German athletes, including specific warnings not to fly flags or play anthems. The quadripartite powers had actually started to consider this idea themselves in Bonn, but the Belgian and Danish representatives on the Committee of Political Advisers came to this idea of developing guidelines for East German travel themselves in response to American comments during the discussion.[30] With this idea arising from the camp that had been pushing hardest for a change in the travel policy, it allowed the quadripartite powers to appear to yield to the views of the other alliance members, while also helping bring more of the states initially wanting a greater relaxation to be able to accept this smaller shift in policy. The Committee of Political Advisers realized they could talk about this topic as much as they wanted, but as it impacted the Federal Republic first and foremost, they would never come to a decision until they had a clear proposal offered by the German delegation.[31] They therefore tabled any policy discussion until the Federal Republic and the tripartite powers controlling the ATO came back to the committee with a policy statement.

The quadripartite powers in Bonn, with guidance from their foreign ministries and their missions in Berlin, spent the next few months working through a revised list of travel categories and regulations. On January 28, three months after the Danish permanent representative in the North Atlantic Council had requested the topic be revisited and the same day the

IOC selected Grenoble to host the 1968 Winter Olympics, the German representative to the Committee of Political Advisers circulated the quadripartitely agreed-upon text for the category that included sport.[32] A revision to the list of categories now subsumed sport within a broader category for "individuals or groups of persons claiming to represent the so-called DDR [GDR] as a state." Instead of an outright ban, the ATO would take into consideration several factors before deciding whether to issue a TTD: "the nature of the sponsoring organisation in the Soviet Zone and its standing in relation to the regime"; "the applicant's employment or position in the Soviet Zone"; "the object of the visit and its probable political significance"; "the behaviour of the applicants or their predecessors on previous journeys of the same kind"; and "the nature of the event." The differentiation in the nature of "national" organizations was important, as the British noted in the development of this new category's details. Whereas the Auswärtiges Amt had still wanted to deny travel to all national groups, "regardless of whether the field of activity is football, ping-pong, stamp-collecting, dog-breeding or what you will," the British felt that view was too rigid. Instead, the tripartite powers "must retain the capacity to discriminate between individuals or groups representing organizations of a more or less objectionable character: i.e. that stamp collectors may be less objectionable than footballers."[33] The visibility of a group and ability to rouse public opinion could thus be taken into consideration by foreign ministries—and the national football team in most countries, as with ski jumpers in Norway, would also draw more attention than stamp collectors or dog breeders. The British had often been the most lenient among the quadripartite powers toward East German travel and wanted this flexibility introduced.

The Committee of Political Advisers agreed on February 17 to the revised East German travel restrictions, which the North Atlantic Council had endorsed on March 4.[34] Before NATO and the ATO could implement this new policy, however, the Federal Republic insisted the question of publicity surrounding the announcement be settled.[35] The German permanent representative to the council stated, "This new policy would, of course, come to public knowledge and be discussed in the press, and it was therefore necessary to give a balanced impression of general Western policy as regards the so-called DDR."[36] The quadripartite powers agreed the statement would be announced in Berlin by the British information officer since the UK chaired the Allied Information Office that month, which won out over arguments against the ATO in Berlin, against the quadripartite powers in Bonn, or from the NATO press office in Paris.[37] With that element finalized, the NATO council approved the statement text itself on March 18 and the relaxation of the travel policy for East German athletes finally went into effect with the announcement in Berlin on April 2—more than five months after the review had begun.[38] The statement began by acknowledging the "Three Powers responsible for the ATO" had modified "the travel regulations for inhabitants of the Soviet zone of occupation of Germany" with the intent to allow more TTDs being approved. However, the statement noted TTDs will be granted "only on condition that they refrain while in NATO countries from political activities in support of the so-called DDR." The statement ended by affirming "the full support of the other NATO Allies."[39] With NATO concerns over public opinion influencing the desire of member states to revisit the travel ban as well as the Federal Republic's desire to stop communist bloc propaganda from controlling the narrative, the exact wording of the statement was not merely a squabbling over text. NATO instead believed this wording helped reorient public opinion to its side and the continued use of some travel restrictions on East Germans.

Shortly before NATO finalized this agreement, the Western press leaked the news, first in the Federal Republic and then in Britain, about a limited relaxation being forthcoming.[40] These brief stories did not impact NATO's decisions on the final text or its timing. With this new policy finally in place, NATO member states hoped their cities would not lose out on hosting sporting events and the events already scheduled within their borders would not face the problems or controversies that earlier events had. None of the countries wanted a repeat of the Chamonix or Colorado Springs disasters from early 1962, nor did they want their events moved to neutral or—even worse—to communist states because of the public embarrassment it would cause NATO and the propaganda benefit that the Soviet bloc would claim. NATO diplomats believed sport carried far more weight than other groups (such as stamp collectors, as the UK Foreign Office had commented) within public opinion, and two years of tight travel restrictions on East German athletes, they felt, had damaged the alliance's reputation. Although still maintaining some restrictions on travel by East German athletes, the quadripartite powers hoped this new policy implemented in the spring of 1964 would still prevent de facto recognition of East Germany while providing the necessary flexibility to allow international sporting events to take place in NATO states.

SPORT UNDER THE NEW TRAVEL POLICY

By the time NATO's new policy went into effect, the IOC had chosen Grenoble to host the 1968 Winter Olympic Games. The French Alpine city's selection assuaged fears within NATO that international sport federations would completely exclude their cities from organizing international sporting events, the direction they had appeared to be heading by late 1963. As cities from a variety of NATO states continued to forge ahead with bids to host European and world championships, they now had to navigate the new East German travel policy. Although NATO continued to not recognize East Germany, the greater flexibility with respect to travel by East German athletes implemented in the years leading up to the Grenoble Olympics saw greater participation by East German athletes in NATO states.

This new policy received its first test before it even went into effect. The Norwegians wanted the process implemented early for the European speed skating championships, which were taking place a mere ten days before the IOC selected the 1968 Winter Olympic host. The Norwegians raised the European skating championships via their embassy in Bonn and with Gerhard Schröder, the Federal Republic's foreign minister, and the four powers in Bonn provided the conditions under which they would grant a TTD: the East German skaters would have to apply to participate as individual skaters and not as representatives of the GDR, and only Norwegian flags could fly around the rink in Oslo.[41] The Norwegian efforts to ensure that the East German athletes could compete at this event coincided with the lengthy NATO and quadripartite discussions over relaxing the travel policy, and the Norwegians consistently raised this event both within NATO and through their embassy in Bonn with the quadripartite powers.[42]

The Norwegian foreign ministry and event organizers eventually agreed to these conditions, and with the athletes applying accordingly, the two East German skaters received the necessary travel documents and competed. The Utenriksdepartement was pleased with this outcome, which demonstrated "that Norwegian guarantees for the future events could be taken seriously."[43] The Norwegian foreign ministry anticipated the Soviet team would withdraw from the event if the East German skaters had not been able to participate. Such action, they feared, "would have provoked sharp domestic criticism of Norwegian compliance with travel restrictions on athletes and provided a basis for anti-NATO elements to broaden sniping at the alliance."[44] Instead, having East German athletes competing at this event in Oslo served "a valuable precedent," which the Utenriksdepartement recognized was able to happen because of the effective cooperation that the government had with the Norwegian Skating Federation.[45] The speed skating event in Oslo thus became the first instance of East German travel under the new guidelines, even though it happened before the new policy formally went into effect. Sporting events scheduled in NATO countries in the ensuing months could therefore have East German participation along these lines.

The ability of East German athletes to travel to and participate in this skating event, which took place days before the IOC's vote in Innsbruck, impacted the Olympic aspirations for Oslo and the other three candidate cities from NATO states. The Norwegian foreign ministry knew a denial of travel documents for the East German skaters would in essence nullify the travel guarantee the government had provided on behalf of Oslo's candidacy for the Winter Olympics and other international events. Both Oslo and Colorado Springs, the site of the 1962 ice hockey world championships, were bidding for the 1965 figure skating world championships. The International Skating Union (ISU) had provisionally awarded Colorado Springs the event in early 1963, before the IOC selected the 1968 Summer Olympic city at its Baden-Baden session. In order to finalize the city's selection, the American delegate to the ISU sought a letter from the Justice Department comparable to the one Detroit and Lake Placid had sent the IOC.[46] Attorney General Robert F. Kennedy provided a letter reusing much of the same text as his letter for Detroit's Olympic bid. Kennedy wrote to the American ISU delegate, who also served as the vice chair of the international committee:

> Satisfactory arrangements will be made for entry into the United States, with a minimum of formality, of all participating athletes, team officials (such as managers, coaches, doctors and so forth), representatives of national sports federations or national athletic committees, and competition judges and officials appointed by the governing international organization. The United States immigration laws are such that it is possible that some participants may be ineligible for admission to the United States. However, the admission of ineligible persons may be authorized by the Department despite the ineligibility. That provision of law will be utilized to permit the

> entry of any *bona fide* participant in the 1965 Worlds [*sic*] Championships in Figure Skating but there may be some restrictions on the movement of those persons admitted under this special procedure while within the United States. Participation in the Championships, however, would not be restricted in any way.[47]

With the *New York Times* reporting that Kennedy's letter stated officials and competitors would be allowed to enter the United States "with a minimum of formalities," other countries became concerned the Americans were acting in opposition to their stated position within NATO and instead were taking actions more in line with Denmark's proposal to repeal the ban on athletes.[48] The Ministère des Affaires Étrangères (MAE) asked its embassy in Washington to seek clarification from the State Department because, with Kennedy's letter, it sounded as though the United States was "express[ing] their readiness to allow unrestricted entry" for the 1965 figure skating world championships.[49] NATO allies raised questions about Kennedy's guarantee provided for the figure skating championships, prompting the U.S. delegation to NATO to inform its colleagues in December that the Justice and State Departments had erred in issuing that letter. They would rescind this letter to the ISU and replace it with a second letter that would also refer to the TTD process being subject to continuous review.[50]

This debate over the nature of a travel guarantee to prevent Colorado Springs from having another disastrous world championships happened concurrently with Oslo's continued efforts to organize other international events. While the Norwegian capital was competing against Colorado Springs to host the 1965 figure skating championship, the city was organizing the 1964 European speed skating championships, which the ISU also governed. Concurrent with these efforts were the NATO negotiations to revise the travel policy. The Norwegian foreign ministry was concerned Kennedy's letter allowing East German athletes to attend an international event in the United States would have a detrimental impact on Oslo's bid if East German athletes could not attend the upcoming speed skating event.[51] Skating, the Norwegian delegation at NATO argued, appeared to be another instance where one of the ATO members (the United States) was receiving an advantage over another NATO state.[52] As a competitor not only against Lake Placid for the 1968 Winter Olympics but also against Colorado Springs for the 1965 skating event (at least according to the diplomatic telegram),

Oslo's candidacy relied on the ability of East German athletes to participate in this event.

As the new travel policy went into effect, the tripartite powers received the dossier compiled by the IOC (addressed in chap. 3), which detailed all of the instances in which East German athletes or officials failed to receive permission to enter foreign countries (in essence, NATO member states).[53] The three states once again consulted on how to reply to Avery Brundage and the IOC. The British letter to Brundage, signed by the parliamentary undersecretary in the Foreign Office, highlighted the April 2 announcement regarding the new regulations, noting "it is likely that more East German sportsmen than hitherto will be able to travel to NATO countries." The letter then placed the onus away from NATO, commenting that "unfortunately the East German regime has brought politics into sport by insisting on the creation of separate East German teams whenever possible."[54] Knowing the all-German team was an accomplishment about which Brundage was extremely proud, this letter was a clear attempt to bring Brundage on the side of the quadripartite governments. The MAE sent a similar letter (albeit in French), and the State Department response included a modified sentence on the Berlin Wall, placing more blame for the loss of freedom of movement on the East German actions.[55] With the East German regime refusing to allow travel other than those journeys that "serve the political purposes of the regime," the British letter further attempted to appeal to Brundage by emphasizing that "in comparison with the human suffering and hardship caused by these policies, I think you will agree that the inconvenience to sportsmen resulting from the NATO regulations is very small."[56] The coordinated reply from all three foreign ministries in the summer of 1964, before the Tokyo Olympics began, once again revealed their desire to influence international sport, and especially the actions of the IOC.

Brundage shared the American and British letters with the IOC Executive Board, who did not interpret the letters as favorably as the tripartite powers had hoped. (The French letter arrived two weeks later.) At Brundage's request the IOC chancellor replied to these letters. He wrote of the IOC and international federations' disappointment that the American and British governments "could not share the point of view of the International Olympic Committee" regarding East German travel, particularly as these actions "will deprive all the NATO countries of most of the leading international sport events which they would normally be in condition to stage if the principle that sport ranks above politics were admitted."[57] Otto Mayer's letter confirmed the idea that NATO states had long feared: their position regarding East German athletes would end all of their hopes of hosting international sporting events. The IOC had already allocated the 1968 Olympics, but with so many European and world championships still open for bidding and almost every NATO member state scheduled to host or interested in organizing these events, Mayer's threat could have serious ramifications.

This potential to lose the ability to host international sporting events, followed by the public problems of the all-German Olympic team in Tokyo and the realization the IOC would vote again on East German recognition at its 1965 meeting prompted another round of discussions in 1965 within NATO over the travel policy. Since the new policy had been implemented eight months earlier, the Dutch representative to the North Atlantic Council called for a review of how the policy had been working.[58] The quadripartite powers recommended maintaining the policy, and the ATO would continue to monitor it and provide statistics on the number of TTDs approved. The ATO continued to require event organizers to take steps to ensure that the East Germans could not exploit the event politically and that the athletes would not be listed with "German Democratic Republic" or GDR (or DDR using the German acronym). As long as they did not recognize the state symbols, NATO states could accept these national team athletes—and the beginning of their détente with the GDR. With these stipulations the ATO granted TTDs to several East German athletes wanting to compete in European or world championships in NATO member states, including biathlon (Norway), wrestling (Great Britain), and yachting (Portugal).[59] The quadripartite powers hoped these recent changes would also help the IOC maintain the all-German Olympic team and not vote for East German recognition in Madrid.

THE MADRID DECISION

The problems with the all-German Olympic team in Tokyo were on display for the world to see and no longer confined to discussions between the IOC and two German Olympic committees. After fifteen years of the communist bloc states advocating for East Germany's separate recognition, the IOC knew this issue was not going away. The East Germans had managed, once again, to have the topic of their recognition placed on the agenda for the IOC's session in Tokyo, two days before the Olympics opened. Brundage, however, wanted the discussion postponed "to have no talk of separation at Tokyo, where a united team would parade at the opening of the Games." The communist bloc representatives argued for a decision to be taken in Tokyo, but Brundage's preference prevailed, moving the discussion to the next meeting in Madrid.[60] The West German government prepared a months-long battle to counter East German recognition in Madrid through a two-pronged approach via sport representatives and its diplomatic corps. The Federal Republic understood the magnitude of the IOC's actions and employed this diplomatic pressure on a nongovernmental organization in the hopes of preserving the status quo within sport and, thus, more broadly within the international community. The IOC finally took decisive action at its 1965 session in Madrid and granted East Germany the recognition it had long desired, in spite of the Federal Republic's diplomatic pressure to prevent that outcome.

The East Germans had been causing problems with the formation of an all-German Olympic team since 1952, but these difficulties had remained largely out of the public eye. Short stories about the challenges of forming the all-German Olympic team in the German press (both East and West) largely constituted the extent of this news.[61] The actions in Tokyo, in contrast, were seen across the world with the publication of the photograph showing the all-German team arriving at the Olympic plaza as the only team not walking behind a flag. During the games a controversy over who would compete for Germany in sailing required Brundage to mediate the dispute, during which he provided three different "final" rulings (none of which were generally acceptable to either German side). The U.S. mission in Berlin reported on the sailing incident to the State Department: "Amid the welter of decisions, objections, charges, and countercharges, most foreign observers were clearly growing weary of the Germans and their seemingly interminable squabbling over an 'all-German' team."[62] The problems of the all-German Olympic team, now visible to the world, led people outside the communist bloc to start questioning the viability of its continuation. The mission noted the East Germans wanted to promote this attitude so they could eventually gain "the right to enter their own 'national' team in Olympic competition."[63] In Tokyo the problems of the all-German team threatened to damage the harmonious atmosphere of the Olympic Games directly with the introduction of politics, which Brundage could not tolerate.

The Federal Republic prepared for a fight in Madrid, with the foreign ministry taking extensive action in the year between Tokyo and Madrid. In January 1965 the state secretary for the Federal Ministry of the Interior, Dr. Hans Schäfer, wrote to his counterpart in the Auswärtiges Amt, Rolf Lahr, that while the IOC did not take action on East German recognition in either Baden-Baden or Tokyo, they could no longer avoid making a decision. Through diplomatic means they therefore needed to ascertain from Western IOC members how they would vote and what the consequences would be. Schäfer wanted the Auswärtiges Amt to take action to ensure IOC members in other countries were personally addressed on this issue, but he recognized having German diplomats approach IOC members would not be effective. Schäfer therefore requested having the foreign ministries in each IOC member's own country speak with them.[64] Lahr immediately met with Willi Daume, president of the Federal Republic's Olympic Committee, and the two developed the strategy the Olympic Committee and foreign ministry would take to ensure they had enough votes within the IOC to again prevent East German recognition. They agreed to approach IOC members via sport and diplomatic channels several weeks before the Madrid meeting. Certain individuals in other countries might also be helpful, such as French youth and sports minister Maurice Herzog for making overtures with French-speaking African governments.[65] They also proposed speaking with Prince Philip during Queen Elizabeth II's state visit to the Federal Republic in May 1965 about the upcoming IOC vote so that he could help influence Lord Burghley.[66]

The West German Olympic Committee created a list of IOC members from over forty noncommunist countries, and the Auswärtiges Amt instructed its diplomats to take action in August, two months before the IOC convened in Madrid. The foreign ministry also shared this list with the tripartite powers in Bonn.[67] On the whole the response to the diplomatic efforts sounded positive, and the Auswärtiges Amt representatives reported optimistically at quadripartite meetings they would receive a satisfactory result at the Madrid meeting.[68] By mid-September the Federal Republic provided to its quadripartite allies a detailed account of how they anticipated the votes going in Madrid: fifteen confirmed in support of their position, another twenty-four or twenty-five likely votes, and another eight that they considered "unsure."[69] With more than half of the IOC members intending to vote against separate East German recognition, both the government and Olympic Committee in the Federal Republic felt confident heading to Madrid.

At the same time, efforts to maintain the all-German Olympic team continued. Brundage sent a letter to the two German Olympic Committees in June 1965 trying to persuade them to continue working together. He opened his letter with these words: "Since I have expressed myself publicly so many times, you must well know that I consider the creation of a United German Team and its continuance through six Olympic Games a great victory for sport over politics, and one of the most important achievements of the International Olympic Committee." He reminded both committees of his role as "one of the originators of this important idea" and that he has "spent countless hours in its promotion." As such, "its abandonment would certainly be a great disappointment."[70] As the powerful president whose desired outcomes the IOC typically approved, Brundage's opinion carried significant weight. Acting against his preferences could result in disastrous consequences, a concern reflected in how the candidate cities for the 1968 games sought to ascertain whether their travel guarantee letters passed Brundage's muster. Following Brundage's outreach, Daume issued an invitation on August 27 to his East German counterpart to meet "any time and any place." Two weeks passed without Daume receiving any response from the East Germans. Privately Daume worked to convince IOC members to vote against East German recognition, but publicly he attempted to promote discussions with the East Germans because, as the Americans in Bonn reported back to Washington, "the IOC is only obliged to consider the German representation question in Madrid if the two sides have not reached prior agreement." Daume hoped reaching out to East Germany would show the IOC the West Germans were open and demonstrating a "forthcoming attitude" in contrast to the East Germans, who were the party unwilling to support the conditions previously set forth by the IOC.[71]

When the IOC gathered in Madrid, the question of East German recognition appeared on the agenda of the Executive Board's meeting as well as of the full body. Of the seven men attending the Executive Board, only one—France's Armand Massard—voted against separate East German recognition. The French embassy in Madrid reported this measure would likely win unanimous support when the entire IOC membership voted.[72] At the full IOC session, the members debated East German recognition for four hours, postponing the vote until the meeting resumed the following morning. When the IOC reassembled the next day, Brundage announced several members had met overnight and "finally found a solution satisfactory to both parties." The Federal Republic's Olympic Committee would be known as "Germany" within the IOC and the East German Olympic Committee would be "fully affiliated for the geographical area of East Germany."[73] The agreement also stipulated the two German teams would still march together into the Olympic stadium and use the same uniform, emblem, flag, and anthem.[74] Using a hand vote, the IOC by a large majority approved this measure with only five opposing votes; East Germany finally secured its own Olympic team. Brundage took personal credit for this solution, particularly the continued appearance (although not reality) of an all-German team by sight.

The Grenoble organizers immediately expressed concern with when this decision would take effect. In Madrid to provide an update on the city's Olympic preparations, the Grenoble delegation suggested to Brundage the possibility of implementing this recognition on a specific date in late February 1968, after the Winter Olympics ended. If such a solution could not be agreed on, or if the French government would not agree to issue visas for a separate East German team, the Grenoble organizers feared the city would lose the games.[75] The final agreement taken by the full IOC calmed the Grenoble organizers' fears, with the requirement of the same uniforms, anthem, and flag not likely to cause the difficulties that would have arisen had those stipulations not been included.[76]

Although not its desired outcome, the Federal Republic's government nonetheless issued a statement emphasizing that this decision "preserved the symbols of German political unity."[77] The Auswärtiges Amt had sent to Madrid one of its staff who had been extensively involved in the efforts to maintain the all-German team in order to provide support during the IOC meeting. He called Bonn to report on the IOC decision, noting it did not in any way fulfill the political wishes of the communist bloc because the outward appearance of the all-German team remained. The one benefit, he reported, was that the Federal Republic's participation in the Olympics would increase as its athletes no longer had to compete with East German athletes to qualify for the games.[78] The Madrid decision was a major news story the following day across the globe, with comments from the prominent political parties in the Federal Republic.[79] The vice chancellor, who also served as the minister for All-German Affairs, commented on the "shocking ignorance of Communist methods and tactics." The spokesperson for the opposition party called the decision "bitter news, whose consequences go far beyond the field of sport." According to the British embassy, the press from across the political spectrum in Germany conveyed "regret, bitterness and some indignation, but also widespread resignation."[80] The *Times* (London) reported West German sports officials felt the "IOC had taken the easy way out" after its thirteen years of "unceasing efforts" to maintain the all-German Olympic team.[81] The East German press, on the other hand, hailed this decision as a "great victory for the Olympic idea"—a pronouncement that the Western press reported.[82]

The diplomatic pressure that the Federal Republic had attempted to use to prevent East German recognition in Madrid had failed spectacularly. Lord Burghley wrote to the Foreign Office about what had happened in Madrid and the sentiment felt within the IOC. He noted the "great pressure" brought by the Federal Republic to prevent East German recognition had mostly "been done on the political level," which "caused considerable resentment and was rather a boomerang."[83] The U.S. mission in Berlin reported to Washington that the West German press coverage of the Madrid decision did not comment on the diplomatic efforts taken prior to Madrid, but the East German papers did. *Neues Deutschland* reported the country had gained its recognition despite "massive political intervention" by the West German government." The paper included a political cartoon (Figure 8) with Willi Daume calling Chancellor Konrad Adenauer on the telephone, with the cord shaped in the five Olympic rings, to say, "Your sword has failed!" Adenauer's broken sword on the ground has "Bonn's assessment" on it, showing how spectacularly wrong the Auswärtiges Amt was in its prediction of the Madrid vote as a result of its diplomatic outreach. In its article the day after the Madrid decision, *Neues Deutschland* did not comment at all on the elements of the all-German team that remained as part of that decision. Only the following day did the paper mention the two teams would still have to march together and share the same uniform, anthem, and flag—a point that diplomats in Berlin noted in their reports.[84]

With the Madrid decision, the East Germans no longer had to go through the agonizing negotiations to create an all-German Olympic team and the tense trials to select the athletes who would represent the combined team. Having monitored this situation for years, the American Embassy in Bonn sent its assessment of the Madrid decision to Washington. The embassy wrote that while the Federal Republic attempted to put "the best possible

Daume aus Madrid: „Herr Adenauer, Ihr Schwert hat versagt!" Zeichnung: Arndt

FIGURE 8. *Neues Deutschland,* October 9, 1965, 2.

face" on the IOC decision, the West German government ultimately could not "disguise the setback which the Madrid decision represents. For sports-minded Germans, acceptance of separate East German Olympic membership will seem a big step toward international recognition of the GDR, even though the decision has no legal significances [*sic*]—as the FRG will certainly point out."[85] The quadripartite powers had spent the past five years discussing the East German attempts to use sport to gain recognition more broadly at the global level, and the IOC's Madrid decision brought the GDR another step closer to that goal.

The importance of the IOC's vote in Madrid prompted the Federal Republic to treat the nongovernmental organization with traditional diplomatic approaches, but the direct use of diplomats to influence the IOC backfired. The IOC asserted its independence from politics by not succumbing to the pressure applied by Auswärtiges Amt diplomats, although by still calling the

Federal Republic "Germany" while qualifying the GDR as "East Germany" did still align with the Federal Republic's politics. Indeed, recognizing the GDR, a country that by that point still remained largely excluded from traditional diplomacy outside of the communist bloc, was clearly a political act. Quiet, behind-the-scenes conversations among sport leaders and diplomats, such as Lord Burghley's letters with the Foreign Office or sporting event organizers meeting with the State Department to ascertain how to deal with an East German entry, were acceptable because these conversations enabled a smoother running of international sport. Diplomatic pressure by one state on other countries' IOC members to force a vote in a particular way, on the other hand, made the IOC feel less autonomous, and it did not want to become a government pawn (although the communist bloc IOC members clearly had to act according to their governments' directions). The compromise and vote in Madrid reflected that sentiment within the IOC.

SPORT AFTER MADRID

The prospect of the IOC recognizing East Germany in Madrid forced sport organizations and foreign ministries to consider the ramifications of such a decision and the impact it would have on sporting events already allocated to NATO member states. NATO once again had to consider how compatible this sport decision was with the revised travel policy and whether it and the quadripartite powers needed to alter their policy. The West German idea of détente and establishing formal relations with East Germany was still a few years away, but the Madrid decision marked the beginning of a shift in the treatment of East Germany in sport, prompting NATO to consider softening the travel policy further. The media also speculated on possible implications for international sport, especially the 1968 Winter Olympics. Almost all international federations had recognized the GDR by 1965, leaving the IOC to face a very different sport and political landscape on the eve of its Madrid meeting than it had in 1951 when the German problem had first arisen. The IOC's recognition of East Germany in Madrid forced NATO to return to this issue, particularly as it directly affected the Grenoble Olympics.

As the East German calls for recognition gained momentum before the IOC's Madrid meeting, the Federal Republic considered a quadripartite boycott of the 1968 Olympics should the IOC allow the East Germans to create their own team.[86] A French boycott would only be possible if the French gave up hosting the winter games in Grenoble; in such a case the German Olympic Committee president Willi Daume promised German solidarity with France. (The State Department, upon hearing of this idea, thought that the Germans "may be interpreting French commitment on Olympics differently from French themselves."[87]) When the Auswärtiges Amt representative raised the possibility of a potential boycott in the quadripartite meeting just days before the IOC session in Madrid, he admitted it was the sport organizations in each country who would have to make such a decision and "none of the three governments could make a binding commitment." Nonetheless, he still suggested the State Department "should do what it could to persuade the American Olympic Committee to reach agreement with its French and German counterparts on a boycott if the East Germans succeed at Madrid."[88] This fleeting boycott idea, which received no support from the Americans, British, or French, demonstrated the challenges that confronted diplomats when it came to sport.[89] Governments might want their sport organizations to act in a certain way, but those organizations were private bodies to which governments could not dictate their decisions.

While NATO discussed the East German travel policy and German diplomats across the world worked to thwart East German recognition in Madrid, the French government was also as invested in the IOC's actions in Madrid. Grenoble's victory was on the basis of the French government's guarantee to allow athletes to enter the country "under the conditions existing in the regulations of the International Olympic Committee," as the original language in the French letter stated.[90] The French were therefore very concerned with any change in the IOC's regulations—namely, the recognition of East Germany. The French minister for youth and sports, Maurice Herzog, met with members of the foreign ministry in April 1965 to consider what kind of impact IOC recognition of East Germany in Madrid would have on Grenoble; similarly, the French embassy in Bonn sought input from the Auswärtiges Amt.[91] While the MAE hoped that by emphasizing France would allow athletes to enter based on the IOC's regulations that were "current" when Grenoble won the games, it was not sure this line of reasoning would force the IOC to maintain the status quo of the all-German team. The MAE also believed taking action with respect to other sport organizations as widely as possible would be helpful in maintaining the French position.[92]

News stories in the spring of 1965 in the lead-up to the Madrid IOC meeting speculated Grenoble would lose the Winter Olympics because of the travel ban on East German athletes. With the headline "Grenoble May Lose '68 Olympics," a wire story reported Avery Brundage had hinted that "a continued French refusal to guarantee visas for East German athletes may force the IOC to take the 1968 winter games away from the French town of Grenoble."[93] Following these stories and in line with the NATO discussions on the East German travel policy, the French sought the views of their North Atlantic Council colleagues in July 1965. In requesting this information, the French stated that if in Madrid the IOC "were to change its attitude, the resulting situation would have far-reaching political consequences."[94] In the Committee of Political Advisers meeting the following day, the representatives unanimously expressed their support for the all-German principle and "agreed that Governments should do what they could, by way of discreet lobbying of their representatives on the international Olympic Committee and the international Sports Federations, to urge that the all-German formula should be maintained."[95] This request for "discreet lobbying" by NATO recognized the independence of national sport organizations and that states could not simply treat the IOC and international federations as they would another country. In contrast to the Auswärtiges Amt's efforts to actively campaign against East German recognition, NATO recommended its members encourage their sport leaders to maintain the status quo of the all-German team. The French reiterated in the quadripartite meetings and as guidance to their embassy in Madrid that the IOC had agreed to the French provisions regarding East German travel in December 1963 when they accepted Pompidou's letter. If, however, the IOC "unilaterally modifies the terms of this agreement, by providing for the establishment of separate teams for Germany and East Germany," the MAE advised its Madrid embassy, "it will be up to them to submit to the French authorities new proposals concerning visas for East German athletes."[96] Following the Madrid decision, the French investigated, in consultation with their quadripartite colleagues, the possibility of using Olympic identity cards to circumvent the travel concerns with respect to East Germany. The United States had used Olympic identity cards for East German athletes on the all-German team for the 1960 Winter Olympics in Squaw Valley and when they transited through Alaska en route to the 1964 games in Tokyo.[97] In the end, the IOC's requirement for the symbolic elements of the all-German team remaining in force even with their granting of a separate team to East Germany quelled any need for the IOC to renegotiate with the French government.

In the months after the Madrid decision the quadripartite powers again reviewed the TTD regulations, sharing their assessment of the first nine months of the year with the Committee of Political Advisers. The changes implemented in April 1964 continued to work well, they reported, with the ATO authorizing travel for all East German sports teams that had applied for TTDs so far that year. The Madrid decision, the report noted, "does not give rise to a need for a change in TTD criteria" as the ATO rules were "sufficiently flexible to permit the issuance of TTDs to any Zonal team travelling to any Olympic competition carried out under the Madrid decision."[98] The IOC had granted East Germany its own team, but the insistence on still using the all-German Olympic flag and playing Beethoven's Ninth Symphony as the anthem for any German gold medal winners meant the East German athletes and officials could receive the necessary travel documents from both the ATO and France for the 1968 winter games.

As Grenoble continued preparing for the Olympics following the Madrid decision, the Norwegians confronted the reality of changed policies because Oslo was hosting the 1966 Nordic skiing world championships.[99] The event organizers, including FIS council member Einar Bergsland, provided a guarantee the East German flag and anthem would not appear at the event.[100] This pronouncement enabled the team, including that year's Four Hills Tournament silver medalist Dieter Neuendorf, to receive TTDs and visas to travel to Norway. Nearly twenty East German journalists, however, had their TTD applications denied as their profession still fell within one of the banned categories, causing public outcry in newspapers across the communist bloc and in Norway.[101] *Dagbladet*, a Norwegian tabloid, placed the blame on the ATO in Berlin, claiming the ATO had "dictatorial control over which East Germans can visit NATO countries."[102] The Norwegian foreign ministry considered directing its military mission in Berlin to counter the East German accusations by telling East German journalists that TTDs cannot in principle be given to "representatives of unidirectional propaganda." Yet the Norwegians themselves wondered whether bona fide sports journalists who wanted to cover the skiing world championships should not, in fact, receive permission to travel to Norway.[103]

Even with athletes receiving their documents and traveling to Oslo, problems arose in the days before the world championships began. The East German team, knowing its flag and anthem would not be used, now complained it could not even have its emblem on team jackets. Emblems usually incorporated national flags and had thus been treated by both the IOC and NATO similarly to flags. This protest led to several meetings between the Norwegian foreign ministry, Einar Bergsland, and FIS president Marc Hodler, as well as meetings between the Utenriksdepartement and the West German embassy.[104] While the Norwegian government intended to uphold NATO policy, the foreign ministry informed the German diplomats that public opinion would not understand if NATO decisions disrupted sporting events. The Utenriksdepartement also warned the embassy representatives "further action could provoke public reaction against the Federal Republic," wiping out the efforts that in recent years had greatly fostered friendly feelings toward the country.[105] Nonetheless, the Auswärtiges Amt demanded its embassy in Oslo lodge a formal complaint, emphasizing that contrary to the FIS president's statement, the signs on the East German athletes' clothing did, in fact, constitute emblems, which violated NATO policy.[106]

Once the skiing was underway the public focused on the athletes, but the Federal Republic continued to press the issue of East German symbols. Only one East German medaled, with Dieter Neuendorf placing second in the individual normal hill.[107] While some people may have noticed the East German emblem on his attire, the Norwegian foreign ministry felt the emblem was not very prominent and therefore not a big deal.[108] The Auswärtiges Amt's diplomats, including Ambassador Heinrich Böx, believed the Norwegian foreign minister had conducted their later conversations in an "*extremely frosty atmosphere*" as compared to their earlier discussions.[109] The Norwegians wanted to avoid being drawn into lengthy discussions with the Federal Republic embassy on the political implications of the East German emblem appearing on athlete uniforms at the Nordic skiing world championships, instead leaving that discussion to the NATO Committee of Political Advisers.[110]

The East Germans also attempted to raise the same issues at that year's European and world championships in wrestling, which took place in Karlsruhe and Essen, Federal Republic, and Toledo, Ohio, respectively. At the European freestyle wrestling championships in Karlsruhe the East German team demanded to have the GDR flag flown. The Fédération Internationale de Lutte Amateur (FILA), however, applied the IOC's recent Madrid decision regarding German flags and emblems, and the East German athletes withdrew from the competition. The following week, at the European championships for Greco-Roman wrestling in Essen, the East German team again demanded the use of the GDR flag and emblems. At the last minute the organizers permitted the team to wear the letters of the national sport federation and use a flag with those same letters. With this concession the athletes competed, winning one gold medal and multiple silver medals. The American diplomats in Germany reported on this event to the State Department as a warning that the East German wrestling team would likely raise these same issues at the world championships in Toledo the following month, as did the Auswärtiges Amt to its consulate in Cleveland.[111] The ATO granted TTDs because the organizers would use the all-German Olympic flag and play Beethoven instead of either German national anthem.[112] Once in Toledo, however, the East German delegation demanded to use its flag and emblem. The FILA congress met and refused to change the conditions for East German participation, with Roger Coulon, the president of the international federation, stating that "the East Germans knew the rules when they came to the United States."[113] The East German athletes, as they did in Karlsruhe, withdrew from the world championships but then sat in their tracksuits, emblazoned with the GDR and state symbols, in the front row of the stands during the event (which the German consulate reported went unnoticed).[114] NATO member states and international federations accepted the détente with East Germany under the conditions agreed upon by the IOC in Madrid, which left the GDR's attempts in 1966 to make propaganda out of international sport fall flat.

The flexibility introduced by the quadripartite powers and NATO in 1964 included the stipulations that the IOC adopted in Madrid the following year, which in essence allowed East Germany to participate with its own national teams but without its flag or emblem. The tripartite powers running the ATO, along with the Federal Republic, continued to review and modify the travel regulations. In 1966 they simplified the categories to permitted and banned, the latter of which included individuals who would attempt to take political action. The sport provisions remained, with the continued clarification regarding emblems and flags from 1964, although the ATO proudly reported that in the two years since that change they had not refused any TTDs to East German athletes.[115] East German political and sport leaders could not rely on sport anymore in their quest for recognition on the international stage as it no longer gave them extensive propaganda that highlighted the challenges East Germans faced or an opportunity to promote the related charges against NATO for blocking those efforts. Although East

Germany still did not have the full equality of its flag and anthem on display at events, its athletes could travel to and compete at all international sporting events in NATO member states. The 1966 Nordic skiing world championships in Oslo demonstrated the stark difference from events four years earlier. Journalists publicized the plight of their East German colleagues who did not receive TTDs, but the sporting event itself went ahead without problems.

CONCLUSION

When NATO reopened discussions on the travel policy in late 1963, the American permanent representative to NATO noted the "feeling generally runs high in NATO" on this issue. He warned the State Department that the delegation expected the discussion in the Committee of Political Advisers "will not be [an] objective common examination of question, but rather [a] direct attack by majority of committee on present policy and on position [of] NATO powers and Germany."[116] His prediction was fairly accurate. With every NATO country (except Iceland and Turkey) hosting international sporting events in the early 1960s, East German travel had directly impacted each member state. Ensuring that the best athletes from across the world could participate in a sporting event helped politicians. Publicly supporting a NATO policy that damaged the ability of a sporting event to run smoothly and that prevented a city and country from appearing in a good light at a global level could, on the other hand, encourage criticism of the government and Atlantic alliance. The Olympics and international sport promote the idea that sport brings the world together, yet NATO's East German travel policy did just the opposite. Historian Hans Otto Frøland noted that Norwegian politicians in the early 1960s considered that NATO's restrictive policies toward the GDR "stood in the way of détente."[117] The country's continuous push for relaxed travel policies in general, but especially for East German athletes, was part of that desire to see détente develop.

The GDR achieved its Olympic recognition in General Franco's Spain, a state built on an anticommunist mentality. That this decision took place at an IOC meeting in Madrid was itself political. After securing power during the Spanish Civil War in the 1930s, Franco's government did not allow Spanish teams to compete against clubs from communist states, a policy that continued well into the postwar era. Only in the late 1950s and early

1960s did Franco begin opening up the country and moving out of international isolation. As late as 1960 the Spanish government still refused to permit the national football team to play against the Soviet Union, but in 1963 and 1964 the government changed course and finally permitted games against the Soviet national team and other Soviet clubs.[118] During this same period of Spain opening itself internationally, its National Olympic Committee offered to organize the 1965 IOC session in Madrid, the first time the country hosted the Olympic body.[119] When the Soviet Union joined every international federation and the IOC after World War II, its representatives demanded the expulsion of Franco's Spain.[120] The achievement of the fifteen-year recognition campaign by East Germany, the Soviet Union, and the rest of the communist bloc in the capital of Spain marked an ironic conclusion to this effort. International politics allowed this meeting to take place in Spain when it did, and with the representatives from the communist bloc allowed to enter the country for the meeting, just as international politics—and a backlash against the West German diplomatic pressure—contributed to East German recognition.

Diplomatic outreach regarding Olympic endeavors had mixed results. France's efforts to have its diplomat speak with Brundage at length were successful and helped Grenoble become the host of the 1968 Winter Olympics. Germany's diplomatic actions in 1965, on the other hand, failed to maintain the all-German Olympic team. Some IOC members might have been favorably inclined to these views, but such blatant efforts on the part of a government to influence the Olympic body instead appalled far more IOC members. The result of this diplomatic blunder was the IOC's recognition of East Germany in Madrid. Diplomatic interventions in Olympic matters, from preventing athletes traveling to competitions to influencing the IOC's votes, however, ran counter to the IOC's view of itself as an apolitical body. Even though politics clearly influenced their decisions, the IOC did not want to be seen as making decisions as a direct result of political interference. Nearly two decades of the German question underscored the IOC's inability to remain separate from Cold War politics.

By allowing East Germany to have its own Olympic team (albeit while still forcing its athletes to march with the team from the Federal Republic and share a common uniform, anthem, and flag), the IOC sought to demonstrate its independence from governmental interference. Yet, as with the earlier decision to award the 1968 winter games to Grenoble, a city located in a NATO country, the IOC's compromise solution in Madrid was an attempt to circumvent the problem of East German travel. Brundage himself had admitted to the French consul general in Chicago that the NATO travel policy had hurt Lyon and Detroit and benefitted Mexico City in the contest for the 1968 Summer Olympics. As Lord Burghley wrote to the Foreign Office in the summer of 1965 about the potential recognition of East Germany in Madrid, sport's "prospect of bringing millions of ordinary people closer together, to the benefit of all mankind, is literally limitless. The opposite is of course equally true."[121] Lord Burghley had seen up close, in both the Olympics and the international federation for which he served as president, that NATO's travel policy had, in many instances in the first half of the 1960s, prevented athletes from across the world from coming together in the name of sport. The IOC hoped that the Madrid solution would end these problems, but with two and a half years to go before the Olympics took place in Grenoble, they could not be sure.

CONCLUSION

TO GRENOBLE AND BEYOND

Two weeks before the 1968 Winter Olympics opened in Grenoble, *Neues Deutschland* proclaimed in the largest headline of the day at the top of its front page: "First Independent GDR Olympic Team for Grenoble." The article quoted Heinz Schöbel, president of East Germany's Olympic Committee, who stated the nearly sixty athletes "will do their best on the independent team for the glory of the GDR."[1] On the top of the front page on February 7, the paper published a photograph of the East German team marching into the stadium during the opening ceremony the previous day, with the second headline of the accompanying article again proclaiming, "Our Republic for the first time with independent team."[2] The East German celebrations of their Olympic team made no mention of the compromise reached in Madrid, which limited that independence. Both German teams marched behind the flag of the all-German Olympic team with the Olympic rings in the middle of the flag and a sign that simply read "Allemagne"[3] (Figure 9).

Although the IOC had made its decision in Madrid in 1965, the French authorities had needed to determine how the East German athletes—now representing a separate East German state—could enter France in 1968 without violating the NATO travel restrictions that the country had both developed and enforced. One month after the Madrid decision the quadripartite powers in Bonn returned to the question of East German athletes participating in the Olympics in a NATO country. With Canada looking to resume the Calgary/Banff bid for 1972, the quadripartite powers also anticipated this question would be raised again within NATO, and they needed to prepare a response on the process for Grenoble.[4] The Ministère des Affaires Étrangères believed the East Germans would favor the use of Olympic identity cards because it would remove the TTD requirement for its athletes. For that process the IOC printed Olympic identity cards and mailed a large number of blank cards to each National Olympic Committee, which then added the names of the athletes, coaches, and officials traveling to the

FIGURE 9. East German team marching into the stadium at the 1968 Winter Olympics in Grenoble, France, behind the all-German Olympic flag and a sign simply reading "Germany" (Allemagne in French). © dpa—sports report. Courtesy of picture-alliance/dpa | dpa.

games. Realizing the use of Olympic identity cards would remove French control of its borders and leave the decision of which East Germans could enter France to the GDR authorities, the Ministère des Affaires Étrangères was reluctant to assent to this bypass of the TTD system.[5]

After much internal discussion, the French government ultimately agreed to allow the Olympic identity cards to serve as permission to enter France for athletes and officials from East Germany (as well as Taiwan and North Korea, which France also did not recognize; Rhodesia, condemned by the United Nations, did not receive the same permission).[6] France's allies in Bonn and at NATO accepted this decision, although the Federal Republic expressed concerns the East Germans would send individuals for "political purposes," as they had done in Tokyo.[7] While the French would attempt to prevent the East Germans from doing just that, the fact that the IOC decision in Madrid had granted the GDR separate recognition left the East Germans with little to propagandize in Grenoble other than that its athletes won medals (one gold, two silver, and two bronze), good for a tenth-place tie for total medals won at the games.[8] The only real drama from the East Germans in Grenoble was the scandal over their women's luge athletes, who were accused of heating their runners and subsequently disqualified, which moved the Italian slider into first place and the two West German athletes onto the podium for the silver and bronze medals.[9]

During its October 1968 session in Mexico City in the days before the Summer Games began, the IOC initially voted (twenty-four for and seventeen against) to postpone any decision regarding "the German problem" to the following year. The presidents of both German Olympic Committees then met with the IOC Executive Board during a special meeting called the night before the final day of the full IOC session where they again pleaded their cases regarding East Germany's status, including how the country's formal name would appear within the Olympic movement. The next day the Executive Board recommended the entire IOC reconsider this issue. During this renewed discussion, Norwegian member Jan Staubo argued that each National Olympic Committee "should have the right to designate its own name" and then requested the IOC consider this issue "from a sporting angle and not from a political one." After much discussion, a "great majority" of the IOC voted to grant East Germany full separate recognition under the name German Democratic Republic with its own flag, anthem, and emblem. This ruling would go into effect November 1, 1968, a few days after the Mexico City Olympics ended.[10]

One reason that factored heavily into this decision was that the IOC had, two years earlier, awarded the 1972 Summer Olympics to Munich. Immediately after the Madrid decision, Willi Daume initiated the discussions with the Munich mayor about a possible bid from the Bavarian city for the 1972 games. Like the cities bidding for the 1968 games, Munich received questions from the IOC about its ability to allow East German athletes to compete at an Olympics in the Federal Republic. The government and National Olympic Committee wrestled with the wording, and the oral guarantee provided by Daume and the city's mayor was sufficient for the IOC to select Munich over Detroit, Montreal, and Madrid in its 1966 vote.[11] The IOC's decision in 1968 to finally allow the German Democratic Republic to use its own flag, emblem, and anthem was necessary for ensuring the ensuing four years would run smoothly in sport. In addition, during the closing ceremony the Mexico City organizers would raise the flag of the next host country. The necessity of using the Federal Republic's flag—and not the black-red-gold flag with the Olympic rings in the middle—helped sway some IOC members to allow the complete separation of the German teams, symbols and all.[12] With this decision in Mexico, the German problem in sport finally concluded after two decades that saw an all-German Olympic team come and go, fights over anthems and flags, and arguments repeated again and again with the almost annual calls for recognition of East Germany. The German Democratic Republic finally received equal status within international sport despite the actions of NATO diplomats, who had tried to influence the IOC and international federations.

A SPORTING DÉTENTE

The appearance of the all-German Olympic team in 1956 at first mirrored the Western view—and especially the position of the Federal Republic—of not recognizing East Germany as a separate political entity. Avery Brundage considered this achievement "a tremendous victory for sport in accomplishing something the politicians have been unable to do."[13] As a quadrennial event the Olympic Games were able to avoid the major international political crisis points, allowing time for tensions to dissipate. The IOC could observe the various ways international federations addressed acute issues such as the immediate break in German-German sporting relations following the appearance of the Berlin Wall in order to guide their own actions. International federations, on the other hand, hosted annual or biennial championships and thus had to confront the political ramifications of the Berlin Wall and renewed travel restrictions much more immediately. International federations forged ahead during this tense period in the Cold War, at times relocating events to allow all competitors to attend. Moving an event for a single sport, especially ones that only need generic indoor arenas rather than more specific venues such as steep snow-covered mountains, is more easily accomplished, particularly at short notice. Selecting a new location for an enormous multisport event such as the Olympic Games is almost impossible.[14] Ultimately, however, the IOC could do as it pleased—or, what its dominating president wanted to do—because the organization knew every country wanted to participate in the Olympic Games. That NATO member states organizing the Olympic Games developed loopholes in their travel policies in order to accommodate athletes on an all-German Olympic team in 1956 (Cortina d'Ampezzo), 1960 (Squaw Valley and Rome), and 1968 (Grenoble), in contrast to strictly enforcing travel restrictions for world and European championships, demonstrates both the aura of the Olympic Games as well as the IOC's influence on diplomacy.

Yet international sport could not ignore politics. Government actions, both domestically and as part of NATO, clearly influenced the IOC and the selection process for the Olympic Games. Political instability will always impact a city's bid, as seen with the lack of serious consideration given to Buenos Aires. NATO's travel policy regarding East German athletes forced the IOC to consider the Cold War in the 1968 contest, first with the demand that every host city obtain a travel guarantee from its national government and then with the selection of Mexico City over Lyon and Detroit. Several factors influence IOC members when they vote for candidate cities, including geography, facilities, finances, and occasionally bribery. The selection for the 1968 Summer and Winter Olympic host cities demonstrates that global politics also play a significant role.

The IOC's 1965 decision to grant the GDR full recognition, separate from the Federal Republic, was a watershed moment in international sport. Lorenz Peiffer has called this decision a turning point in German-German sport relations, but its importance goes beyond sport within the two German states.[15] While the GDR may have appeared in the sport record books before the country appeared on the United Nations' roster, achieving its place within international sport was by no means an easy or simple task. The Federal Republic, tripartite powers, and NATO worked for years to prevent East German national teams from competing in sporting events. Following the Madrid decision, NATO and the quadripartite powers, and especially France as host for the 1968 Winter Olympics, modified their policy regarding travel for East German athletes to reflect the political reality that the GDR was a separate political entity. With other NATO states pushing for change and threatening to take unilateral action—be it the Canadian willingness to provide a blanket travel guarantee so Calgary could win the chance to host the 1968 Winter Olympics or the Danish insistence that the current policy could not remain in the face of public criticism—the quadripartite powers negotiated changes to the East German travel policy.

France's bids for the 1968 Olympics, and especially its preparations for the games once the IOC selected Grenoble as host, must be considered against the country's simultaneous military withdrawal from NATO. France's full support of the NATO travel ban on East German athletes for Chamonix, and encouragement of the United States and other member states to also uphold this policy, was in early 1962, before French president Charles de Gaulle started to distance the country from the alliance. By the time the working group for the four countries with candidate cities bidding for the 1968 Olympics formed in May 1963, de Gaulle had already that year vetoed Britain's application to the European Economic Community (the forerunner to the European Union) and rebuffed U.S. president John F. Kennedy's efforts to strengthen the Atlantic Community. With de Gaulle's additional statement in March 1966 that France would no longer remain part of NATO's military command (thus prompting the organization's relocation of its headquarters from Paris to Brussels), France gained some flexibility with its actions with respect to the alliance.[16] Combined with the IOC's Madrid decision only months before, France could take liberties with its interpretation of the NATO travel policy regarding East German athletes even though, as one of the three states composing the Allied Travel Office (ATO) as well as being party to quadripartite discussions in Bonn, French diplomats helped negotiate the details of those policies.

By allowing the nominally separate East German team, albeit without its own flag or anthem, to enter France on Olympic identity cards instead of official TTDs in many ways mirrored the country's complicated relationship with NATO as a whole beginning in 1963: following some elements of the alliance but not all. Having fought two contests to organize the 1968 Olympics and emerging victorious over five other cities for the winter games, the French government was not going to take any action to jeopardize the smooth running of the Winter Olympics in Grenoble. By using Olympic identity cards, France did not appear to disregard NATO policies while allowing East German athletes to travel to Grenoble. Hosting the Olympic Games fit within de Gaulle's efforts to return France to its great power rank, although losing the summer games to Mexico City and only receiving the winter games as a consolation perhaps reinforced France's diminished status. While East Germany celebrated its athletes competing on the snow and ice at an Olympics for the first time, the world's eyes focused on French president de Gaulle as he proclaimed the opening of the 1968 Winter Olympics in Grenoble's stadium.

At a basic level, the primary negotiations regarding East German travel at the tripartite and quadripartite levels reinforce a notion of NATO as being dominated by the great powers. Yet a closer look at how NATO and its representatives addressed the issue shows that the less powerful member states nonetheless played a significant role. The Anglo-French-American control of the ATO was a clear legacy of the occupation of Germany, but those three countries could not unilaterally make decisions entirely divorced from their NATO colleagues. Canada and Norway, viewing international sport as aligning with their overall diplomatic aims, influenced NATO to try to modify its travel policies relating to East German athletes and teams. Under Canadian prime minister John Diefenbaker, and especially during 1961 and 1962, U.S.-Canadian relations deteriorated.[17] Diefenbaker's unwavering support for Calgary's Olympic bid not only aligned with his goals of elevating Canada on the international stage, but a Calgary victory would come at the expense of Lake Placid—and thus the United States (and European power France as well). Canada had also sought to pursue détente with the Soviet Union throughout the decade, efforts that culminated with the 1972 Summit Series in ice hockey.[18] The country's continual push to weaken or remove the travel ban against the East Germans, including for athletes, thus fit within Canada's broader diplomatic efforts. Throughout the 1960s, sport was an area where NATO member states disputed and negotiated Cold War policy within the alliance, with smaller states pushing against the Western Four. Sport was, on the one hand, an easier field for divisions within the alliance to appear because the stakes with sport were not so high that it would lead to nuclear destruction. Yet, as the lengthy NATO debates demonstrated, sport's extensive media coverage and the perceived impact of these events on public opinion prompted diplomats to engage in these debates on a regular basis for most of the decade.

By 1966 the governments of both the United States and the Federal Republic of Germany had started to make public comments and outward overtures toward a loosening of the hardline Hallstein Doctrine toward the GDR.[19] Sport provided the avenue for concrete action to achieve détente. Stefan Berger and Norman LaPorte, in their study of the British–East German relationship, stated that in the realm of sport, with the appearance of two separate German Olympic teams in 1968, "the door to the world stage was opened to East Germany earlier and more widely than in almost any other field."[20] Indeed, sport was the most visible field in which East Germany fought to be accepted, helped by the national symbols that form a major part of international sporting events. While the East and West Germans no longer jointly selected athletes for a single team in Grenoble and Mexico City, they still used the same flag, anthem, and emblems, forcing the GDR to wait until 1972 to have a visibly separate identity at the Olympics. Yet, as Uta Balbier has noted, "The struggle over flags and anthems lost its force" as détente became the guiding policy.[21] These battles ended not just for the Federal Republic, which allowed the East German flag to fly on its soil for the first time at the 1972 Munich Olympics, but also for NATO, which had increasingly relaxed its travel policies regarding East German athletes by the end of the 1960s.

Officially all of the NATO countries still did not recognize the GDR as a state, but its athletes could, by the end of the decade, compete at events organized in NATO member states. Problems occasionally arose, but unlike in 1962 in Chamonix and Colorado Springs, athletes received the appropriate travel documents and competed at events in NATO states. The French permitted the use of Olympic identity cards for East German athletes for Grenoble, but NATO policies forced the IOC to nominally continue the all-German Olympic team at the 1968 winter games. The additional flexibility in TTD categories implemented in 1966 further simplified the process and largely brought to a close the issue of travel by East German athletes, which had caused immense problems since the Berlin Wall's erection five years earlier. No longer able to prevent East German recognition in international sport, the Federal Republic and its NATO colleagues became less concerned with East German athletes. Travel for athletes, a topic that once dominated Committee of Political Advisers meetings, North Atlantic Council meetings, and tripartite and quadripartite meetings in Bonn, now appeared infrequently. This shift coincided with a greater consideration of détente within the Federal Republic government in the late 1960s and the country's abandonment of the Hallstein Doctrine by the end of the decade.[22]

The years of exclusion from international sporting events in NATO member states helped fuel the East German efforts to gain formal and separate recognition from the international sport community. That acceptance, along with the ability of national teams to travel to NATO countries, enabled the GDR to appear as a dominant country in one area of global interest. By finally competing as the German Democratic Republic at every sporting event and no longer part of an all-German team simply labeled "Germany," athletic success in elite sport became an essential part of the GDR's national self-confidence. Nearly two decades of NATO restrictions on travel by East German athletes and teams contributed to the importance placed on international sport success. Thirty years after reunification, the legacies of East German sport still influence club structures and state involvement in sport in Germany today.[23]

SPORT AND POLITICS FOREVER INTERTWINED

NATO's involvement with sport during the 1960s demonstrates that international sport's decisions regarding political events did not take place within a vacuum but in fact entailed extensive engagement with government representatives, which shaped the actions taken by the IOC and international federations. When the Soviet Union joined the international sport community in the early postwar years, its representatives immediately attempted to take control of international federations and the IOC. The new Soviet members in each organization demanded to have a seat on the executive committee, make Russian an official language, and expel Franco's Spain.[24] Politicians from the democratic West decried this intrusion of politics in sport. The Soviet bloc representatives to international federations and the IOC also complained about NATO involvement in supposedly apolitical sporting matters, most frequently when East German athletes could not travel to sporting events. The democratic West treated these public exhortations as mere communist propaganda at the time, but NATO and the alliance's governments were in fact intimately involved in sporting matters, particularly surrounding the participation of an East German national team and the bidding for the 1968 Olympics.

On the surface, sport might seem completely unrelated to a military alliance, but NATO's Committee of Political Advisers took a broad view of what issues could affect the alliance's security and therefore considered international sport within its remit. The popularity of sport and global media coverage of international events, along with their place as the one field where the two Cold War camps could battle each other head-to-head, contributed to the increased power of sport organizations within the international system in the 1960s. Even with the claims of sport being separate from politics, the IOC and international federations believed they had the power to negotiate with heads of state and related diplomats (such as the ATO) when politics encroached on sport. Kennedy and de Gaulle ignored the Fédération Internationale de Ski protests over the inability of East German skiers to participate in Chamonix, but foreign ministries and NATO recognized the need to engage with domestic sport leaders and international sport organizations in the 1960s because diplomats understood the soft power benefits of hosting major sporting events. They also saw firsthand when politics disrupted those events how those efforts could backfire and the damage that could be done.

The media—in some ways more than the actual playing field—frequently became the Cold War battleground when it came to sport. Since the late nineteenth century, newspapers have relied on sport coverage to drive readership, and the drama of international sport in the 1960s continued in that vein. Papers across the globe reproduced wire stories about sporting events impacted by the East German travel ban, with additional coverage by local reporters and in editorials lamenting the impact of politics on sport. Television during the 1960s increasingly brought images of these events into people's homes, live and in color. These stories, NATO diplomats believed, turned public opinion against the alliance. The press on both sides of the Iron Curtain carried summaries of stories from all over the world, including quotations from prominent sport leaders from the other side of the Cold War. Particularly when East German athletes were not able to compete against their Western counterparts, the media coverage became the only place where the East and West confronted one another. Concerns over low public opinion of NATO and the perceptions of changes to NATO travel policy factored into the alliance's decisions and how it publicized them. NATO and its member states tried to ensure East Germany and the communist bloc would not use the disrupted sporting events as propaganda against the alliance.

East Germany and NATO had both claimed that the other impinged on the freedom of travel, with East Germany only granting politically appropriate individuals the opportunity to travel and blocking travel between East and West Berlin with the wall and NATO not allowing East German athletes and other groups to visit if officially representing the GDR. NATO tried to counter these communist claims and instead sought to demonstrate the alliance's support of freedom of travel, reminding the public it was the East Germans who had stopped those freedoms with the construction of the Berlin Wall. East German criticism of NATO actions often left the alliance behind on the scorecard; countering negative views on this issue in the domestic press inside NATO member states became a difficult deficit to overcome. NATO and its respective foreign ministries strategized how their statements could influence the press to try to achieve victory in the battle for public opinion. NATO had appeared somewhat hypocritical in speaking about protecting the freedom of travel while implementing restrictions in response to the Berlin Wall. With the relaxing of its travel restrictions along with the end of the Hallstein Doctrine, however, the communist bloc could no longer accuse the Atlantic alliance of preventing East German athletes from traveling abroad.

International sport forced diplomats—particularly from the quadripartite powers but in reality from all of the NATO member states—to take action, and to do so quite frequently in the first half of the 1960s. International sport has faced numerous instances of this type of visa refusal in the decades since the end of World War II. Perhaps the most notable example was Indonesia's refusal to allow Israeli athletes to participate in the 1962 Asian Games, which, along with hosting the Games of the Newly Emerging Forces (GANEFO) in Jakarta in 1963, resulted in Indonesia's suspension from the IOC and the 1964 Olympic Games.[25] British Commonwealth states signed the Gleneagles Agreement in 1977, which included a provision excluding apartheid states (but primarily aimed at South Africa) from sport competitions with member states.[26] Israeli athletes continue to confront this problem today. When an Israeli judoka won his weight division at the 2017 World Judo Championships in the United Arab Emirates, the event organizers refused to raise the Israeli flag or play its national anthem. In 2019 Malaysia banned Israeli athletes from competing at events in the country, resulting in that year's World Para Swimming Championships being moved from Kuching, Malaysia, to London. The statement when the International Paralympic Committee announced it was stripping the event from Malaysia echoed the comments from more than a half century earlier: "When a host country excludes athletes from a particular nation, for political reasons, then we have absolutely no alternative but to look for a new Championships host."[27] The proliferation of international sporting events in the era of global live television broadcast and 24/7 media coverage has prompted more states to use sport within their soft power efforts. However, travel bans and refusing to raise flags and play anthems for political purposes continue to result in negative publicity and damaged events today, just as they did for NATO member states in the 1960s.

The efforts to prevent East German participation, while ostensibly led by the Federal Republic, were in fact the result of a coordinated policy agreed on by all NATO member states. Whereas in areas such as trade and formal diplomatic relations countries from one camp could on the whole refrain from having any official contact with representatives from states in the other camp or any country that it did not recognize, the prestige and popularity of international sport made nonrecognition untenable in that field. Unlike a clear act by a single country refusing entry for a specific sporting event, countries belonging to NATO instead placed the blame on other entities to absolve themselves of responsibility so as not to receive any formal punishment from the international sport community. What resulted instead was a multiyear confrontation pitting the two German states, the IOC and international sport federations, and NATO member states against each other. Numerous sporting events, as well as the contest to determine the host city for both the 1968 Summer and Winter Olympics, became caught up in the Cold War issue of the "German question." Timothy Sayle has noted that by the end of 1963 "the NATO policies of the allies were understood by all sides to be based on national interest—and little else."[28] Indeed, member states at times tried to claim national interest to obtain an exception to the East German travel regulations so their sporting events did not turn into disasters like Chamonix and Colorado Springs. The failure of the working group on the 1968 Olympic Games to produce a common response to the IOC regarding a travel guarantee reinforces Sayle's appraisal of the alliance. Earlier agreements supporting the Federal Republic's nonrecognition of the GDR fell by the wayside as governments supported their cities' efforts to secure high-profile sporting events, and especially the Olympic Games.

In response to the Madrid decision, the Ministry for All-German Affairs wrote to the Auswärtiges Amt: "History shows that crucial victories in the world of sport are not achieved by political actions."[29] While that sentiment might have pervaded following the failed diplomatic effort to prevent East German recognition, it is not representative of the 1960s as a whole. NATO and its members' foreign ministries in fact influenced international sport tremendously. Although they did not always achieve their desired outcomes, and they failed to prevent the IOC from granting East Germany a separate Olympic team, NATO's nonrecognition policy of East Germany and its state symbols impacted international sporting events and how sport leaders, particularly the IOC, acted. NATO staved off East German recognition during the height of the Cold War, but international sporting events in the mid to late 1960s took place in a different landscape than previously. NATO, in turn, changed how it responded to international sport. As détente became the accepted norm throughout the entire sporting community by the late 1960s, international sport provided the model that international relations in general then followed. NATO's involvement in international sport over East German participation demonstrated a clear interest by governments in sport, but an interest that they tried to downplay to the public when it appeared they were influencing how sport functioned. The close entanglement of sport and diplomacy only became more entrenched—and more public—in the following decades. When the politically led boycotts of sporting events hit the Olympics with the African boycott of Montreal (1976), the Western boycott of Moscow (1980), and the communist boycott of Los Angeles (1984), the world saw the legacy of NATO's actions and diplomatic interventions from the height of the Cold War in the 1960s.

NOTES

INTRODUCTION: NATO AND SPORT?

1. L. D. Battle, Memorandum for McGeorge Bundy, February 22, 1962, Record Group (RG) 59, Department of State Central Decimal Files (CDF) 1960–63/800.453, box 2239, National Archives, College Park, Maryland (hereafter NA).
2. POLTO A CIRC 175, USRO Paris to SecState, March 8, 1962, RG 59, CDF 1960–63/862.181, box 2645, NA.
3. Barbara Keys, *Globalizing Sport: National Rivalry and International Community in the 1930s* (Cambridge, MA: Harvard University Press, 2006); Alan Tomlinson and Christopher Young, eds., *National Identity and Global Sports Events: Culture, Politics, and Spectacle in the Olympics and the Football World Cup* (Albany: State University of New York Press, 2006), 41–63; Roy Panagiotopoulou, "Hosting the Olympic Games: From Promoting the Nation to Nation-Branding," in *Sport and the Transformation of Modern Europe: States, Media and Market, 1950–2010*, ed. Alan Tomlinson, Christopher Young, and Richard Holt (London: Routledge, 2011), 150–70; Heather L. Dichter and Andrew L. Johns, eds., *Diplomatic Games: Sport, Statecraft and International Relations since 1945* (Lexington: University Press of Kentucky, 2014); Toby C. Rider, *Cold War Games: Propaganda, the Olympics, and U.S. Foreign Policy* (Urbana: University of Illinois Press, 2016); Jonathan Grix and Paul Michael Brannagan, "Of Mechanisms and Myths: Conceptualising States' 'Soft Power' Strategies through Sports Mega-Events," *Diplomacy & Statecraft* 27, no. 2 (2016): 251–72; Kevin B. Witherspoon and Toby C. Rider, eds., *Defending the American Way of Life* (Little Rock: University of Arkansas Press, 2018); Robert Edelman and Christopher Young, eds., *The Whole World Was Watching: Sport in the Cold War* (Stanford, CA: Stanford University Press, 2020); Heather L. Dichter, ed., *Soccer Diplomacy: International Relations and Football since 1914* (Lexington: University Press of Kentucky, 2020).
4. Letter, Marquess of Exeter to J. S. Whitehead, January 11, 1963, Foreign Office (FO) 371/169325, The National Archives, London (hereafter TNA).
5. Allen Guttmann, *The Olympics: A History of the Modern Games*, 2nd ed. (Urbana: University of Illinois Press, 2002), 90–91; Pascal Charitas, "A More Flexible Domination: Franco-African Sport Diplomacy during Decolonization, 1945–1966," in *Diplomatic Games*, 197; Paul Darby, "'Let Us Rally around the Flag': Football, Nation-Building, and Pan-Africanism in Kwame Nkrumah's Ghana," *Journal of African Studies* 54 (2013): 221–46.
6. Simon Martin, "Bikila's Aria: the 1960 Rome Olympics," in *Sport and the Transformation of Modern Europe*, 83–99.

7. Travis Vogan, *ABC Sports: The Rise and Fall of Network Sports Television* (Oakland: University of California Press, 2018).
8. Graeme Davison, "Welcoming the World: The 1956 Olympic Games and the Representation of Melbourne," *Australian Historical Studies* 27, no. 109 (1997): 64–76; Brenda Elsey, "'Because We Have Nothing': The 1962 World Cup and Cold War Politics in Chile," in *Soccer Diplomacy*, 95.
9. Jeremi Suri, "Non-Governmental Organizations and Non-State Actors," in *Palgrave Advances in International History*, ed. Patrick Finney (Basingstoke, UK: Palgrave Macmillan, 2005), 223–46; Aaron Beacom, *International Diplomacy and the Olympic Movement: The New Mediators* (Basingstoke, UK: Palgrave Macmillan, 2012); Sarah B. Snyder, "Playing on the Same Team: What International and Sport Historians Can Learn from Each Other," in *Soccer Diplomacy*, 18–29; Peter J. Beck, "Conclusion: 'Good Kicking' Is Not Only 'Good Politics' but Also 'Good Diplomacy'," in *Soccer Diplomacy*, 221–50.
10. Kevin Witherspoon, *Before the Eyes of the World: Mexico and the 1968 Olympic Games* (DeKalb: Northern Illinois University Press, 2008); Xu Guoqi, *Olympic Dreams: China and Sports, 1895–2008* (Cambridge, MA: Harvard University Press, 2008); Kay Schiller and Christopher Young, *The 1972 Munich Olympics and the Making of Modern Germany* (Berkeley: University of California Press, 2010); Udo Merkel and Misuk Kim, "Third Time Lucky!? PyeongChang's Bid to Host the 2018 Winter Olympics—Politics, Policy and Practice," *International Journal of the History of Sport* 28, no. 16 (2011): 2365–83; Robert Oliver, "The Legacies of Losing: Rethinking the 'Failure' of Toronto's Olympic Games Bids," *Sport in Society* 17, no. 2 (2014): 204–17.
11. Research on NATO has largely studied one country's perspective on a specific issue, typically related to the military or security. Cees Wiebes and Bert Zeeman, "'I Don't Need Your Handkerchiefs': Holland's Experience of Crisis Consultation in NATO," *International Affairs* 66, no. 1 (1990): 91–113; Emil Kirchner and James Sperling, eds., *The Federal Republic of Germany and NATO: 40 Years After* (Basingstoke, UK: Palgrave Macmillan, 1992); Francis H. Heller and John R. Gillingham, eds., *NATO: The Founding of the Atlantic Alliance and the Integration of Europe* (New York: St. Martin's Press, 1992); Andreas Wenger, Christian Nuenlist, and Anna Locher, eds., *Transforming NATO in the Cold War: Challenges beyond Deterrence in the 1960s* (London: Routledge, 2007); Mary Ann Heiss and S. Victor Papacosma, eds., *NATO and the Warsaw Pact: Intrabloc Conflicts* (Kent, OH: Kent State University Press, 2008); Christian Neunlist, "Dealing with the Devil: NATO and Gaullist France, 1958–66," *Journal of Transatlantic Studies* 9, no. 3 (2011): 220–31; Marc Trachtenberg, "France and NATO, 1949–1991," *Journal of Transatlantic Studies* 9, no. 3 (2011): 184–94; Gjert Lage Dyndal, "How the High North Became Central in NATO Strategy: Revelations from the NATO Archives," *Journal of Strategic Studies* 34, no. 4 (2011): 557–85; Timothy Andrews Sayle, "Canada, NATO, and the Berlin Crisis, 1961–1962: 'Slow-Boil' or 'Pressure Cooker'?" *International Journal* 68, no. 2 (2013): 255–68; Linda Risso, *Propaganda and Intelligence in the Cold War: The NATO Information Service* (London: Routledge, 2014); Simone Turchetti, *Greening*

the Alliance: The Diplomacy of NATO's Science and Environmental Initiatives (Chicago: University of Chicago Press, 2019).

12. Robert Edelman and Christopher Young, "Introduction: Explaining Cold War Sport," in *The Whole World Was Watching*, 21.
13. German scholars have largely considered the Cold War German problem as a question of German politics. Martin H. Geyer, "Der Kampf um nationale Repräsentation: Deutsch-deutscher Sportbeziehungen und die ‚Hallstein-Doktrin'," *Vertel-jahrshefte für Zeitgeschichte* 44, no. 1 (1996): 55–86; Tobias Blasius, *Olympische Bewegung, Kalter Krieg und Deutschlandpolitik 1949–1972* (Frankfurt: Peter Lang, 2001); Martin H. Geyer, "On the Road to a German 'Postnationalism'? Athletic Competition between the Two German States in the Era of Konrad Adenauer," *German Politics and Society* 25, no. 2 (2007): 140–67; Uta A. Balbier, *Kalter Krieg auf der Aschenbahn: der deutsch-deutsche Sport, 1950–1972: eine politische Geschichte* (Paderborn: F. Schöning, 2007); Noel D. Cary, "Olympics in Divided Berlin? Popular Culture and Political Imagination at the Cold War Frontier," *Cold War History* 11, no. 3 (2011): 291–316; Jutta Braun, "Learning from the Dictatorship? Sport in Divided and Unified Germany," *German Historical Institute London Bulletin* 41, no. 1 (2019): 50–72; Jutta Braun, "Sports and Society in the Rivalry between East and West," in *A History Shared and Divided: East and West Germany since 1970s*, ed. Frank Bösch, trans. Jennifer Walcoff Neuheiser (New York: Berghahn Books, 2018), 501–50; Uta Andrea Balbier, "'A Game, a Competition, an Instrument?': High Performance, Cultural Diplomacy and German Sport from 1950 to 1972," *International Journal of the History of Sport* 26, no. 4 (2009): 539–55; Karten Lippmann, *„ . . . und für die Ehre unserer Nation(en)": Olympische Deutschlandpolitik zwischen 1960 und 1968* (Hildesheim: Arete Verlag, 2017).
14. Timothy Andrews Sayle, *Enduring Alliance: A History of NATO and the Postwar Global Order* (Ithaca, NY: Cornell University Press, 2019).
15. John Gearson and Kori Schake, eds., *The Berlin Wall Crisis: Perspectives on Cold War Alliances* (Basingstoke, UK: Palgrave Macmillan, 2002); Hope Harrison, *Driving the Soviets up the Wall: Soviet-East German Relations, 1953–1961* (Princeton, NJ: Princeton University Press, 2003); Manfred Wilke, *The Path to the Berlin Wall: Critical Stages in the History of Divided Germany*, trans. Sophie Perl (New York: Berghahn Books, 2014).
16. Mike Dennis, *The Rise and Fall of the German Democratic Republic, 1945–1990* (Harlow: Longman, 2000), 90–3, 101; Rudy Koshar, *German Travel Cultures* (Oxford: Berg, 2000), 176; Patrick Major, *Behind the Berlin Wall: East Germany and the Frontiers of Power* (Oxford: Oxford University Press, 2010).
17. Finney, *Palgrave Advances in International History*; Kenneth Osgood and Brian C. Etheridge, "The New International History Meets the New Cultural History: Public Diplomacy and U.S. Foreign Relations," in *The United States and Public Diplomacy: New Directions in Cultural and International History*, ed. Kenneth A. Osgood and Brian C. Etheridge (Leiden: Brill, 2010), 1–25; Thomas W. Zeiler, "The Diplomatic History Bandwagon: A State of the Field," *Journal of American History* 95, no. 4 (2009): 1053–73; Akira Iriye, "Internationalizing International History," in *Rethinking American History in a Global Age*, ed. Thomas Bender (Berkeley: University

of California Press, 2002), 47–62; Matthew Taylor, "Editorial Sport, Transnationalism, and Global History," *Journal of Global History* 8 (2013): 199–208; David L. Andrews and George Ritzer, "The Grobal in the Sporting Glocal," *Global Networks* 7, no. 2 (2007): 113–53; Souvik Naha, "'Over the Border and the Gates'?: Global and Transnational Sport," *Sport in Society* 20, no. 10 (2017): 1347–53.

18. Additional attempts to locate relevant documents in the Belgian foreign ministry archives resulted in frustratingly little material.

19. Jeanne A. K. Hey, ed., *Small States in World Politics: Explaining Foreign Policy Behavior* (Boulder: Lynne Rienner Publishers, 2003); Erich Reiter and Heinz Gärtner, eds., *Small States and Alliances* (Heidelberg: Physica-Verlag, 2001).

20. Rider, *Cold War Games*, 5.

21. Allen Guttmann, *The Games Must Go On: Avery Brundage and the Olympic Movement* (New York: Columbia University Press, 1984).

22. Garret Joseph Martin, *General de Gaulle's Cold War: Challenging American Hegemony 1963/1968* (New York: Berghahn Books, 2013); Frédéric Bozo, *French Foreign Policy since 1945: An Introduction*, trans. Jonathan Hensher (New York: Berghahn Books, 2016), 35.

23. Lindsay Sarah Krasnoff, "Resurrecting the Nation: The Evolution of French Sports Policy from de Gaulle to Mitterrand," in *Sport and the Transformation of Modern Europe*, 67–82, quote on p. 69.

24. Heather L. Dichter, "Denazification, Democratization, and the Cold War: Diplomatic Manipulation of the German Olympic Committee," in *Defending the American Way of Life*, 173–88; Heather L. Dichter, "The Diplomatic Turn: The New Relationship Between Sport and Politics," *International Journal of the History of Sport* 38, no. 2–3 (2021): 247–63, DOI: 10.1080/09523367.2021.1894135.

25. Adam Chapnick, "The Canadian Middle Power Myth," *International Journal* 55, no. 2 (2000): 188–206.

26. Janice Cavell and Ryan M. Touhey, eds., *Reassessing the Rogue Tory: Canadian Foreign Relations in the Diefenbaker Era* (Vancouver: University of British Columbia Press, 2018); Rhona Richman Kenneally and Johanne Sloan, eds., *Expo 67: Not Just a Souvenir* (Toronto: University of Toronto Press, 2010); Russell Field and Bruce Kidd, "Canada and the Pan-American Games," *International Journal of the History of Sport* 33, no. 1–2 (2016): 217–38.

27. Helge Pharo, "Post-Cold War Historiography in Norway," in *The Cold War—and the Nordic Countries: Historiography at a Crossroads*, ed. Torsten B. Olesen (Odense: University Press of Southern Denmark, 2004), 119–20.

28. NATO, "Political Committee," December 11, 2014, https://www.nato.int/cps/en/natohq/topics_115938.htm (accessed August 20, 2019).

29. Alan K. Henrikson, "Niche Diplomacy in the World Public Arena: The Global 'Corners' of Canada and Norway," in *The New Public Diplomacy: Soft Power in International Relations*, ed. Jan Melissen (Basingstoke, UK: Palgrave Macmillan, 2005), 68.

30. M. E. Sarotte, *Dealing with the Devil: East Germany, Détente, and Ostpolitik* (Chapel Hill: University of North Carolina Press, 2001), 2.

CHAPTER 1: TRAVEL RESTRICTIONS, STATE SYMBOLS, AND EAST GERMAN RECOGNITION IN SPORT

1. Heather L. Dichter, "Sporting Relations: Diplomacy, Small States, and Germany's Postwar Return to International Sport," *Diplomacy & Statecraft* 27, no. 2 (2016): 340–59.
2. Barbara Keys, *Globalizing Sport: National Rivalry and International Community in the 1930s* (Cambridge, MA: Harvard University Press, 2006), 158–80; Jenifer Parks, "Verbal Gymnastics: Sports, Bureaucracy, and the Soviet Union's Entrance into the Olympic Games, 1946–1952," in *East Plays West: Sport and the Cold War*, ed. Stephen Wagg and David L. Andrews (London: Routledge, 2007), 27–44; Heather L. Dichter, "'We Have Allowed Our Decisions to Be Determined by Political Considerations': The Cold War German Question in the International Ski Federation," *Sport in History* 37, no. 3 (2017): 290–308.
3. The one exception was in Saarland, whose athletes had their own Olympic team in 1956 as a result of French efforts to remove Saarland from Germany and make it part of France. Wolfgang Harres, *Sportpolitik an der Saar 1945–1955* (Saarbrücken: Saarbrücker Druckerei und Verlag, 1997).
4. Telegram, Otto Mayer to NOK DDR, February 10, 1952, D-RM01-ALLRD/014—Demande dereconnaissance—correspondance et statuts 1951–1962, Olympic Studies Centre, Lausanne (hereafter OSC); J.S. Edström, Decision of the Executive Committee of the International Olympic Committee Regarding the German Situation, February 11, 1952, Executive Commission, Oslo, February 11, 1952, box 90, reel 49, Avery Brundage Collection (ABC), University of Illinois Archives, Champaign, Illinois (hereafter UIA).
5. Uta A. Balbier, *Kalter Krieg auf der Aschenbahn: der deutsch-deutsche Sport, 1950–1972: eine politische Geschichte* (Paderborn: F. Schöning, 2007).
6. Letter, Avery Brundage to Arnold Bittner, August 7, 1962, Nationales Olympisches Komitee fur Deutschland 1945–1952, box 127, reel 70, ABC, UIA.
7. Konrad Adenauer, *Memoirs 1945–53*, trans. Beate Ruhm von Oppen (London: Weidenfeld and Nicolson, 1966), 183; Elmer Plischke, *The Allied High Commission for Germany* (n.p.: Historical Division, Office of the Executive Secretary, Office of the U.S. High Commissioner for Germany, 1953), 16; Dennis L. Bark and David R. Gress, *A History of West Germany*, vol. 1, *From Shadow to Substance, 1945–1963* (Oxford: Basil Blackwell, 1989), 149–50.
8. AC/52-R/33: Committee of Information and Cultural Relations Summary Record of a meeting held at the Palais de Chaillot, Paris, on Thursday, 5th May, 1955, May 10, 1955, North Atlantic Treaty Organization, Brussels, Belgium (hereafter NATO).
9. "Türkei verweigerte Einreise," *Neues Deutschland*, May 28, 1957, 6.
10. C-R(54)26: Summary Record of a meeting of the Council held at the Palais de Chaillot, Paris, on Wednesday, 23rd June, 25 June 1954, NATO; C-M(54)37: Soviet Grant of "Full Sovereignty" to the East Zone of Germany, June 25, 1954, NATO.
11. William Glenn Gray, *Germany's Cold War: The Global Campaign to Isolate East Germany, 1949–1969* (Chapel Hill: University of North Carolina Press, 2003); Bark and Gress, *History of West Germany*, 374.

12. Bark and Gress, *History of West Germany*, 332, 249.
13. Bark and Gress, *History of West Germany*, 198–214; Lucius D. Clay, *Decision in Germany* (Garden City, NY: Doubleday & Company, 1950), 355–67.
14. Bark and Gress, *History of West Germany*, 435–40.
15. AC/119-R(58)12: Committee of Political Advisers Meeting of the Committee held on Tuesday, 1st April, 1958 Action Sheet, April 2, 1958, NATO.
16. FIFA Minutes of the XXVIIth Congress, Helsinki, 24–26 July 1952, 25th—27th Ordinary Congress, 1946–1952 Activity Report Minutes, FIFA Archives, Zurich, Switzerland (hereafter FIFA).
17. Dichter, "We Have Allowed Our Decisions."
18. Letter, E. J. H. Holt to Max Danz, September 6, 1950, Germany, International Association of Athletics Federations, Monaco (hereafter IAAF); letter, E. J. H. Holt to President or General Secretary, Deutscher Sportausschuss, April 27, 1951, German Democratic Republic, IAAF.
19. Letter, Lord Burghley to Max Danz, September 30, 1955, F.R. Germany, IAAF.
20. Minutes of the Ordinary Congress of the Federation Internationale des Societes d'Aviron, August 23, 1955, Congres PV 1951–1959, Fédération Internationale des Sociétés d'Aviron, Lausanne, Switzerland (hereafter FISA); Procès-verbal du Congrès extraordinaire de la Fédération Internationale des Sociétés d'Aviron, November 13, 1965, Congres PV 1960–1966, FISA.
21. H. D. Thoreau to Messrs. Boyum, Broomhall, Mullin, Palmedo, Raaum, Ruschp, and Schaeffler, May 5, 1959, box 2, folder 24, John Stanley Mullin (JSM) papers, Rauner Special Collections Library, Dartmouth College, Hanover, New Hampshire (hereafter RSCL).
22. Letter, John Stanley Mullin to Alton C. Melville, July 1, 1959, box 2, folder 23, JSM, RSCL; "East Germans Miss Squaw Ski Meet," *Pasadena Independent*, February 16, 1959, 13.
23. Letter, Alton C. Melville to Alfred G. Vidgerman, January 30, 1959, RG 59, CDF 1955–59/800.453, box 4062, NA.
24. Telegram 483, Dillon, Department of State to Berlin, February 6, 1959, RG 59, CDF 1955–59/800.453, box 4062, NA.
25. Telegram 711, Gufler, Berlin to Secretary of State, February 18, 1959, RG 59, CDF 1955–59/800.453, box 4062, NA; Airgram G-301, Gufler, Berlin to Secretary of State and Bonn Embassy, February 21, 1959, RG 59, CDF 1955–59/800.453, box 4062, NA.
26. "USA und Olympia," *Neues Deutschland*, February 18, 1959, 1.
27. Telegram 713, Gufler, Berlin to Secretary of State, February 18, 1959, RG 59, CDF 1955–59/800.453, box 4062, NA; Airgram G-306, Gufler, Berlin to Secretary of State and Bonn Embassy, February 26, 1959, RG 59, CDF 1955–59/800.453, box 4062, NA.
28. Michael Strauss, "Soviet Squad to Ski in U.S.," *New York Times*, January 31, 1959, 17; "Russians to Get Visas," *New York Times*, February 6, 1959, 32.
29. Joseph M. Turrini, "'It Was Communism versus the Free World': The USA-USSR Dual Track Meet Series and the Development of Track and Field in the United States, 1958–1985," *Journal of Sport History* 28, no. 3 (2001): 429.
30. Letter, John Stanley Mullin to Alton C. Melville, July 1, 1959.

31. Sandra Heck, "A Sport for Everyone? Inclusion and Exclusion in the Organisation of the First Olympic Modern Pentathlon," *International Journal of the History of Sport* 31, no. 5 (2014): 526–41.
32. Memorandum of Telephone Conversation, February 2, 1959, RG 59, CDF 1955–59/800.453, box 4062, NA; Union International du Pentathlon Moderne Procès-Verbal du Congrès du 16. october 1958 à Sandhurst, Angleterre, October 16, 1958, CIO FI-PENTA-UIPM-CORR Union International du Pentathlon Moderne (UIPM) Correspondance Bureau Exécutif 1928–1959, OSC.
33. Letter, R. V. Lee to McKiernan, April 7, 1959, RG 59, CDF 1955–59/800.453, box 4062, NA.
34. Letter, Alfred Vidgerman to Robert Lee, April 13, 1959, RG 59, CDF 1955–59/800.453, box 4062, NA.
35. Letter, Jack W. Bernheim to Sven Thofelt, April 16, 1959, Stiftung Archive der Parteien und Massenorganisationen der DDR (SAPMO) DY 12/2172, Bundesarchiv, Berlin, Germany (hereafter BArchB); Letter, Wm. C. Rose to Sven Thofelt, April 21, 1959, SAPMO DY 12/2172, BArchB. Both documents are also contained in the annexes of the minutes from the 1959 UIPM Congress: Union International du Pentathlon Moderne Procès-Verbal du Congrès du 24. septembre 1959 à Hershey, Etats-Unis, September 24, 1959, CIO FI-PENTA-UIPM-CGR Union International du Pentathlon Moderne (UIPM) Congresses 1949–1959, OSC.
36. Letter, G. Dyrssen and Sven Thofelt to M. Mueller, June 10, 1959, SAPMO DY 12/2174, BArchB.
37. Heilmeier, Aktennotiz, September 10, 1959, SAPMO DR 5/913, BArchB; Letter, Sven Thofelt to Rose, August 29, 1959, SAPMO DY 12/2172, BArchB.
38. Union International du Pentathlon Moderne Procès-Verbal du Congrès du 24. septembre 1959 à Hershey, Etats-Unis, September 24, 1959, CIO FI-PENTA-UIPM-CGR Union International du Pentathlon Moderne (UIPM) Congresses 1949–1959, OSC.
39. Telegram 2787, Zellerbach, Rome to Secretary of State, February 5, 1960, RG 59, CDF1960–63/800.4531, box 2239, NA; Telegram 2495, Herter, Department of State to AmEmbassy Rome, February 11, 1960, RG 59, CDF 1960–63/800.4531, box 2239, NA.
40. Telegram 615, Lightner, Berlin to Secretary of State, February 4, 1960, RG 59, CDF 1960–63/800.4531, box 2239, NA.
41. AC/119-WP(60)25: Efforts of the Soviet Zone of Germany to Obtain International Recognition, March 9, 1960, NATO.
42. Despatch 549, Howard Trivers, Berlin to Department of State, March 7, 1960, RG 59, CDF 1960–63/800.4531, box 2239, NA.
43. AC/119-WP(60)26: Policy Towards Visitors from East Germany, March 9, 1960, NATO.
44. AC/119-R(60)14: Committee of Political Advisers Meeting held on 12th April, 1960 Action Sheet, April 13, 1960, NATO; Letter, J. S. H. Shattock, NATO Paris to J. E. Killick, Foreign Office, April 13, 1960, FO 371/154257, TNA.
45. Telegram 864, Bonn to Foreign Office, September 10, 1960, FO 371/154259, TNA; Telegram 3781–84, Courson, Bonn to Diplomatie Paris, September 10, 1960, 105PO/1, box 10, Centre des Archives diplomatiques de Nantes, Nantes, France (hereafter CADN); Telegram 899, Bonn to Foreign Office, September 15, 1960, FO 371/154260, TNA.

46. Letter 394, Helge Groth, Berlin to Utenriksdepartement, September 14, 1960, 18.1/74 Öst-tyske innreisebestemmelser. Bind IV (1/1-60-31/12–60), Utenriksdepartement, Oslo, Norway (hereafter UD).
47. Telegram 867, Bonn to Foreign Office, September 11, 1960, FO 371/154259, TNA.
48. Telegrams 935 and 936, Bonn to Foreign Office, September 23, 1960, FO 371/154260, TNA.
49. AC/119-WP(59)112: Internal and External Situation of the Soviet Occupied Zone, October 27, 1959, NATO; Margarete Myers Feinstein, *State Symbols: The Quest for Legitimacy in the Federal Republic of Germany and the German Democratic Republic, 1949–1959* (Boston: Brill, 2001), 40–51.
50. AC/119-WP(60)3: New Flag of the Soviet Occupied Zone of Germany, January 13, 1960, NATO.
51. For example, the flag also became a problem for shipping, particularly up the Elbe to Hamburg and in the Baltic. Letter 6617, Permanent Delegation of Canada to the North Atlantic Council and the OEEC to Under-Secretary of State for External Affairs, November 5, 1959, RG 25, 4850 50105-G-40 File Part 7, Library and Archives Canada, Ottawa, Ontario (hereafter LAC).
52. Letter, Karl Ritter von Halt and Willi Daume to Avery Brundage, November 27, 1959, D-RM01-ALLEM/005—Equipe unifée allemande aux JO: correspondance et PV 1950–1961, OSC.
53. Sydney Gruson, "Reds' Flag Snags Bonn Olympics Bid," *New York Times*, November 23, 1959, 7.
54. Letter, Karl Ritter von Halt and Willi Daume to Avery Brundage, November 27, 1959.
55. Letter, Karl Ritter von Halt and Willi Daume to Avery Brundage, November 27, 1959.
56. "IOC-Kanzler Otto Mayer: Anerkennen oder zu Hause bleiben!" *Neues Deutschland*, November 25, 1959, 2.
57. Letter, Karl Ritter von Halt and Willi Daume to Avery Brundage, November 27, 1959.
58. "A German Flag Set for Olympics," *New York Times*, December 7, 1959, 3; Telegram, Karl Ritter von Halt to Avery Brundage, December 8, 1959, Halt, Dr. Karl Ritter von, 1956–1964, box 57, reel 34, ABC, UIA.
59. Letter, Avery Brundage to to Nationales Olympisches Komitee der Deutschen Demokratischen Republik and Nationales Olympisches Komitee for Deutschland, January 5, 1960, German Question—W. Germany & E. Germany 1945–1969, box 129, reel 71, ABC, UIA.
60. "The German Flag Controversy," *New York Times*, December 13, 1959, E2.
61. *Neues Deutschland*, November 25, 1959, 2.
62. Telegram 699, Guenyveau, Berlin to Ambafrance Bonn, October 19, 1959, 105PO/1, box 9, CADN.
63. Telegram 3288–89, François Seydoux, Bonn to Diplomatie Paris, November 16, 1959, 105PO/1, box 9, CADN; Compte-Rendu de la réunion quadripartite, November 25, 1959, 178QO/1228, Centre des Archives diplomatiques de La Courneuve, Paris, France (hereafter CADC).

64. Telegram 3151, François Seydoux, Bonn to MAE, November 6, 1959, 179QO/14, CADC.
65. "DDR-Flagge wehte in Paris," *Neues Deutschland*, November 11, 1959, 5; Telegram 739–40, Chalvron, Berlin to Bonn, November 12, 1959, 105PO/1, box 9, CADN; Despatch No. 475/EU, Chalvron, Berlin to MAE, November 13, 1959, 179QO/14, CADC; Telegram 5061–62, Diplomatie Paris to Bonn, November 14, 1959, 105PO/1, box 9, CADN; Memo, External Department, British Military Government, Berlin to Chancery, British Embassy, Bonn, November 16, 1959, FO 371/146107, TNA.
66. Despatch, Ministre des Affaires Etrangères to Ministre de l'Interieur, November 26, 1959, 105PO/1, box 9, CADN; Letter 3112, Maurice Herzog to Ministre des Affaires Etrangères—Direction générale politique EUROPE Service d'Europe centrale, December 1, 1959, 105PO/1, box 9, CADN.
67. Letter, R. F. Stretton, Bonn to W. J. A. Wilberforce, Foreign Office, November 10, 1959, FO 371/146107, TNA.
68. AC/119-WP(60)3: New Flag of the Soviet Occupied Zone of Germany, January 13, 1960, NATO.
69. "Eine gute Lehre für 1960," *Neues Deutschland*, December 28, 1959, 5; Feinstein, *State Symbols*, 51.
70. Letter, R. F. Stretton, Bonn to W. J. A. Wilberforce, Foreign Office, November 27, 1959, FO 371/146107, TNA.
71. Despatch 774, H. G. Torbert, Jr., Rome to Department of State, February 19, 1960, RG 59, CDF 1960–63/800.4531, box 2239, NA.
72. AC/119-WP(60)39: Developments in the Soviet-Occupied Zone of Germany since Autumn 1959, April 7, 1960, NATO.
73. Telegram 358, Trimble, Bonn to Secretary of State, August 7, 1958, RG 59, CDF 1955–59/800.4531, box 4062, NA; Quadripartite minutes, August 6, 1958, 178QO/1228, CADC.
74. Letter, Dr. Weber, Auswärtiges Amt to London, August 5, 1958, B 94/636, Politisches Archiv des Auswärtiges Amt, Berlin, Germany (hereafter PAdAA); Letter, A. C. Buxton, Bonn to J. K. Drinkall, Foreign Office, August 7, 1958, FO 371/137611, TNA.
75. Letter, Dr. Weber, Auswärtiges Amt to Stockholm, August 5, 1958, B 94/636, PAdAA.
76. Letter, M. E. Heath, Copenhagen to J. M. O. Snodgrass, Foreign Office, August 15, 1958, FO 371/137611, TNA.
77. Telegram 358, Trimble, Bonn to Secretary of State, August 7, 1958; Telegram 395, Bruce, Bonn to Secretary of State, August 12, 1958, RG 59, CDF 1955–59/800.4531, box 4062, NA; Telegram 164, Herter, Department of State to Stockholm Embassy, August 13, 1958, RG 59, CDF 1955–59/800.4531, box 4062, NA.
78. Fernschreiben 88, Bethmann, Stockholm to Auswärtig Bonn, August 18, 1958, B 94/636, PAdAA; Letter, J. R. Rich, Stockholm to J. M. O. Snodgrass, Foreign Office, August 23, 1958, FO 371/137611, TNA; Letter, Siegried, Stockholm to Auswärtiges Amt, August 27, 1958, B 94/636, PAdAA.
79. Letter, Stockholm to Auswärtiges Amt, December 20, 1960, B 94/175, PAdAA.
80. Letter, Dr. Meyer-Berkhout, Gothenburg to Auswärtiges Amt, January 3, 1961, B

94/175, PAdAA; Letter, Dr. Mayer-Berkhout, Gothenburg to Auswärtiges Amt, February 7, 1961, B 94/175, PAdAA.

81. Despatch 183, Paul H. Pearson, Gothenburg to Department of State, February 17, 1961, RG 59, Department of State CDF 1960–63/800.453, box 2239, NA; Telegram 1, Meyer-Berkhout, Gothenburg to Auswärtiges Amt, February 18, 1961, B 94/175, PAdAA.

82. Despatch 82/EU, Guenyveau, Berlin to Ministre des Affaires Etrangères, February 20, 1961, 105PO/1, box 9, CADN; Letter, Alfons Fritz to Veranstalter der Weltmeisterschaften im Eisschnellaufen Svenska Skidskoförbundet och Göteborge Skiridskoallians, February 18, 1961, B 94/175, PAdAA; Alfons Fritz, Aktennotiz, February 20, 1961, B 94/175, PAdAA; Dr. Meyer-Berkhout, Gothenburg to Auswärtiges Amt, February 20, 1961, B 94/175, PAdAA; Despatch 704, G. Alonzo Stanford, Stockholm to Department of State, February 21, 1961, RG 59, CDF 1960–63/800.453, box 2239, NA.

83. "Östtyska flaggen Är med i VM Västtyskland hotar lämma Ullevi Rapport till Bonn," *Göteborgs-Tidningen*, February 18, 1961, 1 in B 94/175, PAdAA.

84. "Bonner Flaggenstürmer abgeblitzt," *Neues Deutschland*, February 19, 1961, 1.

85. Fernschreiben, Willi Daume to Dr. Heinrich von Brentano, February 22, 1961, B 94/176, PAdAA.

86. Äusserung des Regierungspreschers auf Presse-Anfrage, March 1, 1961, B 94/176, PAdAA.

87. Fernschreiben, Willi Daume to Dr. Heinrich von Brentano, February 22, 1961; Letter, Willi Daume to Dr. Gerhard Schröder, February 23, 1961, B 94/176, PAdAA; Dr. Sattler, Aufzeichnung für Herrn Dr. Lüders, March 4, 1961, B 94/176, PAdAA; Despatch 118/EU, Chalvron, Berlin to Ministre des Affaires Etrangères, March 9, 1961, 105PO/1, box 9, CADN; Telegram 389–92, Chalvron, Berlin to Ambafrance Bonn, March 13, 1961, 105PO/1, box 9, CADN.

88. Dr. Janz, Aufzeichnung, March 7, 1961, B 94/176, PadAA; "Das Ultimatum des Eishockey-Weltverbandes," *Frankfurter Allgemeine Zeitung*, March 13, 1961, 5.

89. Horst Eckert and Ernst Martini, *90: IIHF 90th Anniversary, 1908–1998* (Zürich: IIHF, 1998), 119–20; "Hallstein Doktrin bringt Niederlage," *Neues Deutschland*, March 13, 1961, 1; Minutes, Emergency Meeting at the 45th Annual Congress of the IIHF, Geneva, March 1961, *LIGH/IIHF Procès Verbaux/Minutes, 1955–1963*, International Ice Hockey Federation, Zürich, Switzerland (hereafter IIHF); Telegram 389–92, Chalvron, Berlin to Ambafrance Bonn, March 13, 1961.

90. "Västtyskar lämnade w.o. 'Flaggstrid,'" *Svenska dagbladet*, March 13, 1961, 1.

91. "Politics Harass German Sport," *Times* (London), March 15, 1961, 11.

92. Fernschreiben 16, Mohr, Bern to Auswärtiges Amt, March 16, 1961, B 94/176, PAdAA.

93. Robert Daley, "Case against Post-Game Anthems," *New York Times*, March 14, 1961, 42.

94. Presseverlautbarung, March 13, 1961, B 94/176, PAdAA.

95. "Hallstein Doktrin bringt Niederlage."

96. "Eishockeypräsident Lebel, Kanada: ‚Schande für unseren Sport!'," *Neues Deutschland*, March 14, 1961, 1.

97. Telegram 389–92, Chalvron, Berlin to Ambafrance Bonn, March 13, 1961.

98. Airgram POLTO G-1536, Finletter, USRO Paris to SecState, March 29, 1961, RG 59, CDF 1960–63/862.181, box 2644, NA.

99. Telegram 960–961, François Seydoux, Bonn to Diplomatie Paris, March 2, 1961, 105PO/1, box 10, CADN; POLAD(61)11: Restriction on travel of residents of East Germany, March 3, 1961, NATO.
100. Heather L. Dichter, "'Football More Important than Berlin': East German Football vs. NATO," in *Soccer Diplomacy: International Relations and Football since 1914*, ed. Heather Dichter (Lexington: University Press of Kentucky, 2020), 116–37.
101. Airgram, POLTO G-1399, Wolf, USRO Paris to SecState, March 10, 1961, RG 59, CDF 1960–63/862.181, box 2644, NA.
102. AC/119-R(61)9: Committee of Political Advisers Meeting held on 7th March, 1961 Action Sheet, March 10, 1961, NATO.
103. AC/119-R(61)10: Committee of Political Advisers Meeting held on 14th March, 1961 Action Sheet, March 17, 1961, NATO.
104. Letter 839, Erik Lykke, NATO Paris to Utenriksdepartement, March 22, 1961, 18.1/74: Öst-tyske innereisebestemmelser. Bind VI. 1/3-61-31/12–61, UD; AC/119-R(61)11: Committee of Political Advisers Meeting held on 21st March, 1961 Action Sheet, March 24, 1961, NATO.
105. Letter 138, Helge Groth, Berlin to Utenriksdepartement, March 16, 1961, 18.1/74: Öst-tyske innereisebestemmelser. Bind VI. 1/3-61-31/12–61, UD; Airgram G-354, Lightner, Berlin to Secretary of State, March 17, 1961, RG 59, CDF 1960–63/862.181, box 2644, NA.
106. Arne Arnesen, Notat: Vest-allierte reiserestriksjoner og östtyske ishockey-spillere, May 29, 1961, 18.1/74: Öst-tyske innereisebestemmelser. Bind VI. 1/3-61-31/12–61, UD.
107. Arne Arnesen, Notat: Vest-allierte reiserestriksjoner og östtyske ishockey-spillere, May 29, 1961.
108. Circular CG-845, Rusk, Department of State to AmEmbassy Bonn, April 4, 1961, RG 59, CDF 1960–63/862.181, box 2644, NA.
109. Telegram G-289, Freeman, Brussels to Secretary of State, April 9, 1961, RG 59, CDF 1960–63/855.181, box 2598, NA.
110. AC/119-WP(61)22: Restrictions on travel by East German Residents, March 23, 1961, NATO.

CHAPTER 2: THE BERLIN WALL AND THE ENDING OF FREE TRAVEL IN SPORT

1. Dennis L. Bark and David R. Gress, *A History of West Germany*, vol. 1, *From Shadow to Substance, 1945–1963* (Oxford: Basil Blackwell, 1989), 468; Patrick Major, *Behind the Berlin Wall: East Germany and the Frontiers of Power* (Oxford: Oxford University Press, 2010).
2. H. Passlack, Deutscher Fußball-Bund to FIFA, 1 September 1961, Correspondence with National Associations GER (FRG) 1955–1961, FIFA; Statement of the Presidium of the NOC [National Olympic Committee] of the German Democratic Republic, August 19, 1961, Republique Democratique Allemagne, Correspondance 1951–1962, OSC.
3. Statement of the Presidium of the NOC of the German Democratic Republic, August 19, 1961.

4. Telegram 192, Lightner, Berlin to Secretary of State, August 14, 1961, RG 59, CDF 1960–63/862.181, box 2644, NA; C-R(61)40: Summary Record of a Restricted meeting of the Council held at the Permanent Headquarters, Paris, 31 August 1961, September 13, 1961, NATO.
5. Heather L. Dichter, "'We Have Allowed Our Decisions to Be Determined by Political Considerations': The Cold War German Question in the International Ski Federation," *Sport in History* 37, no. 3 (2017): 290–308.
6. Letter, John Stanley Mullin to Alton C. Melville, July 1, 1959, box 2, folder 23, JSM, RSCL.
7. Raymond Marcillac, "Des Raisons d'espérer pour le Sport Français," *Le Monde*, January 3, 1962, 9.
8. Telegram 3673, Gavin, Paris to Secretary of State, January 30, 1962, RG 59, CDF 1960–63/800.453, box 2239, NA; "European Officials Willing to Cancel Title Skiing," *New York Times*, February 2, 1962, 34; Telegram 3707, Gavin, Paris to Secretary of State, February 3, 1962, RG 59, CDF 1960–63/800.453, box 2239, NA; Indications donees a Monsieur Cazaux President de la Federation Francaise de Ski a propose de la reunion de Comite Directeur de la Federation Internationale de Ski a Berne le Dimanche 4 fevrier, February 2, 1962, AG/5(1)/1540, Archives Nationales, Pierrefitte-sur-Seine, France (hereafter ANP).
9. Letter N-128, R. L. Rogers, NATO Paris to Under-Secretary of State for External Affairs, January 31, 1962, RG 25, 6081 50341-C-40 File Part 1.1, LAC.
10. Telegram 310, Washington to Foreign Office, February 3, 1962, FO 371/163681, TNA; Telegram 477, Rusk, Department of State to AmEmbassy Bern, February 2, 1962, RG 59, CDF 1960–63/800.453, box 2239, NA; Holz, Notiz, February 3, 1962, B 94/212, PAdAA.
11. Protocol of the Meeting of the International Ski Federation, February 4, 1962, box 3, folder 5, JSM, RSCL.
12. Protocol of the Meeting of the International Ski Federation, February 4, 1962; Per Vennemoe, Notat: Reiserestriksjonere for østtyske idrettsfolk, February 12, 1962, 18.1/74 Öst-tyske innreisebestemmelser. Bind VII (1/1.62–31/3.62), UD. Mullin did not attend the extraordinary meeting, but he cabled his vote from California. Telegram, John Stanley Mullin to Marc Hodler, February 2, 1962, box 3, folder 3, JSM, RSCL.
13. Protocol of the Meeting of the International Ski Federation, February 4, 1962; Telegram, Marc Hodler to Harold MacMillan, February 5, 1962, FO 371/163681, TNA.
14. Telegram, Marc Hodler to John F. Kennedy, February 2, 1962, RG 59, CDF 1960–63/851.453, box 2557, NA; Telegram 479, Rusk, Department of State to AmEmbassy Bern, February 6, 1962, RG 59, CDF 1960–63/851.453, box 2557, NA.
15. "World Ski Championships Appear to Be Doomed," *Lethbridge (AB) Herald*, February 5, 1962, 6.
16. "Verdensleker istedenfor VM i Chamonix," *Aftenposten*, February 6, 1962, 13; "Si les skieurs de l'allemagne de l'est," *Le Monde*, February 6, 1962, 8; "Der Kalte Krieg im Sport," *Süddeutsche Zeitung*, February 6, 1962, 2; "Keine Weltmeisterschaften!" *Neues Deutschland*, February 6, 1962, 6; "Halbwertige Weltmeisterschaften," *Neue Zürcher Zeitung*, February 7, 1962, 4.

17. "Der Kalte Krieg im Sport." The same quote appeared in other West German papers. "Ein Sportultimatum an die freie Welt," *Frankfurter Allgemeine Zeitung*, February 6, 1962, 8.
18. "Keine Weltmeisterschaften!"
19. Telegram 479, Rusk, Department of State to AmEmbassy Bern, February 6, 1962; Telegram 411, McKinney, Bern to Secretary of State, February 14, 1962, RG 59, CDF 1960–63 / 800.453, box 2239, NA; Telegram 766, Alphand, Washington to Diplomatie Paris, February 5, 1962, 179Q / 74, CADC.
20. "Les championnats du monde deviendront-ils les jeux mondiaux de la F.I.S.," *Le Monde*, February 7, 1962, 8; "Soviet Union-Rumania Walkout Mars Chamonix Non-title Skiing," *New York Times*, February 7, 1962, 61.
21. "Climate Right for Skiers," *Times* (London), February 7, 1962, 4; "Bozon First in Slalom," *Times* (London), February 14, 1962, 4.
22. "Climate Right for Skiers"; "Bigger British Ski Team Chosen," *Times* (London), February 8, 1962, 5.
23. Robert Daley, "Politics: A Threat to World Sports," *New York Times*, February 13, 1962, 42.
24. Telegram 664–70, François Seydoux, Bonn to Diplomatie Paris, February 2, 1962, 105PO / 1, box 10, CADN.
25. Telegram 3707, Gavin, Paris to Secretary of State, February 3, 1962, RG 59, CDF 1960–63 / 800.453, box 2239, NA.
26. Telegram 486 / 488, Greyveau, Berlin to Ambafrance Bonn, February 5, 1962, 179Q / 74, CADC.
27. "Ski Tourney Name Changed," *Lowell (MA) Sun*, February 6, 1962, 10.
28. Official Statement by the Presidency of the International Ski Federation, February 15, 1962, box 3, folder 5, JSM, RSCL.
29. Letter, John Stanley Mullin to Merritt H. Stiles, April 24, 1962, box 3, folder 3, JSM, RSCL.
30. R. M., "Ski Nordique et Ski Alpin," *Le Monde*, February 8, 1962, 8.
31. Airgram CA-684, Rusk, Department of State to USBER Berlin, December 19, 1961, RG 59, CDF 1960–63 / 800.453, box 2239, NA.
32. William J. Briordy, "Field of 18 Listed in World Hockey," *New York Times*, December 19, 1961, 44; "World Hockey Tournament Schedule of Games Set," *Colorado Springs Gazette*, December 19, 1961, 18.
33. Airgram A-476, Thompson, Moscow to Secretary of State, December 22, 1961, RG 59, CDF 1960–63 / 800.453, box 2239, NA.
34. Al Colletti, "Officials Hope to Bar Cold War from Rockies," *Winnipeg Free Press*, December 19, 1962, 25.
35. Airgram CA-684, Rusk, Department of State to USBER Berlin, December 19, 1961.
36. Airgram CA-684, Rusk, Department of State to USBER Berlin, December 19, 1961.
37. Airgram CA-684, Rusk, Department of State to USBER Berlin, December 19, 1961.
38. Airgram A-311, Lightner, Berlin to SecState Washington, December 29, 1961, RG 59, CDF 1960–63 / 800.453, box 2239, NA.
39. Telegram 41–44, Chalvron, Berlin to Ambafrance Bonn, January 3, 1962, 179QO / 74, CADC.

40. Telegram 43/44, Courson, Bonn to Berlin, January 4, 1962, 179QO/74, CADC.
41. Airgram A-326, Lightner, Berlin to SecState Washington and AmEmbassy Bonn, January 5, 1962, RG 59, CDF 1960–63/800.453, box 2239, NA.
42. Telegram 903, Rusk, Department of State to USBER Berlin, January 11, 1962, RG 59, CDF 1960–63/800.453, box 2239, NA.
43. Numbered Letter 17, A. Kingsley Graham, Stockholm to Under-Secretary of State for External Affairs, January 8, 1962, RG 25, 6081 50341-C-40 File Part 1.1, LAC.
44. Telefongespräch am 24.1. mit Jochen Grünwald aus Genf, January 24, 1962, SAPMO DY 12/2051, BArchB; Aktennotiz über das Telefongespräch am 25.1.1962, January 25, 1962, SAPMO DY 12/2051, BArchB; Bericht über die außerordentliche Sitzung des Europa-Exekutivkomites der Internationalen Eishockey-Föderation vom 23.–25. 1. 62, January 30, 1962, SAPMO DY 12/2051, BArchB.
45. "Visa Problems Plague East German Pucksters," *Lowell (MA) Sun*, January 11, 1962, 24.
46. "Hockey Games in Springs, Federation President Says," *Greeley (CO) Daily Tribune*, January 26, 1962, 12.
47. "Hockey Championships Site Still Undecided Wednesday," *Greeley (CO) Daily Tribune*, January 25, 1962, 18; "Situation Unsettled As Visa Problem Arises: May Hold World Hockey In Calgary or Edmonton," *Lethbridge (AB) Herald*, January 25, 1962, 7.
48. Letter S-22, External Ottawa to Washington, January 25, 1962, RG 25, 6081 50341-C-40 File Part 1.1, LAC.
49. Statement of Department of State Press Officer on January 26 Regarding Visa Applications by East German Hockey Players, January 29, 1962, FO 371/163681, TNA; Telegram 963, Ball, Department of State to USBER Berlin, January 26, 1962, RG 59, CDF 1960–63/800.453, box 2239, NA.
50. TOPOL 1077, Department of State to Paris, January 29, 1962, RG 59, CDF 1960–63/862.181, box 2645, NA; Telegram 267, Washington DC to External, January 30, 1962, RG 25, 6081 50341-C-40 File Part 1.1, LAC; Max Frankel, "West Bars East Germans in Retaliation for the Wall," *New York Times*, January 27, 1962, 1.
51. Telegram 240, NATO Paris to External, January 30, 1962, RG 25, 6081 50341-C-40 File Part 1.1, LAC.
52. C-R(62)10: Summary record of a meeting of the Council held at the Permanent Headquarters, Paris, on Wednesday, 7 March 1962, March 10, 1962, NATO; Letter, A. E. Donald, NATO Paris to W. J. A. Wilberforce, Foreign Office, January 31, 1962, FO 371/163681, TNA.
53. MEMO(62)2: Publicity aspects of NATO policy on restrictions on travel by East German Citizens, January 31, 1962, 18.1/74 Öst-tyske innreisebestemmelser. Bind VII Fra 1/1.62 31/3.62, UD.
54. Telegram, Robert LeBel to Deutscher Eislauf-Verband, February 2, 1962, SAPMO DY 12/2051, BArchB.
55. "Visa Problems Plague East German Pucksters," *Lowell (MA) Sun*, January 11, 1962, 24; Telegram, Ahearne to Deutscher Eislauf-Verband, February 3, 1962, SAPMO DY 12/2051, BArchB; Minutes of the 46th Annual Congress of the I.I.H.F., March 7–13, 1962, *LIGH/IIHF Procès Verbaux/Minutes, 1955–1963*, IIHF.
56. "The Anti-Red Line," *Toronto Globe & Mail*, February 2, 1962, 6. Newspaper clipping of political cartoon also contained in RG 25, 6081 50341-C-40 File Part 1.1, LAC.

57. Airgram A-438, Lightner, Berlin to SecState Washington, February 11, 1962, RG 59, CDF 1960–63/800.453, box 2239, NA.
58. Letter, Robert LeBel to President Kennedy, February 20, 1962, RG 25, 6081 50341-C-40 File Part 1.2, LAC; Letter, Robert LeBel to John Diefenbaker, February 20, 1962, RG 25, 6081 50341-C-40 File Part 1.2, LAC; Memorandum for the Prime Minister, March 2, 1962, RG 25, 6081 50341-C-40 File Part 1.2, LAC.
59. Telegram 386/388, Chalvron, Berlin to Ambafrance Bonn, January 30, 1962, 179QO/74, CADC.
60. "Plans for World Hockey Play in Springs Continue," *Greeley (CO) Daily Tribune,* January 30, 1962, 12; "If Germans Kept Out: Soviets, Czechs Won't Play in United States," *Lethbridge (AB) Herald,* January 30, 1962, 6; "?" *Aftenposten*, January 31, 1962, 11; "Was wird aus der Eishockey-Weltmeisterschaft?" *Neues Deutschland*, January 26, 1962, 8; "Skiweltmeisterschaften fraglich," *Süddeutsche Zeitung*, February 1, 1962, 2; "Norge til Colorado Springs selv om turneringen ikke går som VM," *Arbeiderbladet*, February 7, 1962, 14.
61. Telegram 386/388, Chalvron, Berlin to Ambafrance Bonn, January 30, 1962, 179QO/74, CADC.
62. Telegram 1439, Lightner, Berlin to Secretary of State, February 5, 1962, RG 59, CDF 1960–63/800.453, box 2239, NA.
63. Heinze, Aktennotiz überein Telefongrspräch mit dem Genossen Alfred Neumann aus Moskau am 7.2.1962 um 16.45 Uhr, February 7, 1962, SAPMO DY 12/2051, BArchB.
64. "Revised Hockey Draw Will Omit Five Nations," *New York Times,* February 20, 1962, 42; Horst Eckert and Ernst Martini, *90: IIHF 90th Anniversary, 1908–1998* (Zürich: IIHF, 1998), 121, 259.
65. "Was wird aus der Eishockey-Weltmeisterschaft?" *Neues Deutschland,* January 26, 1962, 8; "Diskriminierung verurteilt," *Neues Deutschland,* March 11, 1962, 8.
66. "Revised Hockey Draw Will Omit Five Nations," 42; "Eishockey wie geplannt," *Frankfurter Allgemeine Zeitung,* January 31, 1962, 6; Eckert and Martini, *90: IIHF*, 121, 259.
67. Letter, Willi Daume to Dr. D. Sattler, February 19, 1962, B 94/212, PAdAA; Nachstehend wird ein Auszug aus dem Kurzprotokoll über die Konsultationsbesprechung, February 14, 1962, B 94/212, PAdAA.
68. Airgram A-562, Lightner, Berlin to SecState Washington and AmEmbassy Bonn, March 29, 1962, RG 59, box 2239, CDF 1960–63/800.453, NA.
69. Airgram A-728, Lightner, Berlin to Department of State, June 22, 1962, RG 59, box 2239, CDF 1960–63/800.453, NA.
70. Larry Osius, "Reds Looking to Future: Russians Develop New Mat Stars," *Lawton (OK) Constitution*, June 20, 1962, 22.
71. Airgram A-733, Lightner, Berlin to Department of State, June 28, 1962, RG 59, box 2645, CDF 1960–63/862.181, NA; "Ringergegen Diskriminierung," *Neues Deutschland*, June 26, 1962, 6.
72. "VM i vektløfting 1962 i Pennsylvania," *Aftenposten*, September 21, 1961, 16.
73. Telegram 3323, Bruce, London to Secretary of State, March 9, 1962, RG 59, CDF 1960–63/800.453, box 2239, NA.
74. Airgram A-565, Lightner, Berlin to SecState Washington and AmEmbassy Bonn, March 29, 1962, RG 59, CDF 1960–63/800.453, box 2239, NA.

75. Airgram A-565, Lightner, Berlin to SecState Washington and AmEmbassy Bonn, March 29, 1962.
76. "VM i vektløfting i Budapest," unknown newspaper clipping, April 24, 1962, RA /PA-0090/D/Dd/L0355, Norges Idrettsforbund Idrett og Politikk, 1957–1970, Riksarkivet, Oslo, Norway.
77. Letter, Oscar State to Otto Mayer, April 5, 1962, D-RM02-HALTE/003—Fédération Internationale d'haltérophilie (IWF) Correspondance 1926–1971, OSC.
78. Letter, Otto Mayer to Oscar State, April 9, 1962, D-RM02-HALTE/003—Fédération Internationale d'haltérophilie (IWF) Correspondance 1926–1971, OSC.
79. Airgram A-509, Lightner, Berlin to SecState Washington and AmEmbassy Bonn, March 12, 1962, RG 59, CDF 1960–63/800.453, box 2239, NA; "USA gab Weltmeisterschaft zurück," *Neues Deutschland*, March 3, 1962, 6; "World Weightlifting Moved from Hershey," *Lebanon (PA) Daily News*, March 9, 1962, 11.
80. Gottfried Schödl, *Medals and World Records in Weightlifting* (Budapest: International Weightlifting Federation, 1997), 13.
81. "World Weightlifting Titles," *Times* (London), August 21, 1962, 2; "Martin Again World Champion," *Times* (London), September 22, 1962, 3.
82. Letter, I. K. Frith to Otto Mayer, December 19, 1963, contained in IOC Request for visas, January 1964, Republique Democratique Allemagne, Correspondance 1963–1971, OSC; Letter, H. Boehm to Mrs. I. K. Frith, September 25, 1962, CIO FI-TIARC-FITA-CORR—FITA Tir à l'arc: Correspondence of FITA 1935–1969, OSC.
83. Letter, Inger K. Frith to Member Associations, Members of the Administrative Council & Honorary Presidents, September 26, 1962, CIO FI-TIARC-FITA-CORR—FITA Tir à l'arc: Correspondence of FITA 1935–1969, OSC.
84. Proceedings of the Twenty-Second International Congress, July 23, 1963, contained in Robert Rhode, *History of the Federation Internationale de Tir l'Arc, 1962–1983*, vol. 2 (Bridgeton, MO: n.p., 1984), 536–46.
85. "U.S. Archers Lead in Championships," *Times* (London), July 25, 1963, 3; "Woman Archer's World Record," *Times* (London), July 26, 1963, 5; "World Archery Records," *Times* (London), July 27, 1963, 3; "Americans Take All Archery Titles," *Times* (London), July 29, 1963, 4. The *Times* never reported the Grand National Archery Society's relinquishing of the event either.
86. Letter, René Chesal to Otto Mayer, December 18, 1963, contained in IOC Request for visas, January 1964, Republique Democratique Allemagne, Correspondance 1963–1971, OSC.
87. Despatch 343, US Mission Berlin to Department of State, February 2, 1962, RG 59, CDF 1960–63/862.181, box 2645, NA; Airgram A-493, Lightner, Berlin to SecState Washington, March 3, 1962, RG 59, CDF 1960–63/862B.181, box 2673, NA; A-44, Stephen A. Koczak, Berlin to Department of State and Bonn, July 17, 1962, RG 59, CDF 1960–63/862.181, box 2645, NA; A-111, Stephen A. Koczak, Berlin to Department of State and Bonn, August 3, 1962, RG 59, CDF 1960–63/862.181, box 2645, NA; AC/119-R(62)33: Committee of Political Advisers Meeting held on 11th September, 1962 Action Sheet, September 14, 1962, NATO.
88. "Det atkie Sieg beachte den Titel," *Neue Zeit*, February 13, 1962, 5.
89. Airgram A-573, USBER Berlin to Department of State and Bonn, February 5, 1963,

RG 59, Central Foreign Policy File (CFPF) 1963, POL 36 GER, box 3915, NA; Airgram A-188, USBER Berlin to Department of State, September 17, 1963, RG 59, CFPF 1963, POL 36 GER, box 3914, NA; "DDR-Radsportlern Einreise verweigert," *Neues Deutschland*, July 30, 1963, 6.

90. Heather L. Dichter, "'Football More Important than Berlin': East German Football vs. NATO," in *Soccer Diplomacy: International Relations and Football since 1914*, ed. Heather L. Dichter (Lexington: University Press of Kentucky, 2020), 128–31.

91. Procès-verbal du Congrès annuel de la Fédération Internationale des Sociétés d'Aviron, August 22, 1951, Congres Proces-Verbaux 1925–28, . . . , 1930–1938, 1946–1950, FISA; Procès-verbal du Congrès annuel de la Fédération Internationale des Sociétés d'Aviron, July 18, 1952, Congres PV 1951–1959, FISA; Procès-verbal du Congrès extraordinaire de la Fédération Internationale des Sociétés d'Aviron, November 13, 1965, Congres PV 1960–1966, FISA.

92. Procès-verbal du Congrès ordinaire de la Fédération Internationale des Sociétés d'Aviron, August 22, 1961, Congres PV 1960–1966, FISA. At the FISA Extraordinary Congress in November 1965, FISA finally agreed to allow East Germany to participate in FISA events separately from the Federal Republic with a vote of forty-six for and four abstentions. This decision permitted the GDR to participate on its own in the second FISA World Championships in 1966. Procès-verbal du Congrès extraordinaire de la Fédération Internationale des Sociétés d'Aviron, November 13, 1965, Congres PV 1960–1966, FISA.

93. "Das gute Beispiel," *Süddeutsche Zeitung*, March 20, 1962, 20.

94. Robert Daley, "Case against Post-Game Anthems," *New York Times*, March 14, 1961, 42.

95. Minutes of the Conference of the Executive Board of the I.O.C. with the Delegates of the International Federations, February 8, 1963, Commissions CIO—Commission exécutive avec les FI, OSC.

96. Denis Oswald, Flags and National Athems—Historical Perspective of FISA, February 12, 1997, Congres Extraordinaire PV 1997, FISA.

97. Letter, D. T. P. Pain to O. Mayer, January 9, 1964, contained in IOC Request for visas, January 1964, Republique Democratique Allemagne, Correspondance 1963–1971, OSC.

98. Letter, Pierre Ferri to Otto Mayer, December 17, 1963, contained in IOC Request for visas, January 1964, Republique Democratique Allemagne, Correspondance 1963–1971, OSC.

99. John Stanley Mullin to Officers and Directors, USSA, ICC, USOGSC, June 20, 1962, box 3, folder 3, JSM, RSCL.

100. Emphasis in original. Minutes from the meeting with the FIS Council in Athens, May 19, 1963, box 3, folder 10, JSM, RSCL.

101. Telegram 515, Bonn to Foreign Office, May 15, 1963, FO 371/169308, TNA; Telegram 1151, Hulick, Berlin to Secretary of State, May 15, 1963, RG 59, CFPF 1963, POL 36 GER, box 3914, NA; Telegram D 10063, NATO-delegasjonen, Paris to Utenriksdepartement, May 15, 1963, 33.12/45. Pass- og visumforhold m.h.t. Ost-Tyskland. Bind II. (1.1.60–21.12.63), UD; Telegram 3074, McGhee, Bonn to Secretary of State, May 16, 1963, RG 59, CFPF 1963, POL 36 GER, box 3914, NA;

Telegram 772–73, Margerie, Bonn to Berlin, May 17, 1963, 105PO/1, box 10, CADN.

102. Gesell and Schröder to Delegates of the 24th FIS Congress and members of the FIS Committee, Athens, May 15, 1963, SAPMO, DY 12/2111, BArchB; Report by J. Stanley Mullin to the U.S. Ski Association, May 1963, box 3, folder 9, RSCL.
103. Telegram 1308–09, Le Roy, Berlin to Ambafrance Bonn, May 30, 1963, 105PO/1, box 10, CADN.
104. Report by J. Stanley Mullin to the U.S. Ski Association, May 1963.
105. Letter, H. A. J. Staples, Berlin to J. K. Bullard, Bonn, May 22, 1963, FO 371/169308, TNA.
106. Airgram A-733, Lightner, Berlin to Department of State and Bonn, June 28, 1962, RG 59, CDF 1960–63/862.181, box 2645, NA. The telegram and news stories stated the Greco-Roman event, per the East German press, had been allocated to Stockholm, but the event actually took place in Helsingborg.
107. Letter, D. T. P. Pain to O. Mayer, January 9, 1964.
108. Report by J. Stanley Mullin to the U.S. Ski Association, May 1963; Dichter, "We Have Allowed Our Decisions."
109. Letter, John Stanley Mullin to Merritt H. Stiles, April 24, 1962, box 3, folder 3, JSM, RSCL.
110. Robert Daley, "Politics: A Threat to World Sports," *New York Times*, February 13, 1962, 42.
111. Letter, A. E. Donald, NATO Paris to W. J. A. Wilberforce, Foreign Office, February 7, 1962, FO 371/163681, TNA.
112. Letter, R. Brash, Bonn to W. J. A.Wilberforce, Foreign Office, March 2, 1962, FO 371/163681, TNA; Dr. Sattler to Botschaft, Generalkonsulat, and Konsulat der Bundesrepublik Deutschland, March 27, 1963, 105PO/1, box 9, CADN.
113. Circular Letter No. 251 to the International Federations, December 15, 1963, Circulaires 1962 à 1964, OSC.
114. International Olympic Committee, Request for visas for participation in sport events in NATO countries, January 1964, Republique Democratique Allemagne, Correspondance 1963–1971, OSC.
115. Telegram 316, NATO Paris to External, February 6, 1962, RG 25, 6081 50341-C-40 File Part 1.1, LAC.
116. Howard Iverson, "The Lookout," *Lowell (MA) Sun*, February 6, 1962, 10.
117. Letter, P. L. V. Mallet, Bonn to W. J. A.Wilberforce, Foreign Office, February 19, 1962, FO 371/163681, TNA.
118. Heather L. Dichter, "Game Plan for Democracy: Sport and Youth in Occupied West Germany," in *Occupation: Power Politics, Everyday Life, and Social Interactions in the Western Zones of Occupied Germany, 1945–1955*, ed. Camilo Erlichman and Christopher Knowles (London: Bloomsbury Academic Press, 2018), 133–50; Ashley Brown, "Swinging for the State Department: American Women Tennis Players in Diplomatic Goodwill Tours, 1941–59," *Journal of Sport History*, 42, no. 3 (2015): 289–309; George N. Kioussis, "'The Finest Ambassadors': American–Icelandic Football Exchange, 1955–1956," in *Soccer Diplomacy*, 70–93.
119. Iverson, "The Lookout," 10.

CHAPTER 3: NATO'S SMALL STATES ASSERTING THEIR POWER

1. "World Ski Championships Appear to Be Doomed," *Lethbridge (AB) Herald*, February 5, 1962, 6.
2. Robert Daley, "Olympic Fear: Politics," *New York Times*, October 30, 1962, 56.
3. Christian Nuenlist, "Into the 1960s: NATO's role in East-West relations, 1958–63," in *Transforming NATO in the Cold War: Challenges beyond Deterrence in the 1960s*, ed. Andreas Wenger, Christian Nuenlist, and Anna Locher (London: Routledge, 2007), 71.
4. E. John B. Allen, *The Culture and Sport of Skiing: From Antiquity to World War II* (Amherst: University of Massachusetts Press, 2007).
5. Linda Risso, *Propaganda and Intelligence in the Cold War: The NATO Information Service* (London: Routledge, 2014).
6. Timothy Andrews Sayle, *Enduring Alliance: A History of NATO and the Postwar Global Order* (Ithaca, NY: Cornell University Press, 2019), 9.
7. Letter, A. E. Donald, NATO Paris to W. J. A. Wilberforce, Foreign Office, January 31, 1962, FO 371/163681, TNA.
8. Letter, A. E. Donald, NATO Paris to W. J. A. Wilberforce, Foreign Office, February 7, 1962, FO 371/163681, TNA.
9. "Won't Compete in Oslo Tests," *Winnipeg Free Press*, February 1, 1962, 28; "38 mann starter ved skøyte-EM på Bislett," *Arbeiderbladet*, February 1, 1962, 12.
10. Soviet athletes won the overall gold and bronze medals at the European speed skating championships in Oslo. "Sports in Brief," *Times* (London), February 5, 1962, 3.
11. Evelyn Mertin, "Steadfast Friendship and Brotherly Help: The Distinctive Soviet-East German Sport Relationship within the Socialist Bloc," in *Diplomatic Games: Sport, Statecraft and International Relations since 1945*, ed. Heather L. Dichter and Andrew L. Johns (Lexington: University Press of Kentucky, 2014), 61.
12. Per Vennemoe, Notat: Utkast til norsk uttalelse i tilfelle det blir reist spørsmål om hvorfor østtyske idrettsfolk ikke får adgang til å reise til Norge, January 25, 1962, 18.1/74 Öst-tyske innreisebestemmelser. Bind VII Fra 1/1.62 31/3.62, UD.
13. Telegram 10001 U, Utenriksdepartement to Militærmisjonen i Berlin, January 31, 1962, 18.1/74 Öst-tyske innreisebestemmelser. Bind VII Fra 1/1.62 31/3.62, UD.
14. Telegram 282, NATO Paris to External, February 2, 1962, RG 25, 6081 50341-C-40 File Part 1.1, LAC; Letter 317, Kaare Sandegren, NATO Paris to Utenriksdepatement, February 3, 1962, 18.1/74 Öst-tyske innreisebestemmelser. Bind VII Fra 1/1.62 31/3.62, UD.
15. Letter, A. E. Donald, NATO Paris to W. J. A. Wilberforce, Foreign Office, February 2, 1962, FO 371/163681, TNA; Telegram 282, NATO Paris to External, February 2, 1962, RG 25, 6081 50341-C-40 File Part 1.1, LAC.
16. Telegram 282, NATO Paris to External, February 2, 1962, RG 25, 6081 50341-C-40 File Part 1.1, LAC.
17. Letter, A. E. Donald, NATO Paris to W. J. A. Wilberforce, Foreign Office, February 7, 1962, FO 371/163681, TNA.
18. Telegram 316, NATO Paris to External, February 6, 1962, RG 25, 6081 50341-C-40 File Part 1.1, LAC.
19. Telegram 316, NATO Paris to External, February 6, 1962.

20. Letter, A. E. Donald, NATO Paris to W. J. A. Wilberforce, Foreign Office, February 7, 1962.
21. Telegram 316, NATO Paris to External, February 6, 1962; Letter, A. E. Donald, NATO Paris to W. J. A. Wilberforce, Foreign Office, February 7, 1962.
22. POLTO A Circ 151, USRO Paris to SecState Washington, February 7, 1962, RG 59, CDF 1960–63/862.181, box 2645, NA.
23. Telegram 316, NATO Paris to External, February 6, 1962.
24. Telegram 273, Foreign Office to Bonn, February 9, 1962, FO 371/163681, TNA; Letter, A. E. Donald, NATO Paris to J. S. Whitehead, Foreign Office, February 15, 1962, FO 371/163681, TNA; AC/119-R(62)7: Committee of Political Advisers Meetings held on 13th and 14th February, 1962 Action Sheet, February 15, 1962, NATO.
25. Airgram POLTO A-913, Finletter, USRO Paris to SecState Washington, February 14, 1962, RG 59, CDF 1960–63/ 800.453, box 2239, NA.
26. Letter, A. E. Donald, NATO Paris to J. S. Whitehead, Foreign Office, February 22, 1962, FO 371/163681, TNA.
27. Letter, A. E. Donald, NATO Paris to J. S. Whitehead, Foreign Office, February 22, 1962; Telegram S-37, Green, External to NATO Paris, February 13, 1962, RG 25, 6081 50341-C-40 File Part 1.1, LAC.
28. Letter, A. E. Donald, NATO Paris to J. S. Whitehead, Foreign Office, February 22, 1962.
29. Letter, A. E. Donald, NATO Paris to J. S. Whitehead, Foreign Office, February 22, 1962.
30. Telegram 475, NATO Paris to External, February 22, 1962, RG 25, 6081 50341-C-40 File Part 1.2, LAC; Letter, A. E. Donald, NATO Paris to J. S. Whitehead, Foreign Office, February 22, 1962.
31. Telegram 475, NATO Paris to External, February 22, 1962; Letter 532, Sigurd Ekeland, NATO Paris to Utenriksdepartement, February 23, 1962, 18.1/74 Öst-tyske innreisebestemmelser. Bind VII Fra 1/1.62 31/3.62, UD.
32. Telegram 475, NATO Paris to External, February 22, 1962.
33. Letter, A. E. Donald, NATO Paris to J. S. Whitehead, Foreign Office, February 22, 1962.
34. Telegram 585, NATO Paris to External, March 2, 1962, RG 25, 6081 50341-C-40 File Part 1.2, LAC.
35. Telegram 585, NATO Paris to External, March 2, 1962.
36. Letter S-69, Robertson, External to NATO Paris, March 2, 1962, RG 25, 6081 50341-C-40 File Part 1.2, LAC.
37. POLTO A CIRC 175, USRO Paris to SecState Washington, March 8, 1962, RG 59, CDF 1960–63/862.181, box 2645, NA.
38. Letter, A. E. Donald, NATO Paris to J. S. Whitehead, Foreign Office, March 6, 1962, FO 371/163681, TNA.
39. POLTO A CIRC 175, USRO Paris to SecState Washington, March 8, 1962.
40. Knut Hedemann, Notat: Reiserestriksjoner for Øst-Tyskland.—Deltakelse i Holmenkollrennene, March 7, 1962, 18.1/74 Öst-tyske innreisebestemmelser, Bind VII Fra 1/1.62–31/3.62, UD; Telegram 356, Wharton, Oslo to Secretary of State, March 10, 1962, RG 59, CDF 1960–63/862B.181, box 2673, NA; "Norway Bars Skiers from

East Germany," *New York Times,* March 13, 1962, 42; Letter, John Stanley Mullin to Merritt H. Stiles, April 24, 1962, box 3, folder 3, JSM, RLDC.

41. "Charges Fly over E. Germany's Exclusion from Squaw Valley Ski," *Hayward (CA) Daily Review*, February 16, 1959, 10; Telegram A. 10004, Ambassaden i Bonn to Utenriksdepartement, January 7, 1961, 18.1/74 Öst-tyske innreisebestemmelser. Bind V (1/1.61–28/2.61), UD.
42. Letter, Knut Hedemann, Utenriksdepartement to Embassies in Washington, Ottawa, London, Copenhagen, Brussels, The Hague, Paris, and Norges Faste Delegasjon ved De Forente Nasjone, New York, January 16, 1961, 18.1/74 Öst-tyske innreisebestemmelser. Bind V (1/1.61–28/2.61), UD; Arne Arnesen, Notat: TTD til österttyske idrettsfolk, January 18, 1961, 18.1/74 Öst-tyske innreisebestemmelser. Bind V (1/1.61–28/2.61), UD; Telegram 403, Lightner, Berlin to SecState Washington, January 18, 1961, RG 59, CDF 1960–63/862.181, box 2644, NA; Airgram G-298, Lightner, Berlin to SecState, February 4, 1961, RG 59, CDF 1960–63/862.181, box 2644, NA.
43. Letter, Kjeld Vibe, Berlin to Statens Utlendingskontor, January 13, 1962, 18.1/74 Öst-tyske innreisebestemmelser. Bind VII Fra 1/1.62 31/3.62, UD.
44. Letter, Kjeld Vibe, Berlin to Statens Utlendingskontor, February 28, 1962, 18.1/74 Öst-tyske innreisebestemmelser. Bind VII Fra 1/1.62 31/3.62, UD; Klaus Ullrich, "Gratulanten und Heuchler," *Neues Deutschland*, February 27, 1962, 6.
45. Knut Hedemann, Notat: Holmenkollrennet. Øst-tyske reiserestriksjoner, February 28, 1962, 18.1/74 Öst-tyske innreisebestemmelser. Bind VII Fra 1/1.62 31/3.62, UD; "Ski-ing and Olympism," *Olympic Review* 195/196 (January-February 1984), 64.
46. Georg Kristiansen, Notat: Ad melding fra ambassadør Boyesen i dag om øst-tyske skiløpere, March 6, 1962, 18.1/74 Öst-tyske innreisebestemmelser. Bind VII Fra 1/1.62 31/3.62, UD.
47. Letter, Walther, NATO Paris to Auswärtiges Amt, March 6, 1962, B38/57, PAdAA.
48. Letter, Gebhardt von Walther to Jens Boyesen, March 6, 1962, B 38/57, PAdAA.
49. Letter, Gebhardt von Walther to Jens Boyesen, March 6, 1962; Telegram D 10043, NATO Paris to Utenriksdepartement, March 6, 1962, 18.1/74 Öst-tyske innreisebestemmelser, Bind VII Fra 1/1.62—31/3.62, UD.
50. Telegram D 10043, NATO Paris to Utenriksdepartement, March 6, 1962; Georg Kristiansen, Notat: Ad melding fra ambassadør Boyesen i dag om øst-tyske skiløpere, March 6, 1962.
51. Telegram 633, Leger, NATO Paris to External, March 7, 1962, RG 25, 6081 50341-C-40 File Part 1.2, LAC.
52. Knut Hedemann, Notat: Reiserestriksjoner for Øst-Tyskland.—Deltakelse i Holmenkollrennene, March 7, 1962, 18.1/74 Öst-tyske innreisebestemmelser, Bind VII Fra 1/1.62–31/3.62, UD; P. Chr. A., "Holmenkollrennet og øst-tyskerne," *Aftenposten*, March 8, 1962, 14.
53. Letter, Ingendsay, Oslo to Auswärtiges Amt, March 28, 1962, B 94/212, PAdAA.
54. Telegram 370, Wharton, Oslo to Secretary of State, March 19, 1962, RG 59, CDF 1960–63/862B.181, box 2673, NA.
55. Telegram 370, Wharton, Oslo to Secretary of State, March 19, 1962.
56. "Bruken av Recknagel," *Aftenposten*, March 20, 1962, 2.

57. Letter, Ingendsay, Oslo to Auswärtiges Amt, March 28, 1962.
58. Telegram 10044, NATO Paris to Utenriksdepartement, March 7, 1962, 18.1/74 Öst-tyske innreisebestemmelser. Bind VII Fra 1/1.62 31/3.62, UD; Knut Hedemann, Notat: Reiserestriksjoner for Øst-Tyskland.—Deltakelse i Holmenkollrennene, March 7, 1962.
59. Telegram S-74, Green, External to NATO Paris, March 9, 1962, RG 25, 6081 50341-C-40 File Part 1.2, LAC. The action sheet attached to N. A. R.'s Memorandum for the Minister noted that he signed the telegram with reluctance. N.A.R., Memorandum for the Minister, March 9, 1962, RG 25, 6081 50341-C-40 File Part 1.2, LAC.
60. Telegram S-74, Green, External to NATO Paris, March 9, 1962, RG 25, 6081 50341-C-40 File Part 1.2, LAC.
61. Telegram 500, Foreign Office to NATO Paris, March 12, 1962, FO 371/163682, TNA.
62. Telegram TOPOL 1361, Ball, Department of State to AmEmbassy Paris, March 12, 1962, RG 59, CDF 1960–63/862B.181, box 2673, NA.
63. Letter, A. E. Donald, NATO Paris to J. S. Whitehead, Foreign Office, March 13, 1962, FO 371/163682, TNA; Telegram 693, NATO Paris to External, March 13, 1962, RG 25, 6081 50341-C-40 File Part 1.2, LAC; Telegram 10050 D, NATO Paris to Utenriksdepartement, March 14, 1962, 18.1/74 Öst-tyske innreisebestemmelser. Bind VII Fra 1/1.62 31/3.62, UD.
64. Letter, A. E. Donald, NATO Paris to J. S. Whitehead, Foreign Office, March 13, 1962; Telegram 693, NATO Paris to External, March 13, 1962.
65. POLADS(62)17: Travel Restrictions on East German Residents, March 7, 1962, 18.1/74 Öst-tyske innreisebestemmelser. Bind VII Fra 1/1.62 31/3.62, UD.
66. Telegram 693, NATO Paris to External, March 13, 1962.
67. Letter, A. E. Donald, NATO Paris to J. S. Whitehead, Foreign Office, March 13, 1962.
68. Telegram 693, NATO Paris to External, March 13, 1962.
69. Letter, A. E. Donald, NATO Paris to J. S. Whitehead, Foreign Office, March 13, 1962.
70. Telegram TOPOL 1361, Ball, Department of State to AmEmbassy Paris, March 12, 1962, RG 59, CDF 1960–63/862B.181, box 2673, NA; Telegram 693, NATO Paris to External, March 13, 1962.
71. Letter, A. E. Donald, NATO Paris to J. S. Whitehead, Foreign Office, March 13, 1962.
72. Letter, A. E. Donald, NATO Paris to J. S. Whitehead, Foreign Office, March 13, 1962; Telegram 693, NATO Paris to External, March 13, 1962.
73. Letter, A. E. Donald, NATO Paris to J. S. Whitehead, Foreign Office, March 13, 1962.
74. Telegram 693, NATO Paris to External, March 13, 1962.
75. A-119, USBER Berlin to Department of State and Bonn, August 7, 1962, RG 59, CDF 1960–63/862.181, box 2645, NA.
76. "Prof. Peschel in USA," *Neues Deutschland*, August 21, 1963, 7; Telegram 2821/24, Margerie, Bonn to Diplomatie Paris, April 19, 1963, 105PO/1, box 9, CADN; Airgram A-896, R. Glynn Mays, Jr., Berlin to Department of State and Bonn, May 17, 1963, RG 59, CDF 1963, POL 36 GER, box 3914, NA.
77. Greg Donaghy, *Tolerant Allies: Canada and the United States, 1963–1968* (Montreal: McGill-Queens University Press, 2003), 7.
78. Telegram S-26, External to NATO Paris, February 5, 1962, RG 25, 6081 50341-C-40 File Part 1.1, LAC.

CHAPTER 4: THE 1968 CANDIDATE CITIES CONFRONT OLYMPIC DEMANDS FOR FREE TRAVEL

1. Circular Letter No. 209 to the Executive Board of the I.O.C. and to the International Federations, November 21, 1962, Circulaires 1962 à 1964, OSC.
2. Minutes of the Conference of the Executive Board of the I.O.C. with the Delegates of the International Federations, February 8, 1963, Commissions CIO—Commission exécutive avec les FI, OSC.
3. Minutes of the Conference of the Executive Board of the I.O.C., February 8, 1963
4. Robert Daley, "Sound and Fury Emanate from Lausanne Parley," *New York Times*, February 9, 1963, 14. The second headline read, "But View Is That Ultimatum Fails to Solve Problems."
5. Karlheinz Vogel, "Ursache und Wirkung bleiben ungeprüft," *Frankfurter Allgemeine Zeitung*, February 12, 1963, 8.
6. Other European cities had expressed an earlier interest in the bidding for the games, but possible bids from Moscow and Vienna never panned out, nor did bids from Lausanne, Paris, Brussels, or Budapest. Cairo also briefly contemplated bidding for the summer games, informing the IOC of the city's interest in 1960 but withdrawing in late 1962. Detroit faced additional complications in its candidature domestically as Los Angeles contested the United States Olympic Committee's selection of Detroit, forcing the United States Olympic Committee to hold a second vote to confirm Detroit's candidacy. "In Europa kandidiert nur Lyon," *Frankfurter Allgemeine Zeitung*, February 23, 1963, 11; Hugh Dauncey, "The Failed Bid for Lyon '68, and France's Winter Olympics from Genoble '68 to Annecy 2018: French Politics, Civil Society and Olympic Mega-Events," in *Olympic Games, Mega-Events and Civil Societies: Globalization, Environment, Resistance*, ed. Graeme Hayes and John Karamichas (Basingstoke, UK: Palgrave Macmillan, 2012), 87–105; Letter, A. D. Touny to Otto Mayer, July 27, 1960, C-J04–1968/001, Villes candidates, Cairo, OSC; "Cairo Withdraws '68 Olympic Bid," *Albuquerque Tribune*, November 28, 1962, C-1; Letter, A. D. Touny to Otto Chancellor, November 22, 1962, C-J04–1968/001, Villes candidates, Cairo, OSC; Kevin B. Witherspoon, *Before the Eyes of the World: Mexico and the 1968 Olympic Games* (Dekalb, IL: Northern Illinois University Press, 2008), 34–37; "Detroit Gets Nod over L.A. for '68 Olympic Bid," *Los Angeles Times*, October 17, 1962, 1, 7; Allison Danzig, "Detroit Affirmed as 1968 Prospective Olympic Site after Cost Pleas Fail," *New York Times*, March 19, 1963, 16.
7. "Frederick Matthaei Sr. Dies; Detroit Industrialist Was 80," *New York Times*, March 27, 1973, 50.
8. XIX Olympiad 1968—An Invitation to the U.S. Olympic Committee, September 1962, Detroit Olympic Committee, box 20, Burton Historical Collection (hereafter BHC), Detroit Public Library, Detroit, Michigan (hereafter DPL).
9. Detroit Olympic Committee Executive Committee Minutes, March 26, 1963, Joseph Merrill Dodge Papers, BHC, DPL.
10. Ville de Lyon, Jeux de la XIXe Olympiade, n.d., 90 WP 001 5, SPORT ET TOURISME: Tournois internationaux: Jeux Olympiques d'été de 1968, Archives municipales de Lyon (hereafter AML).
11. "Le haut comité des sports s'est réuni à Lyon," *Le Monde*, October 7, 1962, 14.

12. Letter, Otto Mayer to Louis Pradel, October 9, 1962, C-J04–1968/002, Villes candidates, Lyon, IOC.
13. Robert Daley, "Big Idea in Little City," *New York Times*, November 13, 1962, 48; Ville de Lyon, Jeux de la XIXe Olympiade, n.d.
14. Letter, Louis Pradel to various IOC members, June 21, 1963, 90 WP 001 1, AML.
15. Herzog's work in the 1960s with respect to Lyon's and Grenoble's Olympic efforts ultimately secured his selection to the IOC in 1970. Letter, Maurice Herzog to Premier Ministre Pompidou, September 26, 1963, AG/5(1)/107, ANP.
16. Letter, Alberto P. Petrolini and Jose Oriani to Avery Brundage, June 15, 1962, C-J04–1968/001, Villes candidates, Buenos Aires, OSC; Cesar R. Torres, "Stymied Expectations: Buenos Aires' Persistent Efforts to Host Olympic Games," *Olympika* XVI (2007): 50–54; Cesar R. Torres "Tribulations and Achievements: The Early History of Olympism in Argentina," *International Journal of the History of Sport* 18, no. 3 (2001): 59–92; Raanan Rein, "Turning the Country into an 'Immense and Clamorous Stadium': Perón, the New Argentina, and the 1951 Pan-American Games," *International Journal of the History of Sport* 33, no. 1–2 (2016): 29–43.
17. Walter Koenig, "Wer bekommt die Olympischen Spiele 1968?" *Süddeutsche Zeitung*, October 11, 1963, 30.
18. Robert Daley, "Lyons to Use Public Relations in Seeking '68 Olympic Games," *New York Times*, November 29, 1962, 50.
19. Alison M. Wrynn, "'A Debt Was Paid off in Tears': Science, IOC Politics and the Debate about High Altitude in the 1968 Mexico City Olympics," *International Journal of the History of Sport* 23, no. 7 (2006): 1152–72.
20. Claire Brewster and Keith Brewster, *Representing the Nation: Sport and Spectacle in Post-Revolutionary Mexico* (London: Routledge, 2010), 42.
21. Brewster and Brewster, *Representing the Nation*, 45, 82.
22. Organizing Committee of the Games of the XIX Olympiad, *Olympic Report Mexico 1968*, vol. 2, *The Organization* (Mexico, 1969), 71–79; David J. Wysocki Quiros, "*Una Antorcha de Esperanza*: Mexico and the 1955 Pan-American Games," *International Journal of the History of Sport* 33, no. 1–2 (2016): 44–61.
23. Horst Wardenbach, 'Der Kongreß', *Frankfurter Allgemeine Zeitung*, October 21, 1963, 10.
24. Witherspoon, *Before the Eyes of the World*, 32–33.
25. Lake Placid Bid Book, 1963, Lake Placid Olympic Museum, Lake Placid, New York; "Lake Placid's Olympics Bid: Resort Hopes to Bring 1968 Winter Games to Adirondacks," *New York Times*, December 2, 1962, 603.
26. Letter, Dr. A. Michallon to le Président du Comité International Olympique, December 30, 1960, C-J05–1968/001, Villes candidates, Grenoble, OSC.
27. Grenoble Candidature France Jeux Olympique d'Hiver 1968, October 1963, Jeux Olympiques—4R1—Candidature, Les Archives de Grenoble, Grenoble, France (hereafter AG); Andrew Denning, *Skiing into Modernity: A Cultural and Environmental History* (Oakland: University of California Press, 2015), 55.
28. Grenoble Candidature France Jeux Olympique d'Hiver 1968, October 1963.
29. Telegram 3058–61, Le Nail, Haussaire Berlin to Ambafrance Bonn, November 27, 1963, 105PO/1, box 9, CADN.

30. Letter, Maurice Herzog to Premier Ministre Pompidou, September 26, 1963.
31. Protokoll Norges Olympiske Komites möte, April 27, 1961, RA/PA-0090/D/Dd/L0312a Norges Idrettsforbund Norges Olympiske Komite 1965–1969, Riksarkivet; Letter, Brynjulf Bull to Otto Mayer, June 15, 1961, C-J05–1968/003, Villes candidates, Oslo, OSC.
32. "Oslo Welcomes You," October 1961, Rolf Petersen Oslo 1968, Skimuseet, Oslo.
33. "Banff Carries Canada's Colors in Bid for 1968 Winter Games," *Medicine Hat* (AB) *News*, April 24, 1961, 8.
34. Calgary Olympic Bk Galleys, n.d., C-J05–1968/001, Villes candidates, Calgary, OSC.
35. Letter, J. W. Rangell and A. Ruusuvaara to International Olympic Committee, January 10, 1963, C-J05–1968/002, Villes candidates, Lahti, OSC; Numbered Letter 510, Helsinki to Under-Secretary of State for External Affairs, December 28, 1962, RG 29, 2177 file 215-9-2 Part 3, LAC; Letter, Olaf Ditlev-Simonsen Jr. to Avery Brundage, February 11, 1963, C-J05–1968/003, Villes candidates, Oslo, OSC; "!" *Aftenposten*, April 1, 1963, 15; Tor Flakstad, "Bull ikke i tvil: Lekene i 1968 i Oslo," *Arbeiderbladet*, January 28, 1964, OlympiaSport 1.
36. Letter, Olavi Kajala and Osmo Vesiranta to the International Olympic Committee, December 27, 1962, C-J05–1968/002, Villes candidates, Lahti, OSC.
37. Despatch 35, Jacques O'Connor, Lausanne to Philippe Baudet, Bern, March 15, 1963, 89PO/2002021, box 610, CADN.
38. Letter, Serge Margelisch and Roger Bonvin to Marcel Henniger, July 14, 1962, C-J05–1968/003, Villes candidates, Sion, OSC.
39. "Brundage Praises Placid's Efforts," *Lake Placid News*, August 8, 1963, 1.
40. "Sion trekker kanskje sitt kandidatur til OL," *Aftenposten*, December 3, 1963, 17; Letter 323, Dag Bryn, Bern to Utenriksdepartment, December 9, 1963, 74.2/31: Vinterolympiaden 1968. Fra 9.2.1961–31/12–69, UD; "Sion trekker sin søknad om Vinter-IL 1968," *Aftenposten*, December 9, 1963, 9; Despatch 176, Jacques O'Connor, Lausanne to Philippe Baudet, Bern, December 11, 1963, 89PO/2002021, box 610, CADN; Numbered Letter 490, Bern to Under-Secretary of State for External Affairs, December 12, 1963, RG 25, 10528 55–26-OLYMP File Part 1.1, LAC; Circular Letter No. 250 to the Members of the I. O. C., December 1963, Circulaires 1962 à 1964, OSC.
41. "Japan og 1968," *Sportsmanden*, May 18, 1962, 18; "Japan Supports Olympic Bid," *New York Times*, November 16, 1962, 54; Letter, Otto Mayer to Olaf Ditlev-Simonsen, November 15, 1962, C-J05–1968/003, Villes candidates, Oslo, OSC; Telegram 300, Tokyo to External, December 6, 1963, RG 25, 10528 55–26-OLYMP File Part 1.1, LAC.
42. Ann B. Irish, *Hokkaido: A History of Ethnic Transition and Development on Japan's Northern Island* (Jefferson, NC: McFarland, 2009), 184.
43. Hans Eiberle, "Über Sapporo soll die Olympiaflagge wehen," *Süddeutsche Zeitung*, March 27, 1963, 28; "Sapporo søker vinterlekene 1968," *Aftenposten*, November 17, 1962, 14.
44. "1968 Olympics: Detroit, France Have Chance to Get Games Says Official," *Danville (VA) Bee*, March 20, 1963, 3-D; "Lyon, grande favorite pour l'organisation des

Jeux Olympiques en 1968," *Le Soir*, March 22, 1963, 13; "Lyon: 80 chances sur 100 pour les J.O. de 1968," *Le Progrès*, February 9, 1963, 10; P. Chr. A., "Lyon og Oslo!" *Aftenposten*, July 27, 1963, 10; Walter Koenig, "Wer bekommt die Olympischen Spiele 1968?" *Süddeutsche Zeitung*, October 11, 1963, 30.

45. Proces-Verbal de la réunion de la Commission Executive du C . I . O. avec la Commission d 'Amateurisme, March 2–3, 1962, IOC Executive Committee, 1960–1969, 1962 Lausanne, OSC; Circular Letter No. 194 to All International Federations, March 26, 1962, Circulaires 1962 à 1964, OSC.
46. Minutes, 59th Session of the International Olympic Committee, June 5–8, 1962, IOC Sessions, 1960–1969, 1962 Moscow, OSC.
47. Letter, Avery Brundage to David Burghley, August 29, 1962, Exeter, Marquess David, 1960–63, box 54, reel 32, ABC, UIA.
48. Emphasis in original. Circular Letter No. 219, To the Cities candidate to the organization of the Games of the XIXth Olympiad in 1968 and to the Xth Olympic Winter Olympic Games 1968, March 14, 1963, C-J04–1968/001, Villes candidates, OSC.
49. Sidney A. Friefeld, Memorandum for file 11:66-A-60, March 15, 1963, RG 25, 6081 50341-C-40 File Part 3.1, LAC; "Visa Guarantee Sought by IOC for '68 Games: Travel Controlled," *Christian Science Monitor*, March 16, 1963, 14.
50. Robert Daley, "Olympics Insist on 1968 Bias Ban," *New York Times*, March 16, 1963, 8.
51. Letter, K. L. Wilson to George Romney, April 3, 1963, box 222, Governor's Office, Topical File of Margaret Little, 1963, George Romney Papers (hereafter GRP), Bentley Historical Library, Ann Arbor, Michigan (hereafter BHL).
52. Memo, John Martin to George Romney, April 1963, box 222, Governor's Office, Topical File of Margaret Little, 1963, GRP, BHL; Letter, George Romney to Dean Rusk, April 16, 1963, box 222, Governor's Office, Topical File of Margaret Little, 1963, GRP, BHL; Detroit Olympic Committee Executive Committee Minutes, April 17, 1963, Joseph Merrill Dodge Papers, BHC, DPL.
53. Letter, R. Keith Alexander to Norman Robertson, April 10, 1963, RG 25, 6081 50341-C-40 File Part 3.1, LAC.
54. Letter, N. A. Robertson to Joseph W. Willard, April 11, 1963, RG 29, 3284 file 7072–2 Part 1, LAC.
55. Minutes of the Second Meeting of the Interdepartmental Committee on the 1968 Olympic Winter Games, April 16, 1963, RG 84, 2145 U312-4-2 Background File Part 1, LAC.
56. Memorandum, J. M. Weld to Mr. Southam, April 17, 1963, RG 25, 6081 50341-C-40 File Part 3.1, LAC.
57. Memorandum, J. M. Weld to Mr. Southam, April 17, 1963.
58. Memorandum, J. M. Weld to Mr. Southam, April 17, 1963.
59. Letter, G. A. Lahaie to J. H. April 20, 1963, RG 84, 2146 U312-4-2 Calgary File Part 1, LAC; Letter, E. H. Davis to G. A. Lahaie, April 23, 1963, RG 25, 6081 50341-C-40 File Part 3.1, LAC; E. H. Davis, CODA Application to the Chairman, Interdepartmental Committee on 1968 Winter Olympics, April 23, 1963, RG 25, 6081 50341-C-40 File Part 3.1, LAC.
60. Letter, E. H. Davis to G. A. Lahaie, April 23, 1963.
61. Letter, E. H. Davis to G. A. Lahaie, April 23, 1963.

62. Letter, E. H. Davis to G. A. Lahaie, April 23, 1963.
63. Telegram C-528, External to Bonn, April 23, 1963, RG 25, 6081 50341-C-40 File Part 3.1, LAC. External Affairs repeated same sentence in the telegram to Paris.
64. Telegram C-528, External to Bonn, April 23, 1963.
65. Telegram C-527, External to Washington, April 23, 1963, RG 25, 6081 50341-C-40 File Part 3.1, LAC.
66. Telegram C-530, External to Vienna, April 23, 1963, RG 25, 6081 50341-C-40 File Part 3.1, LAC.
67. Telegram C-529, External to NATO Paris, April 23, 1963, RG 25, 6081 50341-C-40 File Part 3.1, LAC.
68. Telegram 899, NATO Paris to External, April 24, 1963, RG 25, 6081 50341-C-40 File Part 3.1, LAC.
69. Telegram 1270, Washington to External, April 30, 1963, RG 25, 6081 50341-C-40 File Part 3.1, LAC.
70. Telegram 94, Vienna to External, May 3, 1963, RG 25, 6081 50341-C-40 File Part 3.1, LAC.
71. Telegram 281, Bonn to External, April 26, 1963, RG 25, 6081 50341-C-40 File Part 3.1, LAC.
72. Minutes of Third Meeting of the Interdepartmental Committee on the 1968 Olympic Winter Games, April 30, 1963, RG 84, 2145 U312-4-2 Background File Part 1, LAC.
73. Memorandum to Cabinet, Request by the International Olympic Committee for a Certificate of Free Entry of Olympic teams and officials—2nd draft, April 30, 1963, RG 84, 2146 U312-4-2 Calgary File Part 1, LAC; 3rd Draft, Memorandum to Cabinet, May 2, 1963, RG 25, 6081 50341-C-40 File Part 3.1, LAC. The $9 million figure disappeared in the third draft.
74. 4th Draft, Memorandum to Cabinet, May 2, 1963, RG 25, 6081 50341-C-40 File Part 3.1, LAC.
75. Memorandum to Cabinet, April 30, 1963.
76. Memorandum to Cabinet, April 30, 1963.
77. Minutes of Third Meeting of the Interdepartmental Committee on the 1968 Olympic Winter Games, April 30, 1963.
78. Telegram 2803, Dowling, Bonn to Secretary of State, April 19, 1963, RG 59, CFPF 1963, POL 36 GER, box 3914, NA.
79. Telegram 3005/07, Margerie, Bonn to Diplomatie Paris, April 25, 1963, 105PO/1, box 9, CADN.
80. Telegram 2893, Bonn to Secretary of State, April 26, 1963, RG 59, CFPF 1963, EDU 15, box 3240, NA.
81. Telegram S-92, External to NATO Paris, April 26, 1963, RG 25, 6081 50341-C-40 File Part 3.1, LAC.
82. Telegram 1609, Ball, Department of State to AmEmbassy Paris TOPOL, April 29, 1963, RG 59, CFPF1963, EDU 15, box 3240, NA.
83. Telegram 974, NATO Paris to External, May 2, 1963, RG 25, 6081 50341-C-40 File Part 3.1, LAC.
84. Minutes of the Ordinary Congress of the Federation Internationale des Societes

d'Aviron, August 23, 1955, Congres PV 1951–1959, FISA; Procès-verbal du Congrès extraordinaire de la Fédération Internationale des Sociétés d'Aviron, November 22, 1958, Congres PV 1951–1959, FISA; Procès-verbal du Congrès ordinaire de la Fédération Internationale des Sociétés d'Aviron, August 21, 1961, Congres PV 1960–1966, FISA.

85. Letter, R. D. Clift, NATO Paris to J. S. Whitehead, Foreign Office, May 3, 1963, FO 371/169308, TNA.

86. Airgram POLTO A 1210, USRO POL Paris to SecState Washington, May 4, 1963, RG 59, CFPF 1963, POL 36 E GER, box 3899, NA.

87. Telegram 974, NATO Paris to External, May 2, 1963, RG 25, 6081 50341-C-40 File Part 3.1, LAC.

88. Letter, R. S. Clift, NATO Paris to J. S. Whitehead, Foreign Office, May 3, 1963; Telegram 10054 D, NATO Paris to Utenriksdepartement, May 3, 1963, 33.12/45. Pass- og visumforhold m.h.t. Ost-Tyskland. Bind II. (1.1.60–21.12.63), UD.

89. Letter, Sigurd Ekeland to Pierre de Menthon, May 6, 1963, 18.1/74 Öst-tyske innreisebestemmelser. Visum-forholdet til Öst-Tyskland. Bind 10 Fra 1/5.63–30/8.63, UD.

90. Telegram 152, François Seydoux, NATO (REPAN) Paris to Diplomatie Paris, May 2, 1963, 105PO/1, box 10, CADN.

91. AC/119-R(63)16: Committee of Political Advisers Meeting of 2nd May, 1963 Action Sheet, May 6, 1963, NATO; Telegram POLTO 1427, Durbrow, Paris to Secretary of State, May 2, 1963, RG 59, CFPF 1963, EDU 15, box 3240, NA; Telegram 152, François Seydoux, NATO (REPAN) Paris to Diplomatie Paris, May 2, 1963; Telegram 971, NATO Paris to External, May 2, 1963, RG 25, 6081 50341-C-40 File Part 3.1, LAC; Letter, R. S. Clift, NATO Paris to J. S. Whitehead, Foreign Office, May 3, 1963.

92. Telegram 971, NATO Paris to External, May 2, 1963, RG 25, 6081 50341-C-40 File Part 3.1, LAC.

93. Airgram POLTO A 1210, USRO/POL Paris to SecState Washington, May 4, 1963, RG 59, CFPF 1963, POL 36 E GER, box 3899, NA.

94. Telegram POLTO 1460, Bohlen, Paris to Secretary of State, May 7, 1963, RG 59, CFPF 1963, EDU 15, box 3240, NA.

95. Letter, Sigurd Ekeland to Pierre de Menthon, May 6, 1963; Telegram POLTO 1460, Bohlen, Paris to Secretary of State, May 7, 1963, RG 59, CFPF 1963, EDU 15, box 3240, NA.

96. Telegram POLTO 1460, Bohlen, Paris to Secretary of State, May 7, 1963; Telegram 164, François Seydoux, NATO (REPAN) Paris to Diplomatie Paris, May 7, 1963, 105PO/1, box 10, CADN; Letter, A. E. Donald, NATO Paris to J. S. Whitehead, Foreign Office, May 8, 1963, FO 371/169308, TNA; AC/119-R(63)17: Committee of Political Advisers Meeting of 7th May, 1963 Action Sheet, May 10, 1963, NATO.

97. Telegram POLTO 1473, Finletter, NATO Paris to Secretary of State, May 9, 1963, RG 59, CFPF 1963, EDU 15, box 3240, NA. For more on the problems of divided Korea and the China-Taiwan split within international sport, see Brian Bridges, "Reluctant Mediator: Hong Kong, the Two Koreas and the Tokyo Olympics," *International Journal of the History of Sport* 24, no. 3 (2007): 375–91; Fan Hong and Xiong Xiaozheng, "Communist China: Sport, Politics and Diplomacy," *International Journal of the His-*

tory of Sport 19, no. 2–3 (2002): 319–42; Yi-Ling Huang and Chen-Huei Wang, "Chinese Question in the Olympic Movement: From the Perspective of Taiwan," *International Journal of the History of Sport* 30, no. 17 (2013): 2052–68; Rachel Vaughan, "'Chinese Rings': The United States, the Two Chinas and the 1960 Squaw Valley Winter Olympics," in *Sport and Diplomacy: Games within Games*, ed. J. Simon Rofe (Manchester, UK: Manchester University Press, 2018), 185–202.

98. Letter, John E. Palevich to Otto Mayer, May 31, 1962, 105PO/1, box 9, CADN.
99. Telegram POLTO 1473, Finletter, NATO Paris to Secretary of State, May 9, 1963.
100. Telegram 506, Bonn to Foreign Office, May 13, 1963, FO 371/169308, TNA; Telegram 3035, Morris, Bonn to Secretary of State, May 13, 1963, RG 59, CFPF 1963, POL 36 GER, box 3914, NA; Telegram 3384–87, Margerie, Bonn to Diplomatie Paris, May 13, 1963, 105PO/1, box 10, CADN.
101. Telegram POLTO 1500, Finletter, NATO Paris to Secretary of State, May 14, 1963, RG 59, CFPF 1963, EDU 15, box 3240, NA; Oncken, Vermerk: Betr.: Lockerung der TTD-Sperre, May 20, 1963, B 38/57, PAdAA.
102. Telegram 506, Bonn to Foreign Office, May 13, 1963.
103. Telegram 506, Bonn to Foreign Office, May 13, 1963; Telegram 3384–87, Margerie, Bonn to Diplomatie Paris, May 13, 1963.
104. Telegram 1394, Washington to External, May 9, 1963, RG 25, 6081 50341-C-40 File Part 3.1, LAC. It is unclear whether the State Department representative who met with the Canadian had read the telegram from Paris, which included the recommendation for the creation of a working group at NATO.
105. Telegram 1394, Washington to External, May 9, 1963.
106. Letter S134, External to NATO Paris, May 10, 1963, RG 25, 6081 50341-C-40 File Part 3.2, LAC.
107. Telegram 95, Hadwen, Oslo to External, May 12, 1963, RG 25, 6081 50341-C-40 File Part 3.2, LAC.
108. Letter, Sigurd Ekeland to Pierre de Menthon, May 11, 1963, 18.1/74 Öst-tyske innreisebestemmelser. Visum-forholdet til Öst-Tyskland. Bind 10 Fra 1/5.63–30/8.63, UD. Although only addressed to the French, the British and Canadians also received a copy of this letter: FO 371/169308, TNA; RG 25, 6081 50341-C-40 File Part 3.2, LAC.
109. Letter, Sigurd Ekeland, NATO Paris to Per Vennemoe, Utenriksdepartement, May 11, 1963, 18.1/74 Öst-tyske innreisebestemmelser. Visum-forholdet til Öst-Tyskland. Bind 10 Fra 1/5.63–30/8.63, UD.
110. Telegram D 10063, NATO Paris to Utenriksdepartement, May 15, 1963, 33.12/45. Pass- og visumforhold m.h.t. Ost-Tyskland. Bind II. (1.1.60–21.12.63), UD; Letter, A. E. Donald, NATO Paris to J. S. Whitehead, Foreign Office, May 14, 1963, FO 371/169308, TNA. Demonstrating the greater importance Norwegians place on skiing, the telegram from NATO to Oslo discussed the skiing decision before the shooting championships, even though the discussion of the latter event happened first at the Committee of Political Advisers meeting and would take place three years before the skiing championships.
111. Letter, N-635, R. L. Rogers, NATO Paris to Under-Secretary of State for External Affairs, May 16, 1963, RG 25, 6081 50341-C-40 File Part 3.2, LAC.

112. Letter, N-635, R. L. Rogers, NATO Paris to Under-Secretary of State for External Affairs, May 16, 1963.
113. Letter, N-635, R. L. Rogers, NATO Paris to Under-Secretary of State for External Affairs, May 16, 1963; AC/119-R(63)18: Committee of Political Advisers Meeting of 14th May, 1963 Action Sheet, May 17, 1963, NATO; Telegram POLTO 1500, Finletter, NATO Paris to Secretary of State, May 14, 1963, RG 59, CFPF 1963, EDU 15, box 3240, NA; Letter, A. E. Donald, NATO Paris to J. S. Whitehead, Foreign Office, May 14, 1963; Telegram 177, François Seydoux, to Diplomatie Paris, May 14, 1963, 105PO/1, box 10, CADN.
114. Letter, R. D. Clift, NATO Paris to J. S. Whitehead, Foreign Office, May 30, 1963, FO 371/169308, NA.

CHAPTER 5: THE NATO WORKING GROUP ON THE 1968 OLYMPICS

1. Letter, N-635, R. L. Rogers, NATO Paris to Under-Secretary of State for External Affairs, May 16, 1963, RG 25, 6081 50341-C-40 File Part 3.2, LAC; Letter, A. E. Donald, NATO Paris to J. S. Whitehead, Foreign Office, May 14, 1963, FO 371/169308, TNA.
2. Telegram 1690, Rusk, Department of State to AmEmbassy Paris TOPOL, May 10, 1963, RG 59, CFPF 1963, EDU 15, box 3240, NA.
3. Telegram POLTO 1539, Finletter, NATO Paris to Secretary of State, May 18, 1963, RG 59, CFPF 1963, EDU 15, box 3240, NA.
4. Telegram S-148, External to NATO Paris, May 24, 1963, RG 25, 6081 50341-C-40 File Part 3.2, LAC.
5. Telegram 1690, Rusk, Department of State to AmEmbassy Paris TOPOL, May 10, 1963; Telegram POLTO 1539, Finletter, NATO Paris to Secretary of State, May 18, 1963.
6. Telegram POLTO 1539, Finletter, NATO Paris to Secretary of State, May 18, 1963.
7. Telegram 1752, Rusk, Department of State to NATO Paris TOPOL, May 25, 1963, RG 59, CFPF 1963, EDU 15, box 3240, NA.
8. Telegram 1192, NATO Paris to External, May 27, 1963, RG 25, 6081 50341-C-40 File Part 3.2, LAC; Telegram 1752, Rusk, Department of State to Paris TOPOL, May 25, 1963.
9. Telegram S-148, External to NATO Paris, May 24, 1963.
10. Telegram 1192, NATO Paris to External, May 27, 1963; Telegram S-152, External to NATO Paris, May 27, 1963, RG 25, 6081 50341-C-40 File Part 3.2, LAC.
11. Telegram 1690, Washington to External, May 28, 1963, RG 25, 6081 50341-C-40 File Part 3.2, LAC.
12. Telegram 1201, NATO Paris to External, May 28, 1963, RG 25, 6081 50341-C-40 File Part 3.2, LAC; Telegram 10059, Utenriksdepartement to NATO Paris, May 27, 1963, 18.1/74 Öst-tyske innreisebestemmelser. Visum-forholdet til Öst-Tyskland. Bind 10 Fra 1/5.63–30/8.63, UD.
13. Telegram 1201, NATO Paris to External, May 28, 1963.
14. Telegram 1201, NATO Paris to External, May 28, 1963; Telegram POLTO Circular 55, Farley, NATO Paris to Secretary of State, May 28, 1963, RG 59, CFPF 1963, EDU 15, box 3240, NA.

15. Telegram 1201, NATO Paris to External, May 28, 1963.
16. Telegram POLTO Circular 55, Farley, NATO Paris to Secretary of State, May 28, 1963; Note, Délégation de la France au Conseil de l'Atlantique-Nord pour la Direction d'Europe (Europe Centrale), May 28, 1963, 179QO/75, CADC.
17. Telegram POLTO Circular 55, Farley, NATO Paris to Secretary of State, May 28, 1963.
18. Janice Cavell and Ryan M. Touhey, eds., *Reassessing the Rogue Tory: Canadian Foreign Relations in the Diefenbaker Era* (Vancouver: University of British Columbia Press, 2018).
19. Greg Donaghy, *Grit: The Life and Politics of Paul Martin Sr.* (Vancouver: University of British Columbia Press, 2015), 191.
20. Telegram POLTO Circular 55, Farley, NATO Paris to Secretary of State, May 28, 1963; Note, Délégation de la France au Conseil de l'Atlantique-Nord pour la Direction d'Europe (Europe Centrale), May 28, 1963.
21. Telegram POLTO Circular 55, Farley, NATO Paris to Secretary of State, May 28, 1963.
22. Telegram POLTO Circular 54, Farley, NATO Paris to Secretary of State, May 28, 1963, RG 59, CFPF 1963, EDU 15, box 3240, NA.
23. Telegram TOPOL 1767, Rusk, Department of State to Paris, May 29, 1963, RG 59, CFPF 1963, EDU 15, box 3240, NA.
24. Telegram TOPOL 1767, Rusk, Department of State to Paris, May 29, 1963; Telegram 1690, Washington to External, May 28, 1963.
25. Telegram S-156, External to NATO Paris, May 30, 1968, RG 25, 6081 50341-C-40 File Part 3.2, LAC.
26. Telegram 1217, NATO Paris to External, May 30, 1963, RG 25, 6081 50341-C-40 File Part 3.2, LAC; Telegram 1221, NATO Paris to External, May 30, 1963, RG 25, 6081 50341-C-40 File Part 3.2, LAC.
27. Telegram POLTO Circular 56, Farley, NATO Paris to Secretary of State, May 30, 1963, RG 59, CFPF 1963, EDU 15, box 3240, NA; Telegram 1221, NATO Paris to External, May 30, 1963.
28. Telegram POLTO Circular 56, Farley, NATO Paris to Secretary of State, May 30, 1963.
29. Telegram 1773, Rusk, Department of State to AmEmbassy Paris TOPOL, May 31, 1963, RG 59, CFPF 1963, EDU 15, box 3240, NA.
30. Telegram 1727, Washington to External, May 31, 1963, RG 25, 6081 50341-C-40 File Part 3.2, LAC.
31. Telegram 1773, Rusk, Department of State to AmEmbassy Paris TOPOL, May 31, 1963.
32. Telegram 1727, Washington to External, May 31, 1963.
33. Telegram 10063, Utenriksdepartement to NATO Paris, May 31, 1963, 18.1/74 Östtyske innreisebestemmelser. Visum-forholdet til Öst-Tyskland. Bind 10 Fra 1/5.63–30/8.63, UD.
34. Telegram 122, Oslo to External, May 31, 1963, RG 25, 6081 50341-C-40 File Part 3.2, LAC.
35. Telegram POLTO Circular 57, Durbrow, NATO Paris to Secretary of State, May 31, 1963, RG 59, CFPF 1963, EDU 15, box 3240, NA; J. L. Toffin. Note pour la délégation française à l'O.T.A.N., June 1, 1963, 179QO/75, CADC; Despatch 66/EU, J. L. Toffin

to Haut Commissaire à la Jeunesse et aux Sports—Délégation Générale aux Sports et à la Préparation Olympique, June 1, 1963, 179QO/75, CADC; Letter 1216, Sigurd Ekeland, NATO Paris to Utenriksdepartement, June 5, 1963, 33.12/45. Pass-og visum-forhold m.h.t. Ost-Tyskland. Bind II. (1.1.60–21.12.63), UD.

36. J. L. Toffin, Note pour la délégation française à l'O.T.A.N., June 1, 1963.

37. Telegram POLTO Circular 60, Finletter, NATO Paris to Secretary of State, May 17, 1963, RG 59, CFPF 1963, EDU 15, box 3240, NA.

38. Anna Locher, "A Crisis Foretold: NATO and France, 1963–66," in *Transforming NATO in the Cold War: Challenges beyond deterrence in the 1960s*, ed. Andreas Wenger, Christian Nuenlist, and Anna Locher (London: Routledge, 2007), 108–9.

39. Minutes, Meeting of the Executive Board of the International Olympic Committee, Lausanne, June 5, 1963, IOC Executive Board, 1960–1969, 1963 Lausanne, OSC.

40. "Olympics Unit in Bid to NATO," *New York Times* (International Edition), June 7, 1963, in RG 25, 6081 50341-C-40 File Part 4.1, LAC; Telegram 1278, NATO Paris to External, June 10, 1963, RG 25, 6081 50341-C-40 File Part 4.1, LAC.

41. Telegram 1851, Wasington to External, June 10, 1963, RG 25, 6081 50341-C-40 File Part 4.1, LAC.

42. Telegram 1812, Rusk, Department of State to AmEmbassy Paris TOPOL, June 12, 1963, RG 59, CFPF 193, EDU 15, box 3240, NA; Telegram S179, External to NATO Paris, June 12, 1963, RG 84, 2148 file U312-4-2 part 4, LAC.

43. Telegram 1812, Rusk, Department of State to AmEmbassy Paris TOPOL, June 12, 1963; Telegram 1888, Washington to External, June 12, 1963, RG 25, 6081 50341-C-40 File Part 4.1, LAC.

44. Telegram S179, External to NATO Paris, June 12, 1963.

45. Telegram 1904, Washington to External, June 13, 1963, RG 25, 6081 50341-C-40 File Part 4.1, LAC; Telegram POLTO Circular 58, Finletter, NATO Paris to Secretary of State, June 13, 1963, RG 59, CFPF 1963, EDU 15, box 3240, NA.

46. Letter, R. L. Rogers to R. W. J. Hooper, June 13, 1963, FO 371/169309, TNA.

47. Telegram TOPOL 1835, Rusk, Department of State to AmEmbassy Paris TOPOL, June 14, 1963, RG 59, CFPF 1963, EDU 15, box 3240, NA.

48. Telegram 826, Foreign Office to NATO Paris, June 17, 1963, FO 371/169309, TNA.

49. Telegram 10067, Utenriksdepartement to NATO Paris, June 17, 1963, 18.1/74 Öst-tyske innreisebestemmelser. Visum-forholdet til Öst-Tyskland. Bind 10 Fra 1/5.63–30/8.63, UD.

50. Telegram 1346, NATO Paris to External, June 17, 1963, RG 84, 2148 file U312-4-2 part 4, LAC.

51. Telegram 1346, NATO Paris to External, June 17, 1963; Letter 1305, Bjørn Kristvik, NATO Paris to Utenriksdepartement, June 18, 1963, 18.1/74 Öst-tyske innreisebe-stemmelser. Visum-forholdet til Öst-Tyskland. Bind 10 Fra 1/5.63–30/8.63, UD; Telegram POLTO Circular 60, Finletter, NATO Paris to Secretary of State, June 17, 1963; Telegram 30, NATO Paris to Foreign Office, June 18, 1963, FO 371/169309, TNA; Note 334 pour la Direction d'Europe (Europe centrale), June 18, 1963, 179QO/229, CADC.

52. Telegram 1346, NATO Paris to External, June 17, 1963.

53. Telegram 1360, Ignatieff, NATO Paris to External, June 13, 1963, RG 25, 6081 50341-C-40 File Part 4.1, LAC.
54. Telegram 1360, Ignatieff, NATO Paris to External, June 13, 1963.
55. Telegram S-214, Wershof, External to NATO Paris, July 5, 1963, RG 25, 6081 50341-C-40 File Part 4.1, LAC.
56. Telegram 1475, Jay, NATO Paris to External, July 8, 1963, RG 25, 6081 50341-C-40 File Part 4.1, LAC.
57. Telegram S-214, Wershof, External to NATO Paris, July 5, 1963.
58. Telegram 1475, Jay, NATO Paris to External, July 8, 1963.
59. Memorandum to Cabinet, 1968 Olympic Winter Games and Berlin Travel Control, July 9, 1963, RG 25, 6081 50341-C-40 File Part 4.1, LAC.
60. Telegram 1394, NATO Paris to External, June 25, 1963, RG 25, 6081 50341-C-40 File Part 4.1, LAC; Letter, A. E. Donald, NATO Paris to J. S. Whitehead, Foreign Office, June 27, 1963, FO 371/169309, TNA; Airgram A-1379, Finletter, USRO/POL Paris to SecState Washington, June 27, 1963, RG 59, CFPF 1963, EDU 15, box 3240, NA; Airgram, POLTO A 10, Finletter, USRO/POL Paris to SecState Washington, July 5, 1963, RG 59, CFPF 1963, EDU 15, box 3240, NA; Note pour le Service des Pactes, July 5, 1963, 179QO/229, CADC.
61. Telegram 1868, Rusk, Department of State to Paris TOPOL, June 22, 1963, RG 59, CFPF 1963, EDU 15, box 3240, NA; Telegram 1394, NATO Paris to External, June 25, 1963.
62. Telegram TOPOL 34, Rusk, Department of State to AmEmbassy Paris, July 7, 1963, RG 59, CFPF 1963, EDU 15, box 3240, NA; Letter, Douglas F. Roby to Otto Mayer, July 8, 1963, C-J04–1968/001, Villes candidates, Detroit, OSC.
63. Telegram 1480, NATO Paris to External, July 9, 1963, RG 25, 6081 50341-C-40 File Part 4.1, LAC.
64. Airgram POLTO A-33, Finletter, USRO/POL Paris to SecState Washington, July 10, 1963, RG 59, CFPF 1963, EDU 15, box 3240, NA; Telegram POLTO 61, Finletter, NATO Paris, to Secretary of State, June 16, 1963, RG 59, CFPF 1963, EDU 15, box 3240, NA; Telegram 1590, NATO Paris to External, July 23, 1963, RG 25, 6081 50341-C-40 File Part 4.1, LAC; Telegram S-236, External to Washington, July 25, 1963, RG 25, 6081 50341-C-40 File Part 4.1, LAC.
65. Telegram TOPOL 116, Rusk, Department of State to AmEmbassy Paris, July 25, 1963, RG 59, CFPF 1963, EDU 15, box 3240, NA; Despatch 1305, Bruno de Leuse, Washington to M. Laloy, MAE, July 26, 1963, 179QO/229, CADC.
66. Telegram POLTO 107, Finletter, NATO Paris to Secretary of State, July 26, 1963, RG 59, CFPF 1963, EDU 15, box 3240, NA.
67. Telegram 1537, NATO Paris to External, July 18, 1963, RG 25, 6081 50341-C-40 File Part 4.1, LAC; Letter, A. E. Donald, NATO Paris to J. S. Whitehead, Foreign Office, July 18, 1963, FO 371/169310, TNA; Note: 1968 OG, July 19, 1963, 1667INVA/405, CADC.
68. Telegram TOPOL 127, Rusk, Department of State to AmEmbassy Paris, July 29, 1963, RG 59, CFPF 1963, EDU 15, box 3240, NA.
69. Letter, L. Zanchi to Douglas F. Roby, July 17, 1963, C-J04–1968/001, Villes candidates,

Detroit, OSC; Letter, Douglas F. Roby to L. Zanchi, July 25, 1963, C-J04–1968/001, Villes candidates, Detroit, OSC; Telegram TOPOL 164, Ball, Department of State to AmEmbassy Paris, August 6, 1963, RG 59, CFPF 1963, EDU 15, box 3240, NA; Letter, Jerome P. Cavanagh to Otto Mayer, August 7, 1963, C-J04–1968/001, Villes candidates, Detroit, OSC.

70. Telegram POLTO 127, Finletter, NATO Paris to Secretary of State, July 31, 1963, RG 59, CFPF 1963, EDU 15, box 324, NA.
71. Note 487, pour la Direction d'Europe (Europe Centrale), July 30, 1963, 179QO/229, CADC; Airgram POLTO A-110, Finletter, USRO/POL Paris to SecState Washington, August 1, 1963, RG 59, CFPF 1963, NATO 3, box 4229, NA.
72. Telegram S-229, Robertson, External to NATO Paris, July 19, 1963, RG 25, 6081 50341-C-40 File Part 4.1, LAC.
73. Telegram S-243, External to Washington, August 1, 1963, RG 25, 6081 50341-C-40 File Part 4.1, LAC; Telegram 2473, Washington to External, August 2, 1963, RG 25, 6081 50341-C-40 File Part 4.1, LAC.
74. Paul Martin, Memorandum to the Cabinet, 1968 Olympic Winter Games and Berlin Travel Control, August 16, 1963, RG 25, 6081 50341-C-40 File Part 4.1, LAC.
75. Letter, N. A. Robertson to Joseph W. Willard, April 11, 1963, RG 29, 3284 file 7072–2 Part 1, LAC.
76. Paul Martin, Memorandum to the Cabinet, 1968 Olympic Winter Games and Berlin Travel Control, August 16, 1963.
77. G. A. Lahaie, Report on Special Meeting of August 27, 1963, to discuss with officials of the Canadian Olympic Association and the Calgary Olympic Development Association the International Olympic Committee's request for a certificate of entry, August 27, 1963, RG 84, 2146 U312-4-2 Calgary File Part 1, LAC.
78. Telegram S-293, External to Washington and NATO Paris, August 28, 1963, RG 25, 6081 50341-C-40 File Part 4.2, LAC.
79. Telegram TOPOL 243, Rusk, Department of State to AmEmbassy Paris, August 29, 1963, RG 59, CFPF 1963, EDU 15, box 3240, NA; Telegram 2757, Washington to External, August 30, 1963, RG 25, 6081 50341-C-40 File Part 4.2, LAC.
80. Telegram S-293, External to Washington and NATO Paris, August 28, 1963.
81. Telegram TOPOL 243, Rusk, Department of State to AmEmbassy Paris, August 29, 1963, RG 59, CFPF 1963, EDU 15, box 3240, NA; Telegram 2757, Washington to External, August 30, 1963; Letter, R. D. Clift, NATO Paris to J. S. Whitehead, Foreign Office, September 4, 1963, FO 371/169311, TNA.
82. Letter, Otto Mayer to Jerome P. Cavanagh, August 24, 1963, C-J04–1968/001, Villes candidates, Detroit, OSC.
83. Telegram 2780, Washington to External, September 4, 1963, RG 29, 3284 file 7072–2 Part 2, LAC.
84. Telegram POLTO 228, Finletter, NATO Paris to Secretary of State, September 4, 1963, RG 59, CFPF 1963, NATO 3–1, box 4230, NA; Telegram 2957, Washington to External, September 16, 1963, RG 29, 3284 file 7072–2 Part 2, LAC.
85. Emphasis in original. Benjamin H. Read, Memorandum for Mr. John Nolan, Department of Justice, September 10, 1963, RG 59, CFPF 1963, EDU 15, box 3240, NA.

86. Telegram POLTO 286, Finletter, NATO Paris to Secretary of State, September 17, 1963, RG 59, CFPF 1963, EDU 15, box 3240, NA.
87. Telegram 1889, NATO Paris to External, September 17, 1963, RG 29, 3284 file 7072–2 Part 2, LAC.
88. Telegram TOPOL 314, Rusk, Department of State to AmEmbassy Paris, September 16, 1963, RG 59, CFPF 1963, EDU 15, box 3240, NA.
89. Telegram POLTO 286, Finletter, NATO Paris to Secretary of State, September 17, 1963; Letter, A. E. Donald, NATO Paris to J. S. Whitehead, Foreign Office, September 18, 1963, FO 371/172194, TNA.
90. Telegram POLTO 300, Finletter, NATO Paris to Secretary of State, September 19, 1963, RG 59, CFPF 1963, EDU 15, box 3240, NA.
91. Telegram 337, Rusk, Department of State to AmEmbassy Paris TOPOL, September 20, 1963, RG 59, CFPF 1963, EDU 15, box 3240, NA.
92. Telegram POLTO 303, Finletter, NATO Paris to Secretary of State, September 20, 1963, RG 59, CFPF 1963, EDU 15, box 3240, NA.
93. Telegram POLTO 300, Finletter, NATO Paris to Secretary of State, September 19, 1963; Releve de decisions de la réunion interministerielle du Mercredi 11 septembre 1963 sur l'organisation des jeux olympiaues de 1968, September 11, 1963, AG/5(1)/107, ANP.
94. Fernschreiben 1234, Blankenhorn, Paris to Auswärtiges Amt, September 9, 1963, B 38/211, PAdAA; Oncken, Aufzeichnung: Betr.: Städte-Kandidatur für die Veranstaltung der Olympischen Spiele 1968, September 10, 1963, B 38/211, PAdAA; Verbeek, Auszug aus der Niederschrift über die Besprechung zwischen Ministerialdirektor Dr. Jansen und Gesandten Lucet, Directeur politique, im französischen Außenministerium vom 11. 9. 1963, September 11, 1963, B 38/211, PAdAA.
95. Despatch 107, J. de Beaumarchais to le secretaire d'etat à la jeunesse et aux sports—cabinet, September 21, 1963, 179QO/75, CADC.
96. Letter, Maurice Herzog to Michalon [*sic*], September 28, 1963, AG/5(1)/107, ANP. Herzog sent the same letter to Louis Pradel, the mayor of Lyon, that day. Letter, Maurice Herzog to Pradel, September 28, 1963, C-J04–1968/002, Villes candidates, Lyon, OSC.
97. Telegram POLTO Circular 29, Finletter, NATO Paris to Secretary of State, October 3, 1963, RG 59, CFPF 1963, EDU 15, box 3240, NA.
98. Telegram POLTO 286, Finletter, NATO Paris to Secretary of State, September 17, 1963.
99. Telegram D 10115, NATO Paris to Utenriksdepartement, September 17, 1963, 33.12/45. Pass- og visumforhold m.h.t. Ost-Tyskland. Bind II. (1.1.60–21.12.63), UD.
100. Telegram 10085, Utenriksdepartement to NATO Paris, September 13, 1963, 18.1/74 Öst-tyske innreisebestemmelser. Visum-forholdet til Öst-Tyskland. Bind 10 Fra 1/5.63—30/8.63, UD; Letter, Sigurd Sigurdsen to Statsministerens kontor, Formannen for Utenrikskomitéen, Justisdepartementet, September 18, 1963, 18.1/74 Öst-tyske innreisebestemmelser. Visum-forholdet til Öst-Tyskland. Bind 10 Fra 1/5.63—30/8.63, UD.
101. Letter 1857, Bjørn Kristvik, NATO Paris to Utenriksdepartement, September 24, 1963, 33.12/45. Pass-og visumforhold m.h.t. Ost-Tyskland. Bind II. (1.1.60–21.12.63), UD; AC/119-R(63)31: Committee of Political Advisers Meeting of 24th September,

1963 Action Sheet, September 26, 1963, NATO; Letter, Sigurd Sigurdsen to NATO-delegasjonen Paris, Ambassaden Bonn and Militærmisjonen Berlin, September 26, 1963, 18.1/74 Öst-tyske innreisebestemmelser. Visum-forholdet til Öst-Tyskland. Bind 10 Fra 1/5.63—30/8.63, UD; Letter, O. C. Gundersen to International Olympic Committee, September 25, 1963, C-J05–1968/003, Villes candidates, Oslo, OSC. The Norwegians also shared this letter with their NATO colleagues on October 8 and can be found in 179Q/75, CADC and FO 371/172195, TNA.

102. Telegram 260, Oslo to External, September 27, 1963, RG 29, 3284 file 7072–2 Part 2, LAC.
103. Telegram 351, Ball, Department of State to AmEmbassy Paris TOPOL, September 23, 1963, RG 59, CFPF 1963, EDU 15, box 3240, NA.
104. Telegram 351, Ball, Department of State to AmEmbassy Paris TOPOL, September 23, 1963; Telegram POLTO Circular 29, Finletter, NATO Paris to Secretary of State, October 3, 1963.
105. Telegram 351, Ball, Department of State to AmEmbassy TOPOL, September 23, 1963; Telegram 2957, Washington to External, September 16, 1963.
106. Telegrams from External: S-199 to Buenos Aires, S-200 to Mexico, S-201 to Helsinki, S-202 to Tokyo, and S-203 to Bern. S-199 is missing from this folder, but Telegram S-205, External to NATO Paris mentions all five telegrams, including the one to Argentina. All telegrams: June 27, 1963, RG 25, 6081 50341-C-40 File Part 4.1, LAC.
107. Telegram 18, Cleveland, Helsinki to External, June 29, 1963, RG 25, 6081 50341-C-40 File Part 4.1, LAC; Telegram 60, Bern to External, July 3, 1963, RG 25, 6081 50341-C-40 File Part 4.1, LAC; Telegram 260, Bower, Tokyo to External, July 4, 1963, RG 25, 6081 50341-C-40 File Part 4.1, LAC; Telegram 108, Mexico to External, July 11, 1963, RG 25, 6081 50341-C-40 File Part 4.1, LAC; Letter 312, Buenos Aires to Under-Secretary of State for External Affairs, July 17, 1963 RG 25, 6081 50341-C-40 File Part 4.1, LAC.
108. Brendan Kelly, *The Good Fight: Marcel Cadieux and Canadian Diplomacy* (Vancouver: University of British Columbia Press, 2019), 133, 160; Stephen Azzi, "The Problem Child: Diefenbaker and Canada in the Language of the Kennedy Administration," in *Reassessing the Rogue Tory: Canadian Foreign Relations in the Diefenbaker Era*, ed. Janice Cavell and Ryan M. Touhey (Vancouver: University of British Columbia Press, 2018).
109. "Klare Sprache," *Neues Deutschland*, March 18, 1963, 3.
110. N. A. R., Memorandum for the Minister: Entry Problem for the 1968 Winter Olympics, August 14, 1963, RG 25, 6081 50341-C-40 File Part 4.1, LAC.
111. Airgram A-1379, Finletter, USRO/POL Paris to SecState Washington, June 27, 1963.

CHAPTER 6: THE 1968 OLYMPIC HOST CITY ELECTIONS

1. Ref. No. 238, Avery Brundage and Otto Mayer, August 23, 1963, C-J05–1968/001, Villes candidates, OSC; Maureen Margaret Smith, "Revisiting South Africa and the Olympic Movement: The correspondence of Reginald S. Alexander and the

International Olympic Committee, 1961–86," *International Journal of the History of Sport* 23, no. 7 (2006): 1195.

2. Letter, Otto Mayer to Olaf Ditlev-Simonsen, March 11, 1963, Ditlev-Simonsen, Olaf, Correspondance 1925–1978, OSC.
3. For more details about the lengths to which the candidate cities for the 1968 games went to win the Olympics, see Heather L. Dichter, "Corruption in the 1960s?: Rethinking the Origins of Unethical Olympic Bidding Tactics," *International Journal of the History of Sport* 33, no. 6–7 (2016): 666–82.
4. In 1963 the only IOC members from the African continent came from Egypt, Morocco, Kenya, South Africa, and Nigeria. Because the Baden-Baden meeting included the vote for the 1968 Summer Olympic host, all of the international federations for sports on the summer games program sent representatives as well, which increased the number of individuals to whom Kenya would refuse visas.
5. Martin S. Hayden, "Detroit's Brains, Brawn: Executives Pitch In to Set Up Exhibit," *Detroit News*, October 17, 1963, 1–2, box 2, Olympic Games—Detroit Olympic Bids, Douglas F. Roby Collection (DFR), BHL; "Detroit Seeks Olympic Bid at Confab," *Holland (MI) Evening Sentinel*, October 14, 1963, 7.
6. Hayden, "Detroit's Brains, Brawn."
7. Hans Maciej, Report on the 60th Session of the International Olympic Committee—Baden-Baden, West Germany, October 14–20, 1963, RG 84, 2150 file U312-4-2 part 5, LAC.
8. Maciej, Report on the 60th Session of the International Olympic Committee; "Lyons Makes a Lavish Pitch to Be Site for 1968 Olympics," *New York Times*, October 17, 1963, 47.
9. Hayden, "Detroit's Brains, Brawn."
10. L. F., "La gastronomie lyonnaise sera présente à Baden-Baden," n.p., October 16, 1963 in 3 Cp 250–3R41 Sports: les jeux olympiques, AML; "Lyons Makes a Lavish Pitch."
11. "Chancen für 1968," *Frankfurter Allgemeine Zeitung*, October 17, 1963, 6.
12. "Der Sport hilft bei der Verständigung der Völker," *Frankfurt Allgemeine Zeitung*, October 17, 1963, 6.
13. Circular Letter No. 240, to the International Federations (of Summer Sports), August 25, 1963, Circulaires 1962 à 1964, OSC.
14. The IOC maintained the schedule, set initially for Nairobi, for Baden-Baden. Otto Mayer to the Cities candidate to the organization of the Games of the XIXe Olympiade in 1968, April 3, 1963, C-J04–1968/001, Villes candidates, OSC; "I morgen faller avgjørelsen for 1968," *Sportsmanden*, October 17, 1963, 11.
15. Maciej, Report on the 60th Session of the International Olympic Committee.
16. Maciej, Report on the 60th Session of the International Olympic Committee.
17. "Mexico City Wins '68 Games," *Oakland Tribune*, October 18, 1963, 57.
18. "Detroit Delegates Bid for 1968 Olympics Friday," *Traverse City (MI) Record-Eagle*, October 15, 1963, 14.
19. "Detroit 'Never Had a Chance' for Olympics," *Traverse City (MI) Record-Eagle*, October 19, 1963, 1.
20. Maciej, Report on the 60th Session of the International Olympic Committee.

21. "Mexico City Picked over Detroit, Lyons, and Buenos Aires for '68 Olympics," *New York Times*, October 19, 1963, 42.
22. "Detroit 'Never Had a Chance.'"
23. "Les jeux olympiques de 1968: Les pays africains voteront pour Lyon," *Le Monde*, October 18, 1963, 17.
24. "Detroit 'Never Had a Chance.'"
25. Horst Wardenbach, "Der Kongreß," *Frankfurter Allgemeine Zeitung*, October 21, 1963, 10.
26. Kevin B. Witherspoon, *Before the Eyes of the World: Mexico and the 1968 Olympic Games* (Dekalb, IL: Northern Illinois University Press, 2008), 116–17.
27. For details about Beliard's career, see "Me. Jean BELIARD, Ambassadeur de France au Canada," *NOUVELLES, Bulletin de l'Union des Français de l'Etranger en Ontario*, no. 2 (March 1982), http://www.ufetoronto.org/wp-content/uploads/2015/10/nouvelles-2.pdf (accessed April 13, 2019).
28. Telegram 52, Beliard, Chicago to Diplomatie Paris, November 13, 1963, 179QO/75, CADC.
29. IOC votes are secret, but this list demonstrates that the IOC president, as well as members from countries with candidate cities, voted in each round, unlike current rules. Jeux Olympiques 1968—Vote de Baden-Baden, n.d. [October 1963], AG/5(1)/107, ANP. An unknown newspaper in France published this exact list, which the Lyon archive holds in a clippings file. "Un pointage vraisemblable," n.d. [October 1963] in 90 WP 001 5—SPORT ET TOURISME:—Tournois internationaux : Jeux Olympiques d'été de 1968, AML.
30. Telegram 52, Beliard, Chicago to Diplomatie Paris, November 13, 1963.
31. The French list was missing the names for five votes, two each for Mexico City and Lyon and one for Detroit. A total of sixty-two members attended the Baden-Baden session, but only fifty-eight members voted. It is not known which of the following people are the five unaccounted for votes: Jean Ketseas (Greece), Prince Alex (Denmark), Ivar Vind (Denmark), Prince François-Joseph (Lichtenstein), Hadj Mohammed Benjelloun (Morocco), Olav Ditlev-Simonsen (Norway), A. Ademolo (Nigeria), Duke of Sparta (Greece), and Marc Hodler (Switzerland). Jeux Olympiques 1968—Vote de Baden-Baden; Minutes of the 60th Session, Baden-Baden, October 16–20, 1963, IOC Sessions 1960–1969, OSC.
32. "Detroit 'Never Had a Chance.'"
33. H. Coury, Note, October 29, 1963, AG/5(1)/107, ANP.
34. "Japan bewirbt sich auch um Olympische Winterspiele," *Frankfurter Allgemeine Zeitung*, December 6, 1963, 8.
35. "Banff Still Has Chance Says Mayor," *Lethbridge (AB) Herald*, December 31, 1963, 13.
36. "C'est M. Pompidou qui devra donner l'assurance que les visas seront délivrés," October 16, 1963, *Le Progrès*, 10; "Le problème des visas doit être résolu par le premier ministre," October 17, 1963, *Le Progrès*, 10; "Feu vert pour les visas," October 18, 1963, *Le Progrès*, 10.
37. Telegram 52, Beliard, Chicago to Diplomatie Paris, November 13, 1963.
38. Letter, G. A. Lahaie to J. H. Messinger, October 23, 1963, RG 84, 2146 U312-4-2 Calgary File Part 1, LAC.
39. Letter, J. H. Messinger to G. A. Lahaie, October 25, 1963, RG 25, 5251 8137–40 File

Part 7, LAC; Letter, M. H. Wershof to G. A. Lahaie, November 1, 1963, RG 25, 5559 12744-A-40 File Part 2, LAC.

40. Letter, Lyndon B. Johnson to Otto Mayer, December 27, 1963, C-J05–1968 / 002, Villes candidates, Lake Placid, OSC.

41. Letter, Georges Pompidou to Dr. Michallon, December 17, 1963, 4R1, Candidature, AG.

42. Telegram 52, Beliard, Chicago to Diplomatie Paris, November 13, 1963; Letter, Georges Pompidou to Dr. Michallon, December 17, 1963.

43. Telegram D 10010, NATO Paris to Utenriksdepartement, January 22, 1964, 18.1 / 74 Öst-tyske innreisebestemmelser. Visum forholdet til Öst-Tyskland. Bind 11 Fra 1 / 10.63—28 / 2.64, UD.

44. Dichter, "Corruption in the 1960s?"

45. "Oslos bidrag til OL-utstillingen imponerer ikke," *Aftenposten*, January 28, 1964, 15.

46. "First Unit Leaves for Innsbruck," *Lake Placid News*, January 16, 1964, 1.

47. Numbered Letter 13, The Hague to Under-Secretary of State for External Affairs, January 10, 1964, RG 25, 10528 55–26-OLYMP File Part 1.1, LAC; R. Fuss, "Le Canada est prêt à accueillir les Jeux olympiques d'hiver de 1968," *Le Soir*, March 22, 1963, 13.

48. Letter, J. H. Messinger to G. A. Lahaie, December 9, 1963, RG 25, 10528 55–26-OLYMP File Part 1.1, LAC; Telegram J-953, External to Vienna, December 13, 1963, RG 25, 10528 55–26-OLYMP File Part 1.1, LAC; Telegram 299, Vienna to External, December 17, 1963, RG 25, 10528 55–26-OLYMP File Part 1.1, LAC; Margaret K. Weiers, *Envoys Extraordinary: Women of the Canadian Foreign Service* (Toronto: Dundurn Press, 1995), 49–61.

49. "Oslos bidrag til OL-utstillingen imponerer ikke," *Aftenposten*, January 28, 1964, 15.

50. Hans Maciej, Report on the 61st Session of the International Olympic Committee, January 26–28, 1964, RG 25, 10528 55–26-OLYMP File Part 1.2, LAC.

51. Circular Letter No. 247 to the International Federation of Winter Sports, December 1963, Circulaires 1962 à 1964, OSC.

52. "Banff looking ahead to 1968 Winter Olympics," *Medicine Hat (AB) News*, January 25, 1964, 9; Hans Maciej, Report on the 61st Session of the International Olympic Committee, January 26–28, 1964.

53. Hans Maciej, Report on the 61st Session of the International Olympic Committee, January 26–28, 1964; Jack Sullivan, "In Bidding for 1972 Games: Canadian Body May Seek Another Olympic Centre," *Lethbridge (AB) Herald*, January 29, 1964, 11.

54. Films CinéPress / Jack Lesage, February 26, 2016, https: / / cinevod.bm-grenoble.fr / news / 2016 / 02 / 26 / films-cinpress-jack-lesage (accessed April 27, 2019); Ski du monde, https: / / cinevod.bm-grenoble.fr / video / LPEZA-ski-du-monde (accessed April 27, 2019).

55. Speech, Lahti Mayor to IOC, n.d. [January 1964], C-J05–1968 / 002, Villes candidates, Lahti, OSC.

56. "Bid Delegation Leaves for Innsbruck Friday," *Lake Placid News*, January 23, 1964, 1; "1968 Winter Olympic Games Bid Material," *Lake Placid News*, January 23, 1964, 3, 6.

57. Ordførerens innledende tale i Innsbruck, January 28, 1964, Rolf Petersen Oslo 1968, Skimuseet, Oslo.

58. Hans Maciej, Report on the 61st Session of the International Olympic Committee, January 26–28, 1964.

59. Robert Daley, "Losers Wonder: Why Grenoble?" *New York Times*, January 29, 1964, 25.

60. "Telegram til Brundage gir efterdønninger," *Aftenposten*, January 30, 1964, 6; Hans Maciej, Report on the 61st Session of the International Olympic Committee, January 26–28, 1964.
61. Sullivan, "In Bidding for 1972 Games."
62. *Le Dauphiné Libéré*, January 29, 1964, 1, 10–11.
63. "Enthousiasme à Grenoble ville olympique," *Le Monde*, January 30, 1964, 17.
64. Daley, "Losers Wonder: Why Grenoble?"
65. Paula D. Welch, "Chamonix 1924," in *Encyclopedia of the Modern Olympic Movement*, ed. John E. Findling and Kimberly D. Pelle (Westport, CT: Greenwood Press, 2004), 283–87.

CHAPTER 7: DECISIONS REVISITED

1. Airgram A-517, R. Glynn Mays, Jr., Berlin to Department of State, February 16, 1964, RG 59, CFPF 1964–66, POL 2 GER E, box 2201, NA.
2. "Dispute on German Team Dampens Olympic Flag Ceremony in Tokyo," *New York Times*, October 3, 1964, 23.
3. Jeffrey Glen Giauque, *Grand Designs and Visions of Unity: The Atlantic Powers andthe Reorganization of Western Europe, 1955–1963* (Chapel Hill: University of North Carolina Press, 2002), 4.
4. C-R(63)63: Summary record of a meeting of the Council, held at the Permanent Headquarters, Paris, XVIe., on Wednesday, 6th November, 1963, November 13, 1963, NATO.
5. Telegram 246, Blair, Copenhagen to Secretary of State, September 23, 1963, RG 59, CFPF 1963, POL 36 W EUR, box 4139, NA; Telegram 274, Blair, Copenhagen to Secretary of State, October 3, 1963, RG 59, CFPF 1963, POL 36 W EUR, box 4139, NA.
6. Letter, David Ormsby Gore, Washington to Harold Caccia, Foreign Office, October 8, 1963, FO 371/172195, TNA; Telegram 308, Blair, Copenhagen to Secretary of State, October 17, 1963, RG 59, CFPF 1963, POL 36 W EUR, box 4139, NA.
7. Letter, Evelyn Shuckburgh, NATO Paris to Harold Caccia, Foreign Office, October 3, 1963, FO 371/172195, TNA.
8. Telegram 1117, McGhee, Bonn to Secretary of State, September 26, 1963, RG 59, CFPF 1963, POL 36 W EUR, box 4139, NA.
9. Telegram 1097, Bonn to Foreign Office, October 17, 1963, FO 371/172195, TNA.
10. Telegram 1097, Bonn to Foreign Office, October 17, 1963.
11. Telegram 1104, Bonn to Foreign Office, October 18, 1963, FO 371/172195, TNA.
12. Telegram 7886/88, Margerie, Bonn to Diplomatie Paris, October 22, 1963, 105PO/1, box 9, CADN.
13. Telegram 3266, Washington to Foreign Office, October 21, 1963, FO 371/172195, TNA.
14. Telegram 3397, Washington to Foreign Office, November 1, 1963, FO 371/172195, TNA.
15. Telegram 1609, McGhee, Bonn to Secretary of State, October 30, 1963, RG 59, CFPF 1963, POL 36 W EUR, box 4139, NA.
16. Telegram 1179, Bonn to Foreign Office, November 4, 1963, FO 371/172196, TNA.

17. Letter, M. D. Butler, Paris to J. S. Whitehead, Foreign Office, November 16, 1963, FO 371/172197, TNA.
18. Letter, M. D. Butler, Paris to J. S. Whitehead, Foreign Office, November 16, 1963.
19. Royal Danish Embassy, Aide Memoire, October 24, 1963, FO 371/172195, TNA.
20. Royal Danish Embassy, Aide Memoire, October 24, 1963.
21. Telegram POLTO CIRCR 36, Finletter, NATO Paris to Secretary of State, October 23, 1963, RG 59, CFPF 1963, POL 36 W EUR, box 4139, NA.
22. Telegram POLTO 621, Finletter, NATO Paris to Secretary of State, November 11, 1963, RG 59, CFPF 1963, POL 36 W EUR, box 4139, NA.
23. Telegram TOPOL 75, McGee, Bonn to Paris, November 16, 1963, RG 59, CFPF 1963, POL 36 W EUR, box 4139, NA.
24. Telegram TOPOL 75, McGee, Bonn to Paris, November 16, 1963.
25. Telegram 8201–06, Margerie, Bonn to Diplomatie Paris, November 4, 1963, 105PO/1, box 9, CADN; Telegram 1619, Diplomatie Paris to REPAN, November 5, 1963, 105PO/1, box 9, CADN; Telegram 9431–32, Diplomatie Paris to Ambafrance Bonn, November 16, 1963, 105PO/1, box 9, CADN.
26. Letter, A. A. Dugg, Bonn to H. T. A. Overton, Foreign Office, November 14, 1963, FO 371/172197, TNA.
27. Telegram 1259, Bonn to Foreign Office, November 23, 1963, FO 371/172197, TNA.
28. Telegram TOPOL 84, McGhee, Bonn to Paris, November 25, 1963, RG 59, CFPF 1963, POL 36 W EUR, box 4139, NA.
29. Telegram TOPOL 84, McGhee, Bonn to Paris, November 25, 1963.
30. Letter, A. E. Donald, NATO Paris to J. S. Whitehead, Foreign Office, November 27, 1963, FO 371/172197, TNA.
31. Telegram POLTO 621, Finletter, NATO Paris to Secretary of State, November 15, 1963; Telegram 662, Finletter, NATO Paris to Secretary of State, November 20, 1963, RG 59, CFPF 1963, POL 36 W EUR, box 4139, NA; Letter, W. B. J. Ledwidge, Foreign Office to A. A. Duff, Bonn, November 22, 1963, FO 371/172197, TNA.
32. Telegram POLTO 1018, Finletter, NATO Paris to SecState Washington, January 28, 1964, RG 59, CFPF 1964–66, POL 23–10 GER B, box 2197, NA; Letter, R. D. Clift, NATO Paris to D. N. Beevor, Foreign Office, January 29, 1964, FO 371/177988, TNA; AC/119-R(64)3: Committee of Political Advisers Meeting on 28th January, 1964 Action Sheet, February 3, 1964, NATO.
33. Letter, J. L. Bullard, Bonn to J. S. Whitehead, Foreign Office, January 18, 1964, FO 371/177988, TNA.
34. Telegram 104, NATO Paris to Foreign Office, February 18, 1964, FO 371/177988, TNA; AC/119-R(64)7: Committee of Political Advisers Meeting on 17th and 18th February, 1964 Action Sheet, February 21, 1964, NATO; C-M(64)12: Restrictions on Travel by Soviet Zone Residents, February 26, 1964, NATO; Telegram 127, UK NATO Paris to Foreign Office, March 4, 1964, FO 371/177988, TNA.
35. Telegram 127, NATO Paris to Foreign Office, March 4, 1964, FO 371/177988, TNA; UK Delegation to NATO Paris, Memorandum: NORTH ATLANTIC COUNCIL, Item IV: Temporary Travel Documents, COUNCIL MEETING: WEDNESDAY, March 4, 1964, March 5, 1964, FO 371/177988, TNA.
36. C-R(64)10: Summary record of a meeting of the Council, held at the Permanent

Headquarters, Paris, XVIe., on Wednesday, 4th March, 1964, March 13, 1964, NATO.

37. Telegram 185, Berlin to Foreign Office, March 6, 1964, FO 371/177988, TNA; Telegram 130, NATO Paris to Foreign Office, March 6, 1964, FO 371/177988, TNA; Telegram 285, Bonn to Foreign Office, March 9, 1964, FO 371/177988, TNA; Telegram 316, Bonn to Foreign Office, March 17, 1964, FO 371/177988, TNA; Letter, R. D. Clift, NATO Paris to D. N. Beevor, Foreign Office, April 6, 1964, FO 371/177988, TNA.

38. C-R(64)14: Summary record of a meeting of the Council, held at the Permanent Headquarters, Paris, XVIe., on Wednesday, 18th March, 1964, March 26, 1964, NATO; Telegram 352, Bonn to Foreign Office, March 29, 1964, FO 371/177988, TNA.

39. PO/64/106(2nd Revise): Restrictions on Travel by Soviet Zone Residents, Draft Public Statement, March 17, 1964, NATO.

40. Telegram 318, Bonn to Foreign Office, March 19, 1964, FO 371/177988, TNA; Norman Crossland, "East German athletes to get permits," *Guardian*, March 19, 1964, 1.

41. B. M. Riise, Notat: Reiserestriksjoner for øst-tyskere, January 24, 1964, 18.1/74 Öst-tyske innreisebestemmelser. Visum forholdet til Öst-Tyskland. Bind 11 Fra 1/10.63–28/2.64, UD; Airgram A-308, Wharton, AmEmbassy Oslo to Department of State, January 17, 1964, RG 59, CFPF 1964–66, EDU 15 NOR, box 370, NA.

42. Telegram D 10157, NATO Paris to Utenriksdepartement, November 27, 1963, 33.12/45. Pass- og visumforhold m.h.t. Ost-Tyskland. Bind II. (1.1.60–21.12.63), UD; AC/119-R(63)40: Committee of Political Advisers Meeting of 26th November, 1963 Action Sheet, November 28, 1963, NATO; Telegram A 10031, Bonn to Utenriksdepartement, December 13, 1963, 18.1/74 Öst-tyske innreisebestemmelser. Visum forholdet til Öst-Tyskland. Bind 11 Fra 1/10.63–28/2.64, UD; Telegram A 10034, Bonn to Utenriksdepartement, December 21, 1963, 18.1/74 Öst-tyske innreisebestemmelser. Visum forholdet til Öst-Tyskland. Bind 11 Fra 1/10.63–28/2.64, UD.

43. Airgram A-308, Wharton, AmEmbassy Oslo to Department of State, January 17, 1964; AC/119-R(64)1: Committee of Political Advisers Meeting of 14th January, 1964 Action Sheet, January 17, 1964, NATO.

44. Airgram A-308, Wharton, AmEmbassy Oslo to Department of State, January 17, 1964.

45. B. M. Riise, Notat: Reiserestriksjoner for øst-tyskere, January 24, 1964.

46. Telegram 681, Department of State to AmEmbassy Paris TOPOL, November 24, 1963, RG 59, CFPF 1963, POL 36 W EUR, box 4139, NA.

47. Emphasis in original. Letter, Robert F. Kennedy to Henry M. Beatty, October 28, 1963, 18.1/74 Öst-tyske innreisebestemmelser. Visum forholdet til Öst-Tyskland. Bind 11 Fra 1/10.63–28/2.64, UD.

48. "U.S. to Allow Entry to Foreign Skaters," *New York Times*, November 19, 1963, 69; Letter 915, B. M. Riise to Norges feste delegasjon ved NATO, November 22, 1963, 18.1/74 Öst-tyske innreisebestemmelser. Visum forholdet til Öst-Tyskland. Bind 11 Fra 1/10.63–28/2.64, UD.

49. Despatch, J. de Beaumarchais, MAE to Ambassadeur de France aux Etats-Unis, December 5, 1963, 105PO/1, box 9, CADN.

50. B. M. Riise, Notat: Reiserestriksjoner for øst-tyskere, January 24, 1964.

51. Telegram UD 10030, Utenriksdepartement to Bonn, December 14, 1963, 18.1/74

Öst-tyske innreisebestemmelser. Visum forholdet til Öst-Tyskland. Bind 11 Fra 1/10.63–28/2.64, UD.

52. Telegram POLTO CIRC 46, NATO Paris to Secretary of State, November 26, 1963, RG 59, CFPF 1963, POL 36 W EUR, box 4139, NA.
53. Letter, W. B. J. Ledwidge, Foreign Office to J. L. Bullard, Bonn, April 13, 1964, FO 371/177987, TNA; Letter, A. A. Stark to Dirk Oncken, April 20, 1964, B 38/59, PAdAA. Stark's letter, which he states he copied to the American and French ambassadors in Bonn, also appears in 105PO/1, box 9, CADN.
54. Letter, Robert Mathew to Avery Brundage, June 22, 1964, FO 371/177987, TNA.
55. Telegram 4095–96, Margerie, Bonn to Diplomatie Paris, June 11, 1964, 105PO/1, box 9, CADN; Despatch 65/EU, J. L. Toffin to Ambassadeur de France près la Republique Fédérale D'Allemagne, July 20, 1964, 105PO/1, box 9, CADN. The MAE finally sent its letter to Brundage on July 7, as noted in Otto Mayer's reply. Letter, Otto Mayer to Ministre des Affaires Etrangères, July 10, 1964, 179QO/229, CADC.
56. Letter, Robert Mathew to Avery Brundage, June 22, 1964.
57. Letter, Otto Mayer to Robert Mathew, July 7, 1964, FO 371/177987, TNA.
58. Letter, W. M. Marsden, NATO Paris to D. J. Hall, Foreign Office, January 13, 1965, FO 371/183141, TNA; C-R(65)1: Summary record of a meeting of the Council, held at the Permanent Headquarters, Paris, XVIe., on Wednesday, 13th January, 1965, January 20, 1965, NATO.
59. Telegram 5360/64, François Seydoux, Bonn to Diplomatie Paris, September 16, 1965, 105PO/1, box 9, CADN.
60. Minutes of the 62nd Session of the International Olympic Committee, October 6–8, 1964, IOC Sessions (1960–1969), OSC.
61. Uta Balbier, *Kalter Krieg auf der Aschenbahn: der deutsch-deutsche Sport, 1950–1972: eine politische Geschichte* (Paderborn: F. Schöning, 2007), 74–87, 120–27.
62. Airgram A-278, Francis J. Meehan, Berlin to Department of State, October 16, 1964, RG 59, CFPF 1964–66, POL 2 GER E, box 2201, NA; John Rodda, "Olympic Games: North Koreans Leave the State," *Guardian*, October 9, 1964, 15.
63. Airgram A-278, Francis J. Meehan, Berlin to Department of State, October 16, 1964.
64. Letter, Dr. Hans Schäfer to Rolf Lahr, January 11, 1965, B 2/155, PAdAA.
65. Lahr, Betr.: Deutsche Olympia-Mannschaft, January 13, 1965, B 2/156, PadAA. Daume and Herzog planned to discuss the issue when Daume would be in Paris for the French Open. Telegram, Willi Daume to Maurice Herzog, n.d. [April 1965], 105PO/1, box 9, CADN; Telegram, Maurice Herzog to Willi Daume, April 23, 1965, 105PO/1, box 9, CADN.
66. Letter, Dr. Gradl to Dr. Gerhard Schröder, March 3, 1965, B 94/331, PAdAA; Letter, Schröder to Dr. Gradl, March 17, 1965, B 94/331, PAdAA; Letter, Dr. v. Plehwe to Noebel, March 19, 1965, B 94/331, PAdAA; Letter, Sattler to Bundespräsidialamt, March 24, 1965, B 94/331, PAdAA.
67. Despatch 1375, François Seydoux, Bonn to Maurice Couve de Murville, MAE, August 21, 1965, 105PO/1, box 9, CADN.
68. Telegram 5036/38, François Seydoux, Bonn to Diplomatie Paris, September 2, 1965, 105PO/1, box 9, CADN; Telegram 615, McGhee, Bonn to Ruehcr/SecState Washington, September 2, 1965, RG 59, CFPF 1964–66, CUL 15, box 336, NA.

69. Letter, A. W. Rhodes, Bonn to D. J. Hall, Foreign Office, September 17, 1965, FO 371/183165, TNA.
70. Letter, Avery Brundage to Nationales Olympisches Komitee für Deutschland and Nationales Olympisches Komitee der Deutschen Demokratischen Republik, June 2, 1965, FO 371/183165, TNA.
71. Telegram 680, McGhee, Bonn to Ruehcr/SecState Washington, September 9, 1965, RG 59, CFPF 1964–66, CUL 15, box 336, NA.
72. Telegram 693/698, Boisseson, Madrid to Diplomatie, October 6, 1965, 105PO/1, box 9, CADN.
73. Minutes of the 63rd Session of the International Olympic Committee, October 7–9, 1965, IOC Sessions (1960–69), OSC.
74. Minutes of the 63rd Session of the International Olympic Committee, October 7–9, 1965; Telegram 347, Duke, Madrid to Ruehcr/SecState Washington, October 8, 1965, RG 59, CFPF 1964–66, CUL 15, box 336, NA; "East Germans to Enter Own Team at Olympics," *Times* (London), October 9, 1965, 8.
75. Telegram 693/698, Boisseson, Madrid to Diplomatie Paris, October 6, 1965.
76. Telegram 699/700, Boisseson, Madrid to Diplomatie Paris, October 9, 1965, 105PO/1, box 9, CADN.
77. Telegram 1005, McGhee, Bonn to Ruehcr/SecState Washington, October 8, 1965, RG 59, CFPF 1964–66, CUL 15, box 336, NA.
78. Note, October 8, 1965, B 2/156, PAdAA.
79. "Separate East German Olympic Team Approved," *New York Times*, October 9, 1965, 10; Karlheinz Vogel, "Der Kompromiß des IOC brfriedigt weder Ost noch West," *Frankfurter Allgemeine Zeitung*, October 9, 1965, 12; Richard Aschenborn "Gesamtdeutsche Olympiamannschaft geplatzt Zone dringt mit ihrer Forderung durch," *Süddeutsche Zeitung*, October 9–10, 1965, 1–2; "La Préparation des Jeux de 1968," *Le Monde*, October 9, 1965, 9; Stein Savik, "CIO-vedtaket et nederlag for Bonn," *Aftenposten*, October 9, 1965, 6.
80. Telegram 1705, Bonn to Foreign Office, October 9, 1965, FO 371/183165, TNA.
81. "East Germans to Enter Own Team at Olympics," *Times* (London), October 9, 1965, 8.
82. "IOC-Entscheidung in Madrid: Olympische Idee siegte," *Neue Zeit*, October 9, 1965, 1; "Travel Rules Affected," *New York Times*, October 9, 1965, 10; "East Germans to Enter Own Team at Olympics."
83. Letter, Lord Exeter to P. C. H. Holmer, November 8, 1965, FO 371/183165, TNA.
84. Klaus Ullricht, "Die dramatischen Stunden von Madrid," *Neues Deutschland*, October 9, 1965, 2; Telegram 346, Calhoun, Berlin to Ruehcr/SecState Washington, October 9, 1965, RG 59, CFPF 1964–66, CUL 15, box 336, NA; "IOC-Kongress in Madrid beendet," *Neues Deutschland*, October 10, 1965, 9; Letter H. F. Stierer, Berlin to J. L. Bullard, Bonn, October 13, 1965, FO 371/183165, TNA.
85. Telegram 1005, McGhee, Bonn to Ruehcr/SecState Washington, October 8, 1965, RG 59, CFPF 1964–66, CUL 15, box 336, NA.
86. Telegram 940, McGhee, Bonn to Ruehcr/SecState Washington, October 1, 1965, RG 59, CFPF 1964–66, CUL 15, box 336, NA.
87. Telegram 835, Ball, Department of State to AmEmbassy Bonn, October 4, 1965, RG 59, CFPF 1964–66, CUL 15, box 33, NA.

88. Telegram 941, McGhee, Bonn to Ruehcr / SecState Washington, October 1, 1965, RG 59, CFPF 1964–66, CUL 15, box 336, NA.
89. Telegram 994, McGhee, Bonn to Ruehcr / SecState Washington, October 7, 1965, RG 59, CFPF 1964–66, CUL 15, box 336, NA; Telegram 5677 / 81, François Seydoux, Bonn to Diplomatie Paris, October 8, 1965, 105PO / 1, box 9, CADN.
90. Letter, Georges Pompidou to Dr. Michallon, December 17, 1963, 4R1—Candidature, AG.
91. Letter, CAB 293, Maurice Herzog to Monsieur Puaux, April 16, 1965, 179QO / 229, CADC; Telegram 2746 / 47, François Seydoux, Bonn to Diplomatie Paris, April 17, 1963, 105PO / 1, box 9, CADN.
92. Telegram 3310–13, Diplomatie Paris to Ambafrance Bonn, April 26, 1965, 105PO / 1, box 9, CADN.
93. "Grenoble May Lose '68 Olympics," *New York Herald Tribune*, April 13, 1965, held in 179QO / 229, CADC; "Grenoble Faces Prospect of Losing 1968 Olympics," *New York Times*, April 13, 1965, 45; Neal Ascherson, "Germans Face Olympic Split," *Observer* (London), April 18, 1965, 20.
94. F. M-B., Note pour la delegation de la France au conseil de l'Atlantique-Nord, July 19, 1965, 179QO / 75, CADC.
95. Letter, W. Marsden, NATO Paris to P. C. H. Holmer, Foreign Office, July 21, 1965, FO 371 / 183165, TNA.
96. Telegram 667 / 69, F. Puaux, Diplomatie to Ambafrance Madrid, October 7, 1965, 179QO / 74, CADC.
97. Telegram 278, Calhoun, Berlin to Ruehcr / SecState Washington, August 28, 1964, RG 59, CFPF 1964–66, Culture and Information, EDU 15–1 Olympic Games JAPAN, box 366, NA; Letter, William Kane to Avery Brundage, September 8, 1964, Schobel, Dr. Heinz, 1955–1959, box 63, reel 37, ABC, UIA; Telegram 6299 / 301, Aumale, Bonn to Diplomatie Paris, November 12, 1965, 179QO / 229, CADC; Telegram 7121 / 22, François Seydoux, Bonn to Diplomatie Paris, December 22, 1965, 105PO / 1, box 9, CADN; Airgram A-987, James S. Sutterlin, Bonn to Department of State, December 29, 1965, RG 59, CFPF 1964–66, POL 28 GER B, box 2200, NA; Identity Cards, n.d. B 94 / 228, PAdAA.
98. C-M(66)12: Restrictions on Travel by Soviet Zone Residents, February 1, 1966, NATO.
99. FIS had decided at its 1963 Executive Council meeting that the same city could not organize the 1966 world championships and the 1968 Olympics. Minutes, FIS Council, Lanz, Austria, February 2, 1963, box 3, folder 10, JSM, RSCL; Letter, Einar Bergsland to Norges Idrettsforbund, April 13, 1962, RA / PA-0090 / D / Dd / L0355, Norges Idrettsforbund Idrett og Politikk, 1957–1970, Riksarkivet; Minutes from the meeting with the FIS Council in Athens, May 19, 1963, box 3, folder 10, JSM, RSCL; Roar Antonsen and Einar Bergsland, "VM på ski i Oslo 1966 eller OL i 1968," *Aftenposten*, May 27, 1963, 16.
100. Letter, Per Landmark to Allied Travel Office, January 19, 1966, 74.10 / 113. Tyskland: Idrett og sport. Bind II. Fra 1 / 1 1960–31 / 12–69, UD.
101. Letter 137, Sigurd Sigurdsen, Moscow to Utenriksdepartement, 18.1 / 74 Öst-tyske innreisebestemmelser. Visum forholdet til Öst-Tyskland. Bind 14 (Fra 19 / 2.66–

30/9.66), February 17, 1966, UD; "NATO weist Visaverweigerung an," *Neues Deutschland*, February 16, 1966, 8; "Øst-tyskerne protester mot norsk avgjørelse," *Aftenposten*, February 16, 1966, 11.

102. "Øst-Tyskerne og VM på Ski," *Dagbladet*, February 14, 1966, contained in 18.1/74 Öst-tyske innreisebestemmelser. Visum forholdet til Öst-Tyskland. Bind 14 (Fra 19/2.66–30/9.66), UD.
103. B. M. Riise, Notat: Innreisetillatelse for øst-tyske journalister til VM på Ski Samtale med Einar Bergsland, February 9, 1966, 18.1/74 Öst-tyske innreisebestemmelser. Visum forholdet til Öst-Tyskland. Bind 13 (1.4-65-18/2–66), UD.
104. B. M. Riise, Notat: Vest-tysk innsigelse mot øst-tyskeres angivelige bruk av "nasjonale" emblemer under VM på ski, February 17, 1966, 74.10/113. Tyskland: Idrett og sport. Bind II. Fra 1/1 1960–31/12–69, UD; Fernschreiben 49, Boex, Oslo to Auswärtiges Amt, February 17, 1966, B 94/352, PAdAA.
105. Fernschreiben 49, Boex, Oslo to Auswärtiges Amt, February 17, 1966.
106. Fernschreiben 31, Carstens, Auswärtiges Amt to Diplogerma Oslo, February 18, 1966, B 94/352, PAdAA.
107. "Neuendorf nur knapp besiegt," *Neues Deutschland*, February 20, 1966, 7.
108. Per G. Schøyen, Notat: TTD-systemet, February 22, 1966, 74.10/113. Tyskland: Idrett og sport. Bind II. Fra 1/1 1960–31/12–69, UD.
109. Emphasis in original. Fernschreiben 55, Boex, Oslo to Auswärtiges Amt, February 23, 1966, B 94/352, PAdAA.
110. Per G. Schøyen, Notat: TTD-systemet, February 22, 1966.
111. Airgram A-1715, McGhee, Bonn to Department of State, May 19, 1966, RG 59, CFPF 1964–66, CUL 15, box 336, NA; Letter, Dr. Kolb, Auswärtiges Amt to Konsulat Cleveland, June 14, 1966, B 94/352, PAdAA.
112. Airgram A-815, Day, Berlin to Department of State, Bonn and PARIS USRO, May 25, 1966, RG 59, CFPF 1964–66, POL 23–10 GER, box 2193, NA.
113. World Wrestling Bulletin, June 16, 1966, B 94/352, PAdAA.
114. Bericht 171/66, Cleveland to Auswärtiges Amt, June 21, 1966, B 94/352, PAdAA.
115. Airgram A-329, McGhee, Bonn to Department of State, September 9, 1966, RG 59, CFPF 1964–66, Political & Defense, box 2193, NA.
116. Telegram POLTO 621, Finletter, NATO Paris to Secretary of State, November 11, 1963.
117. Hans Otto Frøland, "Distrust, Dependency and Détente: Norway, the Two Germanys and 'the German Question', 1945–1973," *Contemporary European History* 15, no. 4 (2005): 517.
118. Juan Antonio Simón, "Football, Diplomacy and International Relations during Francoism, 1937–1975," in *Soccer Diplomacy: International Relations and Football since 1914*, ed. Heather L. Dichter (Lexington: University Press of Kentucky, 2020), 48–69.
119. Spain has only hosted an IOC Session once more, on the eve of the 1992 Barcelona Olympics. Minutes of the Meeting of the Executive Board of the I.O.C., Lausanne, June 26–27, 1964, IOC Executive Board, 1960–1969, OSC.
120. Heather L. Dichter, "'We Have Allowed Our Decisions to Be Determined by Political Considerations': The Cold War German Question in the International Ski Federation," *Sport in History* 37, no. 3 (2017), 291–94; Allen Guttmann, *The*

Games Must Go On: Avery Brundage and the Olympic Movement (New York: Columbia University Press, 1984), 136–37.

121. Letter, Lord Exeter to Lord Walston, July 5, 1965, FO 371/183165, TNA.

CONCLUSION: TO GRENOBLE AND BEYOND

1. "Erste selbständige Olympiamannschaft der DDR für Grenoble," *Neues Deutschland*, January 25, 1968, 1.
2. "X. Winterspiele in Grenoble eröffnet," *Neues Deutschland*, February 7, 1968, 1.
3. Newsreel footage and the official film show this best. At approximately 3:30 into the official movie, two flag bearers stand next to each other, each holding a German Olympic flag. "France: President De Gaulle Opens Winter Olympics 1968," *British Pathé*, February 6, 1968, Film ID: VLVAEH7SVMTNoWBLCI4CN37L2KPAH, https://www.britishpathe.com/video/VLVAEH7SVMTNoWBLCI4CN37L2 KPAH-6-FEBRUARY-1968/ (accessed July 30, 2019); *Snows of Grenoble*, dir. Jacques Ertaud and Jean-Jacques Languepin (1968), online at *The Full Grenoble 1968 Winter Olympic Film*, https://www.youtube.com/watch?v=PnwAYJWygYY (accessed July 30, 2019).
4. Telegram 6299/301, Aumale, Bonn to Diplomatie Paris, November 12, 1965, 179QO/229, CADC.
5. Telegram 5947, Toffin, Diplomatie to Ambafrance Bonn, December 27, 1965, 179QO/229, CADC; Airgram A-987, James S. Sutterlin, Bonn to Department of State, December 29, 1965, RG 59, CFPF 1964–66, POL 28 GER B, box 2200, NA.
6. Proces-Verbal de la réunion international du 3 juilliet 1967 relative aux titres de voyage et à l'entrée en France des personnes qui prendront part aux jeux olympiques d'hiver à Grenoble en 1968, July 3, 1967, 178QO/1229, CADC; Letter, M. Merllie to President du Comité d'Organisation des Jeux Olympiques d'Hiver de Grenoble (1968), August 2, 1967, 178QO/1229, CADC; Letter, Le Ministre de l'Interieur to Le Ministre des Affaires Etrangères Direction des Conventions Administratives et de Affaires Consulaires Conventions Visas, October 5, 1967, 178QO/1229, CADC.
7. Telegram 5663/67, François Seydoux, Bonn to Diplomatie Paris, October 19, 1967, 178QO/1229, CADC; Telegram 394, Roger Seydoux, REPAN Bruxelles to Diplomatie, November 2, 1967, 378PO/6, box 2202, CADN.
8. "Medaillenspiegel," *Neues Deutschland*, February 19, 1968, 7; Letter, Klaiber, Paris to Auswärtiges Amt, March 4, 1968, B 2/187, PAdAA.
9. Klaus Ullrich, "Der Anschlag gegen unsere Mädschen," *Neues Deutschland*, February 19, 1968, 7.
10. Minutes of the Executive Board Meeting, Mexico City, September 30–October 6, 1968, IOC Executive Board 1960–1969, 1968–09- Mexico, OSC; Minutes of the 67th Session of the International Olympic Committee, Mexico City, October 7–11, 1968, IOC Sessions 1960–1969, 1968- Mexico, OSC.
11. Kay Schiller and Christopher Young, *The 1972 Munich Olympics and the Making of Modern Germany* (Berkeley: University of California Press, 2010), 164–67.
12. Lord Killanin, *My Olympic Years* (London: Secker & Warburg, 1983), 110.
13. Letter, Avery Brundage to Roy E. Moore, November 23, 1955, Federation Internationale de Gymnastique, 1946–63, box 215, reel 125, ABC, UIA.

14. While the 1904 games moved from Chicago to St. Louis and the 1908 Olympics shifted from Rome to London, these events were far from the modern mega-event that exists today. Only the 1976 Winter Olympics went to a second city after Denver and Colorado residents voted not to fund the Olympics. The 1964 host city, Innsbruck, stepped in to host the 1976 Olympics. Adam Berg, "Denver '76: The Winter Olympics and the Politics of Growth in Colorado during the Late 1960s and Early 1970s" (PhD diss., Pennsylvania State University, 2016).
15. Lorenz Peiffer, "Die Madrider Entscheidung des IOC im Oktober 1965. Ein Wendepunkt in der Geschichte der deutsch-deutschen Sportbeziehungen," in *Transformationen: Kontinuitäten und Veränderungen in der Sportgeschichte II*, ed. Arnd Krüger and Wolfgang Buss (Hoya: Niedersächsisches Institut für Sportgeschichte, 2002), 118–24.
16. James Ellison, *The United States, Britain and the Transatlantic Crisis: Rising to the Gaullist Challenge, 1963–68* (Basingstoke, UK: Palgrave Macmillan, 2007), 11–39.
17. Greg Donaghy, *Tolerant Allies: Canada and the United States, 1963–1968* (Montreal: McGill-Queens University Press, 2003), 6–7.
18. James Hershberg, "Breaking the Ice: Alexei Kosygin and the Secret Background of the 1972 Hockey Summit Series," in *The Whole World Was Watching: Sport in the Cold War*, ed. Robert Edelman and Christopher Young (Stanford, CA: Stanford University Press, 2020), 59–72.
19. Thomas A. Schwartz, "Moving beyond the Cold War: The Johnson Administration, Bridge-Building and Détente," in *Beyond the Cold War: Lyndon Johnson and the New Global Challenges of the 1960s*, ed. Francis J. Gavin and Mark Atwood Lawrence (New York: Oxford University Press, 2014), 76–94; Helga Haftendorn, *Coming of Age: German Foreign Policy since 1945* (Lanham, MD: Rowman & Littlefield, 2006), 158–59.
20. Stefan Berger and Norman LaPorte, *Friendly Enemies: Britain and the GDR, 1949–1990* (New York: Berghahn Books, 2010), 129–30.
21. Uta Andrea Balbier, "'A Game, a Competition, an Instrument?': High Performance, Cultural Diplomacy and German Sport from 1950 to 1972," *International Journal of the History of Sport* 26, no. 4 (2009): 552.
22. R. Gerald Hughes, *Britain, Germany and the Cold War: The Search for a European Détente, 1949–1967* (London: Routledge, 2007); Garret J. Martin, "An Arbiter between the Superpowers: Charles de Gaulle and the German Question, 1958–1969," in *France and the German Question, 1945–1990*, ed. Frédéric Bozo and Christian Wenkel (New York: Berghahn, 2019), 103; Dennis L. Bark and David R. Gress, *A History of West Germany*. Vol. 2, *Democracy and Its Discontents, 1963–1988* (Oxford: Basil Blackwell, 1989), 182.
23. Jutta Braun, "Learning from the Dictatorship? Sport in Divided and Unified Germany," *German Historical Institute London Bulletin* 41, no. 1 (2019): 50–72.
24. Allen Guttmann, *The Olympics: A History of the Modern Games*, 2nd ed. (Urbana: University of Illinois Press, 2002), 88; Heather L. Dichter, "'We Have Allowed Our Decisions to Be Determined by Political Considerations': The Cold War German Question in the International Ski Federation," *Sport in History* 37, no. 3 (2017): 290–308; Jenifer Parks, "Verbal Gymnastics: Sports, Bureaucracy, and the Soviet Union's entrance into the Olympic Games, 1946–1952," in *East Plays West: Sport and the Cold*

War, ed. Stephen Wagg and David L. Andrews (London: Routledge, 2007), 27–44.

25. Rusli Lutan and Fan Hong, "The Politicization of Sport: GANEFO—A Case Study," *Sport in Society* 8, no. 3 (2005): 425–39.
26. Aviston D. Downes, "Forging Africa-Caribbean Solidarity within the Commonwealth? Sport and Diplomacy during the Anti-apartheid Campaign," in *Diplomatic Games: Sport, Statecraft and International Relations since 1945*, ed. Heather L. Dichter and Andrew L. Johns (Lexington: University Press of Kentucky, 2014), 131.
27. Ron Schleifer and Ilan Tamir, "The Use of Sport in the Arab-Israeli Conflict," *Israel Affairs* 24, no. 1 (2018): 53; James Diamond, "IOC Remind Malaysia over Stance on Political Discrimination after Country Extends Ban on Israeli Athletes," *Inside the Games*, January 18, 2019, https://www.insidethegames.biz/articles/1074358/ioc-remind-malaysia-over-stance-on-political-discrimination-after-country-extends-ban-on-israeli-athletes (accessed August 6, 2020); Nancy Gillen, "IPC Strip Malaysia of 2019 World Para Swimming Championships over Israel Policy," *Inside the Games*, January 27, 2010, https://www.insidethegames.biz/articles/1074728/ipc-strip-malaysia-of-2019-world-para-swimming-championships-over-israel-policy (accessed August 6, 2020); Michael Pavitt, "World Para Swimming Championships Set to Begin in London," *Inside the Games*, September 8, 2010, https://www.insidethegames.biz/articles/1084480/world-para-swimming-champs-set-to-begin (accessed August 6, 2020).
28. Timothy Andrews Sayle, *Enduring Alliance: A History of NATO and the Postwar Global Order* (Ithaca, NY: Cornell University Press, 2019), 99.
29. Letter, Dr. Müller to Auswärtiges Amt, Referat IV 5, October 28, 1965, B 2/156, PAdAA.

SELECTED BIBLIOGRAPHY

ARCHIVES

Archives municipales de Lyon (AML), Lyon, France
Bentley Historical Library (BHL), Ann Arbor, Michigan, USA
Bundesarchiv Berlin (BArchB), Berlin, Germany
Centre des Archives diplomatiques de La Courneuve (CADC), Paris, France
Centre des Archives diplomatiques de Nantes (CADN), Nantes, France
Detroit Public Library (DPL), Detroit, Michigan, USA
Fédération Internationale de Football Association (FIFA), Zurich, Switzerland
Fédération Internationale des Socitétés d'Aviron (FISA), Lausanne, Switzerland
International Association of Athletics Federations (IAAF), Monaco
International Ice Hockey Federation (IIHF), Zurich, Switzerland
Lake Placid Olympic Museum, Lake Placid, New York, USA
Les Archives de Grenoble (AG), Grenoble, France
Library and Archives Canada (LAC), Ottawa, Ontario, Canada
National Archives (NA), College Park, Maryland, USA
The National Archives (TNA), London, United Kingdom
North Atlantic Treaty Organization (NATO), Brussels, Belgium
Olympic Studies Centre (OSC), Lausanne, Switzerland
Archives Nationales (ANP), Pierrefitte-sur-Seine, France
Politisches Archiv des Auswärtiges Amt (PAdAA), Berlin, Germany
Rauner Special Collections Library, Dartmouth College (RSCL), Hanover, New Hampshire, USA
Riksarkivet, Oslo, Norway
Skimuseet, Oslo, Norway
University of Illinois Archives (UIA), Urbana, Illinois, USA
Utenriksdepartement (UD), Oslo, Norway

PUBLISHED SOURCES

Adenauer, Konrad. *Memoirs 1945–53*. Translated by Beate Ruhm von Oppen. London: Weidenfeld and Nicolson, 1966.

Allen, E. John B. *The Culture and Sport of Skiing: From Antiquity to World War II*. Amherst: University of Massachusetts Press, 2007.

Andrews, David L., and George Ritzer. "The Grobal in the Sporting Glocal." *Global Networks* 7, no. 2 (2007): 113–53.

Azzi, Stephen. "The Problem Child: Diefenbaker and Canada in the Language of the Kennedy Administration." In *Reassessing the Rogue Tory: Canadian Foreign Relations in the Diefenbaker Era*, edited by Janice Cavell and Ryan M. Touhey, 103–120. Vancouver: University of British Columbia Press, 2018.

Balbier, Uta Andrea. "'A Game, a Competition, an Instrument?': High Performance, Cultural Diplomacy and German Sport from 1950 to 1972." *International Journal of the History of Sport* 26, no. 4 (2009): 539–55.

———. *Kalter Krieg auf der Aschenbahn: der deutsch-deutsche Sport, 1950–1972: eine politische Geschichte*. Paderborn: F. Schöning, 2007.

Bark, Dennis L., and David R. Gress. *A History of West Germany*. Vol. 1, *From Shadow to Substance, 1945–1963*. Oxford: Basil Blackwell, 1989.

———. *A History of West Germany*. Vol. 2, *Democracy and Its Discontents, 1963–1988*. Oxford: Basil Blackwell, 1989.

Beacom, Aaron. *International Diplomacy and the Olympic Movement: The New Mediators*. Basingstoke, UK: Palgrave Macmillan, 2012.

Beck, Peter J. "Conclusion: 'Good Kicking' Is Not Only 'Good Politics' but Also 'Good Diplomacy.'" In *Soccer Diplomacy: International Relations and Football since 1914*, edited by Heather L. Dichter, 221–50. Lexington: University Press of Kentucky, 2020.

Berg, Adam. "Denver '76: The Winter Olympics and the Politics of Growth in Colorado during the Late 1960s and Early 1970s." PhD diss., Pennsylvania State University, 2016.

Berger, Stefan, and Norman LaPorte. *Friendly Enemies: Britain and the GDR, 1949–1990*. New York: Berghahn Books, 2010.

Blasius, Tobias. *Olympische Bewegung, Kalter Krieg und Deutschlandpolitik 1949–1972*. Frankfurt: Peter Lang, 2001.

Bozo, Frédéric. *French Foreign Policy since 1945: An Introduction*. Translated by Jonathan Hensher. New York: Berghahn Books, 2016.

Braun, Jutta. "Learning from the Dictatorship? Sport in Divided and Unified Germany." *German Historical Institute London Bulletin* 41, no. 1 (2019): 50–72.

———. "Sports and Society in the Rivalry between East and West." In *A History Shared and Divided: East and West Germany since 1970s*, edited by Frank Bösch, translated by Jennifer Walcoff Neuheiser, 501–50. New York: Berghahn Books, 2018.

Brewster, Claire, and Keith Brewster. *Representing the Nation: Sport and Spectacle in Post-Revolutionary Mexico*. London: Routledge, 2010.

Bridges, Brian. "Reluctant Mediator: Hong Kong, the Two Koreas and the Tokyo Olympics." *International Journal of the History of Sport* 24, no. 3 (2007): 375–91.

Brown, Ashley. "Swinging for the State Department: American Women Tennis Players in Diplomatic Goodwill Tours, 1941–59." *Journal of Sport History*, 42, no. 3 (2015): 289–309.

Cary, Noel D. "Olympics in Divided Berlin? Popular Culture and Political Imagination at the Cold War Frontier." *Cold War History* 11, no. 3 (2011): 291–316.

Cavell, Janice, and Ryan M. Touhey, eds. *Reassessing the Rogue Tory: Canadian Foreign Relations in the Diefenbaker Era*. Vancouver: University of British Columbia Press, 2018.

Chapnick, Adam. "The Canadian Middle Power Myth." *International Journal* 55, no. 2 (2000): 188–206.

Charitas, Pascal. "A More Flexible Domination: Franco-African Sport Diplomacy during Decolonization, 1945–1966." In *Diplomatic Games: Sport, Statecraft and International Relations since 1945*, edited by Heather L. Dichter and Andrew L. Johns, 183–214. Lexington: University Press of Kentucky, 2014.

Clay, Lucius D. *Decision in Germany*. Garden City, NY: Doubleday & Company, 1950.

Darby, Paul. "'Let Us Rally around the Flag': Football, Nation-Building, and Pan-Africanism in Kwame Nkrumah's Ghana." *Journal of African Studies* 54 (2013): 221–46.

Dauncey, Hugh. "The Failed Bid for Lyon '68, and France's Winter Olympics from Grenoble '68 to Annecy 2018: French Politics, Civil Society and Olympic Mega-Events." In *Olympic Games, Mega-Events and Civil Societies: Globalization, Environment, Resistance*, edited by Graeme Hayes and John Karamichas, 87–105. Basingstoke, UK: Palgrave Macmillan, 2012.

Davison, Graeme. "Welcoming the World: The 1956 Olympic Games and the Re-presentation of Melbourne." *Australian Historical Studies* 27, no. 109 (1997): 64–76.

Denning, Andrew. *Skiing into Modernity: A Cultural and Environmental History*. Oakland: University of California Press, 2015.

Dennis, Mike. *The Rise and Fall of the German Democratic Republic, 1945–1990*. Harlow: Longman, 2000.

Dichter, Heather L. "Corruption in the 1960s?: Rethinking the Origins of

Unethical Olympic Bidding Tactics." *International Journal of the History of Sport* 33, no. 6–7 (2016): 666–82.

———. "Denazification, Democratization, and the Cold War: Diplomatic Manipulation of the German Olympic Committee." In *Defending the American Way of Life*, edited by Kevin B. Witherspoon and Toby C. Rider, 173–88. Little Rock: University of Arkansas Press, 2018.

———. "The Diplomatic Turn: The New Relationship Between Sport and Politics." *International Journal of the History of Sport* 38, no. 2–3 (2021): 247–63, DOI: 10.1080/09523367.2021.1894135.

———. "Game Plan for Democracy: Sport and Youth in Occupied West Germany." In *Occupation: Power Politics, Everyday Life, and Social Interactions in the Western Zones of Occupied Germany, 1945–1955*, edited by Camilo Erlichman and Christopher Knowles, 133–50. London: Bloomsbury Academic Press, 2018.

———. "Sporting Relations: Diplomacy, Small States, and Germany's Postwar Return to International Sport," *Diplomacy & Statecraft* 27, no. 2 (2016): 340–59.

———. "'We Have Allowed Our Decisions to Be Determined by Political Considerations': The Cold War German Question in the International Ski Federation." *Sport in History* 37, no. 3 (2017): 290–308.

———, ed. *Soccer Diplomacy: International Relations and Football since 1914*. Lexington: University Press of Kentucky, 2020.

Dichter, Heather L., and Andrew L. Johns, eds. *Diplomatic Games: Sport, Statecraft and International Relations since 1945*. Lexington: University Press of Kentucky, 2014.

Donaghy, Greg. *Grit: The Life and Politics of Paul Martin Sr.* Vancouver: University of British Columbia Press, 2015.

———. *Tolerant Allies: Canada and the United States, 1963–1968*. Montreal: McGill-Queens University Press, 2003.

Downes, Aviston D. "Forging Africa-Caribbean Solidarity within the Commonwealth? Sport and Diplomacy during the Anti-apartheid Campaign." In *Diplomatic Games: Sport, Statecraft and International Relations since 1945*, edited by Heather L. Dichter and Andrew L. Johns, 117–49. Lexington: University Press of Kentucky, 2014.

Dyndal, Gjert Lage. "How the High North Became Central in NATO Strategy: Revelations from the NATO Archives." *Journal of Strategic Studies* 34, no. 4 (2011): 557–85.

Eckert, Horst, and Ernst Martini. *90: IIHF 90th Anniversary, 1908–1998*. Zürich: IIHF, 1998.

Edelman, Robert, and Christopher Young, eds. *The Whole World Was Watching: Sport in the Cold War*. Stanford, CA: Stanford University Press, 2020.

Ellison, James. *The United States, Britain and the Transatlantic Crisis: Rising to the Gaullist Challenge, 1963–68*. Basingstoke, UK: Palgrave Macmillan, 2007.

Elsey, Brenda. "'Because We Have Nothing': The 1962 World Cup and Cold War Politics in Chile." In *Soccer Diplomacy: International Relations and Football since 1914*, edited by Heather L. Dichter, 94–115. Lexington: University Press of Kentucky, 2020.

Feinstein, Margarete Myers. *State Symbols: The Quest for Legitimacy in the Federal Republic of Germany and the German Democratic Republic, 1949–1959*. Boston: Brill, 2001.

Field, Russell, and Bruce Kidd. "Canada and the Pan-American Games," *International Journal of the History of Sport* 33, no. 1–2 (2016): 217–38.

Finney, Patrick. *Palgrave Advances in International History*. Basingstoke, UK: Palgrave Macmillan, 2005.

Frøland, Hans Otto. "Distrust, Dependency and Détente: Norway, the Two Germanys and 'the German Question', 1945–1973." *Contemporary European History* 15, no. 4 (2005): 495–517.

Gearson, John, and Kori Schake, eds. *The Berlin Wall Crisis: Perspectives on Cold War Alliances*. Basingtoke, UK: Palgrave Macmillan, 2002.

Geyer, Martin H. "Der Kampf um nationale Repräsentation: Deutsch-deutscher Sportbeziehungen und die ‚Hallstein-Doktrin.'" *Vertel-jahrshefte für Zeitgeschichte* 44, no. 1 (1996): 55–86.

———. "On the Road to a German 'Postnationalism'? Athletic Competition between the Two German States in the Era of Konrad Adenauer." *German Politics and Society* 25, no. 2 (2007): 140–67.

Giauque, Jeffrey Glen. *Grand Designs and Visions of Unity: The Atlantic Powers and the Reorganization of Western Europe, 1955–1963*. Chapel Hill: University of North Carolina Press, 2002.

Gray, William Glenn. *Germany's Cold War: The Global Campaign to Isolate East Germany, 1949–1969*. Chapel Hill: University of North Carolina Press, 2003.

Grix, Jonathan, and Paul Michael Brannagan. "Of Mechanisms and Myths: Conceptualising States' 'Soft Power' Strategies through Sports Mega-Events." *Diplomacy & Statecraft* 27, no. 2 (2016): 251–72.

Guoqi, Xu. *Olympic Dreams: China and Sports, 1895–2008*. Cambridge, MA: Harvard University Press, 2008.

Guttmann, Allen. *The Games Must Go On: Avery Brundage and the Olympic Movement*. New York: Columbia University Press, 1984.

———. *The Olympics: A History of the Modern Games*. 2nd ed. Urbana: University of Illinois Press, 2002.

Haftendorn, Helga. *Coming of Age: German Foreign Policy since 1945*. Lanham, MD: Rowman & Littlefield, 2006.

Harres, Wolfgang. *Sportpolitik an der Saar 1945–1955*. Saarbrücken: Saarbrücker Druckerei und Verlag, 1997.

Harrison, Hope. *Driving the Soviets up the Wall: Soviet-East German Relations, 1953–1961*. Princeton, NJ: Princeton University Press, 2003.

Heck, Sandra. "A Sport for Everyone? Inclusion and Exclusion in the Organisation of the First Olympic Modern Pentathlon." *International Journal of the History of Sport* 31, no. 5 (2014): 526–41.

Heiss, Mary Ann, and S. Victor Papacosma, eds. *NATO and the Warsaw Pact: Intrabloc Conflicts*. Kent, OH: Kent State University Press, 2008.

Heller, Francis H., and John R. Gillingham, eds. *NATO: The Founding of the Atlantic Alliance and the Integration of Europe*. New York: St. Martin's Press, 1992.

Henrikson, Alan K. "Niche Diplomacy in the World Public Arena: The Global 'Corners' of Canada and Norway." In *The New Public Diplomacy: Soft Power in International Relations*, edited by Jan Melissen, 67–87. Basingstoke, UK: Palgrave Macmillan, 2005.

Hershberg, James. "Breaking the Ice: Alexei Kosygin and the Secret Background of the 1972 Hockey Summit Series." In *The Whole World Was Watching: Sport in the Cold War*, edited by Robert Edelman and Christopher Young, 59–72. Stanford, CA: Stanford University Press, 2020.

Hey, Jeanne A. K., ed. *Small States in World Politics: Explaining Foreign Policy Behavior*. Boulder: Lynne Rienner Publishers, 2003.

Hong, Fan, and Xiong Xiaozheng. "Communist China: Sport, Politics and Diplomacy." *International Journal of the History of Sport* 19, no. 2–3 (2002): 319–42.

Huang, Yi-Ling, and Chen-Huei Wang. "Chinese Question in the Olympic Movement: From the Perspective of Taiwan." *International Journal of the History of Sport* 30, no. 17 (2013): 2052–68.

Hughes, R. Gerald. *Britain, Germany and the Cold War: The Search for a European Détente, 1949–1967*. London: Routledge, 2007.

Irish, Ann B. *Hokkaido: A History of Ethnic Transition and Development on Japan's Northern Island*. Jefferson, NC: McFarland, 2009.

Iriye, Akira. "Internationalizing International History." In *Rethinking American History in a Global Age*, edited by Thomas Bender, 47–62. Berkeley: University of California Press, 2002.

Kelly, Brendan. *The Good Fight: Marcel Cadieux and Canadian Diplomacy*. Vancouver: University of British Columbia Press, 2019.

Kenneally, Rhona Richman, and Johanne Sloan, eds. *Expo 67: Not Just a Souvenir*. Toronto: University of Toronto Press, 2010.

Keys, Barbara. *Globalizing Sport: National Rivalry and International Community in the 1930s*. Cambridge, MA: Harvard University Press, 2006.

Killanin, Lord. *My Olympic Years*. London: Secker & Warburg, 1983.

Kioussis, George N. "'The Finest Ambassadors': American-Icelandic Football Exchange, 1955–1956." In *Soccer Diplomacy: International Relations and Football since 1914*, edited by Heather L. Dichter, 70–93. Lexington: University Press of Kentucky, 2020.

Kirchner, Emil, and James Sperling, eds. *The Federal Republic of Germany and NATO: 40 Years After*. Basingstoke, UK: Palgrave Macmillan, 1992.

Koshar, Rudy. *German Travel Cultures*. Oxford: Berg, 2000.

Krasnoff, Lindsay Sarah. "Resurrecting the Nation: The Evolution of French Sports Policy from de Gaulle to Mitterrand." In *Sport and the Transformation of Modern Europe: States, Media and Market, 1950–2010*, edited by Alan Tomlinson, Christopher Young, and Richard Holt, 67–82. London: Routledge, 2011.

Lippmann, Karten. *„ . . . und für die Ehre unserer Nation(en)": Olympische Deutschlandpolitik zwischen 1960 und 1968*. Hildesheim: arete Verlag, 2017.

Locher, Anna. "A Crisis Foretold: NATO and France, 1963–66." In *Transforming NATO in the Cold War: Challenges beyond Deterrence in the 1960s*, edited by Andreas Wenger, Christian Nuenlist, and Anna Locher, 107–27. London: Routledge, 2007.

Lutan, Rusli, and Fan Hong. "The Politicization of Sport: GANEFO—A Case Study." *Sport in Society* 8, no. 3 (2005): 425–39.

Major, Patrick. *Behind the Berlin Wall: East Germany and the Frontiers of Power*. Oxford: Oxford University Press, 2010.

Martin, Garret Joseph. "An Arbiter between the Superpowers: Charles de Gaulle and the German Question, 1958–1969." In *France and the German Question, 1945–1990*, edited by Frédéric Bozo and Christian Wenkel, 93–109. New York: Berghahn, 2019.

———. *General de Gaulle's Cold War: Challenging American Hegemony 1963/1968*. New York: Berghahn Books, 2013.

Martin, Simon. "Bikila's Aria: the 1960 Rome Olympics." In *Sport and the Transformation of Modern Europe: States, Media and Market, 1950–2010*, edited by Alan Tomlinson, Christopher Young, and Richard Holt, 83–99. London: Routledge, 2011.

Merkel, Udo, and Misuk Kim. "Third Time Lucky!? PyeongChang's Bid to Host the 2018 Winter Olympics—Politics, Policy and Practice." *International Journal of the History of Sport* 28, no. 16 (2011): 2365–83.

Mertin, Evelyn. "Steadfast Friendship and Brotherly Help: The Distinctive Soviet-East German Sport Relationship within the Socialist Bloc." In *Diplomatic Games: Sport, Statecraft and International Relations since 1945*, edited by Heather L. Dichter and Andrew L. Johns, 53–84. Lexington: University Press of Kentucky, 2014.

Naha, Souvik. "'Over the Border and the Gates'?: Global and Transnational Sport." *Sport in Society* 20, no. 10 (2017): 1347–53.

Neunlist, Christian. "Dealing with the Devil: NATO and Gaullist France, 1958–66." *Journal of Transatlantic Studies* 9, no. 3 (2011): 220–31.

———. "Into the 1960s: NATO's Role in East-West Relations, 1958–63." In *Transforming NATO in the Cold War: Challenges beyond Deterrence in the 1960s*, edited by Andreas Wenger, Christian Nuenlist, and Anna Locher, 67–88. London: Routledge, 2007.

Oliver, Robert. "The Legacies of Losing: Rethinking the 'Failure' of Toronto's Olympic Games Bids." *Sport in Society* 17, no. 2 (2014): 204–17.

Osgood, Kenneth, and Brian C. Etheridge. "The New International History Meets the New Cultural History: Public Diplomacy and U.S. Foreign Relations." In *The United States and Public Diplomacy: New Directions in Cultural and International History*, edited by Kenneth A. Osgood and Brian C. Etheridge, 1–25. Leiden: Brill, 2010.

Panagiotopoulou, Roy. "Hosting the Olympic Games: From Promoting the Nation to Nation-Branding." In *Sport and the Transformation of Modern Europe: States, Media and Market, 1950–2010*, edited by Alan Tomlinson, Christopher Young, and Richard Holt, 150–70. London: Routledge, 2011.

Parks, Jenifer. "Verbal Gymnastics: Sports, Bureaucracy, and the Soviet Union's Entrance into the Olympic Games, 1946–1952." In *East Plays West: Sport and the Cold War*, edited by Stephen Wagg and David L. Andrews, 27–44. London: Routledge, 2007.

Peiffer, Lorenz. "Die Madrider Entscheidung des IOC im Oktober 1965. Ein Wendepunkt in der Geschichte der deutsch-deutschen Sportbeziehungen." In *Transformationen: Kontinuitäten und Veränderungen in der Sportgeschichte II*, edited by Arnd Krüger and Wolfgang Buss, 118–24. Hoya: Niedersächsisches Institut für Sportgeschichte, 2002.

Pharo, Helge. "Post-Cold War Historiography in Norway." In *The Cold War—and the Nordic Countries: Historiography at a Crossroads*, edited by Torsten B. Olesen, 97–142. Odense: University Press of Southern Denmark, 2004.

Plischke, Elmer. *The Allied High Commission for Germany*. n.p.: Historical Division, Office of the Executive Secretary, Office of the U.S. High Commissioner for Germany, 1953.

Rein, Raanan. "Turning the Country into an 'Immense and Clamorous Stadium': Perón, the New Argentina, and the 1951 Pan-American Games." *International Journal of the History of Sport* 33, no. 1–2 (2016): 29–43.

Reiter, Erich, and Heinz Gärtner, eds. *Small States and Alliances*. Heidelberg: Physica-Verlag, 2001.

Rhode, Robert. *History of the Federation Internationale de Tir l'Arc, 1962–1983*, vol. 2. Bridgeton, MO: n.p., 1984.

Rider, Toby C. *Cold War Games: Propaganda, the Olympics, and U.S. Foreign Policy*. Urbana: University of Illinois Press, 2016.

Risso, Linda. *Propadanda and Intelligence in the Cold War: The NATO Information Service*. London: Routledge, 2014.

Sarotte, M. E. *Dealing with the Devil: East Germany, Détente, and Ostpolitik*. Chapel Hill: University of North Carolina Press, 2001.

Sayle, Timothy Andrews. "Canada, NATO, and the Berlin Crisis, 1961–1962: 'Slow-Boil' or 'Pressure Cooker?'" *International Journal* 68, no. 2 (2013): 255–68.

———. *Enduring Alliance: A History of NATO and the Postwar Global Order*. Ithaca, NY: Cornell University Press, 2019.

Schiller, Kay, and Christopher Young. *The 1972 Munich Olympics and the Making of Modern Germany*. Berkeley: University of California Press, 2010.

Schleifer, Ron, and Ilan Tamir. "The Use of Sport in the Arab-Israeli Conflict," *Israel Affairs* 24, no. 1 (2018): 45–61.

Schödl, Gottfried. *Medals and World Records in Weightlifting*. Budapest: International Weightlifting Federation, 1997.

Schwartz, Thomas A. "Moving beyond the Cold War: The Johnson Administration, Bridge-Building and Détente." In *Beyond the Cold War: Lyndon Johnson and the New Global Challenges of the 1960s*, edited by Francis J. Gavin and Mark Atwood Lawrence, 76–94. New York: Oxford University Press, 2014

Simón, Juan Antonio. "Football, Diplomacy and International Relations during Francoism, 1937–1975." In *Soccer Diplomacy: International Relations and Football since 1914*, ed. Heather L. Dichter, 48–69. Lexington: University Press of Kentucky, 2020.

Smith, Maureen Margaret. "Revisiting South Africa and the Olympic Movement: The Correspondence of Reginald S. Alexander and the International Olympic Committee, 1961–86." *International Journal of the History of Sport* 23, no. 7 (2006): 1193–216.

Snyder, Sarah B. "Playing on the Same Team: What International and Sport Historians Can Learn from Each Other." In *Soccer Diplomacy: International Relations and Football since 1914*, edited by Heather L. Dichter, 18–29. Lexington: University Press of Kentucky, 2020.

Suri, Jeremi. "Non-Governmental Organizations and Non-State Actors." In *Palgrave Advances in International History*, edited by Patrick Finney, 223–46. Basingstoke, UK: Palgrave Macmillan, 2005.

Taylor, Matthew. "Editorial—Sport, Transnationalism, and Global History." *Journal of Global History* 8 (2013): 199–208.

Tomlinson, Alan, and Christopher Young, eds. *National Identity and Global Sports Events: Culture, Politics, and Spectacle in the Olympics and the Football World Cup*. Albany: State University of New York Press, 2006.

Torres, Cesar R. "Stymied Expectations: Buenos Aires' Persistent Efforts to Host Olympic Games." *Olympika* XVI (2007): 50–54.

———. "Tribulations and Achievements: The Early History of Olympism in Argentina." *International Journal of the History of Sport* 18, no. 3 (2001): 59–92.

Trachtenberg, Marc. "France and NATO, 1949–1991." *Journal of Transatlantic Studies* 9, no. 3 (2011): 184–94.

Turchetti, Simone. *Greening the Alliance: The Diplomacy of NATO's Science and Environmental Initiatives*. Chicago: University of Chicago Press, 2019.

Turrini, Joseph M. "'It Was Communism versus the Free World': The USA-USSR Dual Track Meet Series and the Development of Track and Field in the United States, 1958–1985." *Journal of Sport History* 28, no. 3 (2001): 427–51.

Vaughan, Rachel. "'Chinese Rings': The United States, the Two Chinas and the 1960 Squaw Valley Winter Olympics." In *Sport and Diplomacy: Games within Games*, edited by J. Simon Rofe, 185–202. Manchester: Manchester University Press, 2018.

Vogan, Travis. *ABC Sports: The Rise and Fall of Network Sports Television*. Oakland: University of California Press, 2018.

Wiebes, Cees, and Bert Zeeman. "'I Don't Need Your Handkerchiefs': Holland's Experience of Crisis Consultation in NATO." *International Affairs* 66, no. 1 (1990): 91–113.

Wenger, Andreas, Christian Nuenlist, and Anna Locher, eds. *Transforming NATO in the Cold War: Challenges beyond Deterrence in the 1960s*. London: Routledge, 2007.

Weiers, Margaret K. *Envoys Extraordinary: Women of the Canadian Foreign Service*. Toronto: Dundurn Press, 1995.

Welch, Paula D. "Chamonix 1924." In *Encyclopedia of the Modern Olympic Movement*, edited by John E. Findling and Kimberly D. Pelle, 283–87. Westport, CT: Greenwood Press, 2004.

Wilke, Manfred. *The Path to the Berlin Wall: Critical Stages in the History of Divided Germany*. Translated by Sophie Perl. New York: Berghahn Books, 2014.

Witherspoon, Kevin. *Before the Eyes of the World: Mexico and the 1968 Olympic Games*. DeKalb: Northern Illinois University Press, 2008.

Witherspoon, Kevin, and Toby Rider, eds. *Defending the American Way of Life*. Little Rock: University of Arkansas Press, 2018.

Wrynn, Alison M. "'A Debt Was Paid off in Tears': Science, IOC Politics and the Debate about High Altitude in the 1968 Mexico City Olympics." *International Journal of the History of Sport* 23, no. 7 (2006), 1152–72.

Wysocki Quiros, David J. "*Una Antorcha de Esperanza*: Mexico and the 1955 Pan-American Games." *International Journal of the History of Sport* 33, no. 1–2 (2016): 44–61.

Zeiler, Thomas W. "The Diplomatic History Bandwagon: A State of the Field." *Journal of American History* 95, no. 4 (2009): 1053–73.

INDEX

DR. HEATHER L. DICHTER was born in Pennsylvania and studied history at the University of Michigan (BA), University of North Carolina–Chapel Hill (MA), and the University of Toronto (PhD). She is associate professor of sport management and sport history and a member of the International Centre for Sports History and Culture at De Montfort University in Leicester, UK, and has previously taught at Western Michigan University and Ithaca College. She has served as a council member for the International Society for the History of Physical Education and Sport (ISHPES) from 2009 to 2016 and won the ISHPES Award in 2019. Her publications have addressed sport in occupied Germany or the Olympic movement. She edited *Soccer Diplomacy: International Relations and Football since 1914* (2020), *Olympic Reform Ten Years Later* (2012) with Bruce Kidd, and *Diplomatic Games: Sport, Statecraft, and International Relations since 1945* (2014) with Andrew Johns.